RELIGIOUS PARENTING

Religious Parenting

TRANSMITTING FAITH
AND VALUES IN
CONTEMPORARY AMERICA

{⸺⸺⸺}

Christian Smith, Bridget Ritz
& Michael Rotolo

PRINCETON UNIVERSITY PRESS

PRINCETON & OXFORD

Published by Princeton University Press
41 William Street, Princeton, New Jersey 08540
6 Oxford Street, Woodstock, Oxfordshire OX20 1TR

press.princeton.edu

Library of Congress Cataloging-in-Publication Data

Names: Smith, Christian, 1960– author. | Ritz, Bridget, 1992– author. |
    Rotolo, Michael, 1991– author.
Title: Religious parenting : transmitting faith and values in contemporary
    America / Christian Smith, Bridget Ritz, Michael Rotolo.
Description: Princeton, New Jersey : Princeton University Press, 2020. |
    Includes bibliographical references and index.
Identifiers: LCCN 2019027047 (print) | LCCN 2019027048 (ebook) |
    ISBN 9780691194967 (hardback : acid-free paper) | ISBN 9780691197821 (ebook)
Subjects: LCSH: Parenting—Religious aspects. | Religion and sociology—United States. |
    Parental influences—United States. | Intergenerational communication—Religious
    aspects. | Intergenerational relations—Religious aspects.
Classification: LCC BL625.8 .S53 2020 (print) | LCC BL625.8 (ebook) | DDC 204/.41—dc23
LC record available at https://lccn.loc.gov/2019027047
LC ebook record available at https://lccn.loc.gov/2019027048

British Library Cataloging-in-Publication Data is available

Editorial: Fred Appel and Jenny Tan
Production Editorial: Karen Carter
Jacket/Cover Design: Amanda Weiss
Production: Erin Suydam
Publicity: Tayler Lord and Kathryn Stevens

This book has been composed in Miller

Printed on acid-free paper. ∞

Printed in the United States of America

10 9 8 7 6 5 4 3 2 1

For Brian
—B.J.R.

For Olivia
—M.S.R.

For Helen (R.I.P.)
—C.S.S.

CONTENTS

RELIGIOUS PARENTING

Introduction

HOW DO RELIGIOUS PARENTS in the United States approach the task of passing on their religious faith and practice to their children? And what can that tell us about what "culture" is and how it works? This book answers these two questions, one substantive and one theoretical. Substantively, we learn how American religious parents tackle the challenge of intergenerational religious transmission to children. Theoretically, we learn what an inquiry into that substantive concern teaches us about the nature and operation of culture more generally.

We actually know very little about intergenerational religious transmission *from the perspective of parents.* A growing body of research looks at this issue from the side of children.[1] And an established body of literature statistically analyzes the various factors that influence religious retention and switching.[2] Numerous works have also explored American parenting and family life from a variety of helpful perspectives.[3] Social scientists

1. Including Christian Smith with Melinda Lundquist Denton, *Soul Searching: The Religious and Spiritual Lives of American Teenagers* (New York: Oxford University Press, 2005); Lisa Pearce and Melinda Denton, *A Faith of Their Own* (New York: Oxford University Press, 2011); Christian Smith with Patricia Snell, *Souls in Transition* (New York: Oxford University Press, 2009); Marjorie Gunnoe and K. Moore, "Predictors of Religiosity among Youth Aged 17–22," *Journal for the Scientific Study of Religion* 41 (2002): 613–22.

2. For example, Richard Petts, "Trajectories of Religious Participation from Adolescence to Young Adulthood," *Journal for the Scientific Study of Religion* 48 (2009): 552–71; Vern Bengtson, C. Copen, N. Putney, and M. Silverstein, "A Longitudinal Study of Intergenerational Transmission of Religion," *International Sociology* 24 (2009): 325–45; Christian Smith and David Sikkink, "Social Predictors of Retention in and Switching from the Religious Faith of Family of Origin," *Review of Religious Research* 45, no. 2 (2003): 188–206.

3. See, for instance, Rebecca Jo Plant, *Mom: The Transformation of Motherhood in Modern America* (Chicago: University of Chicago Press, 2010); Jack Westman, ed., *Parenthood in America: Undervalued, Underpaid, Under Siege* (Madison: University of

[1]

have also, of course, researched the socialization of children well (although usually paying scant attention to religious transmission).[4] Despite all this work, however, almost no research has explored in depth how religious parents approach the job of socializing their children into their religious identities, practices, and beliefs.[5] That is strange, because we know that parents are the most important factor shaping the religious outcomes of American youth. Yet we know almost nothing about how they approach the task of passing on their faith and practice to their children. This book helps remedy that oversight.

This book is also for readers interested in sociological and anthropological[6] theories of culture, even if they are not especially interested in religion. Our substantive analysis about religious transmission serves as the springboard for advancing a general theoretical argument about culture, one that contests theories dominating in recent decades. So one may have little interest in the study of religion and still find our theoretical analysis and arguments significant and perhaps challenging.

Wisconsin Press, 2001); Paula Fass, *The End of American Childhood: A History of Parenting from Life on the Frontier to the Managed Child* (Princeton, NJ: Princeton University Press, 2016). For a comparative study set in the context of the larger animal world, see Susan Allport, *A Natural History of Parenting* (New York: Harmony Books, 1997); Peter Stearns, *Anxious Parents: A History of Modern Childrearing in America* (New York: New York University Press, 2003); Jennifer Senior, *All Joy and No Fun: The Paradox of Modern Parenting* (New York: Harper Collins, 2014); Elinor Ochs and Tamara Kremer-Sadlik, eds., *Fast-Forward Family: Home, Work, and Relationships in Middle-Class America* (Berkeley: University of California Press, 2014); Christopher Lasch, *Haven in a Heartless World* (New York: Basic Books, 1979); Jan Dizard and Howard Gadlin, *The Minimal Family* (Amherst: University of Massachusetts Press, 1990); Kathryn Lofton, "Religion and the Authority in American Parenting," *Journal for the American Academy of Religion* 84, no. 3 (2016): 806–41.

4. For example, religion as a topic merits only one sentence in Joan Grusec and Paul Hastings's 720-page *Handbook of Socialization: Theory and Research* (New York: Guilford Press, 2007). Ute Schönpflug's *Cultural Transmission: Psychological, Developmental, Social, and Methodological Aspects* (Cambridge: Cambridge University Press, 2009) includes no references to religion at all.

5. To be sure, a nontrivial body of literature examines the influence of family contexts of religious transmission but little of it focuses specifically on the actual perspectives and approaches of parents (one partial exception being Vern Bengtson, *Families and Faith: How Religion Is Passed Down across Generations* (New York: Oxford University Press, 2013).

6. To be clear, we are not anthropologists or expert in the latest debates in anthropological theories of culture, so we are surer about our contribution to cultural sociology. Nevertheless, the theory we employ is drawn from cognitive anthropology, so if nothing else, we hope to lend our endorsement of the merits and value of that school of thought for the larger anthropological enterprise.

Our Research

Our substantive findings and theoretical argument in this book are based on a national sociological study of American religious[7] and non-religious parents that we and colleagues conducted in 2014 and 2015.[8] We conducted 215 personal, in-depth interviews with parents who belong to churches, synagogues, mosques, and temples who by affiliation are white conservative Protestant, mainline Protestant, black Protestant, white Catholic, Latino Catholic, Conservative Jews, Mormon, Muslim, Hindu, and Buddhist.[9] To compare with this religious sample, we also interviewed an additional sample of twenty nonreligious parents. The parents we studied lived in the Chicago, Houston, Los Angeles, Albuquerque, Washington, DC, and New York City areas; and in various parts of Indiana, New Jersey, Florida, Wisconsin, Rhode Island, and Minnesota. We sometimes conducted interviews in locations that in some way typify their religious group—for example, we conducted most of our Latino Catholic interviews with parents in Albuquerque, New Mexico, and Brooklyn, New York, rather than, say, Minnesota.

We selected parents to interview using a "stratified quota" sampling method. This means that we interviewed a set number of parents (the quota) from combinations of categories (the "strata" of types) of religious

7. We define religion as "a complex of culturally prescribed practices, based on premises about the existence and nature of superhuman powers, whether personal or impersonal, which seek to help practitioners gain access to and communicate or align themselves with these powers, in hopes of avoiding misfortune, obtaining blessings, and receiving deliverance from crises" (Christian Smith, *Religion: What It Is, How It Works, and Why It Matters* (Princeton, NJ: Princeton University Press, 2017). This definition, which focuses on religious practices more than beliefs, compels us to count as religious a few parents who were connected to religious congregations but who told us in their interviews that they were agnostics or atheists, at least when it comes to a certain view of God.

8. See the appendix for methodological details. Also see Heather Price and Christian Smith, "Process and Reliability for Cultural Model Analysis Using Semi-Structured Interviews," American Sociological Association Annual Meeting, Montreal, August 2017.

9. Ten of the interviewed parents sampled through religious congregations turned out to be religiously affiliated and more or less practicing but not personally religious believers—for example, they reported not believing in God but nonetheless being religiously involved for the sake of their spouses or children. Three of these were Jewish, two Buddhist, two white Catholic, and one each mainline Protestant, Hindu, and Hispanic Catholic. For purposes of this study, we count these ten parents as religious, since they affiliate and usually at least minimally practice religiously, even if they do not completely believe the doctrines of their religious traditions (which many even more religious American parents do not). See how we define religion in footnote no. 7 and its relevance for this methodological decision.

tradition, social class, race and ethnicity, family structure, and parental religious commitment. We intentionally interviewed parents in middle- and upper-middle-class households and in poorer and working-class households. We interviewed parents in two-parent households and parents who are divorced, remarried in "blended" families, and never married. We interviewed parents who are white, black, Hispanic, Asian, and of some other race or ethnicity. Most of the parents we interviewed were heterosexual, but some were in same-sex parenting households.[10] Many of the children of the parents we interviewed are biological, but some are stepchildren and some are adopted.

Our interview sample is not strictly representative of the populations of religious parents it includes. In-depth research interviews rarely are. Nor does our study include every possible religious tradition. We only studied Conservative Jews, for instance, not Reform, Orthodox, or other kinds of American Jews. Our interviews do, however, provide a large and varied enough sample of different kinds of American parents to be able to identify major themes and differences among these groups of parents in our sampled religious traditions. Our central purpose was to identify the "cultural models" that inform the ways that many kinds of American religious parents approach the challenge of handing on faith and practice to their children. We also wanted to identify and explain apparent dissimilarities between different types of parents. The substantive questions animating this book have received so little study by scholars that we found it enough to undertake these basic explorations. Our interview sample enables us to do that well—although future research with larger samples and including other religious groups can build on and extend our findings here.[11]

The heart of our argument in this book rests on our analysis of the 235 personal interviews we conducted, primarily of the 215 self-identified

10. Our sample was not large enough to draw out reliable comparisons, but our same-sex household parents did not differ at all from heterosexual parents in their views about passing on religion to their children.

11. A second book also produced by this same research project, however, does include nationally representative data and perspective (Christian Smith and Amy Adamczyk, *Handing Down the Faith: How Parents Pass Their Religion on to the Next Generation* [2020]). In addition to analyzing the in-depth interviews, that book also statistically analyzes four existing, nationally representative survey datasets of American parents and congregations that included questions about the transmission of faith and practice to children: the National Study of Youth and Religion survey (2002–13), the Culture of American Families survey (2012), the Faith and Families in America survey (2005), and the US Congregational Life Survey (2008–9). The results of those statistical analyses provide a big-picture, contextual framework that is nationally representative, within which we can set and understand the qualitative findings from our personal interviews in this book.

religious parents. Our purpose is to identify the major themes, differences, and complexities concerning faith transmission to children among American religious parents. Our findings from the interviews, again, do not purport to represent all types of religious parents in proportion to their numbers in the population. Still, we believe they offer great insight. We are confident that our interview-sampling methodology has exposed us to major swaths of different kinds of American religious parents, so that our findings do identify the major cultural models of religious parenting in the United States. Our story is certainly not complete and our findings do not represent in exact proportion the full population of American religious parents. But we are assured that the themes we present in the following chapters are real and roughly proportionate to their reality in American life.

Our interview sample, again, represents *religious* parents, those who have some membership connection to a church, synagogue, temple, or mosque.[12] Our focus is American parents who are religiously connected and invested enough to have a tie to a religious congregation, not the full range of all American parents. We intentionally chose to investigate the religiously "higher end" of American parents because we think they will provide greater insight to better answer the research questions we are asking. Readers must keep in mind, then, that we are not discussing American parents of all levels of religious commitment—even if our sample includes a lot of variation of religious commitment—but relatively more highly religious American parents.

The Overriding Importance of Parents

The single, most powerful causal influence on the religious lives of Americans teenagers and young adults is the religious lives of their parents. Not their peers, not the media, not their youth group leaders or clergy, not their religious school teachers. Myriad studies show that, beyond a doubt, the parents of Americans play *the* leading role in shaping the character of their religious and spiritual lives, even well after they leave home and

12. The nonreligious parents we interviewed were a convenience sample, intended to provide some comparative leverage for our religious sample, not the basis of a study of nonreligious parents in its own right. In fact, we found that the nonreligious parents we interviewed reflected the same underlying cultural models about life, children, and parenting as the religious parents—their basic assumptions, perspectives, and priorities sounded nearly identical—the only difference being that the religious parents naturally spoke more personally about the value and importance of religion.

often for the rest of their lives.[13] Furthermore, this parental influence has not declined in effectiveness since the 1970s.[14] Some American parents seem to think that they lose most of their influence over their children around the early teen years; more than a few American teenagers act as if their parents no longer matter much in their lives. But in most cases those are cultural myths belied by the sociological facts.

The influence of parents on children while they still live at home—including their influence on their religious identities, beliefs, and practices—is paramount, lasting for years, decades, often lifetimes. The best general predictor of what any American is like religiously, after comparing all of the other possible variables and factors, is what their parents were like religiously when they were raising their children. Parents do not of course control or determine the religious lives of their children, and

13. Smith with Denton, *Soul Searching*; Christian Smith with Patricia Snell, *Souls in Transition* (New York: Oxford University Press, 2009); Bengtson, *Families and Faith*; S. Myers, "An Interactive Model of Religious Inheritance: The Importance of Family Context," *American Sociological Review* 61 (1996): 858–66; Lisa Pearce and Arland Thornton, "Religious Identity and Family Ideologies in the Transition to Adulthood," *Journal of Marriage and Family* 69 (2007): 1227–43; Richard Petts, "Trajectories of Religious Participation from Adolescence to Young Adulthood," *Journal for the Scientific Study of Religion* 48 (2009): 552–71; Marjorie Gunnoe and K. Moore, "Predictors of Religiosity among Youth Aged 17–22," *Journal for the Scientific Study of Religion* 41 (2002): 613–22; Christopher Bader and S. Desmond, "Do as I Say and as I Do: The Effects of Consistent Parental Beliefs and Behaviors upon Religious Transmission," *Sociology of Religion* 67 (2006): 313–29; Darren Sherkat, "Religious Socialization," in *Handbook of the Sociology of Religion*, ed. Michele Dillon (New York: Cambridge University Press, 2003), 151–63; J. Kim, Michael McCullough, and D. Chicchetti, "Parents' and Children's Religiosity and Child Behavioral Adjustment among Maltreated and Non-maltreated Children," *Journal of Child and Family Studies* 18 (2009): 594–605; Vern Bengtson, C. Copen, N. Putney, and M. Silverstein, "A Longitudinal Study of Intergenerational Transmission of Religion," *International Sociology* 24 (2009): 325–45; Sarah Spilman, Tricia Neppl, Brent Donnellan, Thomas Schofield, and Rand Conger, "Incorporating Religiosity into a Developmental Model of Positive Family Functioning across Generations," *Developmental Psychology* 49 (2013): 762–74; Pamela King, J. Furrow, and N. Roth, "The Influence of Families and Peers on Adolescent Religiousness," *Journal of Psychology and Christianity* 21 (2002): 109–20; W. Bao, L. Whitbeck, D. Hoyt, and Rand Conger, "Perceived Parental Acceptance as a Moderator of Religious Transmission among Adolescent Boys and Girls," *Journal of Marriage and Family* 61 (1999): 362–74; R. Day, H. Jones-Sanpei, J. Smith Price, D. Orthner, E. Hair, K. Moore, and K. Kaye, "Family Processes and Adolescent Religiosity and Religious Practice," *Marriage and Family Review* 45 (2009): 289–309; K. Hyde, *Religion in Childhood and Adolescence* (Birmingham: Religious Education Press, 1990); E. Maccoby, "The Role of Parents in the Socialization of Children," *Developmental Psychology* 28 (1992): 1006–17; John Wilson and Darren Sherkat, "Returning to the Fold," *Journal for the Scientific Study of Religion* 33 (1994): 148–61.

14. Bengtson, *Families and Faith*, 54–67, 185–86.

many households produce children whose religious lives vary wildly. But a large body of accumulated research consistently shows that, when viewing Americans as a whole, the influence of parents on religiousness trumps every other influence, however much parents and children may assume otherwise.

That profound influence of parents provides the premise for the importance of this book, which speaks to many audiences. Sociologists are interested in understanding processes of social reproduction, how social practices and beliefs are carried on with continuity from one generation to the next. That involves learning about the role of families and other institutions in the process of socialization.[15] Many parents are also invested in how their children turn out religiously, as are many grandparents, religious leaders, clergy, youth pastors, family friends, teachers, and mentors.[16] Since parents are so important in shaping the religious outcomes of their children, their approach to the matter deserves to be understood and explained well.

In fact, however, social scientists have conducted surprisingly little reliable empirical research on the culture of parenting in the intergenerational transmission of religious faith and practice. Sociology contains a massive literature on marriage and family, some of which engages questions of religion, since in America family and religion are so closely tied together.[17] The sociology of religion has also enjoyed a recent burgeoning of studies on the religious lives of teenagers and emerging adults. Sociologists of religion have also long studied religious conversion from one faith (or lack thereof) to another. Some sociologists and political scientists also research institutions involved in socialization generally, including political socialization, such as families, schools, peer groups, and the media. But few have studied the perspectives and approaches of parents themselves

15. For a landmark and exemplary work focused on social inequality, see Annette Lareau, *Unequal Childhoods: Class, Race, and Family Life* (Berkeley: University of California Press, 2011).

16. Some previous studies show that grandparents play a significant role in the religious outcomes of their grandchildren (e.g., Valerie King and Glen Elder, "Are Religious Grandparents More Involved Grandparents?" *Journal of Gerontology* 54 [1999]: S317–S328; Holly Allen and Heidi Oschwald, "The Spiritual Influence of Grandparents," *Christian Education Journal* 5, no. 2 [2018]: 346–62). Our focus in this study and the nature of our data do not, however, lend themselves to an investigation of the role of grandparents in this process.

17. For example, Penny Edgell, *Religion and Family in a Changing Society* (Princeton, NJ: Princeton University Press, 2006); Wesley Burr, Loren Marks, and Randal Day, *Sacred Matters: Religion and Spirituality in Families* (New York: Routledge, 2012).

when it comes to the religious socialization of their children—especially on a national level that includes a broad array of religious traditions and other demographic variables.[18] This book (and a second book produced by this same research project)[19] redresses that deficiency.

Rethinking Culture

This book is not only an empirical analysis of how religious parents in the United States approach passing on faith to their children. We also advance a theoretical argument about the nature and workings of culture. Our argument calls into question a broad set of theories of culture that have dominated cultural sociology and anthropology since the 1980s. We do not critique one specific school or theory of culture. Rather, we address an assemblage of views that nonetheless share strong family resemblances marked by the influence of common reactions in the 1970s and '80s against the previously dominant view of culture.

For present purposes, suffice it to say that we went into our interviews with religious American parents from many backgrounds expecting to encounter diversity, but instead we heard something approaching consensus. We anticipated parental conversations about life, religion, and children to display internal incoherence, but instead discovered an underlying coherence and reasonable intelligibility. We sampled our interview respondents intentionally to examine differences between religious traditions, race and ethnicity, social class, gender, household type, and rural-urban background, but we encountered instead assumptions, hopes, and strategies that are widely shared across those differences. Rather than rummaging their "tool kits" of culturally acceptable explanations to justify their practices, our interview respondents expressed presuppositions, convictions, and expectations that were clearly internalized and dear to their hearts. After completing our interviews, we spent two years meticulously coding and analyzing our data just as the standard "variables sociology" mentality would advise, but in the end we found not disparate outcomes correlated with differing categories, but a general approach shared across the categories, almost as if it had been systematically indoctrinated.

---

18. See, for example, the observations of S. Hardy, J. White, Z. Zhang, and J. Ruchty, "Parenting and Socialization of Religiousness and Spirituality," *Psychology of Religion and Spirituality* 3 (2011): 217–30; Kim, McCullough, and Chicchetti, "Parents' and Children's Religiosity"; P. Heaven, J. Ciarrochi, and P. Leeson, "Parental Styles and Religious Values among Teenagers," *Journal of Genetic Psychology* 171 (2010): 93–99.

19. Smith and Adamczyk, *Handing Down the Faith*.

This book's theoretical contribution grounded in our empirical case, therefore, is to show that culture can be *coherent, consensual, reasonable, internalized,* and *teleological* in its orientation to *guiding* life practices. This is not an argument for a return to antiquated theories of culture. Instead, we wish to move forward into a theoretical space that corrects numerous over-reactions and mistakes of the dominant approach of recent decades. Toward that end, this book reconstructs the "cultural models" that inform how American religious parents approach the transmission of religious faith and practice to their children, through a careful analysis of their extended talking about that and related subjects. Chapter 5 then elaborates our theoretical view on the relationship between such discourse, culture, and cultural models. But first, the next four chapters demonstrate our central empirical case for the reality, coherence, agreement about, and substantive reasonability of cultural models.

CHAPTER ONE

The Purpose and Nature of Life

HOW DO RELIGIOUS PARENTS in the United States approach the job of passing on their family's faith and practices to their children? What assumptions, categories, and beliefs inform their views on the question? Which desires, feelings, and concerns influence the ways they undertake the transmission of their religion to their kids? This chapter answers those questions by systematically analyzing the cultural models that most US parents hold about the issue. To be clear, we are not examining parents' actual faith-transmission practices, their behaviors—although we do consider their reports about their behaviors. Our concern instead is to identify the relevant cultural models that parents hold, which we also have good reason to believe significantly influence their behaviors. In short, we are interested in cognitive frameworks that we think shape practices rather than the practices themselves. We presented the basic idea of cultural models in the introduction, and we will elaborate our theory of cultural models in a later chapter. But first we simply explore the cultural models themselves.

A Constellation of Cultural Models

The dominant cultural model of most American religious parents for why and how they should pass on their religious faith and practices to their children can be summarized this way:

> *Intergenerational Religious Transmission*: Parents are responsible for preparing their children for the challenging journey of life, during which they will hopefully become their best possible selves and live happy, good lives. Religion provides crucial help for navigating life's

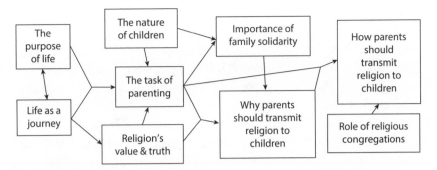

FIGURE 1. The Constellation of Cultural Models Defining Why and How American Parents Should Transmit Religious Faith and Practice to Children. Source: The Intergenerational Religious Transmission Project Interviews, 2014–16 (N = 235).

journey successfully, including moral guidance, emotional support, and a secure home base. So parents should equip their children with knowledge of their religion by routinely modeling its practices, values, and ethics, which children will then hopefully absorb and embrace for themselves.

This is the simplest, most compressed version of the cultural model of intergenerational religious transmission, compacted into which are a host of related and supporting beliefs, metaphors, and meanings that we must decompress, unpack, and examine to understand this matter adequately. Doing so reveals a constellation of cultural models that hang together in parents' cognitive networks, representing and governing their approach to religious transmission. Our interest is with their cultural models of the purpose and means of passing on religion to children. But those make sense because of related cultural models about life's purpose, experience in the world, the nature of children, the task of parenting, family solidarity, religion's value and truth, and the role of religious congregations. Figure 1 represents the full constellation of these models. This chapter and the following three chapters describe each model from the parents' perspective, elucidating the metaphors, beliefs, and language that parents use to express themselves on the issue.

Few American parents think like philosophers. People generally do not consider or discuss life in systematic, coherent, logical terms. When people give verbal accounts of their ideas and actions, much of what they say in the moment can be pretty uncertain, inarticulate, and spotty. But that does not mean people are not reflective or do not have explicable reasons for the ways they live. They usually do. If as scholars we cannot perceive those reasons, the problem is ours, not theirs. To identify and understand people's reflective reasons motivating and making meaningful how they live, we need to listen long and analyze patiently. When we do, people's thinking can become clearer, usually taking the form of networks of clusters of beliefs, which we can represent in cultural models.

To validate and illuminate the propositions comprising the cultural models, we provide numerous interview quotes from parents for each. We want to demonstrate the collectively shared nature of these cultural models, so we err on the side of offering more rather than less substantiating interview evidence. We actually could have supplied many more quotes, but we limit ourselves to avoid extreme evidence overkill. Many of the quotes contain statements that overlap with ideas in different cultural models. Certain themes—such as the importance of being happy and a good person—recurrently circle back and associate with each other across the models. That is because in the minds of parents those ideas really do connect in complex networks of beliefs and metaphors that are intricately linked. It is also because, as we said, people do not ordinarily think and express themselves in highly systematic forms, especially when "on their feet."

In this chapter and in the following three chapters we arrange myriad interview quotes in something like a "mosaic of words" in which pieces of parental talk, like bits of tile, fit together to make a single mosaic that, when stepped back from and viewed as a whole, presents an intelligible picture. Only in our case the picture is not created from the artist's mind but is a representation of the real underlying cultural models of religious parents. In theory, if we showed these cultural models to the parents we interviewed, and if they were thoughtful and honest with themselves, they would react by saying, "Yes, that's just what I think. Thank you for putting it into words." Our sociological task, then, is to reconstruct as accurately as possible from the mass of messy interview materials the cultural models that parents actually embrace but which they can have difficulty making explicit and cogent. In that, we are looking to understand and explain (what critical realists call) "the real" (the cultural models) that operates behind and beneath "the empirical" (the interviews). To do so, we must read not only on the "surface" of interview statements, as if they might only provide direct propositional "proofs" of beliefs, but also discern and ferret out the assumptions and beliefs that stand behind and beneath the interview quotes, ideas that are latent in or must be presupposed by the surface statements and by interviews read as wholes—using what critical realists call "retroductive" and "abductive" reasoning.[1] "Mosaics of words" depict individual cultural models, which then, when arranged in a network by relevant thematic logic, comprise the constellations of cultural models that together answer our research questions (figure 2).

A few words about taking in the many quotes by parents offered in this chapter. Readers may be tempted simply to read the italicized highlights and skim the quotes as mere "yada yada" supporting evidence. However, we recommend spending the time and effort to unhurriedly and closely read all of the parent quotes for two reasons. First, a key theoretical point of our analysis is that the cultural models to which the many quotes point are truly widespread among and shared by the otherwise highly diverse group of parents we interviewed. Unlike some other kinds of sociological arguments, the persuasiveness of that particular kind of claim demands a certain manner of consideration and reception on the part of readers. Skimming will not do. A fair evaluation of our point depends not only on the adequacy of our exposition as authors but also on the reader's manner of reception of the talk of parents. Our theoretical point will be accepted (or not) not merely intellectually but also existentially, we think, as a kind of personal knowledge embraced or refused.[2] Part of the burden of proof of the particular theoretical claim we are making thus rests on readers sustaining a posture of thoughtful but open reception to the reality of the cultural models we reconstruct. And that is best achieved by allowing the weight, richness, and complexity of countless quotes from parent interviews to sink in and marinate in readers' minds.

Second, we hope our exposition makes more than a theoretical point, but also some practical, social, and moral ones. We believe that an attentive and empathetic reading of parent quotes can humanize those parents for readers, even when they represent different religions, races, ethnicities, social classes, and immigration statuses, and even when one does not agree with all they say. Conducting this research humanized these parents for us, and we hope it has a similar effect on readers. But that requires readers to treat the parent quotes not as mere "data" but as the generously shared beliefs, thoughts, feelings, hopes, fears, and joys of very real people with whom we may be better able to relate than we might have imagined. In the world today, such empathetic understanding and connection across differences is imperative and urgent, and sociology rightly contributes to

1. See Berth Danermark et al., *Explaining Society: Critical Realism in the Social Sciences* (New York: Routledge, 2002), 73–114.

2. Michael Polanyi, *Personal Knowledge* (Chicago: University of Chicago Press, 1974).

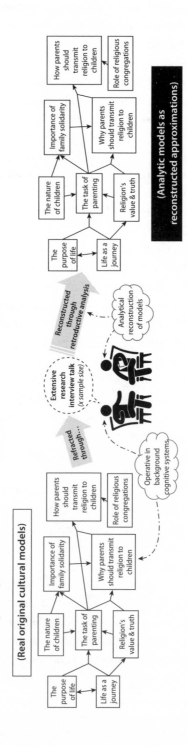

FIGURE 2. The Analytical Reconstruction of Real Cultural Models through the Retroductive Analysis of Extensive Interview Talk.

it. We think the time and effort readers invest in carefully absorbing the quotes below will be rewarded in ways that not only benefit readers but also strengthen the common good.

We focus on the "dominant" cultural models of religious transmission to children, by which we mean the models held by the majority of American religious parents across most religious traditions. We realize that our emphasis on similarity across religious traditions violates the current insistence, especially in the discipline of religious studies, on the detailed particularities of different religious traditions, sub-traditions, and sub-sub-traditions. The days of fitting "the World Religions" into neat analytical typologies and categories or speaking blithely about "*the* Judeo-Christian worldview" are over, and rightly so. Nevertheless, for our purposes, the empirical evidence in fact does point to *sameness* and *convergence* across religious traditions, which we cannot ignore, even if it does not fit the expectations of some scholarly fields. We do note when different kinds of parents accentuate different aspects of the shared dominant cultural models as well as exceptions and contradictions when they arise. But our primary focus is on what is dominant due to its being widely shared. Doing so means exploring the constellation of cultural models representing the approach of most American religious parents to intergenerational religious transmission, which, it so happens, starts where philosophers might have us begin: beliefs about the purpose of life.

The Purpose of Life

What religious parents in the United States believe about the specific issue of intergenerational religious transmission is partly driven by what they believe about the general issue of the purpose of human life. To understand the *specific* we must first comprehend the *general*. For the vast majority of American religious parents, the cultural model of the purpose of life is this:

> *Life's Purpose*: The purpose of living is to lead a happy and good life, in the dual sense of both having life go well (enjoying success and happiness) and living life rightly (doing what is morally right). A good life is one in which self-directed individuals are happy, live ethically, work hard, enjoy family and friends, and help other people. Good lives must be self-determined and pursued in ways that are true to each unique individual self. But they should not be individualistic in the sense of isolated or selfish; they must always be realized and enjoyed with

others, in and with communities, groups, families, and probably marriage partners. Good lives achieve a certain quality of life in this world,
in the here and now; they are not primarily preparing for the hereafter,
eternity, or some ultimate reality. In order to realize life's purpose of
living well, one must be equipped by others with preparation, learning, and competences for the task of self-realization—without which
one may become lost, compromised, or fail in life. Still, each individual
must find his or her own particular way to discover their own purpose
and lead a good life true to who they are as a unique self.

We unpack, validate, and illuminate this cultural model proposition by
proposition, as follows.

*The purpose of living is to lead a happy and good life, in the dual sense
of both having life go well (enjoying success and happiness) and living
life rightly (doing what is morally right). A good life is one in which self-
directed individuals are happy, live ethically, work hard, enjoy family and
friends, and help other people.*

Among the 235 American parents we interviewed for this study, it is
not possible to find even one who does not assume, affirm, and support
these first two propositions of this cultural model. These ideas are "hegemonic," as sociologists say, among parents from every religious tradition,
race, ethnicity, social class, family structure, and region of the country
examined here. These ideas are also expressed equally for boy and girl
children and regardless of the number of children parents may have.[3]
A modest offering of interview quotes—just a few among the many we
could have offered—will help make that point. Remember that sometimes
parents' investment in these ideas are explicit and other times tacit, presupposed, and indirectly evident in what they say.

Consider, for example, the expressed wishes of this mainline Protestant father from New York City: "I hope my kids have friends and good
relationships and be happy. Get married and have a family of their own,
only if that's what they want. I hope they have meaningful relationships
and friendships with people that give them love and friendship." And
those of this mainline Protestant mother from the same area: "I hope my

---

3. More broadly, the sex and number of their children made no difference in the ways
that parents talked in their interviews that expressed the operative cultural models discussed in these chapters. Neither, for that matter, did mothers and fathers differ in the ways
they talked. Nor did single parents or those with low incomes speak differently from those
in two-parent or higher income households.

children find careers they want to be in, that they're both married and have kids and have a house just like me—I have no doubt in my mind they will achieve those things. How much money they earn is not important, because I've learned that money really doesn't do anything, as far as truly being happy, having good friends, money doesn't make any difference. So it's not about that, but really being happy." Speaking of his own life, a white conservative Protestant father from Florida told us: "I pretty much have accomplished just about everything I want to. Money doesn't make you happy, but I have a pretty rich, happy, wonderful life, no complaints. Now, to see my business grow, watch my children grow up, that's really all I look to accomplish in the next ten years, so I'm pretty complacent and happy with where I'm at in life." A black Protestant mother from Houston shared, "I want my sons to be productive citizens, to go to school, graduate, and be productive citizens. I don't want them to fall victim to the monotony and ridicule many black men have to deal with. I just want them to be successful and productive, well-rounded, Christian young men."

Catholic parents spoke the same way. A white Catholic father from New York City said, "I want my kids to be really happy people. Happy people who like their parents, who like their family, to be independent. I want them to explore the world, to be interesting people, good people, to be kind and generous." A white Catholic mother from Indiana explained, "We don't have any major issues. Our kids are healthy and happy and they love their school. My husband has a good job, and we're just comfortable. Our biggest family value is just trying to just be happy, and I tell my kids, no one's happy unless you're being nice to each other [laughs]. I just want everyone to get along and be happy. I just want them to find a path that makes them happy. As long as they're making enough money to live, I don't care how successful they are, if they're successful for them, if they're just happy doing what they need to do." A Hispanic Catholic mother from Chicago told us, "We try to do the best we can for our kids, whether it be a Catholic education, so they become good men in the future. Giving material things, but better with education and teaching them that in the future they will be good people." Another Hispanic Catholic father from Chicago explained: "My dream for my children is they are a good person. I hope when I'm done, I've given them the tools to be able to take care of themselves, both in their personal life and spiritual life. I hope they're doing what makes them happy."

The statements in interviews become monotonously repetitive, but that empirical pattern makes an important theoretical point about cognitions and culture, namely, that very different kinds of people can share the same cultural models of what is real and important in the world and how it works. The repeated perspective continues beyond mainstream Christian traditions. A Mormon mother from Indiana told us, "I used to want them all to be doctors and lawyers, but since we're older now I really just want them to be happy. And good people in society, part of society, actively trying to progress in some way and don't just settle." Likewise, a Jewish father also from Indiana explained, "I may not have had the most exciting life, but family and faith and ethics and all those things are what I value, and they have been there, on both sides of the family. So that's something worth striving for." This Jewish mother from the same area told us, "We have a very comfortable life, a stable marriage, healthy kids who are successful, and we don't want for a lot, so we have a good life. My husband and I have worked hard and stayed focused through our educations to be able to get what we wanted. And we have been successful, so it's nice." And one Jewish mother from New York City said, "I think all those books that say it's not about the destination but about the process are really wrong. It's about attainment, and when there's something that you want really badly and you don't obtain it, there's nothing worse."

A Hindu father from Chicago explained his view of life, "We are not going to live for long, it's a short period, and in that time we should be a good person. Everybody should say they have lived a very nice life, know how to live like a good role model, not a bad life." This Hindu mother also from Chicago said about her daughter, "Overall I think she has to be a good human being at the end of the day, but then, yeah, if she becomes a doctor, that'd be good for her." A Muslim mother from Indiana told us, "I just want to see my daughter married and happy in her life, and my son successful just like his dad and even better. To be able to establish a good life and be on his own and live a respectful life and earn everything and have appreciation for what he has, then I'll be happy" A Buddhist father from Chicago explained about his daughter's possible future religion, "As long as she's a good and happy person, she can believe [religiously] what she wants." And this (non-theist) Buddhist mother also from Chicago said about her girls: "I want them to be happy, whatever that means, and to be independent and strong and smart about it, meaning don't get dependent on a man. That screwed me up. Be your own person first, then worry about men later. Have fun while you're growing up. So I want them to be happy, good people, good happy people. If we had more of those in the world, things would be nicer." These common beliefs lay the bedrock of a most basic cultural model held and expressed by religious parents in the United States about the purpose of life. Additional belief propositions build on them.

Good lives must be self-determined and pursued in ways that are true to each unique individual self.

This proposition is also universally embraced as obvious by all the parents we interviewed. Listen to this Hispanic Catholic father from New Mexico: "In life you have to have it all: to be healthy, intelligent, and everything. But for my children I want mainly that they're well, and that they achieve what they really want, not what I want. What they want." And this Hispanic Catholic mother from New York City: "I would love to see them finish school and become something accomplished, whatever they want to do in life. To see them good in life so that I could move on and do whatever I want to do. I can't do it until I see them happy, so I would love to see them happy." Or this white Catholic father from Chicago: "They can choose whatever religion or beliefs they want, just be successful and happy with whatever you do. Enjoy life, 'cause it's short. That's really what I want. They're free to do whatever they want, just like sports: I'll never force you to do anything. Overall we have done a good job of letting them choose their paths, but also giving them the foundation and structure to build on so they're successful and happy. Even if they choose to change religions or not have the same political or whatever beliefs as me, as long as they're successful and happy, I'm happy."

This view of individual self-determination shaped not only parents' views of children but also their own lives, as is clear in the statement of this Hispanic Catholic father from New Mexico: "I decided to become Catholic. Do you understand me? I had many choices, I could be Mormon, evangelical, Baptist, Pentecostal. Or Catholic, and I decided to become Catholic. Because I liked it, I got to know it, I understood that that was my truth, and now I no longer think on anything else. I have no doubts."

These ideas are repeated by Protestant parents too, as with this mainline Protestant father from Indiana: "Each journey is different, there's so much that says, you're different, a unique person, so I'm going to treat you without the judgment of *my* expectations on you. Yes, we expect you to be honorable and dignified, but not to go out and make a million dollars, though if that happens, glory be to God." The same is expressed by this mainline Protestant mother from Washington, DC: "I try to instill them with their own beliefs and values and to feel good and solid about those, not in a way that's negative to anybody else, just good with who they are and know and are okay with what they believe." A white conservative Protestant mother from Florida said, "I hope my grown kids are different and individual in their own thinking and lifestyle. If they want to travel an RV around, that's fine." Some of the black Protestant parents we interviewed expressed the same idea, though especially emphasized financial independence, as with this black Protestant mother from Houston, "I want for my children that they grow up in the church, be successful, be independent, able to take care of themselves. None of my siblings are at home with my mom, we all grew up and got on our own. That's what I ask, that's our prayer, stay strong in church, be able to grow up and be independent, and don't leave, be helpful to your parents."

This theme continues across other religious traditions. This Muslim father from New York City answered our question about his hopes for his children this way: "Honestly, whatever path they choose, I just want them to be content and happy. Being content is the most important thing to me. The world is their oyster, right?" And this Muslim mother from Indiana told us: "I always want them to be safe, happy, educated. I want them to be in control of their life instead of life choosing for them. I want them to be open to everything and worldly, so that they can decide what they want to be in charge." A Hindu father from central New Jersey said, "If he's different [from me], I'm okay as long as he's happy, if he's happy and safe I'm okay. I will try to guide him to make sure that he follows the correct paths, but I don't really care about the political or religious, as long as he's happy and safe that's my main concern." Likewise, this Buddhist mother from Chicago told us, "He wants to become another religion? By all means, you have the choice, it's your belief. But think it through, not just because friends do it or dad did or family did it, *you* have to believe it now, you have to use your own judgment wisely and then you will see." This Jewish father from New York City explained: "I want them to do what they want to do, basically. But I'd love to see them contributing to society in some way. It doesn't have to be winning a Nobel prize or something, just being a productive member of the human race. It's important for them to figure out how they're gonna fit in to that. I can't prescribe for them what to do. But I want them to be decent people, to think of others, and appreciate what they have."

While pondering the idea of her children switching from Conservative to Orthodox Judaism, this Jewish mother said, "I might not choose them becoming Orthodox [Jewish], but as long as it was a lifestyle where they could be happy functioning in the US, then I'm really pretty open. I don't want them to be a cookie-cutter version of me, but to do their own thinking." Similarly, a Mormon mother from Indiana told us: "I want my kids to learn that in being good they have free agency, that you yourself are an individual free person, you can make choices, they are your choices to make, and you are responsible for those choices, you don't blame other people for them. If I hear one more person say it's their mom's fault that they did something! No, it's not. You can only blame somebody so much for something that's happened twenty years ago, then you've gotta go on. Also to learn it's okay to be different and tolerant. Spiritually, they need to listen to themselves, what some refer to as the Holy Spirit, whatever makes you question situations, to learn that it's okay if you are different from your friends, it's okay to follow that. Just being yourself. You can use religion for that, to some degree, you don't have to be like everybody else." Another Mormon father from the same area related this as what he tells his difficult son: "When you have a kid not doing quite what you want, but at the same time I love him, if that's what he wants, that's his life and I've told him that for years and years, it's your life. I'll give you some advice I know you won't take, because at age 19, at what age do you start listening to people's advice? It's a concern, but at the same time, it's his life and he's gotta live it." The story is thus identical across all of these demographic differences: in life, each individual must be self-determining and true to their unique selves.

Before proceeding, we should note that none of the propositions of these cultural models is humanly obvious, necessary, or universal. If they seem obvious to some readers, it is not because they are objective common sense or necessary, but because those readers happen also to share commitments to these same cultural models—making their power all the more evident. But for perspective, remember that if this study had instead interviewed parents in, say, hunting-gathering tribes, warrior societies, medieval feudal systems, modern communist parties, or Amish communities, we would have had to reconstruct very different cultural models of life, religion, and parenting. To get the most out of this analysis, we do well to remember the sociological imperative to "make strange the ordinary," especially what is ordinary to us.

But they can never be individualistic in the sense of isolated or selfish; they must always be realized and enjoyed with others, in and with communities, groups, families, and probably marriage partners.

This communal imperative qualifies the autonomous individualism just observed, confirming sociologist Claude Fischer's observations about American individualism being a particular type, a "voluntaristic" individualism in which the voluntary joining of associations and enjoyment of chosen social relationships is normative.[4] Many of the following quotes came as immediate responses to our asking what parents' biggest hopes and dreams are for their children. Again, often this belief is explicitly stated and other times only presupposed, implicit, or latent in what is said. One Buddhist mother from Chicago, for instance, said about her children, "Above all I want them to be happy, happy and a good person, good at heart. And good for the community. Right now in society there's difficult and aggressive, selfish people and I don't want my kid to be that way." A Buddhist father also from Chicago explained: "Anything you do to give back to society is practicing Buddhism. The core value for us is family stability, well-rounded kids, that the kids are functioning. Some parents demand their kids be the best. For us, as long as they're functioning well and can benefit society in the future, that's good. You want to make sure they're whole as persons, and you have to provide a stable family for that. So, helping society, doing what you love and being passionate about it, and always give back. Those are the most important."

The Jewish parents we interviewed also emphasized this theme. One Jewish mother from New York City said, "I want my children to feel connected to another person, to have work that has meaning for them, pleased to enjoy their lives, and make some kind of contribution, I don't care what way, whatever that involves." Another from New York City said, "I want them to have the same values as us, valuing family, community, bettering themselves, taking care of themselves, not letting people push them around." And this Jewish mother from New York told us, "I want for my kids to be happy with themselves and their lives, to know not only their needs matter but others' needs as well, and to learn how to negotiate that. I want for them to love deeply and freely and to be loved that way, to be grateful and giving and generous, to give back to the planet. That's what our lives are based on and what we have valued and what I want for them."

American Hindu parents spoke similarly, as with this mother from Chicago: "I want him to become a good father. Then a person who's not standing in one place but moving forward, always checking himself to ask what can I do better? Not lazy, physically, mentally, or emotionally. A humble nature, not being arrogant. That's what I want him to be. The rest all depends on luck and fate, whatever comes to him will come." One

---

4. Claude Fischer, "Paradoxes of American Individualism," *Sociological Forum* 23, no. 2 (2008): 363–72.

Hindu father from central New Jersey said, "I want him to be really happy, happy with his life, no regrets, to do whatever he wants to do. But at the same time be caring and gentle and compassionate, I just I want him to value life." More succinctly, a Hindu mother from Chicago told us, "I just want him to be good human being, treat people with respect, and be more jolly about things."

These themes were equally evident among Christians. Consider, for instance, this view of a mainline Protestant father from Washington, DC: "At the most fundamental level, it's kind of like what the New Testament describes as how you're supposed to form your faith, it's your independent decision, but you live it out in a community with other people." A mainline Protestant mother from Washington, DC, described the kind of life she hopes her children have: "Being a good person, a caring human being out into the community. That's important." Not very differently, a white conservative Protestant father from Los Angeles said: "First I want them to grow up to have Christian faith of their own, and from there for them to serve the community around them as it's needed. I don't really care what they want to be, but that they're able to serve their neighbor in the best way possible—if that means being a garbage man, awesome, we need garbage men; if it means being a doctor, great. Whatever that turns out to be is probably their individual bent." This conservative Protestant mother from Florida said: "I value family, for sure, being tight and supportive and loyal to each other. My kids are pretty close anyway, but I want them to be there for each other, no matter what. So I value family time, and our role in the church, our community, being active in our community. I hope they all have maturing spiritual relationships of their own, individualized, not something somebody else created for them. And service, I want service to be a part of our family life." And this black Protestant father told us: "I grew up going to work, being there for family, going to church, and having a positive attitude and being helpful. We're kinda helpful people. If somebody need help, we'll help 'em, you know. Always trying to reach out and help somebody and being there for somebody. I always say, don't bother nobody, but if somebody need help or something, we'll do what we can." And this Hispanic Catholic father discussed his core life priorities: "Sometimes one gets plagued to think you should live in another city, or a certain house, or have some type of car or live in comfort. I just want to feel happy, to feel free, in this habitat where I am, be calm, and above all to protect my family, my two children, my wife, my mom, my sister, living here in the city. To know they're doing well, to have the closest, feel well with them, and that makes me feel good."

Many parents from various, but not all, religious traditions—perhaps especially conservative Protestant and Mormon families—commonly express their hopes that their children marry and have kids. A Mormon mother from Indiana, for example, told us: "I want my children to be successful, to pursue whatever dream they have, and to succeed. I want them to get married, to have children, to be happy above everything. And to be good people, to whoever they're around." This white conservative Protestant father also from Indiana explained: "I hope they get married, to have that experience. I hope they find somebody to complete themselves as one, two shall become one, somebody that loves Jesus more than they love anybody, especially themselves. I don't care if they dig ditches, if they're in missionary work, in ministry, I don't care what they do, but be in love with Jesus and find a spouse who will love them as Christ loves the church. You'll have joy." A Buddhist mother from Chicago said, "I want them to get married and have kids, that my daughter will meet somebody who is Chinese or Vietnamese, to keep our custom and tradition." A Hindu mother from central New Jersey reported, "I just want to see my girl all settled, find somebody nice [to marry] and be settled, happy, educated, make the right decisions in life. I want her to find the right job that she wants to do, not something she's not interested in. As long as she's happy, money doesn't matter, she will find a way to make it." A conservative Protestant mother from Washington, DC, reported to us: "Thirty years from now I think they'll be a replica of me, their mom, married, they'll be strong and members of a church. Hopefully they'll get married by that time, and be in a career and wherever they go representing what they believe in." And this Mormon father from Indiana said, "We try to encourage them to pursue goals, being contributing members of society, but also to have jobs that pay [laughs]. To have families, which is a source of joy and fulfillment."

But pushing marriage and grandchildren was not on the agenda of all. Hear, for example, what this white Catholic mother from Indiana said of her hopes for her daughter:

> I want her to be independent and know she does not need a man to survive. I want her to balance being independent and knowing you need things in life too, and there's a fine line. I want her not to be so independent that she can't see that she does need help. We all need things from people. We can't do everything alone. But there's a fine line of being too independent where relationships struggle because she feels she doesn't need anybody. That's a hard line I think especially for women.

On the specific point of the priority of finding a mate, this view opposes those just quoted above. But on the deeper cultural point about independent individuals not becoming selfish or isolated but learning how to share and enjoy life with others, it shares the same underlying belief.

Here is a good place to expand on that observation and make a key distinction. We argue that cultural models can be and often are internally coherent and rationally intelligible. But that does not mean that they are uniformly consistent or monotonic about every idea they entail. The cultural models we are examining in fact can hold quite different beliefs in tension, such as self-determining individual autonomy versus the obligation of each person to belong, to relate, to contribute, or the importance of getting married versus not being dependent. The cultural models also combine and balance metaphors that suggest different images or dynamics, such as movement and change ("journey," "path," "track") and stability and immobility ("foundation," "grounding," "base"). This observation we further develop in chapter 5.

Some sociologists, perhaps especially those of the Swidlerian persuasion (as we will discuss further in chapter 5), hear these tensions and differences and interpret them as contradictions, incoherence, and confusion, concluding that people do not make sense and could not be motivated in actions by such confused muddles. We beg to differ. Life is complicated. People's beliefs are often complex. The metaphors people always use to make sense of life are inherently analogical and sometimes equivocal. The whole point of metaphors is that certain things are like others in some but not all ways that need not be precisely specified. The evocative but ambiguous image is more telling than any consistent prose description. So just as we have finally learned that emotions are not mutually exclusive with reason,[5] we also must recognize that apparent oppositions, tensions, contradictions, and multi-directionalities in cultural models need not be at odds with their simultaneously being rational, coherent, intelligible, and motivating of purposive action. Sometimes what seems merely confused on the surface of interviews proves with patient and careful saturation in, re-reading, and detailed analysis simply to represent incompletely or inarticulately what is actually a complex, underlying coherence of beliefs and thought. If we are properly to understand the nature of culture generally and the character of cultural models specifically, we need to grasp and accept this reality.

5. See, for instance, Antonio Damasio, *Descartes' Error: Emotion, Reason, and the Human Brain* (New York: Penguin, 2005).

Good lives achieve a certain quality of life in this world, in the here and now; they are not primarily preparing for the hereafter, eternity, or some ultimate reality.

This proposition highlights part of our methodological point that cultural models cannot simply be read off of the surface of interview transcripts. Sometimes just as important as what people say is what they do not say, not the presence but the absence of attention and talk.[6] Noticing that requires researchers to have personal, substantive knowledge of the peoples and cultures they study in order to be sensitive to what "should" have been said but was not, what might have been expected yet was absent. And then in presenting empirical evidence, the challenge is underscoring the significance of discourse that does not exist. In our case, we can show that the parents we interviewed talked a lot about the quality of life in this world, but few of them, despite their being among the most religious of parents in the United States, thought to mention existence after death, eternity, or an ultimate reality (exceptions to this rule we discuss further on). That absence is an important part of the cultural models we exposit. But working mostly with silence on the topic, readers must simply trust that such talk was largely missing in our interviews. And what we can present here are typical references to this-worldly concerns.

What do parents most want for their children? Even when they emphasize morality and character, very rarely are they tied to heaven, salvation, the hereafter, or eternity. For example, a mainline Protestant mother from New York City observed: "In my life now I feel like I have everything that I want. Basically, the things I was looking for was to be married, have kids in the house, and friends. And I have those things, so for me I have everything." A mainline Protestant father from Washington, DC, answered the question about what he wants for his children: "Happy and healthy, honestly. The world isn't easy, there is so much pressure, and I watch parents put their pressures on their kids. Yes, I really want my kids to do well academically. I would like for them to be great athletes, it's fun, it's wonderful. I just want them to be happy and healthy and they can figure the rest out. Would I love for them to be famous for inventing something good for the world? Yes. Would I like for them to be a renowned architect or doctor? Yes. But at the end of the day, happy and healthy is it." A mainline Protestant mother also from Washington, DC, said, "I want my kids

---

6. More generally, critical realism suggests that social science needs to take much more seriously not just what is present in the actual but also what is absent, missing, negations (Roy Bhaskar, *Dialectic* [London: Routledge, 2008]).

to be successful obviously. I want them to be happy and secure and self-confident in doing whatever it is they want to do. I felt like I was insecure in a lot of ways in high school, college, into adulthood. I wasn't sure I was doing the right thing. I would like for them to feel more confident than I was, to be sure of themselves and not wishy-washy." One mainline Protestant father from New York City said, "I want my children to grow up to be gentle and kind, generous and forgiving, it's more of those kinds of qualities and attributes. Academically accomplished for sure too. I want them to excel, I would love that, but that's definitely secondary to having character."

We might expect white conservative Protestants to talk a lot about salvation and heaven, and some do, but most do not. Conservative Protestants more than most do bring religious and spiritual talk into their discussions, but that normally concerns how faith affects their lives now, not heaven or eternity. Consider, for example, the explanation of this conservative Protestant mother from New York City why she wants her children to have religious faith: "I would love for my three kids to embrace the faith. Because I think they'll have a much better life. I want it for them because I think that they'll, yeah, I want it for them. Why? Why? Because I, yeah, I think they'll have a better life. It's really because they'll embrace a way of living with others and acting with others. In life, you go so much more forward when you open yourself and just accept the bumps and keep going, that's an effect in life. I believe they would have a better life if they have faith." In their vocabulary, white conservative Protestant parents usually sound less secular than those from other religious traditions, but in the underlying content of their concerns they are not much more focused on "heavenly" things. Notice, for example, how the vocabulary of "godly" figures into the aspirations of this conservative Protestant mother in Indiana: "I want my girl to be happy and settled, I want her to find a godly man. She has ideas about what she wants to do for work, but I have no ambition in that area, which is nice because I'm not pushing her in any direction. I tell her you're thirteen you don't have to decide yet." The word "godly" drops into this talk, but substantively it is all about this-worldly happiness and success. Or consider this from a conservative Protestant father from Florida: "I hope my kids follow the Lord, get married, and have a happy life. I know there will be ups and downs, but we'll be there for 'em. I just hope they succeed in life. I want them to experience life like there is no tomorrow. I want them to do things, experience life, go overseas, to another country, 'cause I mean God made all this for us to enjoy, it's just living as best you can."

Again, religious talk is present, but the content of the answer is all about enjoying the good things of life in this world, now, "like there's no tomorrow." We could present scores of similar quotes of conservative Protestant parents, but it would become tedious, because they are mostly the same, focusing on success, education, marriage, children, careers, paying bills, the possibilities of fame or distinction, travel, being good people, being happy, and of course "loving Jesus." Still, one last conservative Protestant quote here is worth noting. We asked a conservative Protestant mother from Indiana how she would feel if her children married non-Christians. Her response is revealing:

> I would have concerns, but I don't know as far as their salvation anymore, don't know what I would think about that. I believe in an afterlife, but am just not sure anymore exactly how that all works. I might be worried more about their quality of life now, living a life in peace, feeling at peace and having God's best for them. Maybe more that, and maybe part of me would still worry about their salvation, I just don't know anymore.

The reality of heaven and eternity and the need for salvation are not ignored or denied, but their relevance is uncertain, and of greater concern is a "quality of life now," "feeling peace," and enjoying "God's best."

The talk of parents from other religious traditions follows the same pattern. This black Protestant father from Houston said, "My goals and dreams for my kids? To keep the faith, work hard at whatever job, be the best that they can be, and able to provide for themselves." A white Catholic mother from Indiana described her aspirations this way: "Well first and foremost, I want them to have a relationship with God, to hold on to their faith. And then I want them to be successful, whatever that means to them, I don't know, but happy and successful. And just have a good foundation." A father from the same tradition and state replied, "Health and happiness, that's it, health and happiness and nothing more important, I mean there's nothing more. Whatever makes them happy and I mean that. My grandfather used to say all the time, that if you have your health you have everything, so I just want them to be happy and healthy and happy." This white Catholic mother from New York City said: "I want them to be really happy people, happy people who like their parents, their family. I want them to be independent, to explore the world. I want them to be interesting people, good people, kind and generous." Speaking of his own life, this white Catholic father from Indiana reported, "I'm happy with my life, and

I can't say I would change anything, I have my family, my health, and great friends. What more can I ask for? We've been blessed with good kids, have a roof over our head, and have food on the table, I mean, just be happy." Another white Catholic father also from Indiana told us, "I don't want my kids to grow up being so focused on religion, because you want to have a balance where you're connected to God but you have to have your feet on the ground too. This life is about balance, so if you have your head in the clouds the entire time, you lose the connection, and I don't want that to happen with them."

Hispanic Catholics discussing their values and aspirations express the same basic commitments to happiness, success, education, family, and so on, enjoyed in this world, but with a few distinctive emphases. Along with white conservative Protestants, they tend to talk more about God than most other parents. And their visions of success for their children tend to be more about upward mobility, "doing better than I did," than children simply reproducing their own material success, which is how other parents tend to talk. One Hispanic Catholic mother from New York City, for instance, said, "I wish they get a little beyond what I've done; I did not do great things, but I feel very happy, very quiet. In the spiritual realm, to be people who are full of the love of God and spirituality. In the intellectual field, as they get a little further, perhaps having their own business." This Hispanic Catholic father from New Mexico told us: "I want them first to know more about God, who he is, why God sent us to the world, that he is our savior. And I would like to see them serving God too. Also that they respect their elders, their parents, their uncles, their grandparents. Then find out what they are interested in studying, whether it's a PhD, a masters, or BA. I want them to study because I think that if maybe I had also studied, I would have [accomplished] something better, another level of life." Again, religion is important in these parental visions, but primarily in order to live good lives on this earth, not as preparation for eternity. Consider the account of this Hispanic Catholic father from New York City: "I have for him many goals! I wish that he be a good man. To make his career. To work. And to make his family. But that he never depart from Christian principles, to keep them, and if you cannot take them to the front, at least that he puts them parallel. Never forget Christian principles. I want him to be a man, that he fights, works, sacrifices, and values everything he has, not what I gave him but that he worked for with much effort, with perseverance." One final accent heard in Hispanic Catholic interviews, especially among the working class, which was absent in the others: the desire by parents for their children to avoid abusive romantic relationships. One Hispanic Catholic mother from New Mexico, for instance, explained:

> I've told my girls, I would like you to live a life not like the one I gave to you, like the past. If you have a violent partner, do not take it. Do not let him touch you. If he verbally abuses, hits you, shreds your clothes, tell the barbarities to your mother. I do not want them to live with such husbands. You reach a breaking point and say, "What kind of life is this?" Some commit suicide. But mine are young, can defend themselves because they went to karate, and as much as you may want a partner, I always instilled in them having a job, buying a home or renting their own apartment, so they can tell their partner, "There's the door. You can go." Be independent. If he does not help, he should not be in the way. And not wish bad things upon him, either. Let him go. Close the door. That chapter is over, get ready for another chapter. Eventually you'll meet another man, despite having a child, who will value you and your child, your family.

We know that abusive intimate relationships and domestic violence are not limited to one race or ethnicity, but of those we interviewed it was Hispanic Catholic parents who included this concern in describing their hoped-for good lives for their children.

Parents from other religious traditions echo the beliefs just expressed. A Muslim father from Indiana said, "I hope my kids get education and are good Muslims, good human beings; and successful in whatever they want to do." A Muslim mother from Indiana reported: "I want to see my kids successful first in their education, being happy. I want to see them married and established and to see my grandkids while I am young. I love to travel all the time. If I can like go on vacation all the time I don't mind it. I like to keep myself busy, between my family and my kids, and always improve with the kids and with my husband. I hope God will give us life and health. Thank God, that's all I'm hoping for." This Hindu father from New York City said he took his newborns to the temple for a prayer that "basically says to the god, 'please help this child to grow up to be a good person and all other things that follow, make her very educated,' so it comes hand in hand, because if you are well educated you'll have good money and likely attract a person to get married and so forth." And what does he want for his daughter now? "To become a person who does what we did, helping people, open minded, to be a person who does something good in life. So I tell my daughter, work hard to get better grades to make sure you can do what you want, because if you don't get good grades you can't go to medical school. Try to do better for yourself, that's your good karmas,[7] if you do good, then good is coming your way." The following particularly Jewish view, spoken by a Jewish mother in Indiana, states explicitly what we find functionally to be the implicit view of the majority of American parents in most religious traditions, whether or not they could say it this bluntly:

> One thing I like about Judaism and why I feel so connected to it is how much it focuses on how you live your life today, here on earth, temporal life. Judaism has very little to say about afterlife, which is a kind of afterthought. What the Rabbi talks about in sermons has little to do with hypothesizing about things obviously unknowable to us. It focuses on how you live your life here, how you treat other people, how you interact with the community. It's more the communal nature, a focus on how you interact with each other, treat them well, caring less about what if anything is outside of us [like an afterlife]. So when I think of God, I focus more on how people are connected to each other and treat each other, not if there might be anything beyond the physical world. That's not a big part of my life.

This Mormon mother from New York City told us, "This church community is preparing my kids for the kind of life I want them to have, that's not sheltered, that sees all people as important, as children of God who have value. They learn they have specific gifts God has given them they can use to help other people, whatever they choose for their vocation, their livelihood. Whether getting married and having a family or not, I don't believe a woman needs to get married or have children, it's a calling, don't necessarily want that for my kids, I just want them to use their gifts, whatever way they can." And this Buddhist mother from Chicago explained, "In the Buddhism we don't have the life after death. When we dead, done. It's like a light, you turn the light off, it's off, we don't have the life after death." And a Buddhist father from Chicago told us, "All religions if you start understanding they all provide you the guide for you living a happy life, that's what I believe."

---

7. Hindu and Buddhist parents do reference karma, reincarnation, liberation, and rebirth (17, 69, 3, and 1 times, respectively), which do concern realities beyond ordinary life in this world, but they are very rarely employed in terms that would seem related to motivations for intergenerational religious transmission, as parental explanations of why they believe it important to pass on religious belief and practice to children. "Nirvana" is only mentioned four times, and only in vague and uncertain ways.

In order to realize life's purpose of living well, one must be equipped by others with preparation, learning, and competences for the task of self-realization—without which one may become lost, compromised, or fail in life.

Here the vision of life's purpose begins to shade into the task of parenting, so we find similarities between parental talk here and that referenced in that cultural model below, providing an instance of how the beliefs and logics of cultural models can interconnect with each other. A black Protestant mother from Houston told us, "You bringing new life into this world, it's something you cannot stop, can't change, something you're gonna have to help grow along the way, you're gonna have to teach them to be strong just like you were." A black Protestant father also from Houston observed about children:

> They can always tell you, "daddy said this" or "momma said that," "daddy and mommy taught us this, it might be right, oh yeah it is right." You know, we been down that road before, so listen to us and we ain't gonna lead you wrong or nothing, down a wrong path. So we just hope what we taught them will help them through life. I just say, "I did my job, we blessed you, the Lord blessed us in what we had to do for you, and now you on your own, and you just pray that the Lord keep blessing you and do the right thing."

A conservative Protestant mother from Florida told us, "I set rules, and as long as they stay safe, safety is a key issue. I try to build their self-esteem by allowing them to feel independent—they think they're doing everything on their own, but I've already put the boundaries up, and within those boundaries they can do things. It's amazing watching and allowing them to grow and explore and figure things out 'on their own,' even though I know what the boundaries are." One mainline Protestant father from Indiana confessed, "You worry about them, making sure they're okay, but we've tried to prepare them as much as we could for things that will come in their life." A mainline Protestant mother from the same area told us, "My goal as a parent when I had them was to make sure they were prepared to live a life of their own." And another mainline Protestant mother also from Indiana said, "You can't do everything for them, you have to teach them independence starting at birth, to teach independence, how to think through things. All three of my sons can cook, 'cause I taught them, can do laundry, can clean the house, and feed their children."

A white Catholic father from Indiana said, "The parent's job is exactly to equip children to be adults. So I think faith is important, not the only thing that you want to teach but certainly one of the important ones. There's a whole variety of knowledge and skills that it is our vocation [as parents] to transmit." A white Catholic mother from Chicago explained this: "It's important for me to have my children learn to be independent. It's a nonstarter for me to always be doing something for them. If I were to always tie their shoes, I'd be like why aren't I teaching them to tie their shoes? Honestly, there's a little price to pay, because sometimes you remember fondly back to mom or dad doing that. But where I'm coming from is I should help them do it by themselves. They feel even better because they can do stuff, they're able to. So in terms of coddling children and doing everything for them, and pre-arranging and making sure they never have any disappointments, I don't really go for that too much." A Hispanic Catholic father from Chicago conveyed that, "I hope when I'm done, I've given my kids the tools for them to be able to take care of themselves, both in their personal and spiritual life. I hope for them to be good people, to be doing what makes them happy." Another Hispanic Catholic mother said, "By raising a kid in the Catholic beliefs or any other beliefs, as long as you teach her what is right and wrong, and knowing about God, giving her the tools to continue her education in religion and what is right and wrong. As long they believe, it's up to her, whatever they decide, as long as parents give them the right education, the right tools to be a good person [they can decide their lives]." Similarly, this Mormon mother from Indiana said, "I feel like one of my responsibilities, although it's really hard for me, is to help them to become independent as they take on things on their own and to foster that. I feel like my job now is to help them to become as they get older to foster independence, but there's a part of me that wants to keep them babies and needing mommy."

A Jewish father also from Indiana explained, "We hope that they're happy and have a satisfied and enriching life and we hope we've given them the tools to do that. To find professional careers that support them and they enjoy. And appropriate mates they love who are respectful and culturally and academically appropriate, life partners in every sense of the word, to find the kind of happiness we've had." This Jewish mother from New York City confessed that, "There's always something to worry about, like, 'are we doing the right thing with the kids? Are they getting what they need?' Not from a religious standpoint but just 'what tools do they need to be self-sufficient, happy individuals as adults?'" A Hindu father from central New Jersey told us, "I want to help him along the way with everything that I can, with the help I didn't get, even though I feel that it made me stronger, I don't want him to have that extra stress in his life. And college, any parent wants to make sure he goes to college, gets a good education. I don't really care what field he does, and I will obviously guide him to make sure the jobs are there, whatever he's gonna pick, that's my number one priority." A Buddhist father from Chicago told us, "We're trying to teach her first of all to be able to survive in this world, don't depend on anybody. We try to help them depend on themselves, financially and with education. We cannot control their lives, they cannot control their life. Whatever happens will happen, but at least they can survive." And a Buddhist mother from Chicago reported, "I don't let my kids stay up all hours of the night. I am lenient, but I try to teach my kids to be independent, to make choices on their own, and I try to guide them with those choices." Likewise, this Muslim mother from Indiana explained, "You gotta teach your kids when they're born, because they don't know anything, it's your obligation to teach them the right way. You gotta teach them the basics and when they grow up they get to learn more and find out if I taught them the right thing." And this Muslim father from the same area told us, "I do not agree about after eighteen you can do whatever you want. I think kids are kids, they need to be guided, right or wrong, with education, till they are on their own. Till they go to medical school I wanna guide them, if you can afford to pay for their school, you pay for them. What else is there for life? You wanna take care of them."

Still, each individual must find his or her own particular way to discover their own purpose and lead a good life true to who they are as a unique self.

The parental task of equipping children is not to prepare them to sustain and reproduce an established inheritance, but rather to discover their own singular, authentic identity and way of life. Preparation during the period of family dependence is precisely to become individually independent. Parent training is thus not so children can carry on stable traditions, like an apprenticeship in an ancient craft. It is rather something more like sailing lessons, so that children are prepared to cast off on their own and sail unexplored waters as they wish. The idea is not "stay on this trail" but "you must find your own path." What matters is not what parents or society wish them to do, but what they want to do, what will make them happy.

Thus, this Hindu father from central New Jersey told us, "Honestly, I just want them to be happy with whatever they do. I know it sounds like such a cliché but I'm not pushing them to be one thing. I want them to find their own path, to be able to have a future." A Jewish mother from Indiana noted that, "I try to hold the reins, they need structure and a framework to find themselves within, rather than total chaos. But I want my kids to find

themselves and to be the best they can be in whoever that is that they are."
A mainline Protestant father from Washington, DC, said, "I want them
to be passionate about something, to develop whatever talent they have
and pursue it, whatever makes them happy. I want to be careful to give
them what *they* need, not what I think they need because I never had it.
I want them to know themselves and not look [elsewhere for direction]."
One Hispanic Catholic mother from New York City said, "It's up to her [to
make her life]. Whatever they decide, then we give them the right education, the right tools to be a good person." A Mormon mother from Indiana
reported, "I try to encourage them to have opportunities to express themselves amongst their peers or other leaders, because sometimes it can be
stifling to always have your parent around. Sometimes they need to feel
like they can be themselves." Another Mormon mother from the same area
explained, "I am not one of those parents who has a strong investment in,
'this child needs to be a doctor' or 'to get a PhD.' I expect them to graduate
from college. They can study whatever they want. I expect them to support themselves. And I hope they make choices that make them happy.
But there's a limit. I'm one of those, 'you're grown-up, you're on your own.
I'll help you if you need help but these are choices that you need to make
for yourself and then live with the consequences.'" "You gotta fail to succeed, you've got to," insisted a white Catholic father from Indiana. "A baby
doesn't get up one day and all of a sudden walk, they gotta fall a few times
before they figure it out. [It's] that way with a lot of things in life." Another
white Catholic mother from Indiana reported: "Our oldest is nineteen and
going to be a sophomore in college. She is a fabulous young lady who is
figuring out her way in life. And there have been some road bumps, but
you know she's a very head strong, independent, bossy lady, but when she
wants to she's got it all together, I would say she's a normal kid."

A white conservative Protestant mother explained, "College is a time
where we make childlike decisions that affect our adult life, though we
don't realize it. There's stages of independence that have value. Those
kinda basic things are huge in the growth process." A black Protestant
father from Houston told us, "I don't want him to have to depend on anybody, he's going to have to be successful because he's the only child, so he's
really going to have to be independent in a lot of behaviors. I ask him, 'Okay,
tell me what's wrong with this situation?' so he will know what actually be
wrong. I want him to be a responsible, successful citizen, that's my hope." A
Buddhist father told us, "I spent a great deal of my life pushing boundaries,
marrying outside my race, changing religions, hauling ass to move from one
place to another. Most people just don't do that, but I've spent a lot of my

life challenging those things. So I kind of expect my daughter to do that too, and I think she will." This mainline Protestant father from New York City said, "I hope my kids will be able to do whatever they want, to be free to follow their dreams and be happy in whatever career they choose and successful. If they're happy in what they do that will make for a better life. I think it's more important to just let them realize their dreams and be happy."

The Experience of Life in the World

Understanding life requires not only grasping its purpose but also knowing how it will be encountered in the living. What is the experience of life in the world like? On this question, most American religious parents also share a similar view—which gives us a second and closely related cultural model—as follows:

> *Life in the World*: Life is a journey out in the world that each individual must venture and do their best to make go well. The world, which exists beyond the walls of the family home, "out there," offers potential for growth, achievement, and fulfillment, but also threats of instability, confusion, danger, and failure. The world presents a variety of paths to travel and options to choose—some good, some bad. "The culture" sends some bad "messages" that, if believed, threaten success on life's journey, which therefore must be recognized and resisted. Even when life's journey goes well, everyone faces trials, makes mistakes, and confronts discouragement along the way; but these can be overcome when one is properly equipped with resources to surmount them. The good and bad influences of the external world always transform people one way or another, so personal change is inevitable. Only by maintaining a solid internal "grounding," a "true sense of self," can life's travelers navigate their journey successfully and happily.

This model is clearly tied to the first concerning life's purpose, both together being mutually constitutive and reinforcing. The talk of American religious parents that reflects this cultural model sounds as follows.

Life is a journey out in the world that each individual must venture and do their best to make go well.

One of the most common metaphors the parents we interviewed used to describe life is as a journey, along with the closely related images of life as a path, quest, stage, road, track, rail, and walk, on which we are all

Table 1. US Religious Parents Using "Journey" and "Foundation" Language in Interviews (counts)

Journey Language	Total Counts	# Different Respondents	Foundation Language	Total Counts	# Different Respondents
Path	408	150	Foundation	248	92
Guide	392	137	Grounding	143	56
Direction	241	104	Base	84	47
Track	181	94	Root	71	45
Stage	127	75	Seed	27	17
Explore	123	57	Anchor	21	9
Road	115	67	**COLLECTIVELY**	**594**	**150**
Come Back	94	60			
Journey	87	42			
Stray	74	34			
Venture	46	24			
Find Self	43	32			
Steer	34	20			
Navigate	32	25			
Ride	30	24			
Drift	23	18			
Obstacle	23	17			
Wander	15	12			
Waters	14	10			
Compass	14	10			
Wave	13	12			
Avenue	13	11			
Hurdle	13	8			
Rollercoaster	9	8			
Sail	6	5			
Quest	6	5			
Roadblock	3	4			
COLLECTIVELY	**2,179**	**235**			

Source: The Intergenerational Religious Transmission Project Interviews, 2014–16 (N = 235 parents).

travelers. The three left columns of table 1 in fact show that 100% of our parents interviewed used some metaphor related to the idea of a journey in their discussions. Every person must make their own individual journey. And each faces the challenge to travel and complete the journey well.

For example, one mainline Protestant father from Indiana told us, "The journey my children have is theirs, my journey was mine, my father's journey was his. Each day we represent our own journey. So they watch us and how we present ourselves to that everyday journey, is our witness to them, saying, I still have the faith, I still believe." A mainline Protestant mother from the same area said, "I've learned that the journey is not for me to know. I can help guide them the best I can along the way. My responsibility is to try to make each day the best day that they can have along with mine." One conservative Protestant mother from Florida reported that, "I'm not seeing my daughter a lot lately, but I think she is still on the right path where she needs to be going." A conservative Protestant father from Washington, DC, said, "My fiancée and I are spiritually similar. At first I didn't think that she knew as much [religiously] as she did, but she was just on her own [path], like a quest." This Florida father from the same religious tradition explained his hopes for his daughter: "I would like to see her stay on the path with God, building that relationship and confidence through him, seeing herself the way God sees her. And her finding her way in life to achieve what she's passionate about career-wise." Another conservative Protestant father from northern Indiana explained his view about his son's delayed profession of religious faith: "My boy's on his own journey with God, and he has to take that journey however it's right for him. He can go through the motions with faith, but it doesn't mean anything. If a kid doesn't make a profession of faith, fine, they're on a journey. Maybe as an adult they join a church and profess faith. I'm not worried about these things. God's in charge here, he's got my boy on a journey." Agreeing that each child must travel their own road themselves, this conservative Protestant mother told us, "I'm glad they get from me the values and learning and going on their own road to the Lord. But I want them to experience their own. I'm glad I'm helping them on their journey, I want them to go on their journey." One black Protestant father also from Houston said, "I let them live their life, let them choose what they want, don't force-feed them. I just want them to be happy and successful and respectful as they journey through life."

American Catholic parents use the same language. This white Catholic mother from northern Indiana told us, "I definitely want them to remain Catholic because I know how much I love it and I know what the Church has meant to me in my journey, and I believe it's the true church." This Hispanic Catholic father from New Mexico explained his desire for his children to learn how to follow their own right path: "We have values we want to show them, so they can make their own decisions, and learn to decide [between] what we teach them at home and what they teach them in the street. We want that they have their norm too, because they also have to do their own ideas, thoughts, and have their own preparation, their own experiences. So we let them have their own experiences, by themselves, but guiding them on the right path, not scaring ourselves from their mistakes."

Mormons too express the same underlying model, such as this LDS father from northern Indiana: "My son, he wants much more to follow his own path, 'cause he thinks that's the best way to go." Another Mormon mother discussed her own life with the images of point, chapter, stage, and path: "I had gotten to the point where marriage was a chapter [in life] I learned from and I was good with myself, my career. But every time I seem to get happy with my stage [in life, something else comes up and] I'm always blindsided by what path comes next, but always grateful for it too."

Non-Christian religious parents also rely on the same journey metaphors to discuss life. One Jewish mother from Indiana explained that, "I've given my girl a road to be on and we love each other dearly. But she has also come packaged with her own goals and track in life she's on regardless of anybody else around her. She's on this road and just independent of us and on her own, too." And this Jewish mother from New York City, for instance, told us that, "In terms of my husband's ethos, who he is as a person, he has me beat by a mile. He's very honorable, ethical, walking the right road, and he lives it, it's who he is." A Muslim father from New York City told us, "There's a saying in Islam that you live in this world as a traveler. So, I want my kids to understand that this is just one stop on the journey, but to make this stop a good one for the next stop of the journey." A Hindu father from Chicago asked us, "What does a father do? At the end of the day, parents have this delusion that children need them. They don't. You can't really hold hands and walk them through life, they do it themselves." A Hindu father from New York City told us, "We are trying hard to keep my daughter on track so she doesn't go off the rail." One Buddhist mother from Chicago considered her daughter's future by saying, "If she decides later on whatever path she wants to take, so long as she's a good human being and not a bigot, no judgment, [I'm happy]." Similarly, this Buddhist father from New York City said, "We have the big obligations to lead my son in the right directions of path. But if he chooses something else, we have no objections." And this Buddhist father from Chicago summarized well what all the parents already quoted: "Everybody has to choose their own path, to find their own life."

The world, which exists beyond the walls of the family home, "out there,"
offers potential for growth, achievement, and fulfillment, but also threats
of instability, confusion, danger, and failure. The world presents a variety
of paths to travel and options to choose—some good, some bad.

Here are the ways that parents talked expressing this part of this operative cultural model. A black Protestant father from Houston told us: "When
they are growing up, you think about them, that they will grow up to be this
and that. But you gotta look at it and guide them in that direction you think,
so they will continue to stay on that path." A black Protestant single mother
from Houston said, "My main concern for them as they grow is to stay on
the right track and use the tools they received from their parents and be the
best they can be. Be role models for someone else, get out of their comfort
zone and reach out to others and share more." A white conservative Protestant father from New York City said, "I think the true meaning of human
existence, our purpose in life is to worship and serve God and be part of his
renewing purposes for the world. That is the way to true contentment and
purpose and meaning. Without that, I would feel that my kids had chosen
the wrong path." And a mother from the same tradition from Florida confessed, "If my kids got to where I once was in life, partying in the wrong are-
nas, that would really bother me. We all stumble and we can always get back
on the path, we always veer, it's not going to be a straight line." Likewise, a
mainline Protestant father from Los Angeles warned us that, "This society
is a place where if you're not careful with children they tend to follow the
wrong path when it comes to friends, a lot of friends out there."

Expressing the same themes, a Buddhist mother from Chicago told us
that, "I try to give my children a path of where we should go and not go."
This Buddhist father also from Chicago explained that, "I go to temple
more now because I think about my kids' futures. Right now there's a lot of
crazy things out there, people don't believe in good things, so I want to take
my kids to the temple. They learned in the community to speak our mother
tongue and learn Buddhism, learn what the Buddha taught is the good
way for them to be good citizens." And a Buddhist mother from the same
city likewise referenced the bad stuff out there: "I feel happy in the temple.
People just relax, respect each other, and we don't talk about bad stuff
about what is happening out there." Similarly, this Hindu mother from
Chicago explained, "I don't make big deal of the god of Hinduism, it's very
flexible, gives freedom, and that's a good way of learning the correct thing.
So I tell my children basically I can't ever point you to a location, or insist
they can or cannot see something [in the media], I can't help them doing
that. I have to use a path to direct them."

Likewise, this Muslim mother from Chicago repeated that theme: "I really feel strongly about what is right, but kids should know what [else] is out there. My mom always said do what you need to in order to get the right grade, but still know what's right or wrong." This Jewish father from Indiana expressed, "At younger ages, it's more important to guide what's acceptable and what's not, because they just don't understand what's out there [in the world]." And this Jewish mother from the same area told us, "We've been somewhat helicopter-ish parents because there's a lot out there and you have to be there and we always were. We both worked but we were always there for every little thing, although I probably didn't expect that I would be such a protective parent, but I have been a lot more hands-on and guiding." And this Mormon mother from Indiana likewise explained that, "You have to make sure you safeguard them, make sure they grow up and stay on the good path. You want to make sure they're hanging around the right people, their friends, so for me it's very important they go to church so they have friends that are not going to be engaging in unscrupulous behavior. That's what church provides me, a refuge for my children as well."

Catholic parents talk in highly similar ways. This white Catholic father from Indiana said, "I would love for my kids to stay in the Catholic faith. There's a lot of influences out there, especially as they get older, that could easily persuade them not to go to church. It's very much a struggle." A Hispanic Catholic mother from New York City confessed, "You can blame yourself because of the situations your child is in. It would affect me if my children in any given moment chose the wrong path. But at the same time, I would continue fighting for them to get back on the right path." A white Catholic father from Chicago told us, "There's lots of people in this world who kill, do awful things, which is sad. I hope my kids don't join those people and do bad things. I also know there are people who are really good, everyone struggles with different things." One Hispanic Catholic mother from Indiana described how she reasons with her son to stay on a good path in life: "You can get sucked into anything, alcohol, drugs, those temptations, out in the world, you can choose your path. You can choose to be successful and take you that way. But if you start doing [bad] stuff, it's gonna take you down the road you don't wanna go, a road you wish you'd never taken. I don't believe he's ever done them [drugs] again, I don't know for sure. But you just don't do drugs, because where is that gonna lead you? You've got two paths to take, down the good road or the bad road. And down the bad road, it's gonna be hard to come back to the good one." And this Hispanic Catholic father from New Mexico told us how he prays for his children: "Do not stray from the path of God, continue on the path of God." Discussing his own life struggle, this white Catholic father from New York City said, "I pray for what I worry about and ask for inspiration to find an answer, to say this is my quest right now, please help me to find clues around me, just to enjoy myself and find my path."

"The culture" sends some bad "messages" that, if believed, threaten success on life's journey, which therefore must be recognized and resisted.

This was the most common response by parents when we asked what are their biggest challenges as parents raising children. In the minds of nearly all religious American parents, a powerful force made up of "the culture," "messages," "technology," and "the media" exists "out there" and makes their jobs very difficult. A white Catholic mother from Indiana told us, "The biggest challenge is being heard over the din of the crazy culture. There's so much relativism, utilitarianism, all the 'isms that influence kids. I think they do see our witness, during their formative years they need to see the authentic witness and be touched by that and value that above all the easy and crass and materialistic things in the world." This Hispanic Catholic mother from Chicago described the view she thinks her daughter holds of her: "Mom is mom and mom is boring [laughs]. She seems to think I wasn't ever her age, I'm just old. And the media and peer pressure, everybody is doing it." A Hispanic Catholic father from Chicago told us: "The older kids, they have an iPad their sister gave them. I only give it to them at certain times, I tell them they have to read books for school. Then their friends make comments to them. Sometimes the friends are there, inculcating [bad], but I'm also there instead contradicting them. It does bother me a lot that friends sometimes inculcate, because they have other beliefs, other customs, values." And this Hispanic Catholic mother from New York City similarly explained that, "Technology is a difficulty. Technology nowadays, you don't allow one thing, but then they go elsewhere. It's practically impossible, a big obstacle, I don't know how to manage these situations. I would like for them to not be so dependent on that, because you see it, bad words, sexual insinuations, everything. And the media, Facebook, Instagram, there's no control over anything. I feel like sometimes it's out of my control."

These beliefs continue across all religious traditions. For instance, one Jewish mother from Indiana related that, "I often think our culture as a whole is like the end of the Roman empire: decadence and waste and the center is gone, there's no value center—though I don't mean that in the way the Religious Right means it when they talk about a 'value center.'"

She went on to explain her belief that, "There's a deep sickness of our culture, in my view. People are just blinding themselves to the reality of most of the world because they're so privileged. You can't even really appreciate what you have because you don't realize it in relation to what other people are suffering." Similarly, one Muslim mother from New York City said, "The dominant culture is just so different from what I'm trying to impart [to my children], whether it's daily rituals or [how to live rightly in] social life and all of that." A Buddhist father from Chicago related his belief that, "The culture actually nudges people away from any sort, okay, when I look at what's happening in the world, he says with CNN on [laughing], there is a conscious or unconscious effort in America today to undercut most traditional beliefs, and really I think ultimately the move is for the powerful to make the political religious. The thing is the media, and I do mean media, because media is the one that actually dictates it. Things get massaged and manipulated in ways that are unhelpful." One Hindu father from central New Jersey explained to us, "There are a lot of crazy things you hear nowadays, like you want to send your kids to school to learn and be safe but nowadays safety can be pretty scary. As she gets older the influences, I'm pretty sure kids are going to experiment and I hope she does not go into the peer pressure or do certain things that will hurt her. It's not knowing, you don't know." And this Hindu mother from Chicago expressed that, "The kids here are told from the beginning about the gender everything and the sexual education. As a parent you don't know many things going on, and at my stage there was no news, no media, so I was not much aware. That's one thing I'm worried about my son here, too much media." This Mormon father from Indiana echoed these sentiments:

> There's not a lot out there to give you support. Especially when we have video games, the internet, garbage on TV, the media I don't think gives a lot of support. There are good things in the media, but it's more difficult to find them. What kind of a society have we become that we've got to put parental guidance software on our media because we disagree with it? I don't know that in the public school kids are getting taught good values. They've watched videos in the classroom we would have never let them watch at home, certain books they've read we would have never let them read.

Many observers of American religion expect white conservative Protestants, like this father from Los Angeles, to express these kinds of views: "Oh, it's a scary world, Just the perversion and violence. As much as I've been letting go, it's still very difficult. My ten-year-old boy, I don't want him to, one day his eyes are going to be opened to porn and just the debauchery that's out there. As things have degraded and what used to be taboo or bad, now you can't even call it bad. It's a frightening, very fluid, lost, spinning world, so that frightens me for them. But I understand that God's in control and I can't get back to being so afraid for them that I make myself crazy. I can't live their lives." But mainline Protestant parents voice the same concerns. Consider this mainline Protestant father from Washington, DC, who said that "the world is just so much more right in your face now. You used to be able to protect your kids from things they shouldn't be exposed to, and now it's 24/7 anywhere you go, media is in your face and that's a challenge trying to manage." Or this mainline Protestant mother from New York City who told us: "I'm always trying to protect my kids from media. Sometimes my daughter gets mad because she doesn't know what's going on, so I'm trying to be more open about it, like the marathon bombing or whatever. I'm trying to protect her and keep her innocent, but at school everyone's talking about things. When they were younger, I shielded them from so much 'cause they wouldn't know, would totally be in the dark. And I actually liked keeping them innocent for as long as possible." And this mainline Protestant mother from Washington, DC: "The media is a big challenge. It's just a barrage of constant media at children that's really intense and overwhelming. I want to not combat that, but harness and balance it, which is a real challenge in today's world. It's like a pendulum swing in society. We've creeped to too accepting, like people are afraid to say, 'I don't think you should do that.' Like crazy things people are afraid to be judgmental about." Similarly, a black Protestant father from Houston worried for his children about:

> So much at their fingertips at a moment's notice, where when I was growing up there was no internet, no smartphone to see everything. It was punishment when they took the phone. Now you've got to turn off the Wi-Fi because every device has access, but it's just so much. And then regular TV and radio was more censored, now it's not. Now you have to drive home the model of Christianity because there's so much on TV and the radio that's not what we desire for them. But you really can't protect them, you have to guide them through what they are seeing and hearing to understand what we desire for them. This is right this is wrong, just sometimes you just have to suffer through listening to what he's listening to, to get an understanding of where his mind's at.

Conservative Christians in the Religious Right are well known to have protested the moral degeneracy of the media since the 1970s. In fact, similar concerns are also felt and expressed by parents across the entire spectrum of American religious traditions. And that helps to define the cultural model of what their children have to face growing up today.

Even when life's journey goes well, everyone faces trials, makes mistakes, and confronts discouragement along the way; but these can be overcome when one is properly equipped with resources to surmount them.

Again, this theme is pervasive across all religious traditions. A white Catholic mother from Indiana told us: "We've equipped them, their whole upbringing, their whole education. You equip them to be agile enough to deal with it. I just don't think they're gonna get too stressed because they're going to be able to figure it out. That's a tribute to the schools they've gone to all the way through college but also that's a mindset, an attitude." Reflecting the risks in life of making mistakes, this Hispanic Catholic father from New Mexico confessed that, "I felt that we were wandering, and for many years I did wander. Not all of my life have I considered myself religious. There was a time in my life, ten or fifteen years perhaps, since we emigrated here, that I only went to Mass, nothing else. I didn't have an intimate relationship with God. So we were wandering in a desert. Right now, though, I see that religion, faith is what gives meaning to our life."

For some parents, what most needs to be taught is independence and learning from mistakes, as with this white Catholic father from Chicago: "It's a combination of having them be independent but also being there and not making everything a teaching moment. Some people always wanna coach your golf swing. But leave me alone. Let 'em go, know what I mean? That's teaching people to be independent, let them make their own mistakes, they'll figure it out for themselves." One mainline Protestant father from Washington, DC, made a similar point: "As long as they have just enough suffering or hardship to develop their character, but not to take over their life, [that's good]. You want them to struggle just enough to learn the hard lessons they need to learn. And then for them to go forth and be productive members of the world, to be good people, the kind you'd want to meet, that'll make the world better, that you'd want to have as a neighbor, as a friend." A black Protestant father from Houston told us: "I think that everybody comes to a stage in their life where they may get lost or just see life a certain way. But you just don't give up on them, you just keep pushing on it and like [Jesus's parable of] the Prodigal Son in the Bible, I think that it happens and we can't really control that." This white conservative Protestant father from Washington, DC, made a similar point: "I tell him his decisions mean a whole lot, because when he's a juvenile, he can make mistakes. But you get to a certain point, you can't make any mistakes, because that can be your life, your job or whatever. A mistake is a teaching moment. Mistakes are going to happen, but what you do after the mistake makes the difference. Same thing as losing in sports. Are you going to work hard to make that up or are you going to pout and quit? That is what I tell him makes a man." As did this white conservative Protestant mother from Indiana: "I want them to see wrong and choose not to do it. We're better parents teaching them you're gonna see all this and be tempted but not to do it. If we just act like it doesn't exist, when it presents itself, they're not gonna have the ability to say no. So we don't hide stuff. I'm not condoning some nasty television program where every other word's cussed. I'm saying there is a balance between hiding everything and letting them do whatever they want. There's a happy medium that allows them to see we all have faults, here's where I made mistakes, don't make them this way. I've always talked that way to my ten-year-old through life. She didn't just get in trouble and sent to her room. I went in and sat down and looked at her and I talked to her about it, explained so she could understand the reasons." And this Mormon father echoes the same themes: "I'm gonna love 'em either way. My older one, I see the path he's on, and I would I want him on a better path, but I realize with our heavenly father, it's the same way with us—that's put a perspective in. I think sometimes, which path am I on again?"

Parents from non-Christian traditions share and express the same ideas, as with this Hindu father from central New Jersey: "Just make them aware, educate them, you can't be there 24/7. You give them a little book, give them the guideline, show them a video, and you hope and pray they don't make a major mistake. It's like driving: you teach, show the rules and regulations, they get their permit, their driver's license, then you hope they follow the laws and don't do any damage to themselves or somebody else." A Hindu mother also from central New Jersey reported that, "I don't really care if he believes in god. But important to me is respecting living beings, those are goals or characteristics you need to instill to help them later in life, being nice and polite to everybody, respectful, putting himself in others' shoes. Those characteristics he's going to need when he grows up, so those are important to me." This Jewish mother from Indiana told us:

> I wonder if my seventeen-year-olds have discovered porn because they have unfettered access to the internet. I mean, they're boys. I don't like all that's out there available now, but it's the world we live in, and if

they make a mistake and look at something they find disturbing, they'll learn a lesson from it. I have faith that the foundation [we parents have provided them] in terms of ethics and values, human relationships, respect for other human beings, even our political leanings that my kids share, just naturally would [help them]. I'm pretty confident they wouldn't abuse or use it in a rampant or inappropriate way. Sooner or later they're gonna encounter it. I don't see the point of laying down harsh laws about everything in the world, because that just makes kids want to go do it. I've never broached the topic of porn. Either way, I kind of trust that if you give them the basic value set and strivings that they need to succeed, they will stumble through and find their way just like we did [laughs]. They'll make mistakes along the way but it won't be fatal. So certain things I just don't see the point bringing it up, because it is distasteful to me.

And this Buddhist father from Chicago expressed the same beliefs:

They'll make mistakes sometimes along the way but at least they know that as parents we're here to help them and they're not afraid to come to us. I think they'll be fine. So letting go. I see a lot of helicopter parents who need to let go and let their kids make their own mistakes, learn on their own. I know they want their kids to do better or succeed, but kids aren't learning anything if you do everything for them. This generation has everything handed to them. If parents step back and let them do it, they can learn to do it for themselves.

The good and bad influences of the external world always transform people one way or another, so personal change is inevitable. Only by maintaining a solid internal "grounding," a "true sense of self," can life's travelers navigate their journey successfully and happily.

Most parents also believe and express the ideas of the need for children to have a stable grounding and a solid sense of self (see the right column of table 1 above). And usually what parents mean by this is something like the same beliefs and values as the parents. That may seem contradictory to the idea of children choosing their own path. But parents make it work by believing that "the foundation" is laid for and in children early in life, whereas independent path-choosing comes later in life. Consider the worry of this Hindu mother from central New Jersey: "They're growing up way too fast, and if they don't have a proper foundation then things can go anywhere. Already conversations come up about pot, piercings, drugs. I tell them about my experience, but because they grow up so fast now, the conversations my parents had when I was fifteen, I'm having with them at nine." A Buddhist mother from Chicago told us: "Partly our kids' friends are handpicked [chuckling], but sometimes when their friends don't make the best decisions, they can see that. I told him to think how he could help his friends make better decisions. It was a learning experience. As long as they're grounded, I make sure my kids are grounded enough and know how to react to different situations. So I'm not so worried about the bad friends." A Buddhist father from Chicago related this story: "I just try, 'cause she's gonna be on her own, to get my daughter to absorb some things. On her seventeenth birthday I actually wrote a long letter from father to daughter all about faith in God, believing in something other than just what people tell you, and not going with the crowd. I think she took it to heart, I was surprised. I tried to hit it from a lot of angles, not just the transcendence part but the whole idea of community, having some rooting in something." This Hispanic Catholic mother from Indiana told us, "I believe if we put enough of the base in there, they will eventually come back to what we taught them." A white Catholic mother from the same area said, "I just want my kids to know what it means to be good to people, to be caring. I'm not convinced they will remain Catholic and I'm okay with that. I just want them to, I mean I don't even know why I'm saying that, I guess just because they may run into other influences in their life, whether it's spouse or whatever, but I just want them to have the foundation." And another white Catholic father also from Indiana explained why he is raising his daughter Catholic:

> I am a free-thinker but you can't just think anything. You need to be grounded in something, and she's grounded in Catholic faith. I find it a solid place to be, to believe. I'm no fundamentalist, but I believe the basic tenets of the Church and believe children need to have that basis. I see the difference, kids that have had that versus those that don't. The ones with that background, as they get older they develop their own beliefs if they want, but they have that solid background that carries them through. You see kids go through that, in late high school and college and suddenly they're off on their own, but later they mature, come back to their basic foundation. We believe it's a foundation important to have, belief in God and Christ and salvation.

Protestants too share this outlook. A conservative Protestant mother from Los Angeles explained to us, "I didn't have a plan growing up. But I'm thinking for them, they will know exactly what they need to do to get where they need to, how to get there. And being Christians, I'm hoping that they're more grounded." One conservative Protestant father from Florida said, "It's very important that my daughters share my beliefs, because that lifestyle, beliefs, the values are all based on my faith in Christ, that faith in God is the foundation for everything else. So it is very important that they understand that foundation so everything else, all the pillars that are built off that, are still grounded in the foundation of understanding who God is." This black Protestant father from Houston told us, "I accepted the Lord into my life when I was fifteen years old and it kept me from a lot of bad things and helped me stay grounded and keeping my path on the right track. I passed those values on to my children and hand them down to my grandchildren, to let them know how important religion *does* play a part in your life."

Mainline Protestants expressed the same beliefs. "Being a bit of a traditionalist, it's important for me that they at least start with the basic value system and beliefs we bring to the table," explained a mainline Protestant father from Washington, DC, "It puts them on a track that works for us and seems grounded. We do talk about ways people choose different paths and the pros and cons, but for the most part our values are important." And this mainline Protestant mother also from DC told us, "We are lenient, and the downside is they're borderline spoiled. But we do things to counteract that, like go out to our farm, where they have to work, which keeps them grounded I hope. I think it works well, in life they're gonna have to figure it out on their own, and so the sooner you start the more likely you are to be successful."

Religious parents in the United States tend to give positive accounts of their ideals, strategies, and experiences. But sometimes they also relate less happy situations as interim reports and cautionary tales, which can express the same operative cultural-model beliefs as the positive accounts. For example, the importance of maintaining a grounding and true sense of self to navigate life well is expressed in this story of failure to do so, told with sadness by a Mormon father from Indiana: "He's so good when he's at home, and really becomes this religious, spiritual kid. But then when he's in that other environment, he takes on that persona. He really just molds, morphs into the environment that he's in." This account is different from those already mentioned but the background beliefs of the governing cultural model are identical.

CHAPTER TWO

Religion's Value and Truth

THE PREVIOUS CHAPTER EXPLORED the cultural models of religious American parents on the foundational questions of the purpose and nature of life. This chapter examines their cultural models specifically about religion, its value and possible truth. Grasping parents' views of these two features of religion is essential to understanding their approaches to the transmission of religion to their children, analyzed in chapter 4.

The Value of Religion

For few American parents does religion singularly determine their understanding of the ultimate purpose and expected experience of life. Instead, the expected experiences of life involve clusters of largely autonomous beliefs forming their own distinct cultural models, perhaps partly shaped by religious traditions generally but not principally determined by the specific views and priorities of those traditions. Those basic cultural models being firmly in place, religion then comes in as its own distinct issue. And when parents think about religion, the primary focus is its practical value, how it helps people, what makes it important in this life. To understand the beliefs of the majority of religious parents about religious transmission, toward which this analysis is leading, we need to next understand their more basic cultural model of the importance of religion, which is this:

> *Religion's Value*: Religion is a normal, valuable, meaningful, and worthy part of life, at least in its general principles, not something deserving of skepticism or indifference. Like anything, religion can be manipulated for bad, but its central teachings are good, valuable, and practical for most people—in ways almost exclusively having to do

with this life now, not eternity or an afterlife. Religion helps people to "have the right values" and to "be a good person." By providing a "bigger picture" on life, among other things, religion provides feelings of peace, comfort, protection, and belonging, which reduces anxiety and increases well-being. Religion also produces pragmatic, humanistic social results, like fostering good citizenship, strengthening society, and upholding morals—all desirable in the world here and now. Religion is good, too, because it can provide cohesion and solidarity in family relationships, and it often helps marriages and families get through hard times. We humans have a natural tendency to stray and misbehave in self-harming ways, but religion is effective at helping "keep people in line," which is beneficial. For these reasons it is almost impossible to imagine being a family without religion (even if for others religion is not necessary for achieving the same values, morals, well-being, and good relationships that religion provides our family).

Religion is a normal, valuable, meaningful, and worthy part of life, at least in its general principles, not something deserving of skepticism or indifference. Like anything, religion can be manipulated for bad, but its central teachings are good, valuable, and practical for most people—in ways almost exclusively having to do with this life now, not eternity or an afterlife.

The parents we interviewed spoke positively about religion and its role in their lives, which makes sense since this was a sample of religiously affiliated parents. On occasion they questioned or criticized aspects of religions, but religion overall was for them a good and valuable part of life. For example, one mainline Protestant mother from Washington, DC, explained, "Every day you just have faith that everyone will be okay, you know things will turn out okay, that you're doing the best you can. You're doing your best and to have faith in yourself. I just can't imagine not having it." A mainline Protestant father from New York City told about his child: "I want him to pray, to have his own rituals, spend time with God by himself, quiet time with God. That's a ritual I want him to do by himself, it's great to connect to God, I so want him to have a ritual regularly so he can seek and get more meaning out of life and understanding about humans and nature and the earth." Similarly, a black Protestant mother said, "It's important to grow up and become a spiritual person because you need that to sustain, just to keep your mind sane, to keep it together, you need faith, belief, that security. I can't imagine not having it, it's very important. You need it and you're absolutely ridiculous if you think you don't [laughing]." And this white Catholic father from Indiana reported: "My two daughters went to a Catholic preschool, which built a foundation. Without that foundation, rather than being good kids that everybody compliments to us, tells us how good they are and well-behaved and smart, I think we could be in a danger zone with them. If we didn't have our Catholic faith, we wouldn't be the family we are, it'd be a bigger struggle for us in a lot of ways."

To be sure, again, these parents were able to criticize certain features or experiences of religion. A Muslim father from Indiana, for example, explained: "When you hear in the media about Islam, it's the bad Muslims are the ones who are affecting Islam. The extremists, people who understand religion the way they want it, any religion in the whole world, you can turn it the way you want. People start changing in their religion, but God never changed and the rules of God never changed. But when they try to get into God's business with your own rules, then it will become something you're adding to. So it doesn't matter if I'm Christian or Jew or a Muslim, it depends on my actions and the way I live my life under God's rules." A Mormon father from New York City told us, "You know Joseph Smith sometimes did things on the verge of despicable, like when he had wives and wasn't honest with Emma [his first wife] and only told some people about the extent of his polygamy. I'm a historian, and we are honest about things in our family." One white conservative Protestant father from Los Angeles told us, "I once knew a woman who claimed God told her things. I was nineteen and didn't have a good foundation in Christianity, to see if it lined up with scripture. She was manipulating scripture and we all believed it and spent months trying to hear from God. Then one of us, a great guy, thought he heard straight from God that God rejected him, that he is not good enough. He just shut down, it's so unfortunate, his walk with God. I talked to him recently, and it's still just like a fresh wound for him. I try to tell him she was wrong, it was a cult, that God does not feel that way, but it really shaped him." And this Hispanic Catholic mother related: "I have a friend who's always telling her daughter, 'I can't always see you, but God can!' I wouldn't say that to my children, they know God is everywhere, so I don't need to go around repeating it. It sounds like she's manipulating her by religion. If you believe in God, well you believe in God, you trust God, and you let your children choose. You give them the teachings, the advice, you guide them. But don't you need to go around telling them that." For that matter, however, some parents also criticized atheism as "belief in nothing," as with this Hindu father from Chicago: "Atheism is not good. Believing in nothing is a cop out. Why should you be polite to somebody else if you don't care, if you are just an accident of ectoplasm or something, just landed up here, then what is there to govern your behavior?"

But these critiques of religion are of particular religious expressions, not religion per se. Religion itself the parents we interviewed held in very positive light, for a vast variety of reasons. For example, one Mormon father from Indiana confessed to us: "I needed religion. My wife said you should be good on your own without religion. Yeah, I should, but that doesn't happen. Religion has made me better. If I didn't have Christ to emulate or belief in an afterlife, what kind of person would I be? Would I go out and take advantage of everything, try to get away with stuff? I can be a very good thief, a very good criminal. Why don't I? Well, it's wrong. Why is it wrong? Because there's a power above us [that says so]. But what if you thought this was the end, when you're dead, life's over, what kind of person would you be?" A Jewish mother from New York City told us, "Learning to read Hebrew and leading services, it gives me a tremendous, very meaningful connection to my grandfathers, who I never met, because of the war, because they knew this. I get scared sometimes having to lead, reading the Torah is not easy, and then I think, well, my grandfathers could do this for sure and their blood is in my veins and I'm gonna do it—that's very powerful for me. And I love the singing, in shul, there's a very transporting quality to it, it has tremendous meaning." Another Jewish mother also from New York told us, "I think of the word 'faith' as having faith in yourself; faith is religion and identity and being secure, so we should teach kids to have a strong identity and feel secure in who they are. I want them to have exposure to all the prayers so if they need to know them in the future, they know them. To know about Israel and feel secure that Israel is there, a safe place for them, and to recognize this culture too is part of their heritage, something important to me." Along similar lines, this Muslim father from New York City explained:

> In our community, our focus is to make our children realize it's not like you have religion and then you have life. No, your life and religion are actually one, faith is intertwined. Growing up I had a Sunday school teacher who always said, "Islam is not a religion. Islam is a way of life." We all made fun of him, mimicked him. But in retrospect I see that makes so much sense, it's true our faith is a way of life because it colors everything we do, from how we dress to how we talk, what we eat.

And this Buddhist mother from New York City explained: "We don't want to force them, they have to study and decide. But for being a parent, Buddhism is the one benefiting us a lot, and definitely we can say that it will help them a lot."

Religion helps people to "have the right values," to "be a good person."

This proposition is one of the most commonly assumed or believed ideas in all of the cultural models reconstructed here. It is patently obvious to all the parents we interviewed in every religious tradition, and nobody ever doubted, questioned, or contradicted it. So obvious was this idea that for most parents it essentially defines what religion *is*, what religion's basic purpose in life is about. Some parents state it straight out, as with this white Catholic mother from New York City: "There's just so much truth that, at the end of the day, religion is about being a good person and living a good life and being good to others, and if everyone could follow that path the world would be awesome. To me there's just this universal peace of love and truth and happiness and I think when you find a community of people who really are living their faith, there's just a beauty and something fantastic in it." Likewise, this white Catholic father from Indiana said, "We are trying to raise our children to become okay, decent adults. It's very tough at times but they're in Catholic school now and I'm trying to teach them their religion and everything. We do not go to Mass every Sunday, but values, just being nice people, honesty, be a good person." Elsewhere in the interview, the same father told us, "Going to Mass doesn't make you a better or worse person. If you don't gain anything out of it, I don't see the point [of going]. I think being a good Catholic is just being a good person, you know."

Similarly, this Hindu father from Chicago said, "Religion, it's a guidance. It's up to people to decide, but for me, I have chosen that way, I need some guidance. It's a good thing to be a little bit god-fearing, so I won't do any mistakes, at least I think about god before what I'm doing, whether I'm doing right or wrong." One mainline Protestant father from Washington, DC, told us, "I've traveled to a lot of countries with different faiths, and they all get at similar moral lessons. So as long as my kids are religious in some fashion that brought them back to good moral, ethical decisions and some way to ensure they're happy, I'd be tolerant of that." A Mormon mother from Indiana explained, "When it comes to children, I expect a church to help instill good morals, strong faith, values, to help me mold them into good, loving people that are happy; to see the glass half full, to see the beauty in everything, they see the silver lining, even in bad things that happen." And a conservative Protestant father from Los Angeles said about his children: "I want them to be real people who understand what it takes to be a good person." Likewise, this Jewish mother from Indiana explained: "Religion is just one piece of everything that we've given our kids, a belief in religion, education, ethical guidelines, and we want them to be as similar to us in all of those things, which is why we've modeled that for them. You want to hand down those values to kids, to make all of those things part of their lives. We want them to be as much like us as possible. We have kids that look like us, we want them to be like us. And we're happy, our shared values on so many topics has made us happy, and one route to happiness is finding a mate who shares those values with you. We also believe in the rightness of our values and so we are gratified if our kids believe that way too." The same outlook is reflected in the words of this black Protestant mother from Houston: "It takes a village to raise a child, so if I leave my child in your care at the church, you are going to teach him how the Bible says we should live, to be taught morals and values, and taught respect, I want you to treat him with respect." And a white Catholic mother from Indiana explained why she wants her children to grow up religious: "You know, not only for eternal life, but I think it really makes you a better person, more compassionate toward others."

Other parents express the same assumption and belief less directly while discussing other aspects of life and religion, although the idea, even if more tacit than explicit, and even when it is sometimes combined with other themes, is still clear and important in parents' talk. For example, the idea is presupposed by this Chicago Buddhist father's explanation of the function of a statue of the Buddha in his house: "When you see that statue, it reminds you to be a good person, reminds you of the teachings. I explain to my kids that the Buddha I have teaches me to be good, teaches me to be careful." Consider too the statement of this conservative Protestant mother from Florida (who very interestingly does not speak about the Bible as teaching true doctrines or the Gospel, but rather being a "base" off of which "values" can be derived having a source greater than mere personal opinions): "If we teach them based off the Bible, then it's not just our values, it's the values that come from the Bible, so it's not just me trying to impress upon them my particular personal opinion. They're going to have different views than me, and I'm not creating robots, I want them to have their own opinions. But I want them to know that it's coming from a source much greater than me, and as long as they follow that source, then their opinions about things are their opinion." This language difference is subtle, but we think marks a profound shift away from traditional evangelical views of the Bible in being focused on "values" instead of truth, doctrines, or the Gospel message. Consider too the statement of this Muslim father from Indiana: "Islam is a way of life, how you carry on, part of the reason why you don't, say, commit suicide, because your religion prevents you. That's your faith, who you are. Without this, you cannot function. It's not as if without a religion you're just like any animal out there. But if you read the Quran or your Bible, there's do and don't, Moses, Ten Commandments, and there's don't commit adultery and what have you." Again, the idea that religion is about making people good is not stated as an overt proposition but is implicit in the statement if it is to be taken as cogent. The same is true about the claim of this New York City conservative Protestant father who attends a Catholic Church with his family: "Putting faith in Christ and God is the most prominent part of Christianity for me, and then it obviously provides a great structure for family and value and answers to questions and a road map for kids." Ditto with the statement of this Hindu mother from Chicago: "I want to be a good parent, give good values to my children, to teach respect, that everybody deserves respect, and to be polite, well mannered, that's what makes you a good person, not a ton of money. I believe that's what makes you closer to God, as opposed to praying your entire day and then doing something inhuman." The implicit belief in religion as being about moral direction is evident in this white Catholic mother's talk as well:

> Church in general, with my kids' spiritual lives, it's guidance. Allowing them to question and have a place to find what answers they can, to the best of any church's ability, because let's face it, it's an open question, all of it is. So the Church is there to support them with that and be a guidepost. It gives you something to say right or wrong, this is how we should be, that brings out the best in you. So church should be a guidepost for them.

That religion provides good values and helps people be good persons is a very practical truth with immediate consequences in the lives of some families. One Mormon father from Indiana, for example, explained: "Without religion, I would be back drinking, I got problems with that, 'cause I enjoy it, and doing drugs, I really enjoyed that too. I really didn't want to give it up. But I did because of my stewardship [i.e., responsibility for life and family as a Mormon]. I enjoy being sober. But I also know who I am, my weaknesses, and I would go right back to it if you were to take religion out of the picture." Likewise, this white Catholic father from Indiana told us: "Our family'd be a mess without religion. Our kids would not be as good as they are, wouldn't have the morals or sense of direction they do. My son learned a very important lesson about dating people who don't go to any church, he just broke up with a girl, that wasn't the reason that she didn't go to church, but we kinda pointed that out to him, like, look at what a mess their family is, they don't go to church." For numerous Hindus and Buddhists, including this Buddhist mother from Chicago, religious values and moral teachings provide the crucial path to reincarnation into a better next life after this life: "We try to live to be good persons, and then in the next life we have better futures. It's not just for me, but also for my children, I teach them to live a good life, to be good persons. So when they go out and talk to people, hopefully people learn what we do, that we have a good family, good communities, and we try to expand, good people around us. Instead of fighting we try to talk to people a nicer way, to be understanding, more loving, instead of arguing."

One of the consequences of the assumption that religion is about good values and morality is the undermining of the importance of the *particularity* of religious traditions. Most religious parents in the United States tend toward an inclusive, ecumenical, sometimes relativistic view of religious pluralism (more on this under "The Truth of Religion model" below). That is largely because what matters about religion is not its particular theological or metaphysical claims, which are considered secondary, but rather its "values" and moral teachings. And most religious parents believe that most or all faiths (except extremist radical religions) share these in common. That view is expressed in a few different ways. One is to accept many religions but to insist on "belief in God" as a non-negotiable least common denominator.[1] Consider, for instance, the words of this mainline Protestant mother from Washington, DC: "Did my kids stay Episcopalian? No and I don't care. Do I want them to believe in God, have a faith in God? Yes, because I think that's good for them." Consider too the statement of this Hispanic Catholic father from New York City: "If my daughter became an atheist, I would try to convince her there is a God. Even if some people don't believe in God, there still is a God. You have to believe in something to be able to be a good person. Not necessarily Catholic, but I say, 'As long as everybody believes in God.'" Another way this inclusive religious ecumenism is expressed is by affirming the similarities across all particular religions, especially "Abrahamic" faiths, as stated by this Muslim father from Indiana: "All religions have the same values, okay? Christian, Muslim, Jews, whatever, they all have the same values. I should not kill, not lie,

---

1. Implicitly and sometimes explicitly, then, nonreligious people and families are thereby "othered" and coded as inadequate. As we noted, however, the nonreligious parents we interviewed expressed the same underlying cultural models about life, children, and parenting as the religious parents—their basic presuppositions, outlooks, and values sounded essentially the same—the main difference being that the religious parents talked more personally about the value of religion and explicitly about their views of how to pass it on to their children.

not steal, that's not just the Islamic value. That's all world major religions on the face of the earth. With the book, that's what make us different. You have a Bible, I have a Quran, the Jews have their Torah." So the particular scriptures of three religions are let to stand, although the practical meaning of the differences between them is removed. All share the same "values," and that is finally what matters. Worth noting here, too, in addition to the ideational power of this cultural belief, the American Muslim parents we interviewed appeared especially intent on stressing the similarities across different religions in order, it seemed to us, to counter widespread suspicions in the media and popular attitudes of Islam as a violence-prone and radical religion generally.[2] Readers by now may also be noticing how much the word "values"—a concept originally spawned in the fourteenth century to refer to economic value, not ethics or morality, and later developed by the academic discipline of economics—pervades parental talk about what is important for children to learn. In fact, 93 percent of our parents used the word "values" in their interviews. By comparison, only 7 percent of parents used the word "virtues," for example, to describe what children need to learn.

By providing a "bigger picture" on life, among other things, religion provides feelings of peace, comfort, protection, and belonging, which reduces anxiety and increases well-being.

Nearly all of the parents we interviewed agreed on this too. Few spoke about religion's demands or trials or the difficulties of, say, self-mortification (some black Protestant parents being the rare exceptions). Instead, parents routinely praised religion for its therapeutic value. The view of this mainline Protestant mother from New York City is representative: "The nice thing about having faith, the benefit of faith, is it's a comfort, right? You have someone to let go to, your higher power, whatever you like or call it, like your Jesus, your Buddha, whomever, Yahweh, Mohammed, but you have something to turn things over to. You lay your burden down [sighs]. If you don't have that, it's rough, so rough. But I just have the sense that there's a higher power, there's a Jesus, and I find that helpful. So I think faith is almost like a crutch, for the bad time. It feels too much to think you control everything and there's nothing protecting us or moving us forward or calling us to our best life." One Buddhist father from Chicago said, "The core the Buddha tried to teach, or any religion teaches, is to be a peaceful person, to be moderate, then you'll be happy and the

---

2. See Smith and Adamczyk, *Handing Down the Faith.*

world will be happy too." A conservative Protestant mother from Florida told us, "The world seems completely unsafe, with worry and anxiety. If you watch the news there ain't nothing good happening, so parents can get fearful for their children, themselves, their lifestyle. But I don't want to live in fear, so I make a conscious decision not to. The way I view it, my faith is in God and I know the end of the story, that no matter what he's going to take care of us. 'God has not given us a spirit of fear, but of power and love and a sound mind.' Sometimes I have to remind myself of that, because things happen and my initial gut reaction is fear. I say that Bible verse to myself over and over and over again, until it sinks in and I get a sense of peace." Similarly, a Hispanic Catholic father from Indiana related, "I teach my children that, if nothing else in the world is important, faith is important, because when tough times come, if you have your faith, then you feel like you have a refuge to go to." A white Catholic mother from New York City told us, "I might not be as calm and focused on the bigger picture without my religion. I might get caught up more in the daily details of life. I think religion allows you to have a certain zen, a certain peace." And providing that for children is primarily the parents' job, as this Hispanic Catholic mother from New Mexico explained, "It is an obligation, we need to give them faith. If I know it is something nice, I want to share it with my daughter, right? That she can always have that protection, feel protected by God. It all starts with the parents, that is important, so that, in addition to be on the right track in life, they can say: 'My mom told me about God, things about God, first.'" This Mormon mother from Indiana spoke about "the foundation I want my sons to have, having values and morals, the foundation, having the faith. I want them to have that, because when you have your religion, your faith, it grounds you. You always have something to hold on to, to keep going, to provide comfort with a family away from home, that's what the church provides for us." And this black Protestant father from Houston said:

> Religion helps you through life, with everything, like getting a job or not getting a job. Some people, if they lose a job and don't know God, they'll lose their mind, blow their head off. We believe God will provide all your needs. If you lose a job, okay, just give it some time. We walk by faith, and then work to make things happen. Without God, I don't know what they would fall back on or have for support to get through hard times, helps you in the good times. They'll struggle or find other means to fulfill their sadness that can harm them more.

Different types of parents emphasize different features of their religions as providing peace, comfort, protection, and belonging. Hindus, for example, tended to talk about the calming environment of their temples. "I go to temple for my spiritual upliftment, to have some mental peace," one Hindu father from New York City explained. "At temple I feel more connected and have some spiritual uplift, feel more peace." A Hindu mother from Chicago said, "We prefer our temple because there's hardly any people there. That quietness, that silence is what I look for in a temple. 'Cause that's where you get peace, with so much going on outside, it's so cruel, there's no end to [noise and conflict outside]." Jewish parents, by comparison, tend to underscore the stability of belonging to their tradition and people, as illustrated by the words of this Jewish father from Indiana: "Judaism provides a self-identification, knowing about a kind of family history, where your ancestors came from and what they have been through, and being proud of having that connection. I guess in a perfect world we would all live in harmony and people wouldn't have their little self-identified groups, but in a world with lots of different groupings, Judaism is a good group to feel identified with." The same Jewish father also said, "I have a strong background in the religious practice aspect of things. I enjoy being part of that community, taking part in leading the services, active in the broader Jewish community here. I feel very close with my synagogue and we've tried to give that Jewish connection to our children, even though I'm not really a spiritual or religious person." Some Catholics talked about the church as a source of comfort and support, as with this white Catholic mother from Indiana: "Church should be a beginning, giving a foundation for their spirituality. Any church would be there to support them through good times, bad times, hard times, fun times. And for me it's also a sense of fellowship, making really good friends, because so often good friends have similar beliefs as you, so church is a good place to meet them, if you have similar beliefs it makes it a lot easier." Other Catholics, such as this white father from Indiana, pointed to the importance of having a familiar religious culture, despite not being sure about God's existence:

I don't go around thinking is there a God, isn't there? If there is a God, he or she will do his or her thing. I'm not in torment trying to figure it out. It just doesn't matter much to me. I don't really care. But the praying part, I don't want our kids to grow up ignorant of our culture. I'm glad that they're going to Catholic school where they teach the Bible and catechism. It's an important part of our culture and education, so I don't want them to be ignorant. I want them to find comfort or meaning in religion, like it's not a strange leap for them to go there, no matter which religion it is. And it's good for our family. Then just the goal of wanting our kids to grow up literate in religion, you don't want to be ignorant. Plus, the messages that they get at school and maybe through us, the positives, that religion could be helpful in growing up. And just to give them that base, in case religion becomes important to them, even if just on their deathbed, to have that vocabulary and that basis, to be able to choose it, could be really important.

Buddhists, like this father from New York City, tended to talk about getting one's mind properly attuned: "The practice of Buddhism on mental health and peace is that everything is mind, mind is the commander, not the body. Buddhist philosophy teaches how to keep yourself happy, healthy, because if you have physical health it is that mental that commands it. When you have knowledge of religion you will be able to stay mentally happy. So those teachings are so precious, living and keeping you always feeling peace of mind." Some parents, like these white Catholics from New York City, told us that meditation and reading are crucial: "My husband does his reading every day and I do my meditation. Because our schedules are different, I have the luxury of reflecting more about these things, but he's in a pressure cooker all day at work. That's why I started doing the meditation, because we just need more tools to cope. You just need to learn new skills for whatever is coming your way. Like my dad got sick a few years ago, really complicated, a cancer diagnosis, and that threw us off." And many parents from different religious traditions talk about the calming practice of prayer. One Muslim mother from Chicago, for instance, said, "That's very comforting, religion. I don't even understand that much about it, but still that's our belief. We pray for God. Whenever we are sad, something goes wrong with us, that's how we can get comfort, that religion." And a black Protestant father from Houston explained, "Once I wake up I pray. And I start my day off when my journey begins. And it's like no matter what, you know, there's nothing to stop me from getting here 'cause I done already prayed on it, ya know?" And for some immigrants, religious communities provide parents the offer of belonging and shelter for their children against an alien dominant culture, as this Muslim mother from New York City described, "Religion has always been like an important part of my identity, but that doesn't mean I didn't struggle, it was a huge challenge for me growing up here and constantly feeling different and not able to participate in the teen social scene in the same way, like no going out with boys and no going to movies and not listening to American music. All of that was something my parents didn't want us to partake in. So they tried to expose us to like alternative kinds of social environments like the mosque and other Muslim families."

Parents repeatedly told us that religion helps them deal with life's difficulties, and that they hope their children will also benefit from that support in their lives. A mainline Protestant father from Washington, DC, for example, said, "It doesn't matter if they grow up believing my religion, but I hope they will be religious for their own sakes, though that's for them to decide. Because life, it's just hard, life is hard, and I think it would be even harder if you didn't have something to help you in that way." This white Catholic father from Indiana similarly related, "Some things are mysteries that can't be answered in this lifetime. But that's where faith comes in, to trust there's a reason you might be going through this [hard time]." One Muslim mother from Indiana explained that religion helped her keep her sanity during a very hard period: "My faith kept me sane throughout the divorce proceedings. It's kept me grounded, to see the truth from the false, but be able to handle the truth. I don't have to understand it, but only to handle it and say, okay if this is what it is then please God see me through and point us in the direction we need to take." Black Protestant parents especially seemed to stress religion's benefits for mental health. One black Protestant father from Houston, for instance, confessed:

> Without religion life would be horrible, because if I miss church my attitude is bad. If I miss devotion, everyone feels it, my attitude, my mouth, my countenance just changes and I understand that I need it. If I didn't have my belief, I would be cuckoo [laughs]. It's that sustaining power and knowledge, and my constant desire and prayer is that he draws me closer. If I didn't have that, my life would be in shambles, worse than it is now. I don't even think I would be able to live 'cause I wouldn't have anything to go on. So I have to have it or my life is gonna be crazy.

Similarly, this black Protestant mother from the same city confessed:

> I have to have faith around me, it's like a shield. When I'm out of alignment or don't align myself with it consistently, I notice I can't think straight, don't handle situations as appropriately as I would when I'm under the total covering. I don't like myself when I'm not consistently drawn and connected. I'm like, oh I gotta get back into church, I've missed too many days. Or I let some situation keep me from church, I'll just be like I can't take it anymore, my life starts to fall apart when my spiritual side is not on a consistent basis.

Because we discuss at greater length the "bigger picture" aspect of this proposition below, we move forward now to avoid unnecessary redundancy.

Religion also produces pragmatic, humanistic social results, like fostering good citizenship, strengthening society, and upholding morals—all desirable in the world here and now.

The benefits of religion are not only personal but also social, cultural, and political, in the minds of religious parents in the United States. A Jewish father from Indiana, for example, explained, "One of the tenets of Judaism is to make the world a better place, that's something my parents tried to do, something that Jewish people tend to, not all of them but some are very philanthropic because of trying to make the world a better place, the belief that we're partners with God in trying to do that." A mainline Protestant father in Washington, DC, said, "Religion is sort of like the regulator [that shapes us to see] that you should be kind to everybody in the world, patient, respectful, trying to seek the best in each other, generous in the community." This Muslim mother from Indiana told us, "I want them to be able to distinguish what's right and wrong, and to draw that from their faith and their humanity, that one doesn't contradict the other. If they're following their faith, they're doing good for humanity, and if they're humane, they're following their faith. It's like a side-by-side thing, and I hope they understand that, and that's one of my aims for them, my goal, that they do that." A white Catholic father also from Indiana related, "I hope Catholicism teaches my kids how to be a good citizen to the community and give back to the community. I think the Catholic tradition offers that."

One Buddhist father from Chicago explained: "I tell my kids that if you achieve in your life, you can use it to help people up. I told them they have to try the best, so when they have a good job they can use their money to donate to the poor, to help a lot of people, to help communities, other people in need. I try to give them a path of where we should go, to live a good life, like helping people." This conservative Protestant mother and schoolteacher from Florida said that, "Kids need morality based on the great morals we have from religion and learned from God, like the Ten Commandments. If [one of my student's] parents aren't paying attention to that, I don't have a problem bridging that gap, because having good morals and a good basis is gonna make a better citizen, and the whole reason why we are educators is to produce citizens. Kids need that little voice inside the head that says, 'Ah, shouldn't do that.'" Therefore, when religion loses its influence, society as a whole suffers, a point this Hispanic Catholic father from New Mexico made: "What I instill in my children is, God is much more than someone sitting up there and watching from afar, God is here, in everyone's heart. But sadly, we have removed God from our daily lives, that we are paying the consequences. Yes, God's absence generates divorce, loneliness, depression, alcoholism, that is the root cause."

The voices of agreement continue. A black Protestant mother from Houston told us, "I hope all my grandchildren become productive citizens of this country and give back what they have learned, that God has blessed you to bless others and share what you have, and pass that torch on." And a Hispanic Catholic mother from New York reported: "I want my children to be good citizens, right? To help the community, all of society, because I firmly believe that within the family, as adults we should continue to become better brothers every day, because if we don't teach our children values, they won't know how to be good citizens in the future." This Mormon father explained how his religion has turned him into a more sociable person in general:

> Christ sets an example but you have to practice it. How do you get better at anything? You practice. So you have to practice being humble, being kind to others, charity, until you get better at it. You can get better at being compassionate, charitable, humble, I figured that out, now I'm getting better at it because I practice it. And my ego and arrogance has gone down because I've stopped practicing being arrogant and egotistical. I mean I was a narcissist to the extreme. And that's not good. But now I finally realize that. And the LDS church helped, though probably any Christian church would.

Religion, parents say, promotes charity in society: "I want them to really be strong in Islam," said one Muslim mother from Indiana, "because by being strong in Islam they are being strong for themselves and for a good life. Then they'll be guided the right way for life, and that way be good to others, charity is real important." Religion promotes volunteering as well: "We've taught them from day one to volunteer and give back," said a white Catholic mother from Indiana; "we've been fortunate, there are people out there with a lot less than us, and the world doesn't revolve around you. I don't think our kids would've been as aware of that [without church volunteering]." It also teaches elementary social cooperation and propriety, as noted by this black Protestant mother from Houston: "I go to a church that has a good, strong teaching ethic for kids, to learn about God but also other little things they need to know for the real world, like etiquette. Not everybody that comes to church knows how to act and respect the church. So church shows children how to act in the real world, 'cause you gotta learn that, so all that can be incorporated together." In addition, religion, when properly interpreted, teaches acceptance of different cultures and religions, as suggested by this black Catholic mother from Indiana: "There's a reason why God made all these different people. For me, if God wanted us all to have the same religion we would. There's a reason why we don't and there's a reason why people are so different, why we look different, think different, act different. And I think that is that we all need to learn how to accept each other, to accept people for how they are, what they look like, and that's a hard lesson for everybody." And some religions promulgate morals that are applicable in a variety of social settings, as pointed out by this Hindu father from Chicago: "In Hinduism everything is situational, there are no absolute truths, it thinks in terms of situational logic. What logic works in this particular situation doesn't have to be universally moral but is effective and moral in a given context." All of these benefits make another reason why parents value religion.

Religion is good, too, because it can provide cohesion and solidarity in family relationships, and often helps marriages and families get through hard times.

The following quotes do not need much commentary but together tell how commonly religious parents assume and believe this idea. "We say a nondenominational grace together," reported one mainline Protestant mother from New York City, "like thank you for our food, for our family, for our friends, for our cat, you know, we love each other, we help each other, we ask for help from each other, we tell each other the truth, we don't say mean things to each other, we just sort of ground ourselves that way." Similarly, this mainline Protestant father from another New York City family said, "We pray always before we eat. Eating together is a very big part of our family, eating food, sitting together at the table and eating, and praying before we eat is a big part of our family, we all hold hands and give thanks. Normally, I lead, sometimes my wife, or sometimes we all participate in the prayer." And this black Protestant father from Houston confessed, "Without religion, our family would be pretty hectic, we'd argue and fight a lot, 'cause we don't see eye to eye with some things. If you don't have that in your life, you see things in the news, like angry guys killing wives and kids and shooting themselves, I think that's because they don't have belief in God or faith, they don't have anything else to turn to. So we would be really hectic if I was without religion or faith."

One white Catholic father from Indiana stated, "You go to church as a family, as a unit. It's not me and you, it's us. Church is a personal thing, but it's a community thing too. When you base your life and it revolves around the church and the church and God are the most important thing in life, it's gotta all be together." A white Catholic father from New York City recalled, "With all the struggles I had with my mom, religion was kind of the glue that kept us together." "It's important for me to continue passing down the generational cultures," said a Hispanic Catholic mother from Indiana, "for the [religious] values, it's very important for the well-being of the family nucleus." And this Hispanic Catholic father from New Mexico told this story:

> Frankly, I would not want to touch the topic of how my family would be without religion. Before, in the past, I was very violent with my wife, my daughters, verbal violence, shouts, insults, accusations. Life before, I opened the door coming from work and my daughters went to hide in the bathroom, below the sofa, behind the curtains. When I approached, they were trembling. My wife did not know how to talk to me, they were traumatized. I do not want that [anymore]. But it's good now because [of faith]. Now, when my daughters are close and kiss me, my wife is compassionate toward me, the first thing comes to my mind is, "I would not change this for anything." I cannot imagine going back to the former, because it could have been a divorce I do not desire.

Similarly, a Mormon mother from New York City said, "Even if God doesn't exist and the church isn't true, it actually really doesn't matter to me, because I'm choosing it, it's an act of faith to believe in God, who can't be proved or disproved, and it's something that makes my life better. It's a way to raise my children, talking openly. We love them and hope they find their own path, but for now it's really brought us closer together as a family to have this faith we all believe in."

A Jewish mother also from New York City related, "I had this conversation with my son this morning, I said, 'I know you think I'm very religious and observant,' and he goes, 'well, you want everyone to be like you.' I said, 'no I just want my family to be like me, I'm just trying to show you what I value.'" A Muslim father from Indiana said, "My job is kind of demanding, but for the most part in the evenings we spend time with our kids. When they were young they needed more help, now they're kind of almost independent. But we guide them and do everything we need to do." A Hindu mother from Chicago reported, "We do meditation, some singing together, we come here on Sundays or Saturdays and sit quietly and pray, like pray singing songs. Once a week we definitely do it, my wife, she sits and makes my son sit [with us]." A Hindu father from central New Jersey explained, "I'll say to my girl, 'why don't you light this' and we'll stand and pray together, and she'll do the Akshara thingy, she does it to herself and then to me. It's important because it builds a bridge that we share. It's very important, being able to celebrate and understand why we do this." Another Hindu mother from the same area reported: "We always do Diwali as a family. We pray every day as a family. Birthdays, you know, we always go out, do everything together, go to temple every birthday as a family." And one Buddhist father from New York City said,

> We told them to have a nice life they need to have a good companion in marriage, not only a Buddhist but one raised in same environment, it will be easier for you. Different habits and traditions make conflicts come up. In America, many don't have any faith, any religion. So conflict comes then, it's common! When the husband and wife live together, definitely some conflict comes up, both start fighting and going away from each other. So religious things help them to lead a normal life too. That's why we say to lead a happy life you need to have someone who believes in same faith.

We humans have a natural tendency to stray and misbehave in self-harming ways, but religion is effective at helping "keep people in line," which is beneficial.

Religious parents from various backgrounds also share this belief about religion as an effective means of personal and social control. "There's a phase in human life," said one Hispanic Catholic father from New York City, "when you do stray, you stray a bit from religion, stray from those spiritual means, to live in and experience the world in its entirety. Maybe not everyone does it, but the majority do, I think it's part of human growth." A black Protestant mother from Houston said, "As a child growing up you will stray, but you will come back to your roots, because growing up, child development, you're going to do stuff, it's just normal, to test the waters, its normal to test, normal to find something new you think you like. But once you get out there and see the problem and trouble, you realize you don't like it, you go back to church and stay grounded." A Buddhist father from Chicago said, "Nobody knows if god is there or not, nobody has seen him. But I think everybody should have a little bit of faith so that we will go in the right way, right path. We need something like a destiny to know what is good and wrong, to know that inside, so we have little bit fear before doing anything wrong." Similarly, this white Catholic father from Indiana explained, "Religion and church provide a community, a moral orientation. It's too easy to just do whatever without a guiding force, a guiding hand, a guiding faith. But with faith we had a set of doctrines or rules or guidelines how to be a parent, to say, this is how you should live, and if you do, you're gonna be a good person and your life will have value. You can do that for your kids. So it was like a paper that says if you follow these rules then you're going to be successful, we had that with religion." One conservative Protestant mother from Los Angeles told us, "Church is necessary because you want to be around other Christians that believe what you believe and do the same things you do. Fellowship is definitely important because the right kind of fellowship helps you stay on the path." A Florida father from the same religious tradition said, "God is someone to be feared. I think the fear of the Lord keeps you in line sometimes. One reason we have gang-banging boys running around killing people is because they've grown up their whole life without a father figure or someone to instill fear into them. Not necessarily fear, but a consequence. A lot of kids today are growing up with no consequences. That's why they'll pull out a gun and shoot a cop in the face, because they've never had a consequence for their actions, never been told 'no,' never been punished. I believe fear of the Lord is very important. He keeps you in line." A Jewish father from New York City explained matters in this typically Jewish way, focusing on identity: "Judaism helps you know who you are and what you are. And if you have a firm basis from that, you can branch out and do a bunch of other things. But if you're not really sure who you are or what you are, it's much harder to."

In all of this, the metaphor of "staying on the right path" is central. "With the hard things happening in our lives right now," one Jewish mother from New York City said, "God is the only thing that's getting me through. I'm always asking in prayers, 'Am I on the right path? Am I not?'" A Muslim mother from Indiana explained how she teaches her children: "I tell them people go through things, and this is how I found my way, you go to the Quran and you read and discuss it and try to understand what the Quran's telling you, and then you pray and try to come to its conclusion. I think God will take you down the right path for it." This Hindu father from Chicago also spoke of being on the right path: "There is a path, but as long as you believe in something that sort of makes you moral, [that is good]. The fact that somebody [a god] is looking down on you from above, it limits [bad behavior]. People also use that as an excuse to say, 'my way is right,' but I think everything in moderation is good." And a Buddhist father from New York City explained, "Ignorance, hatred, and desires, those are the things we say poison. You need to control the mind then you can choose what is right. Bad things stay away from, avoid them. If you are able to avoid them, then you are in the right path, and you will be out free from all worldly problems."

Stated negatively, what parents hope religion helps their children avoid is "straying" away from the path, at least for too long and with too bad of consequences. "I try to keep my kids involved so they won't stray out," a black Protestant mother from Houston told us, "because I know when they do—not saying that they will or they won't, but things happen, life happens—if they have that foundation they know where to come back to. So, I just say he's [God is] the way." Likewise, this black Protestant father from the same city said, "My ultimate desire is to build a foundation for my kids, because they are going to stray, it's going to happen in most kids' lives, you're gonna go wayward. And if you put that foundation in them, they will come back." And parents have a big responsibility to instill religion that can help keep their children in line and not straying from the path. A black Protestant father from Houston explained, "In the end we gonna have to stand in judgment for what [we did]. I believe that. So for my family, I say, I will still love you and I will pray for you, but religion is something that you just don't go astray. Old people say you'll go astray but you don't lose it, don't lose what you have been taught. I look at people when they go and get their [college] education, it does something to some people, we lose some things, shake some things off. But my standpoint, and I'm fifty-seven years old, you better keep that one [religion]." In discussing his child's Buddhist baptism ritual, this father from Chicago explained, "It's really a pledge from the parents that they're gonna bring her up Buddhist, under Buddhist ethics, and teach her the precepts, right thinking, right speech, right behavior." And this mainline Protestant mother from Los Angeles told us, "I've seen some children who have come here, that they can't do nothing with their lives because they have friends out there doing wrong things. It's a challenge. That's why I think, stick with the church, sit with the guidance in the church, and pray that God guide them toward the right path."

For these reasons, it is almost impossible to imagine being a family without religion (even if for others religion is not necessary for achieving the same values, morals, well-being, and good relationships that religion provides our family).

Consider the words of this mainline Protestant mother from Washington, DC: "Every day you have faith that everyone will be okay, that things will turn out okay, that you're doing the best you can, you're doing your best and to have faith in yourself. I mean I just can't imagine not having any of that." And this Indiana mother from the same religious tradition: "It's too late to remove religion from my family. My kids have it instilled in them, even at six years old, she knows. She's been going to church pretty much her whole life. I don't think we could. They already know who God is, what's in their heart, they already have their beliefs." Not being religious is nearly inconceivable. Thus, one white conservative Protestant father from Florida had difficulty thinking about what his family would look like without religion: "I couldn't imagine it. I just don't know. I guess we'd be a bunch of heathens. We wouldn't have any morals, borderline respect, but no deep-rooted hope or understanding that the world's a lot bigger than we are and things happen for a reason. Some things we don't understand and don't really need to. And golly, you would not think you're gonna go to heaven or anything. I don't know, it would be chaos. It would take what makes sense out of it, to me. I don't know, it'd be weird. I just, I don't really ever think like that, so I don't know." One black Protestant mother from Houston explained it this way: "Even primitive man, they worshipped the trees, they were gonna worship something. And so, if you take all the religion out, I'm thinking it would just be replaced by something else. So I don't see myself without religion." The theme continues across the religious traditions. "If you took Catholicism out of our family," thought a white Catholic mother from Indiana, "wow, um [pause], I cannot, I cannot imagine, I don't know that it would be, I really don't know. The biggest thing would be that we wouldn't have the stability and routine of going to church every week and that um [pause] but I don't, I honestly can't imagine not doing it."

Hispanic Catholic parents seemed especially incapable of imagining not being religious. One father from New Mexico also said, "Wow! The truth is I don't even want to think about our life without religion, it would change drastically. Religion is what has kept us together, the truth. We wouldn't be where we are right now, my wife and I, after twenty something years of marriage, if it hadn't been for religion and faith." A Hispanic Catholic mother from New York City said, "Since I was young I have always been with God, I have always wanted to be a nun. It has always been in my mind, so how my life would be without God, it would be something bad, like sin. I would not see myself like that, no." And this Hispanic Catholic mother from New Mexico objected, "No, no, I can't imagine life without religion. I think it would, I would be very sad, maybe. I don't know."

A Mormon mother from Indiana related that, "So many of our family rules come from Gospel rules, like how we spend our time. We would love each other less [without religion] because we would spend less time together as a family, and we wouldn't have that eternal sense that we're in this for the long haul, this relationship is permanent. But I've never really thought about that." A Jewish mother from New York City stated, "I cannot imagine my life without the community, or my marriage without our Jewish life." A Jewish father from Indiana said similarly: "I don't even think I can answer the question how I would be without Judaism, because everything I've said, it's just who I am deep down. It's informed me in ways some of which are probably genetic, some cultural, and some of learned through religious observance. But I mean, I wouldn't be me at all, I just don't even really know how to answer that." This Muslim father from Indiana imagined, "Life without Islam would be drastically different, I couldn't even describe it, because I never experienced that. It has been pervasive, it's all I know, right from when I was child, that's all I have had, I have not known anything different." A Muslim mother from the same state told us, "Religion is the key to life. If you don't have religion, then you have no rules in your life. And rules are made to keep you safe and secure, whether it's the rule of the land or the rule of God, there's a reason for that rule. So you're gonna mess yourself up without religion." This Hindu father from New York City echoed that sentiment: "If I took the spiritualism out, I don't know, because I always believed in it, it would be hard for me to figure out." In fact, of all the religious traditions we studied, only the Buddhist parents generally thought religion was good and helpful but not necessary or unthinkable to live without.

A Minority Concern: Salvation and Afterlife

The dominant cultural model of intergenerational religious transmission held by American religious parents does not involve much of a concern with existence after death. We heard little talk about salvation, heaven, an afterlife, eternity, the other side, or eternal life in the pages above. For the vast majority, religion's purpose and value concern improving life in this world. However, afterlife themes are not entirely absent. A minority of religious parents in the United States does at least reference these ideas when discussing passing on religious faith and practice to children. Overall, forty-three parents used "other world" language of salvation, heaven, afterlife, eternity, the other side, and eternal life, mostly from black Protestant (eleven parents), white conservative Protestant (nine),

Catholic (seven), and Muslim (five) households.[3] Only three mainline Protestant parents used such language, along with only one Mormon and one Hindu parent. No Jewish or Buddhist parents spoke about salvation or heaven (which is unsurprising, since they are not important in the central "doctrines" of those traditions). At times parents from Jewish or Buddhist traditions spoke explicitly *against* a concern with an afterlife. Furthermore, even among parents who did reference salvation, heaven, an afterlife, eternity, the other side, and eternal life, these concerns were not central, but supplemental emphases. No parent elaborated any of these ideas or seemed to hold any substantial notions about what they meant; details were absent. Even black Protestant parents, who were the most likely of all to reference life after death, mostly said that good lives on earth for their children need to involve believing in God and being good so people can go to heaven after they die. Often the idea was how good it would be to continue a relationship with one's children in eternity. To give an idea of the way this minority of parents talked about salvation and an afterlife, we offer these interview quotes, in addition to the few references already given.

A black Protestant father from Houston recounted how he instructs his children as: "I hope to see you on the other side, 'cause I plan on going there, and it's real, it's a part of life. If you do these steps you have been taught, then we'll see each other again when we leave here, because we're going to leave—we don't know when or where, but we're going to go." Among the black Protestants who did discuss an afterlife, some emphasized not the threat of hell for their children (about which sometimes they even laughed) but the burden that life after death lays on them as parents here and now. One mother said, "I'm responsible for them making it to heaven. Well, they really responsible for themself, but I'm the one that's gotta get them in line with that first. And if I don't, then God gonna look at me and say, 'Man, with all that time you had down there, you didn't do nothin'!' You want me to let you in, but your baby ain't gonna make it 'cause you ain't teach him nothing!' So that's my thang now." A related theme is heaven and hell, almost like karma, providing extra incentives to "make good decisions" in life now, as this father told us, "God is watching us at all times, and I've raised them to believe that even though I'm not

3. Specifically, when such a term was used by parents discussing their future aspirations for their children or reasons for wanting their children to be religious, including being the same religion as the parent, and not including instances when parents used the term in general conversations about or trying to help their children understand death or when describing their own personal religious beliefs.

around, the decisions they make, you will have to answer for them, because you're not going to heaven with me, and I don't plan to go to hell with you [laughs]. So what you do, it comes back to you, what you put out is what you get back: you put out good, you get back good; you put out wrong, you're gonna get back wrong—there are consequences for your actions. So in my family we fear God."

The white conservative Protestants who referenced heaven and hell tended to speak more directly about the importance of their children being Christians in order to enjoy eternal life. "I believe in eternity provided by God and I want them to have that," said one father from Florida. "God wants them to have it. They're my children but also children of God, they were designed for him, and it's my role to lead them in that direction." Another conservative Protestant mother from Los Angeles explained, "Eventually we're going to die and experience eternity, so why would you not want to instill that in your kids, help them understand how important that is? The most important decision you ever, ever make is whether you accept or deny Christ, 'cause that is not only for this life but also your eternal life." Similarly, this mother from Florida said, "I want all my kids to be saved and go to heaven and believe in God and have that as their trust and hope." And this conservative Protestant single mother from New York City: "I do believe Christianity is the one true faith, so I think in the long run my daughter would be putting her eternal soul in jeopardy if she turned away from faith. It has nothing to do with being a good person, because I think other people often are better than a lot of Christians. But at the end of the day the scripture says to be saved you have to believe in who Jesus is, so I want to know that when we're on the other side I get to be in a relationship with her, I'm kinda counting on that."

A minority of white Catholic parents also talk about life after death. One mother from New York City mentioned the importance for her children of "giving them a concept of an afterlife, heaven, that when you die it's not the end, that what you do here on earth matters because you have another life to live and enjoy, hopefully, after this one." A Catholic mother from northern Indiana said, "Being religious, being Catholic is their surest way to heaven, and that's what God wants of them, and they can help other people by doing that." When asked which beliefs are most important to her, a different Catholic mother also from Indiana replied, "Well, obviously the belief that if you live a good life you will go to heaven. No one wants to go to hell." A father from northern Indiana told us, "My hopes and goals for my kids? Heaven [laughs], I mean really. And the way they would get there is to find that personal relationship with Jesus and to value that above everything else." This mother from the same area made a point to discount fear about hell, emphasizing happiness and good decision-making in life: "I hope Catholic education gives a strong framework on how to live life that has a consequential end game, understanding that our actions now have potentially longer term consequences, could potentially lead you towards heaven or hell. Not from a fearful perspective, but really more so from happiness perspective on how to make those choices. Please don't ask me the details 'cause I really don't know necessarily [laughing]. But I think the Catholic religion really does offer a good framework for that, and to guide you through some difficult decisions you might have to make." Another Catholic mother from New York City spoke positively about Catholicism by arguing against a concern with heaven after death and instead for the Church making paradise happen today:

> God gave us life, nature, and our freedom, and I believe in the Catholic Church as an entity that wants to regroup and define those values. So that's what I'm giving my children. We need to pray individually, to listen to our inner selves, to have confidence that God created us and we are part of a puzzle, part of the Church, and we have a responsibility to make the world a better place. And if we don't take the time and know who we are and help other people know who they are, we are not going in that direction. I don't know what that direction is, I just know it's a better place than today, because that's a promise, if you pray, if you believe in Jesus, if you love one another, the world will be a better place, and for me that is paradise. I don't wait for the resurrection of the dead to meet paradise, it is today.

Among the Hispanic Catholics who raised these themes, one father from northern Indiana, for instance, mentioned salvation: "When you have been told in your life that Catholic religion is the thing that can get you salvation, and it's two thousand years old, and your parents [believed this], and I believe I'm in the right path, then I want my daughter to be on the right path, and I can't imagine being mistaken about it." And one black Catholic mother from the same area said, "I want my kids to know that God did send Jesus, his only son, to die on the cross, the whole passion and crucifixion, on behalf of their salvation, and hopefully that their salvation is worth saving."

Parents from other religious traditions who discussed life after death did so in ways that related it directly to peace and happiness in this world. One mainline Protestant mother from Washington, DC, for example, said, "I look for my kids to find in a church a good grounding in knowing that there is a God, who made and is active in the world, sent his son, and wants them to go to heaven, wants the best for them. And some of these principles in the Bible that will help you be a better, happier person, a happier person and build a better world for all of us." A Mormon father from northern Indiana told us, "There is great peace in a crazy world when we are doing what's right, choosing goodness, serving, trying to be more Christ-like, an inner peace that comes with that, in this life. I also believe in a reward, that we will get to live with heavenly father again if we learn it in this life. So, yeah, I want that for my boys, to have that peace." One Hindu mother from Chicago used heaven as the reason for her daughter being a good person in this life, which is more important than religious teachings and praying:

> I teach her that if you're a good person you'll go closer to God, to heaven. If you're not that good in life, probably won't get closer to God. There's a darker place, not a happy place to stay. I believe in reincarnation. So basically be a good person, you don't need all that religious teachings. It's true, you be a good person and it gets you much closer to God, who wants you to do good things. You can pray for twenty-four hours and then go out and kill people or say mean things to people, that doesn't take you anywhere. So for me all that doesn't matter, it's just basically who you are as a person.

By contrast, however, one Muslim mother from Chicago said that, "We believe you can do a lot of good things in life, but the only way to get to heaven, if you believe in heaven, is not by doing hundreds of good things, but really because God is merciful, and by the mercy of God you're gonna be granted heaven. So if we lose valuable things in this life, that's not the end-all of existence." And this Muslim father explained what he tells his children, "You will have to face your maker so it's up to you, where do you wanna go? Do you wanna go to hell? Be my guest, I can't help it, I am no longer responsible for you, I raised you up. That's my mentality."

At the same time, if some religious parents think salvation and heaven are reasons their children should also be religious or good, others argue the opposite. One Jewish mother from Indiana expressed her belief that people should be good for its intrinsic value and its making us feel good, not for a heavenly reward: "I believe in righteousness, doing good for goodness sake, not because it's gonna get me to heaven, but because it's the right thing to do, the culturally Jewish thing, to do good. That's an important distinction, because some people's religion says do good or accept certain religious principles to get into heaven, and I don't believe in that. I do good because it's the right thing to do, it gives me warm fuzzies, it's nice, makes me feel good too, that I'm doing the right thing." And one Buddhist mother from Chicago (a convert from Catholicism) told us that all that matters in life is being good now, being grateful today, and appreciating the sacredness and connectedness of everything, explaining that, "I don't even know if there is Nirvana, it doesn't matter if there's a Heaven, Hell, Nirvana, nothing. If there is, great. If there isn't, well, I won't know."

Religious Truth

The dominant view of religion held by most religious American parents is defined not only by its value for life in the world but also by a particular approach to the validity of religious truth claims. Do religions teach authentic truths or is objective truth not even the point of religion? And if the former (authentic truths), how can one make sense of the diversity of truth claims made by different religions? The common operative cultural model of religious truth is as follows.

> *Religious Truth*: All or most religions are after the truth, religions do teach genuine truths, and it is possible (for some parents) for a religion to teach *the* truth. Two religious truths are paramount for children to learn, one vaguely theological and existential; the second, instrumental and functional. First, children should learn to "believe in something" along the lines that "there is a greater picture" out there, "something bigger" going on, such as a God who is with us and answers prayers or the force of karma. Second, religion can help people live good lives in this world. However, exclusivity, superiority, and fanaticism in religions are bad, dangerous, and must be avoided. Even if one believes that no one religion has a monopoly on truth, it is still not a bad idea to belong to some particular religious tradition or community, to be located somewhere specific. Beyond the two paramount truths, however, one can take from one's own religious tradition the parts that make sense and work best, and leave the parts that don't, according to "whatever seems right" to you; nobody needs to accept or be subject to the whole package of a religious tradition.

All or most religions are after the truth, religions do teach genuine truths, and it is possible (for some parents) for a religion to teach the *truth.*

Religious parents in the United States express beliefs on this point of religious truth as we would expect according to the religious tradition to which they belong, based on what we know already about those traditions. Through religious socialization (and some self-selection through tradition switching),[4] the subcultures of various religious traditions as environmental contexts shape the beliefs of parents on questions of truth. Mainline Protestant parents, for example, express a range of beliefs about religious truth, but generally tend toward moderate and cautious positions, as with this mainline Protestant father from Los Angeles: "I would love if my girl were [to remain] Christian, because I truly believe for me that is the truth, I really do. I can't tell you I have never felt so strongly about anything. But I believe." Christianity is true, but "for me," and his "feelings" about it are not as strong as some other beliefs; still, he confesses, "I believe."

By comparison, most white conservative Protestants consider most or all of Protestant Christianity to teach the truth on "the essentials."[5] Their views about Catholicism vary, as some think Catholicism teaches truth and others that it is flawed with errors, and most would hesitate to say that non-Christian religions teach truth. For example, this conservative Protestant mother from Indiana said, "I continue in the faith 'cause I really believe that's where the truth lies. That's really where I'm gonna find the answers, the truth about life." Similarly, this conservative Protestant father from Florida explained, "There comes a point in your life religiously where you accept what you believe and know it to be the truth or not the truth, and you've got to make sure your children get that same belief, because you are gonna die and go to heaven or hell one day. And I am one of people who believe once saved, always saved." One conservative Protestant father from Los Angeles expressed the typical (but by no means exclusive) view of his tradition about the truth of other religions: "We exposed our children to other world religions, teaching it is what someone else believes without considering it true. That's the route we take: this is what Hindus believe, what Muslims believe, what even Catholics believe. Obviously, though, they understand that we are propagating our faith that we have come to know as being the truth." At bottom, conservative Protestants believe that the sole touchstone of religious truth is (their interpretation of) the Bible, as expressed by one mother from Indiana: "What does the Bible say about

4. Religious people with certain views of religious truth may change religious traditions for various reasons and end up intentionally or inadvertently in a tradition that more closely aligns with their view of truth than the one they left.

5. Because they vary wildly about how to correctly interpret the Bible, they have to focus on "the essentials" strategically in order to avoid self-defeating truth claims amid "pervasive interpretive pluralism." See Christian Smith, *The Bible Made Impossible* (Grand Rapids, MI: Brazos Press, 2012).

something? What people think doesn't change what the truth is, word of God is where we start."

Black Protestant parents tend to be confident about what they believe but also fairly ecumenical in downplaying the importance of religious differences. Some tend to hew closer to Christianity as the truth, as with this black Protestant mother from Houston: "My religious affiliation is Baptist because I was raised Baptist, but I've read up on other religions, a little anyway, and from what I can understand I think all of religion has some truth to it, but I think mostly Baptist is closer to the truth, to me." Others are more accepting of all religious truth claims, as with this black Protestant father from the same city: "I'm just a believer. You know I tell people that all the time, I don't try to classify myself as a Christian. Why are we separate when we all trying to get to one goal? It don't make sense to me sometimes. I'm like, why you wanna be called a Catholic or Christian or Muslim or a Jew? We all believe in God, we all trying to get to heaven, I would hope so. I don't think you trying to get to no different heaven than I'm trying to get to." But most black Protestant parents are much more comfortable keeping Christianity as the center of gravity of religious truth, as said by this mother also from Houston: "If my kids married into Islam or Judaism? It could be a problem. The Catholics, I know they want you to convert. Baptists, Pentecostals, and Methodists and Lutheran and all of those, they pretty much the same thing. But when you steppin' out and going over to Islamic, those are a different teaching. I have visited them, the other side, I'll admit, because I just wanted to know for me."

Most white American Catholic parents tend to express fairly relativistic and ecumenical views of religious truth, like that explained by this Catholic father from New York City: "Different religions are fundamentally the same things that people express in different ways. It's like a quest, mankind is on a journey that expresses things different ways. I [happen to] come from a background of parents convinced that there is something in the Catholic religion that is better and the right thing." Most American Catholics view religion as ultimately about "being a good person," which they see most or all religions teaching, ergo all religions teach the truth, as is expressed by this Catholic mother from Indiana: "Church helps give people a foundation, no matter what religion it is. It's that guidepost, living by those rules, which I don't think differ too much between religions, what they [all] want you to do, treating other human beings the same way you want to be treated. It's pretty much the same, kind of universal." Minorities of Catholic parents do take stronger views of the truth of Christianity or of Catholicism, but not many. For instance, one father from Indiana, who attends Mass with his Catholic wife and children, but who (probably not coincidentally) comes from a conservative Protestant background and has purposefully not converted to Catholicism, took this harder position, albeit not without initial self-critical apology: "This might be selfish and self-centered, but I feel that Christianity is the truth. And once you see and know the truth and been involved in that truth, to choose another religion, you're rejecting it."

Hispanic Catholics in the United States are different, with views that are more implicit than expounded. Most expressed surprise and sometimes even shock at our very question of whether, for example, their children might switch to a non-Christian religion—especially those who are more recent immigrants. Hispanic Catholics wish for their kids to remain Catholic, and very much hope they do not become non-Christian. That suggests by implication that they think non-Catholic religions do not contain the truth that Catholicism does. Consider this response by a Hispanic Catholic mother from New Mexico: "If my kids joined another religion, I would try to make them understand it does not suit them. Marry someone from another religion? My word! I haven't thought about that! These are all questions I have never considered. It would be difficult for them, more than for me. The truth is it would cost me. But if they are in love and are happy, I would have to accept it. I want to see them happy and well, even though I wouldn't like it myself. But I think that I would be a nosy grandmother and try to train my grandchildren as Catholics." Belief in the particularity of Catholic faith and practice here more closely resembles that of white conservative Protestants than white Catholics or black Protestants, as, for instance, expressed by one Hispanic Catholic father from New Mexico: "I haven't doubted that God exists. Yes, of course there's always the doubt who is right among all the religions, when they come knocking at your door. But besides that, no, I'm Catholic, and I don't think I have doubts, I like being Catholic, I believe in God, in the saints as well, no, there haven't been doubts." For some, however, in the end "being happy" and "a good person" still trumps particular truth claims, as evident in the discussion of this Hispanic Catholic father from New Mexico: "If my kids became another religion, if they truly have a relationship with God, it would not bother me. Jehovah's Witnesses, I would not like [laughs]. No, they need to be Christians. Even my daughter's boyfriend is evangelical and his mother is the one most involved in their religion. I hope in God they do not become non-Christian! But if it happened, and if they have good behavior in life, good values and morals, if it works for them and they feel good and do well, then I have to accept them. It would hurt me. But being my children I have to accept it. And if they had a change for the better, then perfect. But if they change and do bad things, then there would be even more wrong." Still, others, like this Hispanic Catholic mother from the same state, are not so ready to let children leave Catholicism: "Become another religion, God, I hope not. If that were to happen, my job as a mother would be to pull them to my religion, pull them to the truth that Jesus is the way, the truth, and the life. Keep talking to them, get them out of that mistake, pray for them, so God will remove them from that path, because I don't know how they are going to think, but my hope is in God."

Parents from most other religions express similar ranges of positions on religious truth. Some tend to take stronger stands on the truth of their own traditions, as with, for example, this Mormon mother from Indiana: "I believe we have a living prophet, that priesthood authority was lost after Christ, that Christians were doing their very best but they lost some essential pieces of the truth, and that we the Mormons have been in the process of restoring those essential pieces of truth. Which is why we say we have a living prophet who receives revelation from God." But most take different strategies that affirm the truth in many religions. One approach is to say that, while other religions teach truth, they are all best represented by one's own religion, as suggested by one Mormon father from Indiana: "I've looked into the Muslim religion, I still carry a Koran around with me, read that. I've looked at the Presbyterian, Methodist, the Brethren. And all of the good things of those religions, my current religion, Latter Day Saints, seemed to put all into one." A related approach is to subsume other religions into one's own through a historical-theological interpretation that simultaneously accepts other monotheisms and affirms the preeminence of one's own tradition, as with the approach argued by this Muslim mother from Indiana:

> I think [religious revelation] it's progression. Islam is the oneness of God and praising God all the way through. The original Jewish people were Muslims, so to speak. Then God sent somebody else down, Jesus, and now there's Christianity. Moses and then Jesus, but not going backwards. Then Jesus said there'd be one more [prophet] and that's Mohammed, then that's it. God gave it one more shot with the people, saying this is the way, "one more time guys I'm gonna give you this try, whoever goes with it, fine, but if you leave it, that's gonna be your problem." So the Jews that stayed the true Jews, they're Muslims. Christians who stayed true Christians, they're Muslims. Mohammed came, said the same thing, "hey there's one God, you need to believe in God, to

worship God, it's all about God, okay?" Now if I go away from that, change my religion and go to Christianity, I'm saying none of that ever happened, I just nullified everything that came after Moses. Okay to go forward, but it's wrong to go backward, and those are the only three faiths that believe in God in general. So to step outside of those faiths, you just slammed the door in God's face and he doesn't exist either. Totally blasphemy. It's a done deal. So Islam is the last and final word and everything in between is Islam.

Other parents take a more inclusive approach by saying that different religions are diverse human expressions of the same underlying ultimate reality or truth, as with this Hindu father from New York City: "Because I am a scientist, I look for the truth, and I truly believe it, because truth is one—everything can change, but truth cannot change. The truth is one and [different people just] call it different [things]. Being a Hindu, a Muslim, a Christian, a Jew, we all are going toward the same path, that's where I strongly believe." Buddhist parents express a similar inclusive acceptance of all religions but still insist on the need to "believe in something." One Buddhist mother from Chicago, for example, told us, "Sometimes I'll say, whoever is up there, whatever the plan is, whether it's God, it's Buddha, or whatever. Because it's a lot of the same beliefs, if you go down to the details that's when it becomes complicated. But there's really no big difference as long as you believe in something." And this Buddhist father from Chicago reported that, "Buddhism is a philosophy, a way of life. I want my kids to be brought up Buddhist, because I want them to have faith in something, to believe in something. If you don't believe in anything, it makes life hard when things happen without having a belief in something, it makes it harder to deal with it."

The Jewish parents we interviewed—again, all Conservative, not Reform or Orthodox—approached the question of religious truth with a distinctively Jewish style of explanation. All seemed uncomfortable with the idea that there exists an ultimate religious truth that people should be interested in discovering. Rather, they seemed primarily concerned with the idea that there are genuinely good ways to live, which is what people should seek out. Practices of ethical goodness outdo claims to ultimate truth. At the same time, Jewish parents emphasized the historically and culturally particular nature of good ways of life. In the end, Jewish parents managed to avoid both exclusivity and relativism as they explained what in their tradition was worth sustaining. They would not say that all religions are simply different expressions of the same universal reality or truth. Nor would they take the individualistic strategy of claiming that some religion is the truth "for me." But neither would they claim that Judaism is the one or highest religious truth or way of life. Again, truth is not the main issue. The approach is not correspondence to some objective standard of truth or reality, like the Bible or Brahma, but is rather embedded in and account-able to history, culture, identity, texts, debate, learning, and experience. Consider, for example, the explanation of this Jewish mother from Indiana:

> Judaism is a culture and a way of thinking, it's very text-based, interpretation-based, not hierarchical at all. It's about reading texts in an insightful and informed way. You read the most exciting interpreta-tions and they're playing with many ways of reading the words. I love that, it just feels to me the right way to do spirituality. Judaism is not about, "this is the truth because I said so," it's not like that. But at the same time it's not a free-for-all. It's more based on, here are texts, val-ues, principles that you have to go back to, and if you want to argue against something, you have to create an argument that works. You can't just say, "I don't like that, I'm not gonna do that."

This Jewish father from New York City conveyed the same general approach in his explanation:

> The Exodus, Moses, the Red Sea, is the story of my tribe. It was histori-cal and maybe embellished, but you tell a story from which you want some essence to come across. So maybe the facts aren't as important as the essence of all those stories. I've no doubt there's a divinity. But I've told my children that I believe religions are like a language, that each one has a different way of saying things, different syntaxes, different vocabularies, but they're trying to describe and make sense of it all to us, although you can't argue that English or Italian is better than Russian as languages.

A similar spirit is evident in the commentary of this Jewish mother from Indiana:

> A general principle in Judaism is that rules themselves don't have intrinsic truth or value to them, like certain things in Christianity do [pounding the table], "this is a sin, this is not a sin." The rule itself is not intrinsically the only right or good or true way, it's just the very principle of having self-control and limits and rules giving life holiness and ele-vating us. That we can follow rules that are part of our culture and belief system and regulate the way that we behave, that elevates us, spiritually.

In sum, among the various beliefs of the different cultural models that we are examining here, the question of religious truth gives rise to the greatest diversity of specific approaches by religious parents. Still, underlying most of them is the shared dominant view that religions are after and actually do teach ideas and ways of life that are correct, valuable, and worth following.

Two religious truths are paramount for children to learn, one generally theological and existential; the second, pragmatic and functional. First, children should learn to "believe in something" along the lines that "there is a greater picture" out there, "something bigger" going on, such as a God who is with them or the force of karma.

This theme was ubiquitous among the parents we interviewed. One Mormon mother from New York City, for instance, told us, "Parents ought to raise kids to believe in something stronger or more powerful than themselves, because it's important to see they are not everything in life, the world does not revolve around them, there's something bigger than them that they owe their services, talents, who they are, to something bigger than them. Ideally it would be God, I believe it's God, but I don't want to say that for everyone, because this is my world, right? I love the story of Christ because Christ taught us to think about others before ourselves, what can you do for other people, not what you can get out of somebody for yourself." A mainline Protestant father from New York City said, "I'm trying to make sure the kids are aware that there is something greater than, something bigger out there. I want them to know there's always somebody they can rely on, something within them or outside of them, to help them, what we call God." And this mainline Protestant mother from Washington, DC, concurred, "I would like for them to believe in a God, a spirit, a higher something, something bigger than us. Why? 'Cause I do [laughing]." One black Catholic mother from Indiana commented, "For me it's about passing on morals and wanting them to believe in something greater than themselves, that you don't live in the world alone." And a white conservative Protestant mother from Los Angeles explained, "We're trying to instill in them when they're young, 'What's the purpose of life? Why are we alive?' We always reiterate, 'It's to glorify God. So are we glorifying God in all that we do?' We have this bigger picture of family and how much we love each other and it's all based around this, what we believe and what Christ has done for us."

A Jewish mother from New York City similarly related what she tells her kids: "You can choose something different as an adult, but I have to tell you, what else am I gonna give you but what I enjoy? You're just kids, you haven't had any life experience yet, I could say from my own life that this is what I found brings me joy, connectedness, and a sense of purpose and something bigger, being connected with something bigger than myself, and creating little blocks during the year for little stopping points to reflect and celebrate, this works for me, and I'm sharing it with you." A black Protestant mother from Houston insisted, "You have to be strong and try to feel with it, just try to keep your mind on God so that you get along, and keep the big picture [in mind]." Reiterating the theme, a white Catholic mother from New York City argued this: "Even if you don't believe in church or God, the traditional God, it's a huge disservice to your children if you're not teaching them that there's a bigger picture. Because when shit happens, and it will, and your kid is questioning why, what can you say? 'That's how it is?' 'Pop a medication?' That really doesn't offer much comfort. So whatever religion or values you have, you need to give your child a concept or understanding or belief that there's some deeper, a bigger world, a world outside of this, in a life outside of the physical. That belief, that faith, that's nurture." A Muslim mother from the same city similarly said, "I want them to keep their faith first and foremost as their moving purpose in life, understanding that their purpose is not just to live this life and be done with it, but that there's something more, this is a stop in the *long* haul, and to work toward that. But at the same time not to compromise what they're doing here [for this-worldly achievements], but to constantly be living in this world." A Buddhist mother from Chicago stressed karma as the "big pictures" she wants her children to learn: "We believe in karma. You do good and you'll get good given back to you. You give back to the community and the universe has a way to take care of you."[6] And a Hispanic Catholic father also from New York told us, "God to me is a being, something divine that is above all, something that makes me feel great, it is a spirituality, a being up there and watching, helping us. But God can be anything. The important thing is that our spirit, our heart feels full, and most of all to make things right, that's the way I see it, more or less, is the ultimate God is the creator." And repeating a common

---

6. In addition to the larger realities of karma (and Brahma, samsara, and reincarnation), some immigrants also view their native homelands as part of the "bigger picture" in their religion/culture that they want to instill in their children, as expressed, for instance, by this Buddhist mother from Chicago: "I take them to Thailand every summer to make sure that they have that connection to the motherland, and friends and their own community there, to make sure that even if they don't go to temple, they still have that connection with Thailand that will keep them in the Thai mindset."

theme, a Hindu mother from central New Jersey told us, "As long as they believe in something, I don't want them to just believe in an Indian God, but they need to believe in something, some higher power they can hope to or pray, as long as they do that, that should be okay. As long as they have something they can believe in, it doesn't matter, it doesn't have to be my thing. They have to believe in something, need to have some kind of faith."

This idea of needing to "believe in something" was commonly expressed, perhaps especially by Catholic parents, as with this white Catholic mother from Indiana: "I don't think any of them will abandon God, 'cause I think we all need to believe in something. We can't have the answers to everything, but why wouldn't you think that there was something, something had to make all of this happen." A white Catholic father from Chicago agreed: "I do want them to be involved in some church, whatever church it is, whatever belief, believe in something, 'cause I think that's the best way to go. That'll make them do better as people." For more than a few, including this white Catholic father from Indiana, it appears that what one believes in is less important than simply believing in *something*: "Having belief in something is better than belief in nothing, so I hope they at least take a religion, but make an informed decision with good reasons. I believe in letting my children be free, make their own choices, but I do want them to believe in something and be strong about it. As they get older, make an informed decision and stand behind the decision, whether it's Catholic or Atheist or Jew or whatever, just make sure it's an informed decision." Likewise, this Hispanic Catholic father from New Mexico reported, "I've attended services of other religions and it's not a big deal, because everyone is wanting to appreciate God. But for me it's my God and for them it's their God. I think for this world what's important is faith, you have to believe in something, to take hold of something." And again, this white Catholic mother from New York City said, "Whatever religion or values you have, there's some deeper belief in a bigger world, a world outside of this one, a life outside of the physical. I don't judge what religion you practice, but if you don't practice anything or don't talk [with children] about anything beyond this world, I feel like, 'Hmm, I'm not so sure about that.' That's your call, but I'm a little worried."

Again, for some, the "something bigger" in which one ought to believe need not be God. It might (also) be something like karma, as a mainline Protestant mother from Indiana explained, "I have a lot of beliefs, not just in God, but that if you do bad things, that's gonna come back to you tenfold. If you do good things, yeah you may not get back as much but still good. Some people call it karma [laughs], but for me it's just life experience." But for most religious parents in the United States, the some-thing bigger is a "higher power," such as God, as believed by this main-line Protestant father from Indiana: "God in life gives perspective. People become so self-absorbed, but with God you step out of that, I stepped out of it, then you find out deep down it is a relationship with God, a faith that keeps people going. I know there's something bigger and better out there. I know there's something different." And what most matters is "believ-ing in" God, seemingly as primarily a cognitive affirmation, as apparent with this Hispanic Catholic mother from New York City: "If my daughter decided she was an atheist, I would try to convince her there is a God. We would have to study the Bible together. It's a no-no to not believe in God [laughs]. People can deny God, but there is a God. I don't think there are bad persons, but you have to believe in something to be able to be a good person. I say, 'As long as everybody believes in God.' That's the main reason." But while most religious parents emphasize merely "believing in" something bigger as key, some, such as this mainline Protestant mother from Indiana, also emphasize the importance of a certain kind of affective reverence for or fear of God: "I think you need not so much a belief in God, but the fear of God. If I don't believe in God and die and then find out there is a God, oh my gosh what's going to happen now? I think the fear of God is more important than, at this age of my kids, they need to fear God."

For different parents, believing in "something bigger" serves various purposes. The parents already quoted mentioned that it produces humility, support in hardship, constraints on self-absorption, perspective, moral-ity, life orientation, joy, connectedness, and explanations for trouble and suffering and even existence itself. For others, such as this conservative Protestant father from Florida, belief in "bigger things" produces a trust that helps better to navigate life: "Learning the Bible, you're able to trust on bigger things that may happen in your life and you're able to give more instead of you trying to do everything, you're able to give him more of your life and trusting that he takes care of it, because he's already proven himself time and time again, even when you may not have liked what was happening but he still proved himself." Her "higher being" keeps this black Catholic mother from Indiana "grounded": "Everything I have and do, I owe it to a higher being than myself, it keeps me grounded, and I would like that for her. You don't necessarily need Christianity to feel that way, you could do that with Buddhism, Hinduism, or any other religion of your choosing. But that's my desire for her, because it worked for me as a tool that weaves well into what I feel is a moral value system, and I hope she keeps it." For this white Catholic father from Indiana, "having that greater power" helps him survive the challenges of everyday life: "Having that greater power, a greater belief that there is more to life than just this life, really helps me get through every day, helps get through a lot of my tougher times." For a white conservative Protestant father from New York City, the bigger picture is what gives life purpose: "It's about understanding that this is God's world for which he has a purpose, and it is our job to align our purpose to God's purpose, and so to try and live through the power of the Holy Spirit, to live, to serve God's purposes in the world." For one white Catholic mother from New York City, the "beyond" provides a horizon to keep people from being trapped in materialism: "I don't want them to get caught up in the material world, but to see beyond that. It doesn't matter to me whether they go to church every Sunday. It's just important that they have a strong set of values, a strong spiritual base, even if they don't practice it in a church." And for one Hispanic father from New Mexico, the something bigger is what provides him the power and guidance to raise his daughter well: "The power of God is greater than what the world could teach my girl. What God is going to teach me to guide her is bigger than what she can see outside."

Second, religion can help people live good lives in this world.

This cultural belief we have already heard in various ways in the quotes above, so we will not belabor the point here. But it is a clear theme across all of the religious traditions we studied. A Buddhist mother from Chicago, for instance, told us, "All religions, if you do it right, interpret correctly, they all teach you to be a good person. That's what I believe. I don't think any religion try to teach a bad thing, it just how you interpret the priest." A Hindu father from central New Jersey reported, "Religion played a very important role in my life, because we were taught you do certain things because religion makes you a better person. We were told you respect adults, you don't lie, you don't do anything bad, you believe in God, in higher power, celebrate all the festivals. You know when you're in trouble or when things are not going well, you look to God for guidance, support, and signs, I was taught all those things at a very early age." A Muslim mother from Indiana said, "The same God sent Jesus and Moses, he sent Mohammed with the same rules. Each religion has their rules, but we complete each other, the basics are the same, we believe in one in the same Creator. So when you understand religion is the same basic stuff, the same belief, then you become a good person." A Jewish father from Indiana similarly said, "Judaism really is the way to live your life as a principled human being that respects other people. It provides a really

strong grounding for living a good life, an appropriate life on this earth."
And one Mormon mother from Indiana explained the same thing this
way: "When I found my church it was the best thing that happened to me.
Growing up very dysfunctional, I never knew how a family was supposed
to function, and it showed me how families are supposed to be, and what
I can have. I think as long as you have a foundation in God and, and do
what he wants you to do, that everything else will kind of fall into place.
And nowadays so many people are lost and confused. It doesn't matter
really what faith they're from, as long as they're being a good Christian, a
good Catholic, good Muslim, just the best person that you can be, 'cause
the world is so negative and so bad, what we need is good, positive people
and, most importantly, love." A Hispanic Catholic mother from Chicago
similarly said, "Religious faith, it's very important 'cause it will keep them
grounded, just keep them grounded. Being just a better person, and stuff
like that, I think it would." Likewise, a Hispanic Catholic father from New
York City told us, "If she wants to follow another religion, I don't mind, as
long as she follows the ways God wants us to live, as long as she's doing
the right thing. God is for humankind, to be good, to do the right thing.
I don't think religions matter. I'm not a fanatic Catholic. I come to church
because I want to learn more about God and to be a better person. To be
a good Catholic, or religious person, you have to follow whatever God is
telling us in the Bible. I want to be a better person." This black Catholic mother from Indiana essentially agreed: "It's important that my sons
share my religious beliefs, but I wouldn't force it. You know, if they chose
another faith, just as long as it's a path that's going to God, [then okay],
that's basically how I would feel. I can respect all religions, parts of them,
even Muslim, although I don't understand it. I can respect Jewish, parts of
it I guess I don't know, like the doctrination, the full doctrinarian of being
Jewish, all it entails. But I know it's peaceful, I know it's not about harming others, and it's about praying to a creator of some sort. So therefore
we've got a commonality." Note that doctrinal differences between beliefs
do not matter here, since it is assumed that all religions are paths "going
to God" and that what really matters is being peaceful and not harming
other people.

The theme continues. One white Catholic mother from Indiana
reported, "I probably could be a little more authoritative but I am trying to
remind them about Catholic choices, like 'how are your choices, how is that
improving your life? Are you wasting your time or is this something that's
gonna make you a better person?' I try to still instill values in them while
I'm parenting them." Reiterating this theme, a black Protestant father

from Houston said, "Church helps you stay grounded, because you know what the Bible say, you go to church, listen to the word, and you're convicting yourself, because what you did last week was wrong and now you're trying to right your wrong. Therefore, it helps you to work on yourself to become a better person." Similarly, a white conservative Protestant mother from Indiana explained, "My personal thing is believing in the Bible and it ultimately makes you a better person. It makes you try not to judge, try to love the neighbor, help somebody out, give to somebody that needs it. It's just overall the best book ever written." And this mainline Protestant father from the same state observed:

> I see other families without religion, there seems to be no direction, like they're on their own trying to figure things out, which values in life, the way they're treating other people. So if my kids are around people who have a little higher values, that's a good role model for them. I think that people with faith have a different way, a different relationship with friends, think they're more caring. Going to church, reading from the word, and hearing stories of God taking care of people, helping the sick, there's a compassion there. People that have the faith have some compassion toward other people.

However, religious exclusivity, superiority, and fanaticism are bad, dangerous, and must be avoided.

This cultural belief is also ubiquitous and clear. Not one parent from any tradition we interviewed disagrees with it. For most parents from every tradition—not only including but actually especially Muslim parents—radical Islamist extremism is the archetypical example of what must be avoided. Committed but moderate Islam is necessary, as one Muslim father from Indiana explained, "I act very normal. Don't misunderstand me, I don't allow myself to do things against the Islamic religion, but we're living in an open society and you have to be an open and moderate Muslim. We cannot be fanatic, that's wrong." Another Muslim father from New York City even voiced worry that extremism has tainted the identity of being "religious": "I'm not a big fan of the word 'religious,' 'cause to me we follow the religion, we did the required stuff, but I don't think we were extremists or anything like that." Some Muslim parents we interviewed speak with some chagrin about the religious practices of their home countries and family members, as with this Muslim mother from Indiana: "Culturally, the way Islam has been practiced in South Asia, where we're originally from, is often misguided. There's no understanding, people will say wacky things, ideological. Every time any issue comes up in the family, you have to explain, it's a constant learning process, and older people don't understand these things, you have to explain that Islam is not like that, so education is the key." Many Muslim parents, however, criticize not only Muslim extremists but also "the media," which they see as obsessed with Islamic extremism that sheds a generally bad light on religion. One Muslim mother from Indiana, for example, criticized the media preoccupation with, even as she criticized the egoism of, radical Islamists: "The media are always concentrate on the bad people, extremists, to make the religion sound bad. I don't agree! Extremists like to impose their thoughts because they have a problem with their selves, number one, deep down, they think they are better than others, so they want to make everybody else follow, they wanna be in lead, and that's what gets us all the problems." Nearly all of the Muslim parents we interviewed nonetheless relied on the moderation of their own life practices to counter the negative influences of the media, as, for instance, this Muslim father from the same area explained, "The media right now projects Islam as terrorists. But I have colleagues and friends who are non-Muslim, they see who I am and understand that. But by the same token in every religion I think there are some extremist elements and you cannot control everyone."

Radicalized Islamism as the negative model of religious extremism runs in the background of most of the discussions on this topic across all religious traditions. For instance, one Hispanic Catholic father from New Mexico objected: "Muslims who are planting bombs, it's the stupidest thing I've heard, who say that 'Allah told me.' My God! God is love, God never commanded to destroy anyone. The Lord preaches love. If you get hit in the face, turn the other cheek, so you get another. God never says, 'Kill those, because I do not love them.' No. It is the ambition, it is the devil who's involved in all those things." But violent Islamicists are by no means the only concern of parents. What parents consider religious fanaticism can also be evident in aggressively proselytizing members of Christian groups, as one white Catholic father from Indiana said, "One of the things that scares me about religion is some groups go around recruiting people to their faith, in a way that can be very fanatical, and I think there's a very easy path to that mentality with religion. That might be another reason why from my perspective I don't push religion hard on my girls." Extremism can also take the form of lamentable features of one's own religion, evident in one white Catholic father from New York City's comments about his daughter's time on a church mission trip: "She didn't have a great experience overseas. Catholicism there is very different, can be very misogynist, sexist, women subservient to men, for some of the older guard priests, and it doesn't resonate. Our group, it's definitely not like that, it's more inclusive and open." Likewise, this Hispanic Catholic father from New York City warned against Catholic fanaticism close to home: "Fanaticism, for my children, I don't want that. Fanaticism toward the saints, or even including God himself. They should have a healthy belief, that I don't think would be harmful to others." According to one white Catholic father also from New York City, people's inability to talk frankly about religion only aids extremism in all religions, which can be countered by open dialogue:

What kills religion today, it's all the taboo and all the walls put around it. The less we talk about it, the more taboo and the stranger it gets, the more rejected people feel, the less they want to open up. Extremist religious movements are not only one religion, it is all religions. If we could break those barriers of talking about terrorism and so no one is at the mercy of having their religion leveraged to gain political power and to influence others. Tyrants and despots are going to have less influence in the future because there is more communication, and the more you talk, religion is moderated, talk to share with other religion. I think the Pope does a great job at it, we have the best Pope [Francis] for the job.

One of the main effects of parents' objection to religious exclusivity and fanaticism is to dampen their own religious fervor, as evident in the father quoted above who observed, "That might be another reason why from my perspective I don't push religion hard on my girls." Perceived religious extremism, in other words, tends to push many relatively moderate parents toward what seems to be even more restrained, perhaps sometimes even bland expressions of their own faiths. For some, like this mainline Protestant mother from Washington, DC, opposition to religious fanaticism pushes them if anything toward skepticism about religion, including their own: "I would rather my kids be skeptical than fanatical or superconservative to the point where they were worrying about what everybody else is doing and not taking care of their own backyard. I don't like religion used as a weapon or justification for all kinds of hatred. I would rather they be skeptical, but if they fully embrace some moderate religion, I'd be totally supportive." Others, such as this Mormon mother from Indiana, react against too much religious intensity by downplaying aspects of their religious traditions in favor of contemporary concerns: "Being a progressive Mormon, I'm not fanatical about Joseph Smith, all those other things, I am more progressive. I focus more on what is the church now." And instead of fostering open dialogue, sometimes attitudes of religious superiority make parents simply not want to get into discussions about religion, as expressed by one black Protestant mother from Houston: "Sometimes religion can cause arguments between 'superior people' or saying others are 'Holier than thou.' I don't wanna argue with them about God, 'cause everybody has they own opinions. How I feel about him might not be how you feel about him." Perceived extremism also tends to turn many parents away from a concern with religious doctrines and instead to refocus them on "the basics" of ethics, on being a "good person," as evident in the testimony of this black Catholic father from Indiana (whose image of zealous religiousness as carrying "a big cat on my head" we voted to win the Best Metaphor Award of the Project):

> I am a repentant Christian. I do wrong, I ask forgiveness, period. I don't carry religion like an ideology, like a big cat on my head. I don't. I just live a very simple life, do what you are asked to do. Just love God with all your heart, love your neighbor and treat them as you want to be treated, that's what I live by. I'm just a spiritual person, not a fanatic to carry the Bible over my head. Just simple everyday things. I'm comfortable with everyone as long as they're not invading my space, ya know?

For many religious parents in the United States, their general openness to their children choosing other religions ends at the thought of some extremist faith. One mainline Protestant mother from Washington, DC, for example, told us: "You raise children to become independent adults and then if they embrace some other religion, wonderful. Unless it's radical Islam or something [laughs], yeah then we would have a problem." A father from the same tradition and city similarly said, "They can marry whoever, I really just want them to be happy and healthy. If he marries a Jewish girl and wants to practice Judaism, fine. I mean, at least nothing like radical, a radical religion that brings harm to other people, that's where I have problems." And another mainline Protestant father from Indiana said about his kids: "They can be what they want religiously as long as they're not going to kill somebody for their belief, extremist."

Unsurprisingly, many mainline Protestant parents tended to view "conservatives" and "the right" as regrettably religiously exclusivist if not fanatical. "I don't want a lot of judgment," said one mainline Protestant father from New York City, "some religions have a lot of judgment about women and gays. I don't believe those things, rules that are hard to break, judgment and prejudices." Many Jewish parents held similar outlooks, as, for instance, this Jewish mother from Indiana: "Religious people on the right, those kinds of people are stupid, uninformed, incapable of thinking, analyzing. It's shallow, it's hatred based and fear based. It's demagogic, the worst of humanity. I mean, the words they use, Putin does the same thing in Russia. You can call anything whatever you want, but if you really look at what's happening, it's hatred based, it's fear based, it's prejudice based. It has nothing to do with what they claim it has to do with." Another Jewish father from the same area offered these somewhat-hyperbolic (but also somewhat self-correcting) arguments typical of the so-called New Atheists, like Christopher Hitchens and Richard Dawkins: "Unfortunately, everything that's wrong in this world, all the wars that are going on everywhere, are religious wars, everything is just religious wars and it's too bad. Well maybe not everything, Ukraine and Russia are not having a religious war, that's not religious. But over the millennia, the overwhelming number of wars have always been about religion. And it's too bad because I really believe that it would be better if people could just live in the culture that they are in and accept other people's rights to have their culture and religion and I do but of course we know that so many don't. But I think that's evidence that there's no all-powerful God and that this is all created by man. You know all the religion I mean is created by humans." Perhaps more unexpectedly, however, some conservative Protestant parents took similar views about conservative Christians. One evangelical mother from New York City, for instance, while discussing her daughter's religious future, actually contrasted what she believes to be true Christianity with common conservative Protestant beliefs about same-sex relationships: "I'd be really disappointed if she turned away from Christianity and became some evangelical wacko, a right wing homophobic nutcase. That would freak me out. We have a lot of gay friends and I just want her to be faithful to who God is, who he calls her to be, and not to get caught up in really legalistic, judgmental, all-talk-and-no-action kinda faith where she's not caring about other people." This is not the common view of conservative Protestant parents. This mother's particular case is at least somewhat conditioned by her larger social context living in New York City and her having converted from a formerly secular background into a somewhat progressive evangelical church. Our main point here is simply the reminder that, while adherents of different religious traditions do tend to represent the dominant views of their traditions, not all do, and some of those stereotypical dominant views may also be gradually becoming dated with time and the rise of younger generations.

For some immigrant parents, pulling apart what exactly comes from their home cultures and what from their religions is not easy, especially when it comes to sorting out features of their heritages that they do not wish to perpetuate. This Hindu mother, for example, struggled with the relative influence of culture and religion on perceived patriarchal attitudes in her tradition: "I have seen a kind of mindset in certain men, it runs in families, male superiority in certain families, having more than one wife, unfair things. But over here I don't want to pass on that religious mindset, it's not even religion, religion has certain concepts, and cultures [can influence them wrongly]. So it's a part of religion and culture, but a part of my culture I don't want my son to pick up." Finally, Buddhism tends strongly to emphasize the importance of moderation, multiplicity, and flexibility in faith and life, so a strong aversion to and reaction against fanaticism was not explicit among our Buddhist parents, we think because it simply is not such a big issue within that tradition. Buddhist parents instead make comments such as this father's from Chicago: "Buddhism teaches you to be a peaceful person, to be moderate then you'll be happy and the world will be happy too. Others who teach if you are not Christian you would go to hell, I think they're a bit too extremist. You don't know that, I don't know." One Buddhist father from New York City told us, "You need to have your mind nature come through at all times, if you able to control your mind, then choose whatever you will. Just lead your mind to avoid what is bad, then you are in the right path and you will be out free from worldly problems." And this Buddhist mother from Chicago explained, "It's like any religion, killing is bad, adultery is bad, the same core things you would find in any religion. But along that is balance, and peace, finding inner peace, inner balance, hence the meditation. Not killing is huge in Buddhism, you don't kill anything, even insects. My husband makes fun of me because if there's an insect, I won't do anything about it, I'll call my husband to come take care of it [laugh]."

Even if one believes that no one religion has a monopoly on truth, it is still not a bad idea to belong to some particular religious tradition or community, to be located somewhere specific.

This belief helping to define this cultural model of religious truth was not as obvious as some others in our interviews with parents, but it still emerged as a significant aspect of their background understandings, amid the push and pull of religious particularity and religious universality. Parents expressed it in different ways, but the same underlying belief was evident. As might be expected, parents from religious traditions with more exacting or exclusive cultures of correct belief tended to offer the strongest arguments for belonging to a (their) specific community. This more "confident" black Protestant mother from Houston, for instance, explained how she would respond if her daughter became not religious:

> I'd be like, "Baby, where'd you get that from? That's not how you were brought up, not how your grandma raised baby. I be like no, we do church here." I'd say, "I don't know where you're coming from baby, I'm gonna have to get on that [whipping] cane and we gonna get you to some church [laughing], we gonna get you some good *old* school church around here." No nuh-uh. Nuh-uh. Even Catholic or Baptist is okay, but not no Jehovah's Witness, that's not how we were brought up. So let's open that Bible. Given the foundation of what I have been through, what my parents have been through, for you to not to go to church. No. Nuh-uh. I'd have to let her know.

By comparison, this black Protestant mother also from Houston stressed the social rewards of membership in a specific congregation: "Belonging to a church is a benefit, it makes you feel wanted, warm, that you are somebody, that you belong somewhere, there are other people like you." While discussing his own religious doubts, one white conservative Protestant father from New York City—who, in a way relevant for this quote, works in the city's central financial services sector—expressed his belief in the importance of religious particularity this way:

> I have doubts and confusions fairly regularly. My faith is completely and utterly central to my life and yet sometimes I think to myself, "and I believe this exactly why?" Because it's not the most rational thing to believe. I'm generally a very rational person and I like evidence and logical argument. And then I look around and the church gets so much wrong. We've gotten so many things wrong so many times, then why do we think we hold truth, you know? You'd have to be a little unthinking not to have doubts. But in the end, I think that we cannot come to God other than through Jesus. The claims of Christ are exclusive, we cannot claim there is something else, another route. What God chooses to do is God's business, I think we're called to submit to Christ and that's the bit we have to concentrate on.

And this Mormon mother from New York City related, "Mormon is all I've ever done and of course I question, have doubts, and fall short, but for whatever reason I just keep doing it, there's just not a question. It's the framework through which I make sense of life and so I'm a devout and practicing member of my church." One traditionalist white Catholic mother from Indiana stated simply this: "The Catholic faith is the best way for everyone, and especially if their parents are raised with it, why would they not raise their kids that way?" This white Catholic father from the same area settled on his children perhaps not being Catholic as okay, as long as they stayed within some kind of Christianity. "I'd really like to think they're not going to grow up to become Muslim. I guess if they became Jewish I wouldn't have an issue with that. If they were Satanists I would have an issue, that's completely opposite of what I believe. I would say as long as they stayed in the Christian religion, I'm good. But if you're not in a Christian religion then you're denying the existence of Christ."

Those are examples of more "strict" religions. But even parents from other traditions with more open or relativistic views about religion still seemed to think it is important to be religiously located somewhere particular. One mainline Protestant father from Washington, DC, for example, explained why he places himself in a specific institution, despite taking a broad approach to spirituality: "Spirituality is an important thing regardless of a particular religion. At the same time, I have a hard time doing that on my own. I need an organized religion to be more spiritual, I need the institution for that to work." In a very different way than the more insistent parents quoted just above, another mainline Protestant father from New York City nevertheless expressed his desire for his children to embrace not only Christianity generally but his own specific Episcopalian tradition specifically: "The core of my religious faith is my experiences, valid in the context of Christian faith. You can't believe all religions are ultimately equally valid because that doesn't make sense as an idea. But my sense of what the good life is, how you should live the good life is to do the best you can to make the most of one's little piece, to make the world a better place. Clearly I'd like to see my kids following a similar kind of path. And I like the mildness of Episcopalianism, in that, as somebody who is verbal, I like the fact that it's built around a set of seventeenth-century words and it expresses beautiful things in simple ways. I would, I'd love to think that they would discover that for themselves and make that part of their lives." This white Catholic mother from Chicago expressed the same approach: "I can't really [tell my kids what religion to be], that would make me being a hypocrite; you have to find your own path, if you don't like this, go another way. However, I do want them to be involved in some church, whatever church it is." Similarly, a Hispanic Catholic father from New York City said, "Frankly I do not address the Catholic religion directly, I'm more about faith, to believe in a living God, a being that helps us, hears us, someone who is leading us, and through our spirituality keeps us well, happy, doing right things, to love our neighbor, to help others. That's important, whether Pentecostal and Jehovah's Witness, I think we're all going to the same God. But I am a Catholic because I always professed that religion, in fact I studied in a Catholic school, and I feel happy here." Another Hispanic father from New Mexico, struggling to balance respecting his children's choices with the need to choose what is "normal," told us, "As long as they are united in some church, to me it's okay. Well, within what's normal, from what you would consider normal, what you have instilled in them. Because going to another extreme maybe you would feel a bit uncomfortable. But I can't imagine my children deviating to such an extreme degree, so drastic."

Jewish parents tended especially to be adamant about the importance of particularity, despite their being not very concerned with exclusive religious truth generally. One Jewish father from New York City, for example, told us, "It really goes back to tribal identity, I think, it just helps you to know who and what you are. And if you have a firm basis in that, then you can branch out and do a bunch of other things. I think there's too much vanilla out there, better to have distinct flavors, though not extremism." Many displayed a pressure that their tradition not be lost through intermarriage and attrition. A Jewish mother from Indiana confessed that, "I would really be upset if my grandkids were not Jewish. I want the history to remain Jewish, the religion dies if we keep having all these intermarriages and assimilations and people don't stay with religions, so in general I hope that all Jewish families continue to raise them Jewish, and so many people are not today it's very frightening to me." This Jewish father also from Indiana had this to say: "I don't believe in bringing kids up in two religion families, 'cause it doesn't make any sense. You can't believe one and believe the other because they contradict each other, which is not to say that one is right and the other is wrong, I actually don't believe that about religion. It's just part of your culture and who you are, and whatever religion you're part of, that informs your community, your worldview, so it's not necessarily about ultimate truth, I think in some way they're all right in certain ways, but the one that's right for you is the one that's who you are. So it doesn't make sense to combine two because they clash, the different beliefs, different tenets even habits of mind and ways of approaching things, they clash." Likewise, a Hindu father from Chicago, who holds a universalistic approach to religions generally, explained the importance of belonging to a specific religious group this way: "In a heterogeneous society, religion is an identity thing. Sooner or later you fall into some group, and even if you don't believe in anything, there is still a group for you. And if you don't belong to that group, you feel isolated, since we are all social beings." Another Hindu mother from New York City explained that actually the acceptance of all religions is precisely one of the things that bonds her to her particular temple: "The thing I absolutely adore about my temple is the spiritual leader there is very open to other religions. He says, 'If this is water, it doesn't matter whether I call it agua, pani, or water, it remains the same.' So you call God, Jesus, Allah, it doesn't make the difference, they're more inclusive, it is not really dogmatic, and you can have your own ways or relationship with God, it's more based on a personal relationship of God, right?" Or consider the conclusion of a Hindu father who first told us that, "just yesterday we were at a Christmas party and met a pastor of a big megachurch. I'm not a Christian but I love to respect all religions, whatever they believe in, and I even have a Jesus Christ picture in my Gods collection. Just be a good person and that should be it, it's all one God so what does it matter?" But when asked if he might ever consider embracing another religion personally, he replied, "I've been religious through and through all the time, but converting, no, I'm very happy with Hinduism." This Muslim mother from New York City explained how she committed to her Muslim roots despite questions: "I took a Religion 101 college class, and the professor was really amazing. I spoke to him about my religious questioning and his advice was, 'well, unless you have a really good reason to walk away from your religion, it's better to just stick with what you have and try to figure out who you are within that framework.' That was really important advice, a turning point in terms of me being more inclined to go back to my roots, when before I didn't want to deal with it and was starting to have a feminist awareness. So that whole experience just made me reconnect better." And this Buddhist mother from Chicago, who like most Buddhists has little investment in religious differences and particularities, argued this about her tradition: "To be safe for citizens in society, a religious person is better. At least you have something you believe in, and you might be afraid of something [e.g., fear of God] and you might believe in doing good. Buddhists teach peacefulness, modesty, politeness, and you don't have a lot of [social] problems with Buddhists, right?"

Beyond the two paramount truths, however, one can take from one's own religious tradition the parts that make sense and work best, and leave the parts that don't, according to "whatever seems right" to you; nobody needs to accept or be subject to the whole package of a religious tradition.

This belief, again shared by parents across the religious spectrum, flows logically from the commitment of most American parents to the inviolable autonomy of the individual.[7] Religious traditions are primarily resources from which to benefit, not authorities that help to define what one should be and want in the first place. For most parents, the latter is up to individuals to decide, as we have already heard a great deal. Still, the significance of this point varies by religious tradition, according to the official structure of authority it proposes and the organizational consequences of disagreement. Roman Catholicism, for example, is centralized, hierarchical, and extensive and precise in its promulgated doctrines. So disagreement with the official Church is a significant issue with which some Catholics struggle, if they care enough about it to pay attention. Mormonism is roughly similar, even though it lacks formal schools of theology and ordained clergy, and its mechanisms for regulating conformity are much more rigorous than in Catholicism. So individual disagreement with official church positions is also a big issue.

By contrast, the standard means in Protestantism for processing disagreement is to leave the church with which one disagrees and start or join a new one that fits one's beliefs and sensibilities. So disagreement is mostly relevant within denominational organizations that need to maintain some semblance of concurrence about common policies, such as the ordination of women or gays and lesbians, which normally get hammered out through standard intradenominational political means. Disagreement is also relevant for certain transdenominational religious movements, such as American evangelicalism, that as "imagined communities"[8] comprise immense internal diversity and disagreement, and whose strategies for sustaining cohesion and unity therefore focus on emphasizing agreed-upon "essentials" and discounting "secondary" points of disagreement.

American Judaism is functionally roughly similar to Protestantism on the specific point of disagreement and tradition differentiation. On the one hand, most American Jews generally expect fairly strong identification with and adherence to Judaism, but that is to be expressed through a quite limited set of expectations: identity continuity, ethics and values, and hopefully some ritual observances. On the other hand, depending on the vast range of possible approaches to Jewish belief, practice, and culture, one can choose to be Orthodox, Conservative, Reform, or another minor tradition that suits one best. But compared to even mainline Protestantism, most of American Judaism is less concerned with doctrinal beliefs,

7. See Robert Bellah, "Is There a Common American Culture?" *Journal of the American Academy of Religion* 66, no. 3 (1998): 613–26.

8. Benedict Anderson, *Imagined Communities* (London: Verso, 1998).

so issues of dissent and fit mostly concern finding a tradition and congregation that matches one's convictions and proclivities. That is to say, Jews can resolve their disagreements by selecting into different traditions, temples, and synagogues. Finally, in religious traditions that are organizationally decentralized and lacking an official orthodoxy, like Buddhism, Hinduism, and even to some extent Islam, divergent individual beliefs and attitudes that may involve individuals picking and choosing are not major concerns.

Within that larger context, how do religious parents in the United States talk in ways that disclose their belief in this proposition above? American Catholic parents, despite the centralized authority of their Church, are among the most self-authorized to believe and behave as seems right to them as individuals. Consider this typical statement by a white Catholic mother from Indiana: "My daughter has a friend who's gay and I said okay. I might feel guilty sometimes as a Catholic and not being as staunch about some of these beliefs the Church hands down, because I do try to think it through a little bit. But I'm not just going to do something because the Church tells me to do it, with those types of controversial issues at least." Or think about the implications of this report by a white Catholic father from New York City: "We chose our church based on location, boiled down to just location. Then it fit us, we liked the priest, the schedule worked for us, it was convenience. Then again if we didn't like the priest and felt out of place, we would've tried to find something else, or maybe we'd have stopped altogether." One white Catholic father was self-conscious about what he thinks is the normal human tendency to use religious beliefs highly pragmatically: "Jesus if nothing else was a fantastic storyteller, you can always take something he said and apply it to your life, somehow, some way. I'm sure other religions claim the same thing, and us being human beings we tend to take what we want and somehow make it work for a situation. So I just choose Christianity over, say, Buddhism."

Most American Catholic parents view themselves as entitled to select and reject from the Church whatever seems right to them—with the possible exception of the importance of the Eucharist and a sacramental outlook generally, around which most Catholics rally—although, at the time of our interviews, the question of same-sex relationships was the point of greatest struggle and often dissent for white Catholics. One white Catholic father from Indiana, for example, contrasted official (negative) Church teachings with "real life" and opts for the authority of "real life": "Gay marriage, I really struggle with that one. I get what the Church is saying about it but I look at it from real life. That's the one I really struggle with, I don't have a problem with it, and the Church is like, oh no, no, no, no." And this white Catholic mother from New York City told us, "I don't consider myself strictly a traditional Catholic. I am Catholic, I identify as Catholic. However, I do hold views that contradict some Catholic rules, like on homosexuality, abortion, I have gay friends and I have no problem with that, at all, ever." By comparison, Hispanic Catholics in the United States seemed to dissent less about same-sex relationships, but were more focused on other policy and authority issues. One Hispanic father from New York City, for instance, told us, "I have some disagreements with the Church. They're not always saying the truth, I'm pretty sure. Like about the remarriage [after divorce] question, and other things, like the Vatican itself, I have some doubts, about the organization." And this Hispanic Catholic also from New York expressed doubt about heaven: "I really don't know if I believe in heaven. I think when you die, you die, and who knows where your spirit is going, nobody knows. I mean, in the Bible it says heaven, but me personally, I don't know if it's heaven. [So is the Catholic Church a teaching authority?] Sometimes I get a little bit skeptical."9

Mormon parents do not talk a lot about their disagreements with their church. But on occasion, some dissent does surface. One Mormon mother from Indiana, for example, told us, in contrast to what her church teaches, that "I think it's okay to have sex with somebody you care about. We've prepared our boys, with conversations, even with condoms. It's their body, as long as they're responsible. The church says be married to have sex. I've always thought that was the worst idea ever, 'cause what if you didn't like the person? Have you ever been with a person? What happens if you do not get along in that way? That's why I've disagreed with it. I think even if my daughter was in college and found somebody she

---

9. Hispanic Catholics from New York seemed more likely than those from New Mexico to pick and choose from Church teachings what they were willing to believe. The poorer and newer-immigrant Hispanic Catholics in the Southwest we interviewed did not tend to display "cafeteria Catholic" mentalities, although they were not hesitant to criticize the Church. One father from New Mexico, for example, said, "I do look for priests to be prepared, because I am no longer just going to listen to a sermon, and when the priest is not well prepared, I get frustrated a lot." And a New Mexican mother who had previously worked with youth in the Church in Mexico vented: "It bothers me in the Catholic Church there is never anything for young people, which is why young people are leaving, we have nothing for them. And people in charge of the youth in the US don't want you to intrude. So, even though I know how to do it, and that the young people follow me, I can't do it, because there is someone who is already in charge, and I'm going to step on their heels. That frustrates me about the Catholic Church, that we don't have the right programs, we don't think for the children, the young people. So then what is the attraction of our Catholic Church for young people, there is no such attraction."

really cared about, I don't think I would have a problem with them having sex." Even less hypothetically, this Mormon mother explained: "My son exhibits feminine qualities, which I think are awesome. But let's not kid anybody here, I'm a Mormon, I don't want him to be gay. But we're very prepared for that being a reality and things are changing in the church. If it turns out he is gay, he's gonna have good parents, he's in a good family as Mormons go. I want him to be reaffirmed the way he is." Even in as strict a religious tradition as Mormonism, then, we see a readiness to set aside church teachings for beliefs and practices that seem more pragmatically realistic and caring.

What about Protestants? One mainline Protestant father from New York City confessed to being not a Christian Trinitarian but a polytheist (formally a heresy in his tradition): "For me, God is one and many, so in a way I'm polytheist. God is within me and you and every living creature and every nonliving being as well. The universe, we're all one being, all humans and life, it's all one and we're all interconnected. We don't always recognize it and the human species has been spiraling more and more toward a dehumanized, desensitized trend for forever." He clearly feels authorized to choose the doctrine of God that suits him best, and as a member of a liberal United Methodist Church congregation, he faces no negative consequences. The conservative Protestant parents we interviewed addressed their individual rights to believe the theological points they wished by casting the disagreements they naturally cause as unimportant, secondary matters. One conservative Protestant father from Los Angeles, for instance, explained, "If we eliminate the far extremes, disagreements about the minutiae of Christianity, really it's just the fundamentals of the faith that hold true. As long as my kids have those fundamentals of the faith in place, the secondary and tertiary things are a little less important." And this conservative Protestant mother from Florida observed: "You can always find something to disagree with. Churches are known for that, you know, some churches believe this or that. It doesn't matter. Even in the Bible, Paul preaches don't get caught up in that. Everybody has an opinion on something, don't get caught up. Stay with the root of what Jesus taught while he was here on this earth and that's all you need to really worry about." Individuals are thus free to make up their own minds on all but the most core doctrines without any trouble. Black Protestants were the least likely of all Christians to display an individualistic authority to judge on religious matters, although some did criticize recommended religious practices they didn't like, such as this black Protestant father from Houston: "I don't pray as much as I used to pray, I talk to God all during the day. I used to [pray on a more rigid schedule], but that's what got me with Islam too, I thought that was too strict, saying God telling you to tell me to pray at this certain time every day. I'm like, no I don't believe that, that's not what I want to do."

We interviewed Conservative Jewish parents, not Orthodox or Reform, and the vast majority were very happy with their current tradition. Most of their talk that reflected their belief in the proposition in question concerned leaving Orthodoxy and the decisions made about exactly how to practice Judaism afterward. One Jewish father from New York City, for example, recounted his story:

I was raised Orthodox Jewish but was ostracized by that community when my parents divorced. So I became completely not religious for a long time. I returned to Jewish practice when we became parents, and decided we had to be observant, conservative, kosher, etcetera. I liked conservative synagogue because it is progressive and had a woman Rabbi. I didn't want Reform because it was just, pardon me, but it's too churchlike. It's much more someone sitting up there and you're down here, and that whole tradition it's just too watered down.

This New York Jewish woman raised Orthodox recounted her religious journey in a way that reveals the authority of the individual over the community: "At a fairly young age, I realized that I did not want to marry a man. I can't say that I had a language for knowing I was gay, but I certainly knew I was really different. And I knew that ultimately in Orthodox Judaism there wasn't gonna be a place for me. To say that would be problematic wouldn't even begin to cover it. Plus, the nonegalitarian nature of Orthodoxy was extremely troubling, and just the closed-mindedness of so much of the Orthodox community. So I joined a conservative synagogue." A similar general assumption of individual authority to take or leave from a religious tradition whatever seems good or not good is evident in this Jewish mother from Indiana's explanation of why she does not embrace Reform Judaism:

I'm definitely not Orthodox by any stretch of the imagination. But in my experience, for the most part Reform Judaism is just an assimilation to typical American Protestant culture. It's like, eh kind of go through the motions but without any expectations of anything. So Reform Judaism in most cases doesn't agree with me. I don't keep strictly kosher, I drive on Shabbat, I don't follow the letter of the law, but I have total respect for the knowledge and the learning and the tradition of the Orthodox, and that dismissive attitude just doesn't do it for me. So Reform is not a good fit for me, even though my observance level would fit with Reform. But the attitudes and the mindset, not at all.

Finally, again, Buddhist and Hindu parents, and even some American Muslim parents, have less reason to wrestle with disagreements with their religious traditions, since their traditions themselves allow some if not a lot of internal diversity of beliefs and practices. So when accounts of doubts about those traditions do arise, they tend to sound like this, told by a Hindu father from Chicago: "I believe in karma, and reincarnation also probably follows from it logically, and a divine being, Brahma. But probably not much of the other stuff, the other side stories, legends like Rama and Krishna, they're real people, but I don't think a lot of their feats were truly real." One Muslim mother from New York City said, "Growing up in this culture has made me more individualistic about faith, I'm just much more open to the idea that it's a person's choice [what to believe], and even Islam teaches you have to choose, it's up to you and what you believe whatever." But such concerns seem to be of little consequence.

Children, Parenting, and Family

HAVING EXPOSITED AMERICAN religious parents' background cultural models about life and religion, we examine in this chapter three other important cultural models that condition their approach to religious transmission to children—those concerning the nature of children, the task of parenting, and the importance of family solidarity.

The Nature of Children

The dominant view of religious American parents about intergenerational religious transmission is also informed by a particular understanding of children's nature and potentials. This view somewhat represents the personal side of the cultural models of life's purpose and life in the world, described above. The cultural model is this:

> *The Nature of Children*: Every child possesses within themselves a "best self they can be," something like an inherent, unique, and inalienable ideal personality and optimal life-to-be-lived. Children are unrealized bundles of personally unique "ideal outcomes" that need to be prepared and cultivated if they are to develop, endure, and reach their full potentials. Each child's "best self" exists internally as a latent yet real potential that must be actualized and manifest through growth and experience, driven ultimately by each child's own personality and wants. Children can only realize their "best selves" by venturing upon and effectively navigating the challenging journey of life, especially the first half of life. Success means not only enjoying life's opportunities and pleasures but

also effectively facing and surmounting the problems and trials in one's quest through the world, which promotes positive growth, maturity, and understanding and reveals and progressively unfolds one's ideal personal self. The frightful but real alternative is for growing children to become compromised or wrecked by an inability to overcome the hardships, temptations, and misfortunes that assail them in life's journey, and so to fail to realize the "best selves" they could have been.

Every child possesses within themselves a "best self they can be," something like an inherent, unique, and inalienable ideal personality and optimal life-to-be-lived.

Many parents we interviewed talked explicitly about their children reaching their potential in this way. For example, one black Protestant father from Houston said, "As they continue to grow, my main concern for them is to stay on the right track and use the tools they received from parents and be the best that they can be." A Jewish mother from Indiana reported, "I want my kids to find themselves and to be the best they can be at whoever it is that they are." Similarly, this mainline Protestant father from New York City told us, "We want to make sure they have the opportunity to be the best that they can be." A Hindu father from Chicago said, "The best a parent can hope is provide a convenient space for their children to reach their best potential." And a Muslim mother from Indiana said, "My number one priority is my children to be the best they can to be."

Parents often talk about the best selves their children can be as rooted in their fixed personalities. One Mormon mother from Indiana, for instance, said, "You can't protect your children from difficulty, they need to learn through difficulties. But they are also God's children, their personalities, they come with fully developed personalities, they already are the person they are. And it's your responsibility to help them be the best version of that that they can be, but not to think that you can fundamentally change them." A Jewish mother from New York City told us, "Their personalities are really different, you could see that from babyhood, they were who they were, and they each go their own way." This conservative Protestant mother from Florida said, "Certain personalities are just the way they are. Their personalities literally have not changed at all since birth. It's just the way they have been ingrained." A Buddhist father from Chicago said, "When she was around age twelve, I stepped away from my daughter a little bit, not because of any emotional thing, I just started to realize she was really being her own person, so I became a bit more laissez-faire. My daughter's her own person." Similarly, a Mormon father from Indiana said, "I have four beautiful daughters that are so talented and different, just completely opposites. They have their own little personalities."

This then leads to the belief that the most important thing for children is simply to be themselves, as this white Catholic mother from Indiana expressed: "The biggest thing I tell my kids is just be genuine, be who you are. Have faith to lean on and don't be fake, be genuine. Go into things with a pureness of heart." A mainline Protestant single mother from Los Angeles: "That she has a sense of who she is and is okay with that, that's success to me." This conservative Protestant mother from Florida hopes her daughter will be "content to be herself": "In my ideal world she would be a hair stylist or an artist, she's very creative, and that she would have a husband that totally supports her creativeness and quirkiness, and that she is content to be herself. That is what I would love to see." For some parents, what matters most is children doing their best in life to become their best selves, as one Hispanic Catholic mother from New York City said, "I would like for my children to keep moving ahead, find something nice in the future, that they can do it the best for themselves, that's what I would like, as a mother one wants the best for the children." Likewise, this Muslim mother from Indiana told us, "You like to see your kids better than you and the most successful people with everything, everybody hope for that. But people have limitations, which gotta understand how much they can handle, and as long as they're doing the best they can, they're trying, as long as they're doing their best." And for some parents, their children's best selves will produce truly great things, as expressed, for example, by this white Catholic mother from Indiana: "We have really high hopes especially for the older one 'cause he's so talented, he has gifts, you can just see them, you can just see how God wants him to do great things, leadership and all kinds of good stuff, so we do our part in raising him right, so he can go out and do good things for God and help a lot of people." Similarly, one conservative Protestant father from Los Angeles said, "I pray every night that my sons become godly men and husbands, that they'll lead lives in ways that I'll have left a legacy, a Christian family legacy, the way they raise their kids, that's what I want to see."

Children are unrealized bundles of personally unique "ideal outcomes" that need to be prepared and cultivated if they are to develop, endure, and reach their full potentials. Each child's "best self" exists internally as a latent yet real potential that must be actualized and manifest through growth and experience, driven ultimately by each child's own personality and wants.

Children's "best selves" do not automatically happen. They must be nurtured and achieved. Nurturing is the parents' job, and achieving is the children's job. Parents need to prepare their children to flourish by providing them with life skills such as critical judgment, encouragement toward independence, opportunities to learn, relationships with other adults, and opportunities to learn to make decisions. For example, a white Catholic father from New York City told us, "It's important to give them critical judgment, to give them a sense of who they are as a person and how they find themselves by giving to other people, through other people." A Mormon mother from Indiana explained: "There's a natural rite of passage to move out of mom and dad's house after high school and stand on your own two feet and see how that goes, to exercise more agency than ever before. It's an opportunity to really learn who you are when push comes to shove. College, making families, to serve a [Mormon] mission, because I did that and learned so much about me that I don't think I could've come another way. I want them to have that experience, to complete two years of serving, completely detached from home." One black Protestant father from Houston linked his son's "special potential" with the connections that other adults give him: "Anybody who really takes the time to get to know my boy, who takes a liking to him, just sees that he has potential to be something special, and they really reach out to talk to him." A Hispanic mother from Chicago explained the value of exposing children to multiple options in life to help cultivate their autonomy: "Parents should expose kids to alternatives to give them something to compare to, 'cause if you don't have nothing to compare, then what's your other option? You can't force your religion on somebody. We're Catholic and my daughter loved going to both Catholic and [Protestant] Christian churches, 'cause of the praise and worship there, so if she finds that she likes it better there, then that's her choice." Similarly, this white Catholic father from Indiana described the delicate balance between providing boundaries and fostering autonomy: "I'm giving her the opportunity to explore something else, you give them the free-for-all to explore whatever they want. But they are children so you have to be careful, they have to be careful, there's some weird stuff going on and you can get sucked into believing some really 'interesting' things. So have some formal foundation is good, but you also don't wanna force-feed somebody."

Children, then, for their part, need to exert themselves fully to achieve their ideal selves, as is evident in this Jewish father from Indiana's advice for his children: "You follow your passion, your heart, your talent, those three things, and then you work damn hard at it. You may not see now the picture that's going to emerge, where you're gonna be, and how all your passions and interests are going to come together later in life. But if you do what you're born to do, what you love best, what you're best at, and you work hard, then you're gonna find a way, somehow or other, to make it work." A mainline Protestant father from New York City put it this way: "I want my kids to develop and achieve the abilities they already have, finding and developing them and showing up, not hiding or suppressing them. That's a really great thing God gave us individually, that's profound, amazing. That's a really healthy way we grow up. My son has a lot of skills and abilities, he's quite smart. I want him to be happy, independent as much as possible, really helping other people too, and be nice to others and himself, and really develop his skills and achieve what he is able to do. I want him to do more, just a little more pushing, just a little bit, to make him more developed." This Hindu father from New York City explained how a belief in the determinism of karma should motivate his daughter to become her best self in this life in order to be reincarnated in a better next life: "I believe everybody is born for a reason, I always tell my girl you were born for a reason and try to make the best of it. My grandmother used to say that your destiny in this life is fixed when you were born, but you work to make it better or worse, now it's your karma to make it better on the journey because our life is definite." A white conservative Protestant father from Florida expressed a similar thought using the idea of "God's personal calling" on his kids' lives: "Success for my children is doing what God has called them to do, he gives you the desires of your heart, then following that in the design that God's called them to do. Achieve in education and an occupation, being financially sound so they can give. I wanna say be happy, but more doing what God's called you to do, because you do that and everything else will fall in its place, and you'll have a peace about what's going on, whatever's happening."

Crucial in this growth process is children learning personal independence and not becoming dependent on or influenced by others. Consider the view of this Buddhist mother from Chicago, for example:

> I worry about bullying, mean girls, cliques, and her not being a strong enough personality to be herself and not just go along with the crowd. I hope she's more like me growing up; I've never been that type of person that needed anything, never needed a boyfriend. I'm strong, I am very much a woman, hear me roar! [laughs] I want her to be a strong, independent woman, not that girl that needs a man. To be able to survive on her own two feet. I'd have a problem if my daughter had a husband who was controlling and didn't allow her to be herself.

A Mormon father from Indiana explained, "My children are not me, not little me's, they're them, and not going to always agree or feel the same as me. What's important is that I help them with broad strokes, in what they want to pursue, like my son is into karate, I'm not, but we support his interest because it makes him happy, it's a fine pursuit. The realization that they're different and that's okay, that is faith oriented, knowing that God is our parent and all of us are different." Hence this Muslim father from Indiana said, "We sometimes disagree. These kids wanna take more chances, society has some influence, but we let them be. We try and tell them what is best, but they can make up their own mind."

Parents know that their children can and will make mistakes, which can be hard, but also from which they can learn, so they prepare themselves for that near inevitability. A Hispanic mother from Indiana said, "You can lead a horse to water but you can't make them drink. You can teach them the best you can and then you have to let them be, they have to be their own person. Even if they make mistakes, you just have to sit there and hope that they learn from that mistake." Similarly, a Muslim mother also from Indiana reported: "She has her own mind, her own strong personality, her own things, you gotta accept nobody is the same, everybody has their own choices and personality. They can in their mind like stuff that's different, that's their own choice and they're not gonna find out about it until they became a grown up and have their own family. I make mistakes and learned, and they can learn to." Immigrant parents trying to navigate two cultures describe wrestling with the same dilemmas, as noted by this Hispanic Catholic father from New Mexico:

> We bring a Mexican culture, here in the house we live one way, but outside they also see other ways of living. We can't force them to think like us, because they don't have our experiences. We have to adapt ourselves. That doesn't mean that I'm going to adapt if they get marijuana. With the values that we have as a family, how we want them to grow, not to take them down, that are going to make you healthy: they are the values we have, that we want to show them, so they can make their own decisions.

Through this kind of life experience, parents hope that children learn resilience and flexibility but also inner strength, as described by a Muslim father from Indiana using a growing-tree metaphor: "You gotta let children live their own lives, let them have their own personality, straighten them up like a young tree when they are children, and as they're growing up they might blow with the wind a little bit but then they straighten out."

Children can only realize their "best selves" by venturing upon and effectively navigating the challenging journey of life, especially the first half of life. Success means not only enjoying life's opportunities and pleasures but also effectively facing and surmounting the problems and trials in one's quest through the world, which promotes positive growth, maturity, and understanding, and reveals and progressively unfolds one's ideal personal self.

These ideas are so obvious to parents that they rarely feel the need to express them explicitly. They are assumed by and implicit in much of what all parents say, however. The existentially most pressing and difficult issue for parents while their children are still living at home is learning how and when to ease their children into life's journey so they are adequately prepared but not overwhelmed. Consider, for instance, the dilemmas expressed by this Hispanic Catholic mother from Indiana:

It's hard to keep her sheltered, but kids are really smart, they know what's going on, that there's a lot of danger out there. I remind her there is always danger, always people who want to outsmart her. I'm trying to keep her aware and innocent at the same time. Like she's not supposed to open the door to anyone or answer the phone if she's home alone. I taught the danger of pedophiles, of grownups talking about kissing, to look out for things that don't look right or look dangerous. But I can't really shelter her, because I don't want her to eventually go into life and suddenly find herself like, "Oh this is not the world that I know." She needs to find out too that everything out there is not that great.

Many parents can only with great difficulty refrain from intervening into their kids' lives to help them. But most also, like this white Catholic father from Indiana, know that they must allow their children to begin to risk life's journey, since encountering its challenges is the only way they can become their best selves: "I wish many times that I would've been told, 'This is good for you.' I see it now with the girls, and my first instinct is to protect them and get rid of whatever situation is making them sad or scared. But I look back and see no, they really do go through some things to learn and come out better on the other side." A conservative Protestant mother from Florida conveyed a similar idea using the religious ideas of dangers of idolatry combined with a football metaphor: "I'd hate to know my child was out there thinking some idol [instead of God] was gonna do it for them, and have to learn [otherwise] the hard way. But

I did what I think I'm supposed to do. So eventually, they're gonna take the ball and run with it." Again, in the end the child must through lived experience achieve their own best self. Again, a Hispanic Catholic father from Indiana explained his strategy: "I am not a helicopter parent, I don't hover. There's times I'm in the background, but I do believe they need to take risks and learn on their own. I'll be there if there's something's gone wrong, I'll step in, but most of the time it's up to them." Some parents, such as this Jewish mother from Indiana, express worries that their children will not exert the effort to live up to their ideal potential: "The biggest challenge right now is getting him to succeed to his potential, to actually perform what he's capable of, and that's taking a lot of sweat, the challenge of just getting him to succeed to his potential and just not like daydream his life away." A Mormon mother from Indiana told us, "I want my kids to get on with their lives and be progressing. It's hard for me to see people who are stagnant, not trying to reach their potential, that is hard." Most, however, are optimistic that their own children will rise to the challenge.

Knowing that their children face difficult life journeys ahead, the best consolation that parents can give themselves is the hope, already noted in the previous section, that their children will at least learn from their mistakes and thereby move closer to achieving their true selves. "As a parent you learn sometimes you have to let them make their own mistakes," one Mormon father told us. "There is a learning process that's important, and the learning can only happen in a first person, you can't convey the experience." A Buddhist father from Chicago said, "Buddhism teaches you have to learn from your mistakes and everything happens for a reason and then another opportunity will come. So for parents, just letting go, not being a helicopter parent." This Muslim mother from Indiana explained, "We are gonna face our creator and when he asks you, 'did you do it the right way,' you have to answer, 'yeah I did.' I'm not saying perfect or anything, every stage in life is a learning opportunity, and if you've made a mistake, learn from that mistake, ask how can I improve?" One black Protestant mother from Houston said, "I do have to be aware of [bad] situations, but also you need to let them grow up and experience the world and learn from their own mistakes, because if I always say 'no you can't do this' and 'no, no, no,' they won't be able to learn from their own mistakes." And this Hispanic Catholic father from Chicago told us, "If my children grew up different from me, I would have to accept it. Not that I would like it and I would try to talk to them to change it, but I don't try to change anybody. They would have to probably trip and fall and learn on their own."

Different parents express different thoughts and feelings about their children learning from mistakes. Some, such as this mainline Protestant mother from Indiana, explicitly teach it as part of their children's training: "I'm pushing them to be better kids, better every day. I want them to know it's okay to make mistakes, we learn from our mistakes and we get up and we move on and we learn, we just keep pushing, don't give up. That's my biggest thing, don't give up. So I hope that they will be successful. I hope that they're happy. I hope they always know they're loved and wanted." Such parents make learning from mistakes an explicit part of a strategy for life. "They're their own beings," explained a black Catholic father from Houston, "When they're grown, they have to make their own mistakes, their own successes. But we try to show them all sides of it." Parents providing their children a good "foundation," however, is a necessary part of their knowing how to learn from mistakes, as this white Catholic mother from Indiana presupposed: "I hope they will take the things we've given them for their foundation and learn from their mistakes, learn from our mistakes, and help guide them to do that." Other parents, such as this mainline Protestant mother from Washington, DC, seem less proactive in actively preparing kids to learn from mistakes, but seem to think instead it better simply to let it happen naturally: "I've had to learn to try to step back and let him make mistakes. He has to learn it by himself, he doesn't want to take anyone else's word for it, so part of me is letting him find that stuff out for himself."

Most parents think the loose oversight and boundaries they can provide while their children still live at home will lessen the pain of learning from their mistakes later in life, as observed by this white Catholic mother from Indiana: "I'd rather see my children make mistakes when I can help them instead of telling them, 'no you can't do this, you can't drink, you can't go party, you can't do that.' Giving them space, trusting them to make their own decisions." Similarly, this conservative Protestant father from Florida said, "My own parents were very relaxed, but at the same time you knew there was discipline. It was great, it was ideal. They let me make mistakes and learn from my own mistakes, 'cause that was the only way I was gonna figure some things out, but it was really good." A black Protestant father from Houston also told us, "I have to protect them until they get to that certain age they feel they have to make their own mistakes. But then she has to make her own mistakes until she bump her head and see where she fall back." For many but not all parents, learning how to let their kids do this takes real work on their part. For some, such as this Hindu mother from central New Jersey, the effort is for patience and self-restraint: "I need to work on being a little more patient and not trying to take over her thoughts, let her make her own mistake and stand back. I want perfection, everything perfect, but something I have to develop is to be patient and not be so type-A, because I hated when my mother was type-A and I'm becoming like her now. So a little bit more relaxed and not focus on so much irrelevant stuff." For other parents, however, the work is simply not to constantly live in fear about just how bad and damaging the mistakes in their children's life's journeys will be, as illustrated by this mainline Protestant mother from Washington, DC: "That's a place where faith really comes in, realizing they're gonna be fine, they're gonna be fine. My husband says I need to let it go, they're gonna be fine, or else accept that they've gotta make the mistakes they've gotta make. He's like, 'let 'em, let 'em, let 'em, let them, they've got to figure it out, it's gonna be okay.'"

The frightful but real alternative is for growing children to become compromised or wrecked by an inability to overcome the hardships, temptations, and misfortunes that assail them in life's journey, and so to fail to realize the "best selves" they could have been.

Nearly every parent we interviewed was hopeful that their own children would successfully rise to the challenge of life's journey and so realize and fulfill their true selves. But pressing on that hope is also an acute awareness and fear that for many young people life does not always turn out well. Amid their optimism and confidence, parents recited a litany of failures and fears and cautionary tales about much they hope their children will manage to avoid. For example, a mainline Protestant mother from New York City reported about her adopted daughter, "My biggest fears for her? She had a traumatic background so I fear some sort of abuse, like sexual abuse, domestic violence, drugs, alcohol, you name it, I'm fearful about it." A mother from the same tradition living in Washington, DC, noted, "We're really lucky, they're good kids so far but who knows what happens later in life. If they get drug addicted or mental illness, I don't know what happens." This mainline Protestant father from New York City explained, "I have seen a lot of people who are highly educated, smart, and financially secure but internally unsuccessful as humans, they are miserable or having low self-esteem or don't use their genius in positive terms, but instead to hurt others. So I think basic human development, like learning compassion, needs to be primary over intellectual development, that's important to me in our family." And this mother from the same religious tradition and city said, "I would be disturbed if she gave up herself for someone else, that she didn't feel like she had agency in the world, in a situation where she was powerless or didn't feel like she could rely on herself. She has this fantasy mentality, like some man will come on a white horse or I'll marry a rich man and everything will be fine, so I say, 'you will make your own money even if he is rich.' And of course if she gets stuck in any sort of addiction that would be heart-breaking."

One conservative Protestant mother from Florida confessed this fear: "I'd hate if they did something crazy and it broke my heart, but the ball is in their court after a while. Our job is to raise productive adults, but adult kids do weird things. There are many parents who have so many sorrows over their adult kids, it's ridiculous. I just hope that doesn't happen. But it's like rolling dice. You do all the things you felt were right, and then your adult child does crazy stuff, and what do you do? I know from too many other parents it doesn't always work out." Another white conservative Protestant mother and schoolteacher from Florida reported: "When you have a kid without conviction and conscience, you pretty much have a sociopath. And I've seen them, no morals, nothing, feel no remorse. One of the main things that I wanna see when I talk to a kid who's done something wrong is remorse. I have this kid in class, she's a train wreck. There's not intentional parenting, sure they'll beat their kid's butt or verbally abuse her, but there's no like, 'Why? Do you know why you probably shouldn't throw that bat at your sister's head?'" And an African American father attending a conservative Protestant church in Washington, DC, noted that, "I want them to be much better than I am, with their choices, because it's difficult out here for a black male, you know? You see they are getting shot over simple things, by an officer or just in a wrong neighborhood." A black Protestant mother from Houston told us this cautionary tale about a neighbor girl she knows: "She was a straight A student and a leader, but then she started acting out in middle school and got caught up, took a negative turn and it down-spiraled from there. She got on drugs real bad, started knowing older guys and fast money and all that—opposite of how she was brought up. And that tells us religious parents, we still have to keep our eyes open to our children, to stay focused on where they are. But when they become adults, you're limited in the things you can do for them." Another black Protestant mother also from Houston noted the many "devilish things out there, drugs, could be liquor, unhappiness, people not feeling loved, some kids never had love and affection and discipline, they don't know what love is, so they just go out and just do whatever." And one black Protestant father from the same city confessed,

"Our family right now, it's kind of like a struggle. My son is trying to be pulled to the streets. But I keep praying for him."

A white Catholic father from Indiana reported, "We've had some major incidents in this community with kids dying of drugs and alcohol, suicide, it really makes you refocus and double down on what you're doing." A white Catholic mother from the same area said, "It's your duty to raise kids in a church to have that basic foundation. When you don't have that foundation, you grow up lost. I see a lot people today who are lost." One white Catholic mother from Chicago related this story: "There's a lot of kids addicted to drugs. A very dear friend of mine, married, two children, and his younger brother, thirty years old, just died of an overdose, addiction problems. He was a great guy, a musician, poet, a really gentle soul, but when you're addicted, there's two outcomes, either kick the habit or die. He died. And there's a lot of grief there, a lot of sadness." Explaining why she severely limits her son's time playing video games, a white Catholic mother from Indiana explained, "He was born shortly after Columbine [a mass murder in a Colorado high school], and that's been imprinted in my mind, these kids who were messed up, probably didn't have much parenting at home, played nothing but violent video games, wanted to be the weird outcast. Dress weird and people are gonna treat you that way. I have to trust that I've done the right things with him and he knows the difference between right and wrong, but why give the devil a foothold?" This Hispanic Catholic mother from New York City told us:

> I found a box of cigarettes in my son's room and started crying, "Ay, my God, he is going to become addicted." To a mother, what comes to mind is he is going to become addicted, smoking all the time. So I talked with him. I said, "I know, I went through what you are in, you have to try everything, because you can't say no, you have to try. But after, realize it's a bad thing, because it affects you negatively everywhere."

"Oh wee, there's a lot of challenges for parents now," reported this black Catholic father from Indiana. "The media, peer pressure because of the internet, people can say things on there, just run off with their mouth or entice them. And some kids don't have parents that come to talk to them."

The anxieties and cautionary tales continue. One Mormon mother from Indiana told us: "My younger brother still lives at home with my parents and he is twenty-eight. He has a wealth of physical and mental health problems, it's very hard on them. So I use him as a cautionary tale with my children actually, I say, 'You are not going to be like Uncle

Rob, are you?' When I see something that looks a little off, I nip it in the bud right there. 'No. We're not having that behavior in this house.'" A Jewish mother from the same area reported, "Both of my brothers did drugs, one of them a lot more than marijuana and it made his life very difficult. It cost him a lot. That's what happens with drugs. Even teen-agers just experimenting, marijuana is a gateway drug, it was for my brother, it led to acid among other things and people die. I'm just glad he didn't, he could have died. It's just scary, a good way to ruin your life."[1] This Muslim mother also from Indiana explained how young people go wrong this way: "There is no point of our living only like an animal, eat-ing, sleeping, and having sex, that's the difference between human beings and animals, self-control. Like alcoholics, they lose everything, if you let your needs control you, you're gonna have a bad life and lose everything. What stops you from that is the religion, there is no point for living with-out belief. Like Hollywood stars, you may have everything but be empty, without God there's no point for my living, and that's why some of them decide to kill themselves." A Hindu father from Chicago confessed to us, "I'm always worried what's going to happen with him. I want him to be very disciplined, having a humble attitude, to be nice, but I'm scared of him getting lost in the whole changes with this culture." This Hindu mother from central New Jersey actually brings her children to work to show them concrete examples of the life compromises they must avoid: "I always tell my kids about real-life stories, people who make mistakes that hold them back with limitations. Like a teenage mom I work with had to drop out of high school, so I take my kids and show them that she's smart, she could have done something better in life but made bad choices. Her parents told her but she still did them. It's sad that people have such greatness in them and one silly choice makes their path that way. So, what the consequences are, I make them aware. And I hope they follow all the laws and don't do any damage to themselves or somebody else." Finally, this Buddhist mother from Chicago related, "No matter what happens, we try to raise our kids to make them happy because I see there's a lot of kids out there who doesn't have either mother and fathers, and that make them sad. And we don't want our kids to go in that path." Clearly, in the dominant cultural model of the nature of children held

---

1. In general, however, Jewish parents expressed by far the fewest concerns about their children failing in life, as reflected in the statement of this Jewish mother from Indiana: "If for any reason one of them didn't go to college it would be an epic fail, it would be stupid [chuckles]. So yeah, that's not gonna happen."

by religious parents in the United States, kids are not destined to realize their ideal, true selves; that must be achieved and there always remains the possibility of failure.

The Task of Parenting

American religious parents have a cultural model not only of the nature of children but also the job of parenting. What is it? The answer to this question is determined by all of the preceding cultural models. Having accepted all of the aforementioned, the cultural model of the task of being a parent turns out to be clearly defined, as this:

> *The Task of Parenting*: The central job of parents is to prepare and equip their children not only to enjoy all that is good in life but also to successfully navigate, endure, and overcome difficulties in their personal life journeys in the world. Good parents provision their children with the grounding, learning, and resources they will need to surmount life's difficulties and come out stronger and truer on the other side. How parents do this will be shaped a lot by their own experience growing up in their families. Parents may simply enjoy their offspring as children, but the true quality of their parenting work will be tested when their children face life's trials and tribulations down the road. The demanding task of parenting is made especially difficult by two major complications: parents must never violate their children's ultimate self-determination nor trigger teenage rebellion. These demand that parents carefully navigate the narrow, difficult straights between lax and overbearing parenting.

The central job of parents is to prepare and equip their children not only to enjoy all that is good in life but also to successfully navigate, endure, and overcome difficulties in their personal life journeys in the world. Good parents provision their children with the grounding, learning, and resources they will need to surmount life's difficulties and come out stronger and truer on the other side.

Once again, parents across all of the religious traditions we studied assume and embrace these ideas. For instance, one mainline Protestant father in Washington, DC, said, "Helping them learn how to navigate hard relationships on their own, that's the goal, and that's hard and tiring, 'cause you have to be in the know of what's going on and it gets harder to know that when they become more closed with us." Similarly, a conservative

Protestant mother from Los Angeles said, "I was never given direction growing up. So with our kids we're talking about whether they want to go to college, and take sports, we try to really get them thinking about the future. I was never shown that, if this is my goal, here's how you reach that goal. I just felt lost, but becoming a mom made me feel purpose." More forcefully, a black Protestant father from Houston insisted, "God say that's your duty to get your child on the straight path, you don't let him make the decision for hisself, if that was the case, then he could take care of hisself. Since he can't take care of hisself, then he do what [tapping table] *I say do*. And I'm not gonna tell him nothin' wrong." And this white Catholic mother from Indiana told us, "We've equipped them their whole upbringing, their whole education, so I'm not worried. You equip them to be agile enough to deal with life. I don't think they're gonna get too stressed because they're going to be able to figure it out." A Hindu mother from Chicago said, "Parents need to ensure children know what is good and not good so they make the right decisions. That is their responsibility, to tell them what is good, what is not good, and then make sure they are mature enough to know how to make the right decision." Similarly, this Muslim father from Chicago related that, "With parenting, I hope the first ten or fifteen years I can build some type of foundation for my kid. And then eventually when he goes off to college, he has that foundation where he sees right and wrong, he'll be able to make that decision." One white Catholic father from Indiana even read us his "Parental Accomplishment Checklist" that enumerates the competencies he wants his children to learn before they leave home—including everything from knowing about sex, drugs, and alcohol to how to paddle a canoe from behind, volunteer, and bake potatoes.

Again, the key to good parenting in these ways is providing a "foundation," support, and oversight for their children, as this black Protestant mother from Houston told us: "Parents are there for the basic, your base, your foundation, also your support, they're your monitors, your guides. They make sure you following through, so kind of like your hawk-eyes." This Hindu father from central New Jersey agrees: "Parents should lay the groundwork of the family foundation, to lay a good foundation strongly, and whatever else they decide to do, you support them. The foundation should be strong." For some parents, including this black Protestant mother, for example, having learned in their own experiences that much their parents taught them was true and valuable, emboldens them to prepare and equip their own children in ways they believe are right: "When you're young, your mother teaches you things and then you think, well, she is right but you want to see for yourself, and then you rebel, do things on your own. Then you realize, wow, my mom was right, I just didn't want to listen, 'cause you want to do what you want to do. Through my experiences and looking back at what she taught me, it has gotten tremendously stronger for me to show my son too, and I hope and pray that he doesn't rebel along his life." Parents of course need to provide a base, support, and oversight in age-appropriate ways. When children are very young, for instance, parents may teach them to pray as a way to cope with their basic fears, as one Mormon mother from Indiana explained, "I told them prayer is important and then when they're scared of the dark, like well pray. When scared, that's when you need to talk to God the most, so I think prayer is the best thing you can do." For some parents, equipping their children means setting firm guidelines when they are young and then training them gradually to know how to handle life in the world, as this black Protestant mother from Houston explained, "You can't give 'em a choice at a young age, because if you let them, they're not gonna ever do it, so you gotta put it [the requirement] there. She don't know what she believes, so I got to start [to teach her] now, we gotta start practicing. That's in the part of training. I've got to make sure I have equipped them with everything that they need to go out in this world. I don't want to hold 'em back. I've found myself having to step back because I'm [normally] that mother that wants to take care of everything." It also means helping children learn to become strong by navigating difficult relationships, as with this Buddhist father from Chicago: "She got bullied from her friends a lot, and crying because she don't know what to do. So I say okay, then we have to just deal with it, learn to deal with the problems, that will make you stronger in life. That's what we talk about." Also important that children be prepared to face at the right age as potentially difficult challenges are porn, drugs, alcohol, smoking, and sex, as one Hindu mother from New York City observed: "I am against premature exposure to bad things, because everything is available on this planet depending on what you accept, like pornography is everywhere, but whether we look at it is a different story, it's your choice, you are the one making the choice, so that's what I inculcate in her. I hope she understood that I am the one making the choice to take the drug, to smoke, to drink, to have sex, to go to a party where they should not be. I think it is better if they deal with those things when they are older and mentally and physically more mature." Exposing children to many different positive experiences and opportunities, however, and supporting their interests is also important. "We expose her to as many activities as possible, encourage her with the ones she seems to favor," said one black Catholic father from Indiana. "Just help her to navigate through whatever it is she's comfortable with. I'm doing that now, whatever it takes, driving her to her appointments and cheering her on, providing whatever she needs, morally and health, relationships, that she's well rounded, just whatever I can do to help her out." Then as children grow up, parents have to pull back and provide support and guidance from a further distance, as this Jewish mother from New York City noted: "Getting a little older, I'm trying to be more lenient with him and his time, but guide him in a way. I want them to know not to do something bad to someone if they're hurt, don't hurt them back—they see kids do that all the time at school. So to have some sort of inner moral compass for themselves and to feel confident in that." In the end, however, as one mainline Protestant mother from Washington, DC, put it, "our job as parents is to put them in a position to carve their own path based upon success and failure, learning, trying new things."

How parents do this will be shaped a lot by their own experience growing up in their families.

The most important reference point for nearly all American parents about how to raise kids is their own early-life experiences as children and teenagers growing up under their own parents. How they were raised by their own mothers and fathers—versus, say, the teachings or advice of their religious traditions or congregations—provides parents the most important influences on their own parenting, whether positive, negative, or mixed. Their own experience as children one generation earlier remains for them the obvious, unquestioned standard that informs their own parenting as adults. This applies to their general parenting methods and styles, the "values" and morals that they seek to instill in their children (which many parents equate with religion), and their specific approaches to passing on religion to children. The parents we interviewed, however, did not often explicitly spell out in detail how they were reproducing or revising the ways their parents raised them religiously. They often simply observed that they were following (or revising) the way their parents had raised them.

American religious parents fell into three general categories of how their parenting is influenced by their own parents. Many had positive experiences growing up, which they were seeking to reproduce with their children. Others had mixed experiences and were working to replicate the positive and avoid the negative. A minority reported negative experiences growing up under their parents and were purposively attempting to raise their children differently in certain ways.

The most often expressed experience was positive, which many parents simply mention in passing. One Jewish father from Indiana told us, for instance, "I want them to be like my parents taught me [to be], I want them to and I fully expect they will grow up that way." A Muslim father from the same state said, "We value education a lot, like my parents did." "Parenting was not really a hard task," a black Protestant mother from Houston remarked, "because I knew what I was supposed to be doing as a parent by watching my parents raise me." A black Protestant father from the same city likewise told us, "You can't parent all your kids the same, it doesn't work. Being a sibling of eight, I could see the difference in how my parents treated us, and it has helped me to be able to parent differently." "I believe in honor in all things," a mainline Protestant father from Indiana told us, "Honor becomes a point of respect, which my parents held up very highly." Said a Mormon mother from New York City: "How we talk to our kids about what is important, I've passed that on from my parents." A white Catholic father from Indiana related, "I believe my dad has a lot to do with my guidance because I try to emulate him. He was a good man, liked by a lot of people, always cared for his family. And, to me, that's my job." And this Buddhist mother from Chicago explained, "I learned a lot from my childhood. So when I had family, I adopted what I got from my parents to raise my own kids. I haven't changed that much."

Positive experiences being raised by their own parents tend, as we've seen, to get translated into current parenting behaviors, as, for example, this Hispanic Catholic father from New Mexico explained: "My parents weren't super strict with me. They didn't leave a bad taste in my mouth by making me do things I didn't want to do. And maybe that's why I haven't been like that with my kids." This Hindu father from Chicago likewise said, "It sort of like follows a pattern of my parents, it's not really very different, a similar template kind of thing." Parents tend to reproduce the ways they were raised even when they realize things did not work exactly as their own parents had thought. One conservative Protestant father from Florida, for example, told us, "I don't wanna be that overprotective dad, I wanna trust that we've taught our daughters to do the right thing and make the right decisions on stuff, the same way my parents taught me. But yet I didn't always make the right decision." How parents were raised as children also sets expectations for what parents anticipate from their children, per the report of this Mormon mother from New York City: "Our theory is, the oldest is sort of a rebel and tries a lot of things that normal teenagers do, and the others just sort of followed suit. I'm not condoning it, but that's sort of how my parents raised us as well." Parents' experience as children can also determine their general comfort levels with different kinds of lifestyles and practices, as mentioned by this Mormon father from New York City: "My wife opens up everything she has for people. And there's no doubt that's easier for me because I watched my parents do it. It wasn't unusual for me to come home and there be some person on our couch, or sleeping in the next room in a fold-out couch, or we'd take in cousins or someone who lived with us for two years. So that had to have affected me."

Other parents, such as this Hispanic Catholic mother from Indiana, even muse about their children reproducing the same practices they learned from their parents: "It's funny, it's like a little flashback. Somehow bringing up your own family you pass it on, so if I do something with her like my parents did, maybe she'll do it later too." And some parents, like this white Catholic father from Indiana, continue to learn from their own parents even as they raise their children today: "Our parents are pretty good about not acting like parents toward our kids, their grandchildren. So I think that's a good goal for me to try to emulate, not try to micromanage how they grow up." For most religious parents, their primary reference point of their own experience being parented influences how they pass on religious traditions and identities to their children. To give one example, consider the sometimes halting words of this Jewish father from New York City: "There's something about being Jewish that has, I don't know, there's something about being, I . . . it's hard to explain. Maybe 'special' is the right phrase for it, and I think it's important to continue that. I guess I have my parents' attitude."

Even when parents diverge from the way they were raised, their own parents serve as the foremost reference point guiding their choices. Parents who mentioned ways they try to differ in parenting from their own parents usually mention wanting to be emotionally warmer and more lenient with their children. One conservative Protestant father from Los Angeles, for instance, told us, "I want to do something my parents didn't, which was actively participate in my life. So I am actively participating in all of my kids' lives." A Hispanic Catholic mother from Chicago reported, "I talk to her about things all the time, because my parents never did." Similarly, this Hindu father from Chicago mentioned, "I think I should talk to her more about religious practices in the home, because my parents didn't, never did talk to me about any of this stuff." A black Protestant father from Houston explained to us that, "I wasn't as strict as my parents. If my parents said 'Be home by 10,' you had to be home by 10. And I don't remember telling them 'you have to be home by 11 or 12,' I don't remember saying anything like that." And this Hispanic Catholic from Indiana reported, "I don't believe I'm strict, because I'm comparing myself to my parents and they were pretty strict, but I give in to my kids." Then again, some parents would like to reproduce the parenting of their own parents, but view themselves, as does this Muslim mother from Chicago, as having different personalities, which make things difficult: "My parents talked a lot, that's what I remember. It helped me a lot and I think I learned a lot. But my husband and I are not like big talkers, so I don't know if we're going to be able to sustain discussions at the dining table like my parents did."

In between the reproduction and change strategies, a few parents spoke explicitly about selectively changing only a few targeted practices. One Mormon father from Indiana, for instance, explained that, "I always assumed I would be a parent quite a lot like my parents. Except there were a few things I felt that they had done wrong that I was gonna do differently, which is how I think most people feel." And a conservative Protestant mother from Los Angeles reported, "I'm a really involved mom, I'm cooking and cleaning for them. My mom didn't do any of that stuff. But I also am reproducing a lot of what I was raised with that my parents did well. We had a lot of traditions that I still do."

For some parents, the passage of time has led to a greater appreciation for their own parents and the value of how they were raised. One Muslim mother from Indiana, for instance, explained: "When I grew up, I used to be against everything like my parents did. But after I had kids and family, I understand more about my parents maybe or decisions they've made in their life. And I tried not to pass on their mistakes, but learn from their mistakes and improve my life. That's how I am and how I hope my kids learn and improve themselves, hopefully." And this Hindu father from Chicago told us, "I really think a lot about what has passed on from my family, not taking anything for granted, to be more focused on the how my kids grow up and how to wrap the values right. I was exposed to a lot of different thoughts, contradicting many things that my parents would say, but now I see when I look back why they were saying. It was my mother mostly who influenced me, I feel."

Complicating the picture for some parents is a perception that the larger context of society and culture has changed so much since they were children that simply reproducing the ways they were raised is not possible. A Jewish mother from New York City, for example, said, "I'm very aware of how different it is for me raising my girl as a religious child than it was for my parents raising me, because I grew up in a religious world and she is not." This Muslim mother from Chicago emphasized challenges in dealing with the ubiquity of media: "I would like to raise my children like my parents raised me, but I know that's not going to happen. My parents made sure we didn't watch any TV. That's hard. We didn't watch any TV growing up. My parents used to actually like enforced that. Now that I look back, I don't know how they did it." Immigrant parents, such as this Hindu father from Chicago, are especially aware of how the change of context makes the reproduction of parenting difficult: "The way I had grown up is so different, I cannot bring up my child like my parents did." Still, most parents, despite perceiving such difficult contexts, still believe in transmitting to their children at least the same "values" with which they were raised, as expressed by this mainline Protestant father from Indiana: "It all goes back to the way I was raised. I know times are a lot different now, but I still firmly believe in those values. I guess it's just that sense I got from my parents, I don't know how else to explain it."

Parents may simply enjoy their offspring as children, but the true quality of their parenting work will be tested when their children face life's trials and tribulations down the road.

Parents tend to be more focused on the present with their kids than the future. But future ramifications of present parenting help to inform their current approaches to parenting. Parents do have running in the background the ideas of what will count as their success and failure. Thus, one conservative Protestant mother from Indiana said, "The test of how well a parent has done in the values communicated is found out as it proves itself out over time. You hope you've done a good job but there is seeing how things work in a child's life. You want to do the best for her but you can't do it all for them, they have to find a way too." For many, as with this Muslim father from Indiana, transmitting good "values" is of paramount importance for measuring parental success: "We all value life, we're here to worship and pray and earn a living, raise a family. And once you leave, you're gone, you give what sticks to your kids, you're judged on how you raise your kids, you know? That's very important, so when you carry on, it's not leaving them money, it's values." Parents hope that their doing a good job will translate into their children's success in life, broadly defined, but they are not always sure either, as expressed by this mainline Protestant father from Washington, DC: "We hope they find their own relationship with God that will sustain them over life. We hope they go through the journey and find a passion that's suited to them, and land on their feet with relationships and family that today we take for granted but are things you work hard to perfect over time. If my efforts to ground them in faith don't translate to the next generation, you wonder I must not have done a good job. If you believe that's a good path, you would hope others would stay on that path." Sometimes parents' ideas of success and failure are not overt, but only implicit in their talk. For example, this Buddhist mother from Chicago told us, "Thai and American cultures are different. I want my girls to finish college before they have a boyfriend. I don't want my daughter pregnant before she's finished college. I have already talked to her, saying life is hard, when you have a family you have so many responsibilities, so get more education and not a baby. Not only your life is hard but your kid's, how your kids gonna grow up to be good people and be secure, it's so many things after babies." This mother feels responsible positively to influence her daughter, and she thinks she will have succeeded in the future if she finishes college before having babies and failed if she does not, even if she does not say that directly.

Occasionally, a parent will prove the rule about the testing of the quality of parenting in the future by disagreeing with the dominant model. One white Catholic mother from Chicago, for instance, placed all responsibility for outcomes on "what is within" children—that is, carrying the autonomous individualism of children to an extreme—and so relieving parents of that burden: "I can't be disappointed in how my kid turns out, because a child is not an outcome. There's no outcomes in this life. That's somebody's life. I'm not an outcome to my parents. You can't look at it like that, cannot start thinking about your child as extensions of your own parenting ability or creating little personalities. They're an independent person. They're going to thrive based on what is within them." Similarly, this Hindu father from Chicago expressed skepticism about what he thinks is American parents' standard "delusions of grandeur": "Parenting has become a profession in this country, just too much of it. Parents try to do everything, but the idea that parents play such a fantastic role I just don't buy. Parents here are terribly involved but I'm not, I don't feel any burden of being a father. Parents have this delusion of grandeur about their role in their children's lives. It's not that much. It's very minimal." But, again, these rare exceptions prove the rule by recognizing the dominance of the views they are against. Much more typical are statements such as this from a Hispanic Catholic father from New York City: "If she turned out badly, that as a parent, you'd feel let down, it's very painful. Even in middle school, if she does not work hard to do better, as a dad or mom you feel a bit cheated. I'm a strict person even with myself, I've blamed myself in certain occasions, saying 'I'm at fault,' I get paranoid feeling guilty, even when it's obvious I'm not to blame. So, yes, sometimes you blame yourself because of the situations your child is in." Similarly, a Mormon mother from Indiana stated:

> I think parents have as much of the pie as they want to take. Absolutely. It's all how involved the parent is. Some parents have given up and it's a self-fulfilling prophecy, they have no interaction and let children do what they're gonna do. But as a parent you can decide to be involved in your children's lives and have an influence, as long as you recognize that your children are not you, they are individuals. But at the same time, I can help them and point them and be a guidepost and be a sage in some respects when they're younger. We can have a huge influence in their lives.

Because of these beliefs that parents exert enormous influence in their children's lives, many believe that if their children do not turn out the way they raised them to be, then they the parents somehow failed. "I will have failed if . . ." comes up surprisingly often. Some parents, like this Mormon mother from Indiana, can already detect ways they have failed: "Sometimes we'll be having conversations and I'll realize there's something they just don't know, and I will say, 'I have failed as a mother. You're supposed to know that.'" Similarly, this white Catholic mother from the same area reported, "We are trying to raise men of high character and ultimately saints, so with the older one now it's very difficult lately, we feel like we're totally failing [laughing sardonically] because he's just not where we think he should be." Others, including this conservative Protestant mother from the same area, are already anticipating future realizations of their failures: "I'm not the perfect parent, I wish I were different in certain ways. They might as adults look back and think mom failed in some ways, some day when they're in therapy, it'll all come out how their parents failed them [laughing]. I'll only say 'I'm sorry, I wasn't that person, I wish I had been.'" And for still others, such as this white Catholic also from Indiana, the possibility of failure seems real but more hypothetical: "It's our job to transmit the faith so I think if they don't buy in, then we failed in a sense."

For some, stories of parenting success and failure are framed by their own experience growing up with what they think were failed parents, which they usually managed somehow to overcome, enabling them to be better parents to their children. Consider the tales of two Jewish mothers, for instance, the first from Indiana:

> Being a mother helped me to break away from a lot of the very negative patterns that I learned growing up, which is the opposite of what

usually happens, that people repeat their dysfunctional patterns. But from the time I was three, my mantra was, "I will not do this to my kids. I will not do this to my kids." I was very conscious of it. Which doesn't mean you know exactly how to make that happen. So it's a process of trial and error over time, it takes a lot of self-control and patience and self-reflection. I don't know how much it has to do with my Judaism, but my kids are the best part of my life now, they made me a better person, and they've enriched my life in so many ways.

The second story is told by this Jewish mother from New York City:

My mother was a pretty bad parent. She was in a lot of pain, a lot of chaos, didn't have a supportive partner, felt like a single mother because she had to do everything herself, made all the decisions herself. So she was overly nurturing, claustrophobic, and at the same time not really giving emotionally what I needed. She didn't know what to do with me. I wasn't a good student, I was chaotic, didn't take medication for ADHD so I could never be on top of school, I had no organization skills, and she didn't know how to help me because she was the same way. So there was all this stress over me having to be normal, get good grades, lose weight, so she could marry me off. And I couldn't do anything she wanted, couldn't live up to any expectations she had of me in any area, which caused a lot strife, even though we loved each other, she didn't know how to parent me. She needed me to be an extension of her. And after all that drama, I just said, "Why would I do this to somebody?" I never thought maybe I could have a child and not do that, it never occurred to me I could get healthy. I just thought I would always make the mistakes my parents made.

Nonetheless, this mother considers herself a reasonably good parent now.

Some parents, including this Muslim father from Indiana, face the prospect of failure with a matter-of-fact uncertainty: "I've done my best to show them the right choice, but if they choose the opposite, I'm not gonna be able to do anything. I have to advise them and pray for them, but if they choose something else, I'm gonna feel like I failed, I'm a failure parent or I did not do my job the way I'm supposed to. But then there's nothing to do about it." Others, such as this black Protestant father from Houston, fear bigger consequences for their failure: "No man can give you God, you have to go seek for yourself. Still, I don't want God to look at me and say I failed as a parent, I'm more afraid of disappointing God than anything. And if at thirty-five, forty years old he is not spiritually grounded, then I failed as a father." In any case, parents with children at home know that only time will tell how the quality of their parenting will be tested.

The demanding task of parenting is made especially difficult by two major complications: parents must never violate their children's ultimate self-determination . . .

About this, all the parents were clear. "There's things I would like to see my kids get involved with," reported one mainline Protestant father from Indiana, "but I'm not overbearing, so that way it doesn't come across as a disappointment [if they don't]. I try not to over-exuberate, push, push, push. Let the natural thing happen." This conservative Protestant mother from Florida told us, "I'd be okay if my kids dropped out of church for a long while because I know they know what's right and maybe they just need [time away]. Like who am I to judge, because my husband and I definitely went through our highs and lows. I would definitely encourage them to stay active and get involved, but I don't want to be the pushy, overbearing mother that pushes them away." Similarly, a black Protestant mother said, "It would bother me if they chose to not have a religion. But now you're dealing with adults so you can't really control that. You can give them words of wisdom, and I would try to get 'em back on the right track, but they're adults at the end of the day, so you can only do what you can." And a white Catholic mother from Indiana related, "I'm not forcing, I'm hoping they develop the same beliefs that I have, but I need *them* to come to that so they really believe it. If I'm forcing it on them just because mom says so, doesn't mean it's a true belief of yours. Then I don't think it's genuine." A white Catholic mother from the same state also stated, "I wouldn't say I prefer her to go to Mass every week. I think where she's at, giving her some latitude to be herself and to find herself, and if she chooses not to go to Mass, then I'm okay with that."

This principle of children's autonomy and self-determination applies to all areas of life, not only religion, as evident in the words of this Hispanic Catholic father from Chicago: "I would love my girls to be maybe a doctor or an architect, God knows if they ever will be, but I'm starting to learn that as long as they do what makes them happy, I'll be happy. I hope that if they marry, they find that happiness in their personal life. I just want to know that they'll be okay, both spiritually and physically, to be okay, be happy." This Mormon mother from Indiana also said: "They need to have their own agency. I can't really do much about them sharing my values. I think from personal experience, being in the church is gonna make them happier, but if they choose not to and go away and do their own thing or make really bad decisions, it's my job as a parent to love them no matter what. I'm hoping she stays with Mormon beliefs and doesn't move in with her boyfriend. I would like her to go to college and not have sex until she's married. But at the same we have our free will, our agency to make our own choices and she's gonna be an adult so she's free to make her own. So I'm hoping for the best and will love her either way." This same Mormon mother also noted, "My daughter decided to go to orchestra instead of church, but like my husband says, that's her choice. I don't agree with that choice, and I hope they can make good choices when they're older, but my husband is the head of the household and I have to support him no matter how difficult, but I don't agree with that." Continuing the theme, this Jewish father from the same state told us, "We always make it clear that we want you to be able to be yourself and not influenced by what anybody else thinks you should be doing. We know what standards we've set in our lives for what is important and I don't want you to run away from those, so I make the point very clear that I don't want to tell you what to choose in your life, but I also don't want you to be someone that you're not."

For some parents at the extreme, belief in the principle of children's autonomy and self-determination causes them to doubt the legitimacy of their formative influence even on their own toddlers and babies. For example, a Jewish mother from New York City told us: "When we had our son, I just thought it was weird to have him do Jewish things, like Shabbat or putting a little yamaka on his little head. I was like, 'it's so weird.' I just thought it weird to make him Jewish 'cause he was just this new person, a baby, and all the sudden he's Jewish just because his parents are Jewish? I don't know, that was a real, hard thing for me to understand. I didn't know what to do with him. I felt like it was almost a decision *he* had to make, like the way I was Jewish was my decision." This general theme in less extreme forms also pervades parents' talk about their older children. A Muslim father from Indiana, for instance, explained: "When we grew up, the only difficulties we saw was kids not being interested in studying, or smoking or drinking. Now there's like lot more, like on the internet. So I think the challenge with kids is we gotta keep telling, that's all you can do, is kind of guide them, saying there's a right and a wrong thing. Beyond that, it's their life." A Hindu father from New York City said, "It is her life, and she has to choose, it's not my life, I am living my life, that is what I always tell her. You learn what you learn as a young person growing up and I'm quite sure every parents try to teach something good, and if they take it, fine, if they don't, they don't, you cannot really force them." Therefore, as a Hindu mother from central New Jersey explained, "Parents should lay the groundwork of the family foundation, a good foundation strongly, and whatever else they decide to do, you should support them." Children must determine their own lives because each has his or her own path, in the words of a Buddhist father from Chicago: "She has a good foundation to be a good human being, regardless of where she goes in the future. She's going on twenty-one, so we've done as much as we can for her, including the basics of our faith and religion. But the Buddha taught, don't believe what I say just because I say it; question it, challenge it, study it for yourself, find out, walk your own path, your path may not be my path."

. . . nor trigger teenage rebellion.

Religious parents in the United States commonly believe they need to tread carefully with their children lest they provoke them to rebellion and produce outcomes that backfire on their intentions. Parents generally do not think every teenager will necessarily rebel, yet rebellion remains a continual danger worth averting. And in the minds of many parents, religion is the very area of life most likely to inflame rebellion, as some parents know personally from their own youth. The key to avoiding rebellion is to "not force" religion on children. The following quotes help us better understand how religious parents think about the threat of rebellion. This conservative Protestant mother from Indiana told us, "We didn't go to church every single week, more like every couple weeks. At age sixteen we encouraged her to stay in it. But ultimately I think I wouldn't want to push so much, 'cause I'd be afraid they'd be rebellious." A mainline Protestant father from the same state reported, "The main thing I did raising my kids religious was to not force things on them so much that they would just totally rebel against it." A black Protestant mother from Houston said, "I don't want to force you into doing something and then you turn around and be rebellious to me when you old enough, a lot of kids are like that." This white Catholic mother explained how she talks with her children: "I'll say to them you might want to go to church, but it's their decision and I never wanted to force them into something, because then they'd want to rebel against it." Fear of rebellion caused this Jewish mother from New York City not to have her youngest child receive the Jewish education she wished she had: "One of my greatest regrets is that I did not give her a Jewish education, so she doesn't know how to read Hebrew. At least my other kids all do, so they can go into a synagogue anywhere in the world and feel somewhat at home participating. I never forced Judaism on them, I didn't force Hebrew school on the last three, I just encouraged it, and bar mitzvah's, but I never wanted them to rebel against it." Some parents, such as this Hindu mother from New York City discussing career choices, not religion, fear their children's possible rebellion because they themselves were rebellious as youth: "I was told by my parents what career I had to take, which I totally rebelled against, so I wouldn't do that, I'm very loosey-goosey in so many ways. I let go, I pick and choose my battles." And this Hispanic Catholic from Indiana said, "When they are rebels it's a challenge, that is the hardest, 'cause you want the best for your children but when they are rebels, they don't understand. I went through adolescence too, and we may not come to understand until married, have children, that you go through stages and say, 'really, as my mom told me this, and it was true.'" And a white Catholic mother from the same state recalled, "Church wasn't a requirement, just a thing we did as a family. I didn't want to force it on 'em, 'cause I was afraid doing something they didn't want to do they would fight me tooth and nail." Similarly, this white Catholic father also from Indiana explained: "We've never said they have to believe. We've let them know we've questioned it at times and it's okay. Part of why I rebelled against church when I did was that it was always seen as, 'you're going to do this, you're going to go to church, you're going to CCD, you're doing it no matter what, we choose this for you.' I didn't want to push my kids in that direction where they would rebel against it for that reason." Other parents, like this white Catholic father from Indiana, see rebellion in their friends' children: "We have friends who are clamping down so hard on their kids, but when they get to college and freedom, they're the ones who get hurt and drunk and have problems 'cause they've never been on their own. So we're always exposing our kids to things when we're still in control and let them have freedom, even though it's monitored, so when they get there, it's not all new like jumping out in the world and [going crazy]."

Immigrant parents from home cultures where greater respect for parents is normative seem especially to struggle with their encounters with youth rebellion in the United States. For example, this Hispanic Catholic mother from New Mexico explained:

> When I was young, I had a certain intimidation of my dad, much respect, he said what was right and wrong and we listened. That environment was very healthy. I did see bad things, but they never caught my attention and he always turned us the other way. But now, young people find it easy to fall in all things, drugs, homosexuality, rebellion, there's a lot. My youngest tells me all that goes on in school. There is a time when children enter that rebellion, they start rebelling, in family, school, something outside of school and family, church rebellion. If this

happened to one of my daughters, I would pay attention, not to be pressing, but to help at the right time, to talk to her. But I don't know what I would do, what words I would have to say.

One Buddhist mother from Thailand currently living in Chicago related this about her teenage daughter:

> She depends on herself more because she's grown up and she thinks she knows everything. I want to teach her how to cook but she won't listen. She likes to give me lessons. We have conflict over her messes in the house, I want it to be clean. In Thailand I listened to my mommy when I was young. But she pays more attention to her father and argues with me. Sometimes my husband says I am too strict to her, that she is big already and just let her go.

Some parents, including this conservative Protestant mother from Los Angeles, were struggling with rebellious children at the time we interviewed them, and they shared with us how they try to make sense of their mistakes, revised strategies, and hopes for the future:

> At first we made it too rules-based, rather than grace-based. We're making up for that now, as he's tested us, like, "What if I don't do anything you want me to do? What if I'm everything you told me not to be? What if I'm not a Christian? Are you gonna love and support me? Will you be a Christian toward me?" That's difficult for a lot of parents, because you feel let down. But we just said we're going to accept you for who you are because we know who we were before God changed our hearts. We do have boundaries, like he can't come home drunk. But he also knows we adore him and celebrate him. He's a part of this family and it's okay that he's not there [living a Christian life] yet. But we couldn't get to that point until we understood it wasn't our job to save him. Christian parents, even though it's not said outwardly, you're often taught it's your job to save your kid or else you did something wrong. But after two years of me being depressed about that, God showed me we are only called to give our kids stability and love, teach them our need of God, show them who God is, be an example for them of what Christian life looks like, and then let go. I was missing the let go part. I thought my job is to force feed God to you, make your heart want him. How did I ever think I could make my kid's heart want God?

Some Mormon parents tended to be something of exceptions to this "avoid rebellion at all costs" rule. They do share the idea that teenagers rebel, but it is less clear that they believe parents need to be so careful about what they make their children do in order not to exacerbate rebellion. More common was the idea that parents have the right to make their kids attend church as long as they are living under their roof. Mormon parents thus share much of the dominant cultural model here, but they engage the implications differently when it comes to forcing kids to go to church. Typical of this view, a Mormon mother from Indiana expressed:

> If one of my kids came to me and said, "I don't like church. I don't want to go to church anymore," my initial response would be, "As long as you live in my house and are eating my food, then you are going to follow my rules and go to church whether you like it or not." But when they live on their own they can do whatever they want. But yes I would force their attendance as much as I possibly could, because you don't develop the testimony by not going to church. But I would also try to take comfort in the fact that many people do return to their roots as they mature. I would try to keep the lines of communication open, just keep talking to them like everything was fine. But hopefully it will never come up.

In any case, for parents the perceived underlying problem remains: teenagers do not know what is best and often cannot be reasoned with. "When they become teenagers, they don't understand," lamented a Hispanic Catholic mother from New Mexico, "they don't come into reasoning, don't listen to any advice." A Mormon mother from Indiana echoed the sentiment: "When they become teenagers and more independent, it's harder, because they want to have boyfriends before they're supposed to have boyfriends, wanna date behind your back and go to parties, drinking. So it's harder when they get older, but it's really easy when they're young, 'cause they're so eager to please when they're kids. But teenagers are more selfish, sad but true, it becomes like, 'let me be happy.'" In the face of this challenge, most parents hope that "not forcing anything" on their children, especially religion, will succeed. Beyond that, starting from a young age to try to explain the reasons for certain actions and avoiding hypocrisy are important too, as this black Protestant father from Houston explained: "If you want a child to really listen to you and not be rebellious, show them why, and act on what you're telling them to do, don't just tell them to not do it, if you're doing it, be an example, lead by the example." For those parents who think that rebellion is probably inevitable, they at least try to take solace in the hope that, having hopefully raised kids well, the rebellion will not be too protracted and destructive. "We raise them up in a way they're not gonna go wrong for so long," reported a Muslim father from Indiana. "Even if they go wrong, they're not gonna stay there forever, they will come out of it. But again you don't want to push too much." Always avoid pushing and forcing.

These demand that parents carefully navigate the narrow, difficult straights between lax and overbearing parenting.

Given all they believed about children and parenting described above, most parents see the strait between being too slack and too strict as tight and tough to navigate. A Hispanic Catholic father from Indiana explained the dilemma: "If I was authoritarian and told 'em, military style, they'd rebel against that. And if it was all lovey-dovey and trying to convince them to do things, they'd eventually rebel against that." A Muslim father from Chicago explained the difficulty this way: "My practical side says you should give them the option to choose for themselves, that they become who they are and not be influenced by anything. But my other side says I should have a strong say. This is my struggle." A Jewish mother from New York City said, "It's hard when you're bringing up your kids 'cause I want them to know it's important to me, but I don't want to like push it down their throats in any way." And a black Protestant mother from Houston described this way the difficulties parents have in not wanting to hurt their own children: "When parents make kids go to church all the time when young, they get older and have kids and tell theyself, 'I ain't gonna make my kids go,' and that's really crippling them. But [claps hands and pauses] who am I to tell you that you crippling them? But you are crippling them—so that's our problem, parents want to be their kids' friend, but they not your friend." The tension between granting independence and still protecting children can wear on parents, as with this Hindu mother from central New Jersey:

> I feel sometimes I'm a broken record repeating myself, like "study hard, study hard, do this, do that," and sometimes I wonder if the message is registering. When I was growing up I didn't know anything, but she knows more about cell phone apps and technology, and that worries me because kids get lazy and I want her to strive for the best. I also worry about the kind of friends and influences she is going to have outside of me. But you know I have to let her grow up and be independent, but a part of me wants to shelter her for as long as I can.

The most common strategy for addressing these dilemmas is to attempt a delicate balance. The Hispanic Catholic father above ended up concluding that, "it's got to be a combination" of authoritarian and lovey-dovey. A mainline Protestant from New York City told us: "I have a friend who is a really good parent. She gives her kids a lot of freedom and lets them be independent but she's also very strict about some things, so it's a good balance between freedom and structure. A bad parent would be someone who doesn't give their kid any attention, just uninvolved. A good parent is involved but not controlling, involved but letting them have their independence." This black Protestant father from Houston commended a mix of free choice and monitoring: "My grandparents were the rock that set the path of religion what we should follow. I don't force religion on my children, they have the right to choose which one that they want to participate in. But I do go back and check and make sure they're on the right track as far as their belief and growth, I'm very much concerned about that." Some parents, such as this white Catholic father from Indiana, intentionally try to govern their children's behavior without letting them realize: "It's a question of how to maintain control over them without [them feeling that control]. We don't want our girls to feel like we're controlling them, but we want to maintain control." Similarly, a Mormon father from Indiana explained, "We're very careful about taking away certain agencies. While we like setting boundaries, we still do all we can to make it their first choice, though sometimes it's not, no matter how pretty you paint the picture."

In navigating these difficult waters, parents talk about how they want religion to be their children's own free choice in the end. But for some, acceptable outside parameters also emerge beyond which children should not go. A conservative Protestant mother from Florida, for example, strongly affirms choice and eschews force, but also expects her kids' final choice to be some denomination of Christianity: "Definitely expose children to religion and then let them choose. I never would force religion on them at all. If they went to church for eighteen years I definitely would want it to be their decision, not forced. Coming to church, that's what our family does, but if it's not them it's not gonna work, it's not real. I wouldn't expose them to other religions now, like, why don't you try Buddhism. I would definitely offer what we [Christians] have to offer and if it's not found in this church, fine. They know what we believe as far as Jesus, and I would like it to be that." Other parents seem to knock themselves out to balance the potential legitimacy of every point of view, even while wanting to respect and affirm their own religion's traditional teachings. One white Catholic mother from Indiana, for instance—who views moral convictions as "opinions" and potential parental influencing as "unfair"—described how she related to her daughter after a church youth group discussion on the topic of abortion: "I want to play the neutral role because I want her to formulate her own opinions. I wanted her to see the Church's side of things and to see the majority of society's view. But I didn't want her to be swayed by my personal opinion, I don't think it's fair. She's at the age to form her own opinions and it's not fair for people to persuade somebody one way or the other. I think that's where the Church may go astray sometimes, they try to push their opinion so much. Still, I had to be careful because I didn't want her to blatantly go against the faith, because we believe in it."

A variety of forces impinge on parents as they try to steer the course between too strict and too slack. One is the baggage of their own experience growing up under their own parents, especially when two parents in a couple differ on the matter. The conflict this can generate is described by one Mormon mother from Indiana: "I think that for now when they're in our household, under age eighteen, they should abide by our rules, our beliefs, and when they're older, they can make their own decision. My husband doesn't believe that, since his father forced religion on him, he's very anti, that you don't force anybody to do anything. That's where we clash the most." Similarly, this Jewish mother from New York City told us:

> My husband doesn't want to force our kids to do anything 'cause he feels so like he was always forced to do this stuff. People of our generation feel like we were forced to go to Hebrew School, and he doesn't want them to feel that way. It's hard, because I'll start breaking out in some Shabbat song, if we have friends over and he will be like "We don't usually sing Shabbat Shalom." I'm like "Whatever! We can sing 'Shabbat Shalom!' it's freakin' Shabbat!"

Another pressure parents feel as they try to steer between being lax and overbearing are differences in their own certainties of conviction about religion itself. Some, such as this Muslim mother from Indiana who believes that Islam really is the truth, find it difficult, while wanting their children to be free to choose anything, to grant them the full space to do so: "It's very important that my girls share my Islamic faith and practices, because I feel strongly it is the right way. By praising and loving God you love the people and life around you, and you're good to everyone, so that is very important to me. Other than that, they don't have to think like me. I don't want them to think like me in religion, I want them to understand and choose that for themselves. Because as strong as I feel it, I would love for that to be their choice, 'cause I really feel that is the only way."

Others, however, such as this Jewish father from Indiana, hesitate to be too strong with their children in part because of their own uncertainties: "I wanna give them the resources they need, to let them know I'm there and I'll talk to them. But not force it on them, because I don't see the point in laying down the law about anything, because I don't even know what it [the final truth] is, outside of the context of a particular relationship." And then other parents like this Mainline Protestant mother, who simply want their children to be religiously happy and satisfied, seem to fear that being too overbearing might make them personally responsible for their kids eventually ending up becoming nonreligious, a guilt they do not want: "I don't want to force anything on them. I would feel hypocritical saying you have to be this or that, though I hope they find something that fulfills and satisfies them. And if that turns into nothing [religious] I don't want it to be because I restricted them or prevented them or didn't provide the religious opportunity for them, I want to give them access and let them make their own decision."

In the end, while the underlying tensions and dilemmas faced are the same, some parents seem to feel more satisfied than others with the balances they strike in raising their children. A white Catholic father from Indiana, for instance, reported, "I can't tell her what to do. There are some things she's gonna have to do. But I'm trying to give her space and not be overbearing, and more than anything just telling her to enjoy life." A Muslim mother from Indiana said, "I want them to have that underlying understanding that God is there. I want them to come to that realization on their own, and they need a little experience and age for that, but if the foundation is there I feel like it'll come." Other parents, however, such as this Mormon mother from Indiana, feel much less confident about their parental balancing act: "I encourage them to develop their own relationships with God, but I'm not sure I do enough. I like to be the boss and in charge, but I also didn't like other people telling me what to do as a kid. I know parents that make chore charts, 'Did you clear your dishes? Did you make your bed?' and also, 'Did you say your prayers? Did you read your scriptures?' I'm not comfortable with that. I think somebody's relationship with God is so personal that having it regimented by an outside authority is not helpful. But I also realize regular practice of prayer on your own is very important, and so I'm not sure how to encourage my children to pray without requiring them. This is an area I feel like I'm falling short. I'm still working on it."

Either way, life moves inexorably forward and parents continue with more or less angst and success to wrestle with the challenges of their job.

Excursus: A Distinctive Black Protestant
View of Parental Authority?

The black Protestant parents we interviewed struck a chord that was notably different from other American religious parents on the question of parental (and divine) authority. We think it is worth noting here, though with great caution. Our sample of black Protestant parents is very far from being nationally representative (we interviewed thirty black Protestant parents from three churches in Houston), so we offer this descriptive observation as highly tentative and needing more research to disconfirm or validate. However, our observation does seem consistent with prior research about a distinctive style of parenting authority among black Americans.[2] We observed from our interviews that, while most parents in every other religious tradition tread lightly when it comes to their parental authority to teach, command, and discipline their children, many of the black Protestant parents we spoke with clearly felt authorized and responsible to do that with greater authority. This contrast is not absolute—sometimes the discourse is similar across traditions—but a difference was still evident. One example of this stronger approach was expressed by one black Protestant father from Houston: "When they get older, their ass still better be going to Sunday road that we taught them the way to go [laughing]. We instill this in their life, and they're like, 'that's what daddy and momma did, and it seemed right.' Ain't no *seemed*, it *was* right!" Consider too these statements repeated from the quotes above, which seem characteristic of the view of the black Protestant parents we interviewed and yet rarely heard among parents in other religious traditions:

- God say it's your duty to get your child on the straight path, you don't let him make the decision for hisself.
- I'd be like, "Baby, where'd you get that from? That's not how you were brought up, not how your grandma raised baby, I be like no, we do church here."
- Every parent should train their child up in the church, that it be mandatory they go to Sunday school and Bible study.
- They know "daddy said this" and "momma said that," and it might be right, "oh yeah it is right."

2. See, for example, Christopher Ellison and Darren Sherkat, "The 'Semi-Involuntary Institution' Revisited: Regional Variations in Church Participation among Black Americans," *Social Forces* 73 (1995): 1415–37; Christopher Ellison and Darren Sherkat, "Identifying the 'Semi-Involuntary Institution': A Clarification," *Social Forces* 78 (1999): 793–802.

- Since he can't take care of hisself, then he do what [tapping table] *I say do.*
- Just listen to us parents, we ain't gonna lead you wrong or down a wrong path.
- I'd say, "I don't know where you're coming from, I'm gonna have to get on that cane and we gonna get you to some church."
- Today you have to drive home the model of Christianity.
- Religion is something that you just don't go astray.
- If it was something I didn't agree with or knew that they wouldn't be raised right or healthy, I would say something.
- I'm more afraid of disappointing God than anything.
- Be helpful to your parents.
- Some things you can change, but religion shouldn't be changed.
- My house, my rules, you're coming with me. You can decide to do whatever you want when you start paying your own bills, that's how my mom did it, that's how I'm gonna do it.

Note that this list of fourteen interview quotes does not represent the repeated views of only a few parents but come from fourteen different parent interviews. (This difference in tone was also clear to us in the nearly one thousand interviews we conducted with adolescents and emerging adults in our previous research in the National Study of Youth and Religion, during 2002–13, although the point went unremarked in publications from that study.) Needless to say, as sociologists we simply describe observed differences as our data allow, making no value judgments about them, as to whether this suggested distinctive black Protestant view of parenting is better or more problematic than the dominant view.

To underscore and further illustrate this point, consider one more epitomizing black Protestant quote: "I hope he stays firm believing in God and not straying from that. If he started believing the total opposite, doing bad things, I would have to put a firm foot down. And if he stops going to church or being the person he was taught to be, I would be concerned." In this view, children are not cultivated so they can freely decide for themselves. They are by their elders "taught to be" a specific kind of person. Their "stopping going to church" would mean doing the "total opposite" of their raising, a point of real concern. And the proper parental response to such "doing bad things" is not to respect their autonomy, to carefully raise a concern in a well-timed conversation, to simply pray and wait. The proper response is for the parent "to put a firm foot down." To be sure, some black Protestant parents quoted above did emphasize their children's freedom as adults to choose for themselves, the tendency to go astray from church, and the need to wait patiently for their return. Still, for many others, their assumptions about parental responsibility, authorization, and expectations simply sounded quite different from the dominant approach expressed by parents in other religious traditions.

This observation, if validated by additional research, also highlights a larger theoretical point. We think this black Protestant accent on both parental and divine authority is not coincidental but cognitively logical, the two mirroring each other. The God of many American black Protestants is loving and comforting, yes, but also holds high and unbending expectations for behavior. God in the minds of many black Protestants is very much a strict parent who lays down the law, is not messing around, makes demands, can harshly chide, and holds his children accountable. Likewise, the image of good parents in the minds of many black Protestants is of one who is divinely authorized and supremely responsible to teach and direct children, speak their minds clearly, demand conformity to certain behaviors, and to call children to account when they stray. The God of many black Protestants also seems to present a palpable reality distinctive of that tradition, as expressed, for example, by this black Protestant father from Houston: "Every religious experience I've been through and am going through now, I want them to go through the same thing, because that's gonna let them know that he [God] real. Oh, he real, he real. He's so real you can touch him, if you wanna touch him, you can touch him, but you gotta believe that you can touch him." Likewise, the presence and authority of black Protestant parents in their own view of parenting is very real too. The images of God and parent here are homologous. The nature of the divine and the relations between God and his children on earth are transposed to those of parents and their children in family households—or perhaps the other way around (the causal ordering is impossible to determine historically or developmentally). The theological image of God shapes the sociology of human roles and relations (or vice versa, or both)—a point argued more generally by the classical sociological theorist, Émile Durkheim.

By contrast, one listens in vain to hear parents in other religious traditions speaking of God and parenthood the way black Protestants do. "I would have to put a firm foot down" is a phrase simply not heard from the mouths of any other kind of Protestant parent, including white evangelical parents, or Catholic, Mormon, Jewish, Muslim, Hindu, or Buddhist parents. They tend to talk instead about "creating contexts for learning," "building kids' confidence," "looking for opportune moments to make a

'God point,'" "helping children become their authentic best selves," and in the end "allowing kids to be free to do whatever will make them happy." Whether our observation is generally true beyond our limited sample and what exactly may account for it, if so, only more research with much larger samples comparing across races and social classes could determine. But the empirical difference and the theoretical point it suggests seem to us worth noting and deserving of further research. Again, to be clear, as sociologists we attach no value judgments about these suggested observed differences in parenting cultures, whether positive or negative. Our only purpose is to accurately describe and attempt to explain.

The Priority of Family Solidarity

Returning to our main cultural models, conversations with religious parents about passing on religion to children brought to the surface a distinct cultural model with its own beliefs and associated feelings about the importance of family solidarity. This outlook is related to the cultural models of the nature of children and the task of parenting described above, but not reducible to them. We need to grasp this distinctive web of beliefs (and related emotions) in order adequately to understand how parents think about the intergenerational transmission of religious faith and its relative priority among the demands of family life. It sounds like this:

> *The Importance of Family Solidarity*: Parents desire to have warm, close relationships with and among their grown children in the future (harmony while children live at home is not necessarily to be expected). Major differences or divisive conflict with or alienation from or between adult children would be deeply saddening. Anything parents can do in the present to foster a family cohesion that will continue into the empty-nest decades—such as fostering common recreational interests like sports, political views, and basic life values—is therefore important, including working to pass on the family religion. Families that agree on the same religious beliefs, practices, and ways of talking enjoy a particularly strong basis of harmony and cohesion, because shared religion is a potent source of family solidarity. However, if religion ever gets in the way of other activities that also build family solidarity (such as league sports), then religion may have to give way, for the very same reasons. Shared religion can also be set aside in specific cases by the higher-priority imperative of family solidarity. Furthermore, if a child

eventually marries someone of a different religion, that would not be ideal but also not a serious problem, as long as they shared the same "basic values" of the family.

Parents desire to have warm, close relationships with and among their grown children in the future (harmony while children live at home is not necessarily to be expected). Major differences or divisive conflict with or alienation from or between adult children would be deeply saddening.

This sentiment is common across the parents we interviewed. Its ubiquity and power are best apprehended simply by listening to parents talking around it. One mainline Protestant father from Indiana, for instance, reported happily: "We're very close and I think as time goes on we get even closer as a family." A New York City mother from the same tradition smiled when she told us, "We're friendly now, which is almost a problem. We'll be hanging out, talking, and I'll be, 'Okay, we have to go do this now,' and they're like, 'But we're just hanging out!'" One conservative Protestant mother from Florida told us, "I don't want them to ever not be in my life, never want that to be a block, so if it's something I don't agree with, I'm still gonna be their mom, actively involved, and just pray they eventually do that right thing. As long as we're still all loving each other, I don't ever want to not be in their life, so I hope nothing ever happens for that to happen." Another from the same tradition living in Los Angeles said, "If he believed differently than us, I would talk to him, continue to be his mother, love him and continue to pray for him. But that would crush me, that would suck." "I hope they always love each other, be there for one another," said a black Protestant mother from Houston, "and always love their parents [laughs], and know we're always in their corner, their number one fans." This father from the same tradition and city said, "I hope God keeps me close to my grandkids so I can direct them in the right direction, even if the parents didn't, then grandpa and grandma would do it."

White Catholic parents talked the same way. This mother from New York City told us, "I would love to if possible live close to some of my kids, and to see them on Sundays would be beautiful, at church, would be beautiful. Like the extended families you see at church, it's kind of amazing, the old-school Italians or Irish who've been in the neighborhood for one hundred years, multigenerational, there's something very beautiful about it." And this father from the same city said, "I really want them to be good friends, the two of them. It's important because I benefit from that too. I want my sons to be best friends when they grow up." Ditto with Hispanic Catholic parents, as with this mother from New Mexico: "When they are going to do something, they always ask for support. We have always said we are there to support them in whatever decision they take, we are there. We are like a friend, more as a friend." And this newly empty-nester Hispanic Catholic father from New York City said, "Now that they are all adults, we're friends. That's what I like. We talk." One Mormon mother from Indiana described her ideal future daughter-in-law as fitting well into her family: "I want them to have families of their own, because that's where my biggest joy is, my family. I want them to be good in their communities, in their families, good neighbors, problem solvers, and be self-sufficient. And I want them to find the perfect spouse they'll enjoy, and who'll be fun and fit in our family, I hope I like her." And this Jewish father from Indiana said, "You hope as a parent that your children are close to their siblings whether or not you're around to see it."

The enthusiasm of some parents anticipating warm family relations in the future was palpable, as with this Muslim father from New York City: "I hope we maintain that close relationship. I always tell my wife, 'I can't wait until the kids get older,' and at the end of Ramadan they'll all be over at our house, kids and grandkids. That's my hope and dream. I hope my business does so well that I can pass it on to them. My dad never gave me a dime, and I want to do the opposite with my kids, like, 'Here's fifty-thousand dollars each, go put a down payment on a house.'" A Hindu father from Chicago said, "I would like them to be nearby, if possible. One of my goals is I retire and make enough money that even if they move away I am able to follow them." A non-theist Buddhist mother from Chicago echoed these themes: "I'm so selfish, the first thing I'm going to say is I want to be near them. I'm gonna move and follow them to the ends of the earth." This Indian immigrant, Hindu mother from New York City explained, "In Western society when a child moves out, he's independent, we rejoice and say wow, we did something right, we have launched him, the child is independent from us. But in India we think, whoa, what did we do wrong? Why did she move away? Ideally, my child would be close by somewhere, with her spouse. If she moves far away that means I have driven her away." The home country theme—important among many immigrant parents—is repeated by this Buddhist father from Chicago: "In Thai communities, kids are very close to their parents. Here if you're married and your parents want to visit you, they got to make an appointment. But in Thailand it's just in the morning bring the dog, bring some rice. So I want them to be like that too, that I'm your dad, she's your mom, we want to visit you, we sacrificed so many things for you, you know? Family is first is an Asian thing that stands." And a Chicagoan Buddhist mother from a different family said likewise, "I will be the first to admit my fear when it comes to my son, that he'll find a wife and forget about us [laughs]. I'm like, 'my family comes first, I'm sorry.' Our family comes first, I'm like I don't care who you date, or who you marry, just remember that we still come first." Another Buddhist mother from Chicago told us, "My son, if I'm lucky I want him to marry an Asian woman, that is good for him. But my daughter, I don't care. Maybe I want the daughter-in-law to look like me and be easy to get along."

Most of the above is stated positively. But the same beliefs and interests emerge in negative form when parents ponder facing potential basic differences, especially but not only about religion, between them and their grown children. "If my kids converted to another religion," a conservative Protestant mother from Indiana told us, "that would make me sad, that would create distance between us in some way. Of course, I would always love them and be in their lives, but there would be a point where we didn't connect anymore, yeah. There would be some loss there." A Floridian father from the same tradition confessed, "If he grew up to live very differently from me, it depends on the lifestyle, but I would be very disappointed, I'll be honest with you, I could be very disappointed. Like if my son grew up to be a homosexual, as backwoods redneck as that sounds, that's what I am, I can't help it, that's how I was born and raised, I would be very crushed about that. I don't think he will, but I'm just saying it really would affect me severely, if that happened, I don't know, a lot of prayers, I don't know." Likewise, a black Protestant mother from Houston told us, "If they grew up really different on religion or sexual orientation or politics, I'd be very heartbroken, it'd a be a stronghold letting myself know that I let myself down, that I didn't teach them well."

Continuing, a white Catholic mother from Chicago said, "You always hope they'll grow up to be somewhat similar to you and your values. I guess if they are extremely different I'll try and be as accepting and loving as I can, I certainly wouldn't ever disown them if they became, you know, a radical Republican or something [laughs]. I mean they're still my kid, I'm still going to love them, maybe there'd just be some topics we wouldn't discuss." Hispanic Catholic parents recurrently used the word "sad" to describe how a loss of shared views with adult children would make them feel. "If my girls took another path in life very different than mine," one mother from New Mexico reported, "it would give me great sadness, to make a decision different from our way of thinking, living, culture or religion. I'd be very sad." A father from the same state said, "If my grandchildren were not religious, the truth is for me it would be a great sadness. When we pray as a family, we pray for our children and for future generations, that the legacy of our faith is maintained. And it is very difficult, especially in this society, but that's where we have to have faith, pray, and above all teach our children that they do the same with their children." Mormon parents have a particular theological reason to feel sad about possibly losing their adult children, since they believe that faithful families will live together in heaven, as noted by this Mormon mother from Indiana:

> It would be harder for me if my kids left the church. I would feel like it was a judgment on me as a mother that I had failed in some way. I know people think Mormons are crazy, so I have thought about the kids leaving. I would be sad and I would tell them I was sad. But I would not let it become acrimonious because obviously I'd hope they would come back. And they're certainly not gonna come back if I'm yelling at them. But I would immediately find common ground that we could say, "But we still have these things in common." I hope that would be helpful. I would be sad because we believe in eternal families, but that being together as a family in heaven is dependent on each individual person's choices. So if you make a choice to leave the faith, then you're not gonna be right there with us. Here on earth we can still be together as much as we want regardless of church. It's the eternities that we wouldn't be together.

Likewise, this Muslim father from Chicago echoed the themes of failure and self-judgment: "If they grew up and said they didn't want to be Muslim anymore? Oh I'd be mad. I would be mad. I wouldn't stop loving them, but I would find it disappointing. Like maybe I failed in doing something. At the end of the day you can't control what anybody else does, when they're older. They'll do whatever they want. Even between me and my parents, I'm less [religiously] practicing than they are, it's just generally gonna happen. But if they told me I don't want to be Muslim anymore, I'd feel like a failure, like we did something horribly bad." And a Hindu father from central New Jersey told us, "If our kids grew up and lived very differently than us, it is scary 'cause it can happen, yeah, definitely. But there's nothing you can do."

Anything parents can do in the present to foster a family cohesion that will continue into the empty-nest decades—such as fostering common recreational interests like sports, political views, and basic life values—is therefore important, including working to pass on the family religion. Families that agree on the same religious beliefs, practices, and ways of talking enjoy a particularly strong basis of harmony and cohesion, because shared religion is a potent source of family solidarity.

Religious parents in the United States do many things to foster family solidarity, most of which are not religious. For instance, this white Catholic father from Indiana told us, "Most of our extracurricular activities are just about being together, whether it's sports, playing a video game together, a board game, or going to the park. Doing stuff like that, we're fixated on just trying to be a strong family and spend time together." A Buddhist mother from Chicago reported: "I dropped a day from my work schedule so I could be at home more with the kids. Drive them around, I feel like a chauffeur, driving them from one class to another to another. It's great. I don't have him go to preschool all week, just because I actually feel it's more important for him to have me and for me to have that bond with him. I had so much time with my daughter before he came along, he didn't ever really have alone time, just mommy or daddy time." And a Muslim father from New York City said this: "She's not a great athlete but she's started playing soccer. I coached her soccer team, I'm very involved in sports with my kids, and her interest in art. And right now my relationship with her, we're like buddies. She views me as the cool guy. She likes me because we do things together, go to the soccer game, basketball game, we've done all these things. Maybe this is subconscious 'cause I never did that stuff with my father, he never took me to sports, to him it was all about working, bringing in money. So I do all these cool things with my kids, vacations and all."

Sharing religion, however, also emerged as a major part of most parents' strategies for building and sustaining family solidarity. That is partly because our interviews focused on religion, and so our questions primed parents for that emphasis. But it is also partly because many religious parents view religion as a uniquely powerful family bonding agent. A Jewish mother from New York City, for example, related this: "I try to show my kids the joy and love of being Jewish, and creating a routine, being part of the larger Jewish community, and doing a lot of rituals that, even if right now don't feel touchy-feely, still gives us family experiences together and memories. It's not strict or about heaven and hell or doing the right thing, but just showing them that, with structure we're creating something, and doing it year in, year out, celebrating a holiday and creating memories, you're gonna appreciate that later on. But if they left Judaism, I'd say you're still invited to the table. It would sadden me a lot but I would be okay with it, I'm sure one of them will, just because odds, right? But I would hope while I'm alive they come to our house for holidays.

That's really it." And a Jewish father from the same city said, "We have a place upstate, a bungalow summer community where we have a little house we envision as a place where the kids and grandkids can come back to. I would be surprised if they raised children where Judaism isn't at least on their consciousness. It's natural and we will continue to live it and be part of who we are and what we talk about." The particular concerns of passing on a religion much based on a sense of "peoplehood" shows up especially among parents of adopted children, as voiced by this mother of an adopted toddler from overseas: "I think I'll be heartbroken if at some point [she rejects Judaism]. I have a cousin who's adopted and when she became an adult she said, 'Look I'm not Jewish,' and I think I'd be very sad if that happens. I'm trying not to be too attached to it, but that's the only way I know how to raise her is Jewish."

A Mormon mother from Indiana told us, "It's important our boys share our beliefs. Both our parents are LDS, so our religion is an all-day, every-day experience, not just what we do on Sundays, it's our lifestyle. My one daughter who is not choosing Mormonism right now, we don't have as much in common, we see her less, and it's not our choice, just the way our paths have gone, so religion is part of what unites us." Another Mormon mother from the same area explained: "My expectation would be that they marry a Mormon. And if they don't, that is something else I will come to peace with, I would not allow it to become a wedge that ruins our relationship. Grandchildren raised a different religion would bother me, it's kind of hard to imagine that, I hope to have a close relationship with my grandchildren."

Religion as family glue seems to be an especially strong view among the Catholic parents we interviewed. Consider, for instance, the statements of these white Catholics from Indiana, two fathers and a mother, respectively:

We try to have a strong family backbone, try to be on a good schedule where we go to church regularly and the kids feel like it's their church. I like tradition, so I would love for them to be able to have that one church they've always belonged to for their life. Having a good family base and then creating good habits, so as the kids get older they hopefully will continue those habits, just 'cause they're used to it.

Religion's a part of the values we believe in and follow, it's really at the core of who we are as a family. Sometimes I hear about one spouse is very religious and does everything and the other doesn't have anything to do with it. But whatever we do, we do together, so it's part of the core of what makes our marriage work. We believe strongly in the commandments and raising our children with those beliefs. We discussed that when we got married.

I would love for us to all go to church together. It's hard when my [Protestant] mom has come to the kids' confirmations, she doesn't know when to kneel or stand, she's a great sport, but there's always that little bit [of difference] there. So sure, I would love for my whole family to all be together [religiously]. And I think we will, I really do. But I want to guide them hopefully into that direction, but not force them into it.

Similarly, this Hispanic Catholic mother from New York City explained: "It would be nice if they continued being Catholic, because it would be part of the good communication we have. When another belief exists, I'm no longer living it firsthand. If my father was Catholic like me, we could communicate better on certain topics. But since he's another belief, there's no way. So I think that it would be important they continue being Catholic. I hope to God they do continue, it's something that's fundamental."

Protestants said the same. "It is very important for them to have their religious background," a black Protestant father from Houston said, "because that's part of our roots. Some things you can grow up and change, but religion, I don't think it should be changed because it is a very important part of our life." One conservative Protestant father from New York City said, "A family that has the same faith base can work through their struggles. There's always going to be struggles, but if they keep God as the center of their life, everything else will emit from that. My first marriage wasn't that, it was very much the opposite, and the trouble that I went through, it was destabilized, you need to share faith as a very basic life principle or the foundation is not there." And this mainline Protestant mother from Indiana confessed, "If one of my kids didn't believe in God [pause], it would be an absolute rejection of the way the world turns, an absolute rejection of life for us. I want to know that at the end of this journey, we're still all going to be together." Similarly, one Buddhist father from Chicago said, "Our kids know we are Buddhist. And one of the values of religion, and I'm not talking about what religion is good or bad, just saying I can see the family has a value, kind of the bond." And a Hindu mother from Chicago said, "To see a kid growing is a religion in itself, you don't need any books or anything if you are dedicated to the kids, the way they think, completely spending the time with them. It takes courage because it's a very risky business because you invest your time and don't know what happens with them. Anything can happen."

However, if religion ever gets in the way of other activities that also build family solidarity (such as little league sports), then religion may have to give way, for the very same reasons. Shared religion can also be set aside in specific cases by the higher-priority imperative of family solidarity.

Consider the words of this conservative Protestant father from New York City, who is not a religious slouch, but a serious Christian: "In my upbringing it was ingrained in me Sunday is for church. But I've tried to be lenient, recognizing when issues come up that keep us from going. I'm not gonna be the one to bring the hammer down and say 'no, we're going, you're gonna give up everything and we're going to church.' One of the things I promised myself as a dad was to not limit my kids from doing all the things they like doing just because I want them to go to church. I didn't want faith to get in the way of them enjoying life, but to be a part of their life." Likewise, this black Protestant father explained: "Our biggest thing as a family that's brought us closer is all of 'em playing basketball. My wife, she's really into that, she really likes the traveling, the tournaments, the excitement, meeting people, bonding with other parents. Recently we went to a tournament, we all ended up going for like a mini vacation, it was a lot of fun, it brought us closer, we enjoy the games together. And shopping, going to the mall, Wal-Mart. I think [those are] the two biggest things. Of course we love fellowshipping, just going to church, but out-side of that, the basketball games and restaurants." A mainline Protestant mother from Washington, DC, related, "Hockey and practice and games are on Sunday mornings, so I've just let it [church attendance] go the past few years, it's a phase we're in, I just tell myself this is a phase, it's okay, we go for Christmas and Easter. We do go every once in a blue moon, and she acolytes and I'll take her and I go when I can, sometimes just me. But the last time all of us went to church, my son just sat there like he was on death row, just sat there." For his part, the father in the same family said, "We've been pretty weak with confirmation class at church lately. Hockey practice is 6:30 in the morning on weekends, so by the time he's done he is exhausted and you have to drive an hour to games, so he gets a big pass [on church] in the winter."

Catholics are the same. One Hispanic Catholic father from New York City explained, "They are busy with other things and sometimes it calls us in the social field to do other things, sometimes we miss Mass for a social event, but I do not think that at heart they are rejecting it." A Hispanic Catholic mother from New Mexico said, "We always try for both of us to be at church on the weekends. And when there is a game for our boy, regularly it is me who goes to church, and he goes to our boy's game. We agree on it." The white Catholic father from Indiana who said above that Catholicism is the core of his family and marriage said this elsewhere in his interview: "We try to keep track of scheduling so we don't overwhelm them, because we want to balance our home life, school, religious life, and whatever else. But we've seen it take the hit this time of year when our religious life always gets really crunched down to almost nothing." A white Catholic mother from the same state observed, "Religion's always been a part of our life. But I know a month goes by where we've had soccer tournaments or swim meets away [and miss church], we do need to wrangle ourselves back into church." Likewise, this white Catholic mother from Indiana observed that, "My husband and I, we keep ourselves very healthy. We're both cyclists so we cycle together and I'm a runner. So we try very hard to teach our kids to stay healthy and to eat right, have fun and play hard. I have to say we have done a very good job of teaching our kids to be healthy, but I can't say that we've been as good at keeping our faith healthy because of our constraints, because of our busy schedules. There are days where I say 'Gosh, maybe we shouldn't do this' because we're always seeming to fit something in and it's a little crazy." Some parents, such as this white Catholic father from Indiana, feel uncomfortable missing church: "Growing up, you're used to church on weekends, that's what you did, it's all you know. But we go through spells when, this is so bad, but sports take over weekends, that just comes up and we do that. We have the friends who after sporting events, they always go to the 5:30 Mass. But we don't always make those last-chance Masses, and I feel bad about it, 'cause my gosh here I am trying to teach my kids this, and it's not actually a priority." Another white Catholic father from the same state explained how demanding his daughter's sports routine is: "She's been playing travel volleyball for two years, and travel softball for five years, so for the last two years she's been doing both. It is so busy and hard, 'cause she does travel softball and travel volleyball and we're gone every weekend, get up early, first of all, she plays Saturday and Sunday from 6:00 a.m. to 11:00 p.m. at night and we're driving and driving." As an adult convert, he says, "I now find it very appealing, the whole Mass, prayers, the whole liturgy, all of that is very appealing to me," but he also says he really only likes going to his home church, so does not attend when on the road. "I'd have to find a Catholic church somewhere and go to a different Mass, and I'm not comfortable at that Mass because it's different, you're used to your home, different priests and different church." And when he is home on Sundays, "it's been really difficult, sometimes when we have a weekend off we sleep all weekend. That's even worse, 'cause then we don't have any excuse." And when his wife asks if they went to Mass, "we're like, oh my gosh." According to this father, his daughter actually wishes they attended church more. "I think she wants to go to church more, and that's my fault as a parent that we just are so busy. We drive past the church all the time and she says in passing, 'I miss going to church.'" But, he says, "sometimes when we'd be done with a tournament and it's just during like the middle of Mass, she'll be too sweaty and dirty." He concludes, "She gets a lot out of Mass she really does. So it was my Lenten Promise to go to church more frequently, which we did, and she was so excited about that."

Parents in other religious traditions wrestle with the same issues. A Jewish father from New York City told us:

> We're gonna run into trouble because there are games on Friday nights and afternoons, when the Sabbath begins early in the winter. Maybe if they don't have to travel, she can do it. If it's an away game, we have to figure it out. Maybe I'll say "Okay, you can travel as long as you're home for Shabbat dinner." It's been interesting watching myself go pretty far out of my comfort zone to try to make things work for her. But I feel like it's been working. And I feel like she appreciates that, it's made us closer. I mean we're very close, very connected. But I don't know where I would draw the line on Shabbat.

And this Mormon mother from Indiana explained:

> All our kids resist church activities, even me sometimes. We used to say you're only giving 3 hours out of 168 hours in a week. But the girls hate it, and now that they're older they do sports or something, so we miss. That used to be hard because of judgment from other people over your kids missing church because of sports. But I said, "Life's different now, you have a [diverse] population, you can't just expect people not to play on Sunday because you're religious. Some people, Jews don't wanna do sports on Saturday and why are we better than them?" Life's changed. There's certain things you're gonna have to do different or you're not going to be able to do them at all.

Religious practice does have an opportunity cost. Similarly, this Hindu mother from central New Jersey spoke of how her daughter's involvement in "many different activities" prevents them from much involvement in the local temple: "One mile away from my house they're building this temple, the third largest Hindu monument in the world. People always say 'oh I should join,' but I don't want to commit to anything because my priority is my daughter and she keeps me very busy, because she's involved in many different kinds of activities. So for now I don't want to be involved in anything other than just praying and visiting."

Clearly, then, religion, no matter how important parents consider it, is often not as important as other priorities, especially sports—even among many parents in more "strict" traditions, such as Mormonism and conservative Protestantism. When they believe religion will help their kids and family, most parents will push it to some extent. But when religion itself threatens to disrupt internal family peace and unity, religion often gives way. To this rule we encountered rare exceptions, such as a Chicagoan Muslim family whose children fast despite playing sports: "My kids fast. Even being on the school soccer team, even though it's hot, they have to play, but they still fast." But most parents adhere to the standard rule. For instance, this Muslim mother from Indiana hesitates to push important religious instruction in the name of "not pressuring" her children: "I always encourage my kids to read more Arabic, to go back and learn [to read the Quran in Arabic], but they're satisfied with what they got. I always tell them maybe you're gonna regret it when you have kids but there's only so much you can do. I wish there was better Arabic school in the mosque, but it's gonna get harder and you don't want to put pressure on the kids too much too." A Jewish father from New York City makes concessions about his scruples over Jewish observances in part in order to avoid conflict with his daughter over texting on the Sabbath, which he "works" to be a happy experience: "I want to make sure she thinks of Shabbat as a time when we have a house filled with friends and laughter, working it so she doesn't experience it as a deprivation. And [pause] I know she texts on Shabbat. And would that be my first choice? No. Is it gonna kill her? No. Is it gonna ruin my or her enjoyment of Shabbat? No. And I've let her know that. We sort of have an agreement, she does it in her room. Her practice doesn't need to be exactly the same as mine. In our joint space, I'd like her not to do anything problematic for me, but what she does in the privacy of her own room, I'll turn a blind eye, don't do it in front of me." And this Buddhist mother also prioritizes her daughter's broad education over practicing religion: "I don't want to be a dictator on religion, I'm not gonna do that. I always teach my kids to be more focused on the education right now, just the education, and not only in school, but like dancing. If you love dancing, like my girl does, I bring her to different dances, because dancing has so many kinds of dance, or get her to experience, like try this, try this, try this, and then she can pick, so focus on education."

Furthermore, if a child eventually marries someone of a different religion, that would not be ideal but also not a serious problem, as long as they shared the same "basic values" of the family.

Nearly all the religious parents we interviewed expressed the identical view here. A mainline Protestant father from New York City said, "If my kids wanted to marry someone who was Jewish, Muslim, Buddhist, I don't think it matters. They should go with the individual who they love. It doesn't matter what that person is, as long as they're a good person." Another mainline Protestant father from the same city said, "With marriage partners and grandchildren, whatever works, as long as it's not harmful to the kids or the partner is imposing something. What are you gonna do? People are gonna be who they are and you can't really [oppose it]." A black Protestant mother from Houston said, "He should marry whoever he wants, that's his decision, because he has to live with them. It shouldn't matter about religion, as long as you believe in God, that's all that matters to me." This white Protestant father from Florida explained, "I would want her to marry somebody that has the same beliefs as she does. So not necessarily Baptist but there are other religions that believe pretty much the same things we do." A white Catholic mother from Indiana answered: "Would I rather they marry a Catholic? Not having done so myself, not necessarily. I'd rather they find someone they love, they're compatible with, share their values and beliefs, and if it's not a Catholic, well, you know. Grandchildren? [Inhaling deeply] I would like them be Catholic, because the way I was raised and how we're raising them, I'd like to see that continue. But would I turn them away if they're not? No, I can't imagine that." And this Hispanic Catholic father from New York City said, "If he marries a person of another religion, it is to be respected. You respect my religion, and I respect yours, put aside what's personal as a couple, and I think it will work, just like in politics. Leave political parties at the door, and enter inside only as a couple, I think it will work." Similarly, a Mormon mother from Indiana explained: "I think it depends on how you are together. Some people don't even care. We know a Mormon who's married to a Jew, and the problem is the kids have to attend both, which I always thought was kinda rough, that's a lot of religion. But as long as they can agree, be tolerant, and help each other, then I don't think it's a big deal." A Jewish mother from New York City said, "In an ideal world, it would be wonderful if they married someone Jewish, to be able to make sure that the culture got kept up. But I would never say that to them. I want them to have partners that will love and cherish them, to find someone who is wise and spiritual and supportive, I think that's very important. It's more important to have somebody who's in sync with your belief systems. So I don't push it, but in my heart of heart, of course I would want them to have Jewish mates." In agreement, a Muslim mother from Indiana told us: "I prefer my kids marry the same religion. But I don't mind if my son married a Christian or Jewish lady, as long as they agree on the same basic belief. But for my daughter, it's forbidden in Islam for a girl to marry non-Muslim, unless he becomes Muslim, because the kids follow the religion of the father. I have to advise her, but if she does not listen to me it's her choice. After she is eighteen, I cannot force her or lock her in and tell her she cannot marry. It's better to go with somebody who has same common thoughts. It doesn't matter if he's American or Pakistani or Indian or Arab or non-Arab as long as he's a good person, and he believes in God, and practices the same belief as her." A Hindu mother from New York City shared the same outlook, making one possible exception on historical and practical grounds: "She doesn't need to marry a Hindu. As long as he treats her right and knows the basic values. She needs to be respected, to have spiritual freedom to practice her own religion. If somebody is willing to do that, fine. I do not think I would be uber excited if she marries a Muslim because of very deep-rooted dislikes between Hindus and Muslims, the years of trauma and abuse that goes both ways, that would be a recipe for disaster. But other than that, whatever, I don't care." And this Buddhist father from Chicago said, "My girl has dated atheists, Christians, but it would be up to her. For us, so long as they treat her nice and are willing to accept us and not come in and try to convert us."

CHAPTER FOUR

The Whys and Hows of Religious Transmission

HERE WE ARRIVE at the substantive heart of what this book is about. What cultural model runs in the background of and helps to guide American religious parents' approach to handing on religious faith and practice to their children?

Why Parents Should Pass on Religion to Their Children

The answer to the question just posed is determined by the content of all of the cultural models examined above, as is clear here:

> *Why Parents Should Pass Religion on to Children*: Parents do good and well to pass on religious faith and practice to their offspring, because religion can help growing children successfully navigate the journey of life in the world that they will soon face. Life's journey can be a difficult one, and parents' primary job is to prepare and provision their children for safety and success on the road. Religion offers particularly valuable help in the forms of guidance, comfort, and rest stops offering rejuvenation and aid along the way. Religion also provides a "home base" or "grounding" that serves, among the vagaries and troubles of life, as a stable reference point by which to navigate life, and a foundation upon which to build a life that need not go ruinously off course or be shaken. When a child's life's journey takes the wrong path, she or he can always "return home" to and through religion, reset themselves, and start again on the right road. Shared religion also glues families

together, which, besides being a desire of parents, is good for growing children. Therefore, parents instilling the right foundation of religion in their children effectively provisions them with crucial life resources that greatly enhance their chances of living good lives as they proceed on their journeys in the world.

Parents do good and well to pass on religious faith and practice to their offspring, because religion can help growing children successfully navigate the journey of life in the world that they will soon face. Life's journey can be a difficult one, and parents' primary job is to prepare and provision their children for safety and success on the road. Religion offers particularly valuable help in the forms of guidance, comfort, and rest stops offering rejuvenation and aid along the way.

"I pray that God shows them, gives them the grace, that they can live a life as a Christian," said a conservative Protestant father from Florida. "That's important. Life is hard even for a Christian as well, it's not an easy life, there are plenty of struggles." A black Protestant mother from Houston explained, "You need something to fall back on, a spiritual being inside, something that's gonna keep you rooted and help you get through your daily journey, 'cause life is not easy. There's challenges and if you don't have something you can fall back on, not just mommy and daddy, but somebody you can take to your prayer closet and pray, you're gonna have a tough time." And this mainline Protestant father from Washington, DC, said, "I hope they will join me in heaven but also that their faith would be part of their success and happiness in life and guide them to make good decisions and have good relationships. They'll live a richer life in a relationship with God, and be able to survive the highs and lows that they're inevitably going to experience when I'm not around, knowing that God is around to love and take care of them. I've always found my faith as a centering aspect of life, as you get distracted or the highs get too high or lows too low, coming back to having the ritual of a weekly church service or the reflection around what's right and wrong, is an important part of life." A mainline Protestant mother from Indiana told this story: "How do you deal with life's difficulties as you age? My father, the last week of his life was horrible, worse than I can imagine, and I'm crushed 'cause he did not deserve that, he was a wonderful, wonderful man. He could hardly speak, but he recited the words of hymns. 'Oh Lord my God, when I in awesome wonder,' trying to recite 'How Great Thou Art.' So he was able to walk the end of his journey drawing on hymns he learned as a child. I want that for my family [gets emotional]. Sorry. I want that for everyone. I want everyone to have the opportunity to have a core, a strength, some inner sense of balance and peace that they can draw upon in life's difficulties." "Kids have no idea how hard life is, it's very hard," a white Catholic father from Indiana told us. "And for me it has been a great comfort imagining this benevolent planner, this intelligent force out there, it's given me a light to follow, I can't imagine life without that, and I wouldn't want them to think they had to live hard somehow, held to some realism, to scientific facts. I would hope they'd be expansive enough in their imagination to imagine this comforting force out there." And this white Catholic mother from the same area said, "Life is difficult, and you need some place to turn to in difficulties. That's what religion provides. You can turn to it and find some comfort, someone to talk to and help you make the right decision, and guide you when you need guiding, to show you the path and keep you [on it] if you're trying to decide which way to go." A Hispanic Catholic mother from New York City related: "I firmly believe having spiritual peace is important in life. Having faith, something to believe in. When you go through difficult times, when someone is spiritually weak, when the serious problems come, many people break, they don't know how to continue on, like the world is falling down around them. Religion helps to level out your life a bit, to give importance to the things that really have importance. Religion helps give you balance. That's the word: to achieve balance in your life. My son, he's a very intelligent boy, but I want him to go to heaven, I want him to achieve everything that he wants in life, but also keep on being a humble person, not brag, and he keeps balance in his life." And this Hispanic Catholic mother from Indiana explained, "My concern is trying to keep my daughter grounded in a Catholic base, making sure she's okay, that she and I will be always in a good place, and to keep everything safe. But at the same time make her aware that life is not what she thinks, as she grows up she will find out more. But always want to make sure she always keeps her religion so that she has a good ground to be a Catholic." Likewise, this black Catholic mother from Indiana predicted: "As they go about their life and run into all kinds of people, they'll be able to carry themselves with the strength of knowing that God is in them. [They can say] 'I don't have to prove anything, God is in me.'"

"Remove religion and we wouldn't be grounded, would have no morals," reported a Mormon mother from Indiana. "It would be chaos, chaotic. Religion is more for a guiding compass, how to help you navigate through life, through different challenges, like a road map." A Jewish mother from New York City admitted, "There's always something to worry about, like, 'are we doing the right thing with the kids? Are they getting what they need?' Not only from a religious standpoint but just, 'what tools do they need to be self-sufficient, happy individuals as adults?'" A Muslim father from Indiana repeated this concern: "I don't know how God's gonna judge me if my grandkids lose religion, I'm responsible as well. I mean, I raised their parents right, so if they don't raise their children right then a curse can go on the father, not on me. I hope not, I hope not me." A Chicagoan Buddhist mother and convert from Catholicism who believes in God explained the importance of passing on religion to children nonetheless in this way: "Religion is a guide, even a philosophy like Buddhism. Kids need some kind of structure early on. It's hard being atheist and trying to explain to a child why they can't steal or beat someone up. We needed something. When I was growing up it was, 'You're gonna go to hell if you do this,' and you didn't do it anymore. It's efficient and effective. Some people need religion or else they would be in prison all the time. I know I came from a pretty bad neighborhood and the only reason some gang members didn't kill people was they believed God was watching them, they'd say 'Madre de Dios' and all make the sign of the cross, that was brakes for them. So I think everything is the parents' responsibility, almost all of it up until kids can take care of themselves. For us, it's Buddhism, not God related stuff, but the morals are there." And a Hindu mother from Chicago told us this: "She will be a teen soon, so I should tell her what is right, what is good. She should know how she should be in the life that is important, we should teach them more. I help cross the stage. I'm not going to go in the wrong way, I know what is good and what is wrong. My husband knows, so we don't need any guidance, but yeah our children needs the guidance."

Religion also provides a "home base" or "grounding" that serves, among the vagaries and troubles of life, as a stable reference point by which to navigate life, and a foundation upon which to build a life that need not go ruinously off course or be shaken.

The metaphors of religion as a "base," a "basis," a "foundation," a "grounding," "guidance," a "rooting," and an "anchor"—which they want for their children—were pervasive in our interviews with parents (recall table 1). The following are only some of the examples of how parents talked in these ways. "I was very aware of myself as a single mom trying to raise this child," reported a Muslim mother from New York City. "I wanted him to have a good religious grounding, given all the frustrations and internal identity crises I'd had growing up. I wanted to give him a strong foundation, so I started him in a Muslim school when he was in pre-K till eighth grade." A Hindu father from central New Jersey said, "At least when she was young she had a foundation in teachings and practices, whatever she chooses to do now, I could care less. But when she was growing up, I needed to give her those foundations." This Buddhist father from Chicago said, "Becoming a parent, religion became more important, partly the whole Hebraic and Christian idea of renewing the world, and some of it was just the concern with her growing up and falling into certain pitfalls if she didn't have any sort of solid foundation or shared belief." A Jewish mother from New York City reported, "All our kids grew up kosher, I don't think any of them are now, it actually doesn't bother me. They know what's what, they're gonna figure it out. What they're doing at twenty may or not be what they do at thirty or forty, but we wanted to give them a foundation, both in the community and in literacy and in practice." That confidence is evident in the words of this Jewish father from the same city: "After our youngest grew to a certain age, I stopped spending a lot of time with the kids collectively and individually. They have enough of a foundation to be able to go from there." And a Mormon mother from Indiana told us, "I want them to be religious, from generation to generation. When they don't have that origin, they're like lost sheep, just wander in the wilderness. Religion is like home, it grounds you."

Catholic parents used the same language. "I trust the process and the plans God has for them," said one white Catholic father from Indiana. "We have tried hard to give them the best foundation for life, because if you have a rock foundation you can weather the storms of life, as long you're anchored in this foundation of faith, and you know you have a purpose in life, and it's your job to keep those communications open with God to be used." A white Catholic mother from the same area reported, "What they do with their religion when they grow and leave home, it's gonna be up to them. But they have had that foundation, we've given it to them, we've tried to live our lives that way. Without religion I don't know that they'd have as much of a base." Another white Catholic mother from Indiana explained: "When they get older and have a family of their own, they'll have a basis to go to, a home base to see what they want to do. They won't be uncertain if they stay in the Catholic Church, they're comfortable and know it, so some of the searching may already be done. Maybe the Catholic Church won't be what they're looking for, but they'll have a basis, an idea. But maybe that is what they'll want. I hope it is, because it's a foundation and they know the Catholic Church is a family to fall back on, it has been for us." Such a sense motivated this white Catholic couple from Indiana to return to regular church attendance after they had babies, as explained by the mother: "When we were first married, we didn't go to church and our family life was not a whole lot different at home than it is now because we both had a religious upbringing. We said, as long as we believe and do what we think God would want, we're okay. But if we wouldn't have [started going to church when we had children], my kids wouldn't have had that same security. What they do with their religion when they grow, leave home, it's gonna be up to them. But they have had that foundation, we've given that to them. [Without that] I don't know that they would have had as much of a base." A Hispanic father from New York City told us, "I believe the church is a special foundation for the youth, the church has a very important value, inside the family and inside the people so they can come out ahead. I do believe in that." Another from Chicago said, "I want them to go through life having that foundation, so that they don't have to suffer through their lives, don't have to go through something that really hits them, to be able to go back and say, okay this is what I need. To me, it's very important they have this foundation from an early age and just keep on through life." This Hispanic Catholic mother from New Mexico explained, "I'd like them to get to know my way of living, because the world is changing much, and technology, how to see things in the world. I want them to know the basis of ideas and ways of life of their dad and me, because they are foundations that have helped us to live well. I want to see that kind of teaching, religious, moral was not lost. It is one of the most important works as a parent, religion, that they believe in something that is true, then they have a base in religion." And a Hispanic Catholic father from Indiana concurred, "Parents have a responsibility to form children, to make them to be moral, have them be socially adept, learn manners, so why shouldn't you have them learn religion? Yes, they're eventually gonna choose on their own, but you can put a good base in there."

Protestant parents of all traditions use identical metaphors to describe religion. "Religion is part of who you are, part of your foundation, especially when you grew up with it the way I did," explained one mainline Protestant father from Indiana. Another from Washington, DC, told us: "My church growing up, I got from it a sort of worldview, thinking about others who are less fortunate, trying to make a difference, trying to be a good person. There's a deeper level to that when you feel there's a power greater than yourself looking over you. It gave me a sense of right and wrong for myself, like it wasn't just my parents. It gave me a moral compass, I would feel like I shouldn't do this because it doesn't fit with my beliefs for myself. That's something I really want my kids to have." Likewise, one mainline Protestant mother from Indiana said: "There's a lot of guidance in some of the religious things you gain in childhood, foundations of faith. So I wanted my daughters to be in an environment where they would learn those things that would serve them in adulthood. I wanted them to connect with church and a generous spirit and a good heart and a compassion for people and to know why and have an understanding of why they believe this, that confession, 'I believe in God, the father almighty, maker of Heaven and earth.'" None of those beliefs guarantee that these parents are diligent and effective in passing on religion to their children. Some of them, like this mainline Protestant mother from New York City, are anxious: "I sometimes worry, am I giving them enough religion? I worry that I don't give them enough spiritual foundation at home." Others concede that they have not invested in religion as much as they should have, even while insisting on its importance in their lives, as with this mainline Protestant father from Indiana who said above that religion is "part of who you are": "Do I put it on the back burner a lot? Yeah. But if it wasn't important I wouldn't have put my kids in Christian school, and I would have stopped going to church completely. So it's not that it's not important, it's just easy to push it aside, unfortunately." Nevertheless, parents of all kinds still insist on the importance of religion for providing people a ground and roots, as this black Protestant father from Houston said, "They're gonna grow up and live their own life. But if you keep 'em grounded and rooted in the word of God, they won't do some of the things you don't want 'em to do. Every parent knows when they walk out that door, when you don't see 'em, when he or she gets away from his parents, ain't no tellin' what he gonna do. So you have to let 'em be kids, but you gotta stay on 'em early. If you keep 'em rooted and show 'em what God want 'em to do, they'll honor that." A conservative Protestant father from Los Angeles also told us, "My Christian life is what drives me to do the things I do. I feel having a good grasp of scripture, a good theological foundation helps drive daily decisions. Having a playbook so to speak that you're able to draw from in any given situation." This conservative Protestant mother from the same city said, "I'm hoping they're a little bit more plan-oriented. I didn't have a plan, but I'm thinking for them, they will know exactly where and what they need to do to get where they need to get there. And being Christians, I think they, I'm hoping they're more grounded." Such a strong sense of the importance of this feature of religion drove this conservative Protestant mother from Indiana to exclaim, "I don't know how people can do life without the base, without what is solid, the line. If you don't have that, there's no foundation and it's hard to build anything, it's impossible to build anything."

When a child's life's journey takes the wrong path, she or he can always "return home" to and through religion, reset themselves, and start again on the right road.

Religious parents in the United States have a tremendous, though not absolute, faith in the power of religion to draw wayward children home after periods of error and confusion. Parents of all religious traditions believe this, although Christians seem especially confident in the idea, often referencing Jesus's parable of the Prodigal Son (Luke 15:11–32) and the verse of Proverbs 22:6 ("Train up a child in the way he should go, and when he is old he will not depart from it."). Black and white conservative Protestants tend among all traditions to take the Bible most straightforwardly, and so they talk like this. "I hope as they get older, they would come back, you know?," noted a black Protestant mother from Houston. "'Train up a child in the way they should go, and when they get old, they will not depart from it.' So I can only hope and pray they will come back, 'cause they will stray, they will stray, that's a given, I just want them to come back." Another from the same city claimed, "If they grow up and want to do something else, that's them. People do stray away. But if growing up what we've instilled is in there, you'll choose God, Jesus as your Savior." This black Protestant father from Houston too told us, "The Bible says if you train up a child in the way he should go, he may leave but he'll come back. And really all you can do is wait till they come back, so that's what we doing." The early religious instruction will never disappear, according to another black Protestant mother from Houston: "Even though you're not going to church, and you are out there [in the world] and like you wanna go clubbing or whatever, deep down that experience, that messages that you heard, even if you said you weren't listening, it's still there. Trust me, it's there. If they eventually try to stray, we just have to let them know that they are still people too, they trying to find themselves." Likewise, this black Protestant mother from Houston related, "I would hope they would grow up and come back to the realization like I did, that everything my parents said wasn't bad. That foundation that was laid for me was a good foundation and put me in the right direction, even when I rebelled against. That would be my hopes and dreams for them."

White conservative Protestant parents talked very similarly, sometimes even positively, about children straying for a while. "If they left church, I would let them go, because the exploration I went through was really important, it helped me solidify myself in a much more solid perspective than what I had," explained one conservative Protestant father from New York City. "I think it's part of everyone's spiritual growth, everyone needs a period where they feel they can ask the questions and have other people in their lives who are different than them to talk to and understand where they're coming from, it helps solidify who they are. And if the foundation is strong, they'll recognize where they come from." This conservative Protestant mother from the same city explained how her thinking had changed over time on the matter: "I grew up believing it was all about a decision to accept Christ as your savior and then you were in, when before you were out. I don't think it's quite that simple now, and so I think that children could drift away as part of a process of coming to God in their own way. If they didn't come back, I would feel that as a loss for them." Such beliefs are reassuring to parents who know how easy it would be for their children to wander off the correct path. One conservative Protestant father from Los Angeles predicted: "I would guess they are all going to follow after the Lord and model their lives like that. I mean, who knows? But I'm guessing they'd all be married with kids, because that foundation's been laid and we are not preventing them from seeing what life is really like. I think they'll all come back around. That's my prayer. But either way, we know God's in control, so I can't impose his timing on them either. But my guess is they will all come around." "If she strayed from the faith in college, I would be very upset about that," said a conservative Protestant mother from New York City, "but I also would like to think I wouldn't panic because college isn't the end of the story." And another from Florida explained, "She is learning her books of the Bible and is excited about it, and she's never, 'Oh, do we have to go to church?' I'm sure at some point that's gonna come when she hits teenage years, but my hope and prayer if that you start 'em young, as the Bible says, they will always come back to it, that's my hope and prayer for her."

Other Christian parents speak in the same terms. A mainline Protestant father from Washington, DC, told us, "It wouldn't bother me if my kids dropped out of church for a while, because dropping out of religion doesn't mean you don't believe in God. About going to church, I think we all have been through our vagaries of life." And a mother in the same tradition from Indiana related this story from her own life: "I grew up in the church, and then when I turned sixteen, got my driver's license, started experiencing other forms of life out there, I said, hey, I'd rather go there than church. It was okay. I realize now there was a stability in the people that stayed at church, showed up to church, that tradition. The prodigal son thing, returning, you go out, you learn about life out there, but your real home is where your heart lies." This Hispanic Catholic father from Indiana analyzed it more sociologically: "If we ground them well in what the Church believes and they leave, eventually they're gonna have kids and send them to parochial school, and all of sudden they'll be back into the community, they'll probably be brought back in. That seems to be the norm for a majority of the population, they leave church, have college years, then I'm gonna send them to Saint Whatever. Okay, we'll have to participate, I got confirmed so I'm really Catholic, okay, well, you coming back? Yeah. And all of a sudden they start coming back, that's just the norm." "I love the community of church," declared a white Catholic mother from New York City, in somewhat less precise terms, "the understanding that people are [just] human, that we're fantastic and wonderful and also flawed and make mistakes, and it just always comes back."

Shifting traditions, Jewish parents also subscribe to this same cultural model, but on quite different grounds—not based on referenced biblical promises and parables, but rather on the view of Judaism as a valuable community, tradition, and identity. Jewish parents do not want their children to lose their Jewish identity, and they make that very clear to them, even if religious observance is negotiable. Most American Jewish parents are also not Scripture thumpers and obviously do not have the New Testament's Prodigal Son parable to reference. This makes them different from what many Christian parents express, namely, that they do not want their kids to lose their faith, their beliefs, their relationship with God. The Jewish parents we interviewed (who, again, are not a representative sample) were also generally more confident than parents in other religious traditions about the quality of their parenting work and their close relationships with their children, as many of the Jewish quotes above have reflected. So they seemed less concerned in general with the idea of their children straying very far. But some Jewish parents still do worry, as with this Jewish mother from Indiana, yet hope that romance and marriage will pull them back: "I hope my son comes back because he has dropped out quite a bit, out of the youth group mostly because his other peers dropped out and he had a lot of homework so they all sort of fell apart for his group. I hope he comes back to it but I think the only way he will is by meeting and marrying a Jewish woman who will bring him back. That's the only chance and so I worry that he'll meet a non-Jewish woman and then really drop out."

Finally, note the similar ideas present in the words of this Mormon mother from Indiana: "After age sixteen there is a big falling away from church, you graduate, get your job, have kids, and then you want that religion back for your family—it's a trend within the church and we've seen it with our boy, the falling away part. We hope he will come back and find his anchor. I would predict no problems and struggle as far as religion goes, just because of who they are now." A Buddhist father from Chicago observed: "I have some friends who have converted but they will come back. Because Buddhism and Thai culture are so closely intertwined, it's hard to say what is part of what. I hope they keep some of it but if they become Christian, whatever works for them is fine. I just want them to keep some of their traditions. If you don't know your past or keep some of your past, you can't really progress to move forward. You have to embrace it to flourish. So I see a lot of college students who growing up now want to learn about their culture and learn where they came from, who now wanna find their roots and they come back to the temple or say, 'I wish my parents taught me this. I wish I knew more about this.'" Likewise, this Muslim mother from New York City told us: "The first part of life is really important for laying a foundation. My parents provided that for me, yet I chose to question it, I almost walked away from it. But the depth of that connection and firmness of that foundation does matter, it's part of your anchor. So I'm hoping by being the Muslim I'm trying to be, he'll have that anchor, a space he can come back to wherever he goes, a place that's stable for him."

Shared religion also glues families together, which, besides being a desire of parents, is good for growing children.

This proposition is an integral part of this cultural model, but it also overlaps with parallel propositions in the model about the "Importance of Family Solidarity" above, so we will not offer redundant quotes here. The reader can reference that section to see how it obviously connects.

Therefore, parents instilling the right foundation of religion in their children effectively provisions them with crucial life resources that greatly enhance their chances of living good lives as they proceed on their journeys in the world.

In a way, this final proposition of this model repeats much that has been said above. Yet it represents the logical concluding inference that completes this cultural model. Some of the parent quotes that illustrate it include this statement from a mainline Protestant mother from Los Angeles: "I've worked so hard to make Christianity her foundation because I knew that there was no way that she was gonna grow up feeling safe and comfortable and okay with who she is if she didn't have a strong foundation. And it's been such a blessing that she comes to church six days a week [for a children's program], all through the week and then on Sunday, that's amazing, that's solid!" A conservative Protestant mother from Indiana said, "It's important to have that established faith because as you get older and get out in the world it's going to be a challenge. And if you have that base and have that foundation, it's a lot easier to stand up to those challenges." "I think by God's grace they will save themselves a lot of pain and heartache," predicted a conservative Protestant father from Los Angeles. "I think they will come to know the Lord in a greater way than we have. Just by laying the foundation that we're laying, that wasn't laid for me."

A Mormon mother from New York City said, "We're laying the groundwork, but the church hangs together in a magical way that it only can for children. And my boy thrives off order, that things have to make sense, right?" This Jewish mother from Indiana recounted: "We've had such a unified approach in our philosophy and values that has come across pretty clear, that I don't think they've heard alternative messaging. They've been able to ignore other side-influencing messaging because we've had such a unified approach. They are very involved in the media and my son reads everything and is involved in every aspect of what messaging is out there, because he wants to be involved debating it. I think they have a strong foundation in how we've tried to guide them, and they listen to media with that in in mind, with a clear focus of where they are." And this Muslim father also from Indiana told us how he instructs his children: "Don't try to please me—you better have a stronger belief that you have a destiny. You are on a road, you are traveling, that's what life's all about, you're traveling, you're on a bus. Someday you're gonna come down, be six foot under, and there's nothing I can do for you then." Consider too the words of these three white Catholic parents, all from Indiana, two mothers and a father, respectively:

> The biggest thing is you go to church and provide that foundation with your children, so as long as they continue on that, I feel I've done my job and hopefully they can do the best with what they do and be well-adjusted.

> It's an obligation, you need to give them a solid foundation. They're gonna make their own choices at some point, and you have to be good with that, but you have to believe you've given them a strong enough foundation that they're gonna make a right choice then. Do I drink? Do drugs? Have sex? So many different things. If they've been given a proper foundation, they're gonna make the right choices.

> We've given them a good foundation, in church, with our friends, and different experiences at church, [so we hope] they're good enough and will find that to be a valuable part of their lives. Hopefully we've given that indication with how we live.

Similarly, a Hispanic Catholic father from Chicago insisted, "It's very important they be Catholic. I want them to go through life having that foundation, so they don't have to suffer through their lives, to go through something that really hits them in their life, to be able to go back and say, okay this is what I need. So to me it's very important that they have this foundation from an early age and just keep on through life." Likewise, this Hispanic Catholic father from New York City told us, "I want my children to be prepared for the future of their children, to see them with a well-formed family, where they instill religion in their children as I have taught to them. And that they don't turn away from God, to teach them that the one who is going the way of the Lord is on track, to guide their children, know that they will do that for your grandchildren." A black Protestant mother from Houston agreed: "As a parent now I have to prepare them, so when the trials and tribulations come, he won't say, 'I don't believe in God.' That happened to me. 'Took my mom and my dad from me and now I'm here by myself. I don't got nothing.' I'm not gonna be here forever and you got to understand that God takes us through certain things to elevate us to a different level. He not gonna put you through something to bring you down. So anytime you going through something, it's gonna be a blessing that come out of it. I don't care what it is, how it's going, at the end of the journey he has a blessing with your name on it. So you just have to be there to receive it." Finally, this black Protestant father insisted, "Every parent should train their child up in the church, growing up, going to church, that it be mandatory they go to Sunday school, Bible study, encourage them to learn about God as much as they can, participate in different activities, like volunteering, help somebody in that aspect, because one day it might be you who needs help."

The Proper Role of Religious Congregations

Before exploring religious parents' cultural model of *how* to transmit religion to children, we need first to take note of a separate model concerning their view of the proper place and role of religious congregations in that process.[1] It runs as follows:

The Role of Religious Congregations: The primary responsibility for passing on religious faith and practice to children rests with parents;

---

1. Smith and Adamczyk (*Handing Down the Faith*) also explore this topic from a somewhat different perspective.

religious congregations are secondary and primarily supportive. Religious congregations should reinforce what parents teach at home, not determine it. Reasonable parents hold only modest expectations for what congregations offer them and their children. Most helpful is when congregations provide a general sense of an inviting, comfortable community and some positive experiences for children. Kid-appealing programs and some teaching of the moral "basics" (e.g., the Ten Commandments, the parable of the Good Samaritan) are also great. Congregations that do things to make time spent there fun for children help the getting of kids to participate less of a headache, and so are particularly attractive and appreciated. But specifically "religious" aspects of congregations—like theology, liturgy, and doctrinal teachings—are not especially important when it comes to parenting.

The primary responsibility for passing on religious faith and practice to children rests with parents; religious congregations are secondary and primarily supportive.

A mainline Protestant mother from Indiana exemplified this point by telling us: "Me teaching them as a parent is more important than the church teaching them. The church has a little bit more to offer. Everybody's going to have a different perspective as to how they interpret things, and just because I view it one way doesn't mean that you have to view it that way. The person at church is going to be able to show you something different than I will, so one of the reasons I don't want [exclusively] to teach my kids is they hear it from me all the time. I probably have the more important role but church can reinforce and back me up." One black Protestant father from Houston said, "Church is there to put icing on the cake. We the parents are the bread, the foundation. The church is support, just there to smooth everything, smooth all the edges out, put the icing on." And a black Protestant mother from the same city explained, "The parent is more important than church because parents encourage them to be there, it's an institution, you get them to the church, it's the parent's role to get them there." Another black Protestant father from Houston explained, "It starts in your house. When Jesus sent his disciples out, he said, 'Start here in Jerusalem, then spread.' So you're supposed to start in your house and get their foundation strong, raise them, then sending 'em to youth ministry, show 'em that it's possible to be active in the church and have a life too." And another black Protestant mother from Houston elaborated, "Parents should be the main role model, the main teacher. You can't rely on Sunday school and pastors, it has to be the parents first and foremost. If you really want it to be a real faith, it has to be the parents, 'cause that's who they see day in and day out, who's influencing them every day. If you only rely on Sunday, it's not gonna happen. You need to be explicitly talking about it, also your walk, how you're living your life. And going to church to supplement what you do. That's when they see we do this together with other people and other people have these same beliefs and live their life similarly. Obviously, you need both, but I think parents are definitely the primary." A similar relation between parents and church is expressed by this conservative Protestant father from Florida: "Next to me and their mother, church is probably the next most profound relationship shaping them, just very important." This Mormon father from Indiana likewise said, "It's your very important responsibility as a parent to teach your kids, it's not the church's responsibility, although they do and there's teaching experiences you get from church, but it's the parent's responsibility." A Jewish mother from New York City agreed, "Actually not being hypocritical, like if you want them to do something you have to do it and believe in it yourself. You can't send them to a Jewish school to learn about stuff and then do nothing at home—which a lot of families do, the kids learn what Passover means and then Passover vacation they go to Bermuda and do nothing with ritual, I mean I don't get it." And this Hispanic Catholic mother from Indiana also agreed: "If the parent doesn't do it, who else is gonna? The world is not gonna teach them anything good. If they're not taught by their parents, they're in trouble. I have an obligation to my children to give them religion. You can't just plant a tree and never water it. It's gonna die. So if you don't teach those children faith, where are they gonna get it?" As did this white Catholic father from Indiana: "The parish isn't gonna be able to do anything unless the parents take them to there anyway, so it's got to be the parents' involvement. Even if they're hands off and they say, 'Go to CCD, this is what we used to do,' and at CCD lo and behold they meet just the right person, that's how it works. But it's the primary responsibility of the parent." Hindu parents took the same perspective. One mother from central New Jersey insisted, "Definitely parents, you cannot leave anything to anybody, I'm not comfortable leaving my kid with anybody. I'm going to be in charge of her, I don't want other people to raise my kid. Even certain things, I don't want my parents to teach her, it's gonna be all me." And this Hindu father from Chicago reported, "My daughter knows about Ramayana now from school. Actually I didn't teach her, but she learned it from the school. So I was really glad [chuckles] because that's my duty, I should have taught her that." Finally, this Muslim father from

Chicago reiterates this very common view of the priority of parents over religious congregations:

> Ninety percent of [children's learning is in] the Muslim homes, sometimes clergy come to their homes, sometimes they go to the mosques. So right from there they started learning, we started teaching them. I am of the opinion that parents need to teach them instead of clergy. When parents themselves are involved, they know the real values. And if they are blessed with the education, knowledge, that's their duty to start that instead of clergy. That's my opinion. Many people have that opinion also. So that's how we started with them, and then Sunday also, we would pray and now when we pray at home, we ask them let's pray together, like a congregation. Muslims, we can pray anywhere. We don't have to go to the mosque, or church, or anywhere. So every home is a mosque, basically. We have the material to study and they become interested most of them themselves.

Religious congregations should reinforce what parents teach at home, not determine it. Reasonable parents hold only modest expectations for what congregations offer them and their children.

"Church is something you grab hold of to reinforce what you believe," a conservative Protestant father from Florida said. "It is a good place for people to explore what they believe as a family. If you're my family member though, I believe I [as a parent] have a priority over the church." A Buddhist mother from Chicago told us, "When they go to temple, they have friends there and learn from their friends and also learn from the teachers. Just learning from us and learning from the teacher at school, I don't think that's enough."[2] This mainline Protestant mother from New York City explained: "I don't know if church has a responsibility with kids. The responsibility is probably mine if I bring them there. Once they get to church, they're exposed to the ideas, I like that aspect, the church

---

2. The topic of children's friends raises the question of the extent that parents attempt to control or guide their children's peer relationships in order indirectly to influence their religious outcomes—what is known as the "channeling hypothesis" (see, e.g., Todd Martin, James White, and Daniel Perlman, "Religious Socialization: A Test of the Channeling Hypothesis of Parental Influence on Adolescent Faith Maturity," *Journal of Adolescent Research* 18 [2003]: 169–87). Some scholars believe that parental "channeling" is an important mechanism of religious transmission, but the parents we interviewed spoke little about it. Whether this is because channeling is actually less important in parental religious transmission than is often thought or because parents are simply not very conscious of their actual channeling strategies, our data are not able to tell.

values that are aligned with our values, so it's another reinforcement to be exposed to those values. Going to church helps reinforce the values we share and it's also a good community-building. They have a lot of activities where people get together, just not for Sunday service but other nights." This conservative Protestant mother from Florida said the same: "Church just reinforces what we talk about at home and how we live at home. I'm looking for people at church to love them, just as I'm loving their kids, and hold them accountable if they see them doing something they shouldn't do, then they're able to tell them that." A Catholic father from Indiana agreed: "Rather than saying, I'm the big parent, I can handle this, no, I want the kids to understand we have these different avenues, different choices. But as parents, my wife and I make the choices of how we're gonna guide our children, and the Church is certainly one of those ways. But I don't believe it's up to the Church to raise our kids for us." Expressing modest expectations, one Hindu mother from Chicago explained this about her congregation: "Temple should be a place where you just go and get peace of mind, right? That's what I look for. Not necessarily having to try to follow A, B, C, that thing, right but just go, relax, try to not think of all the things are going on, for at least one hour, change your state of mind, and then come home. That's what I'm looking for." A Muslim father from Indiana agreed: "We are devout in the sense yes we pray five times a day. They recommend you to go to mosque as much as possible, but it's not a must. We would definitely go once a week, but most of the prayers we do at home."

Said this black Protestant father from Houston, "Church is a place for kids to get an extended, more professional lesson on God. I teach and I tell them, but you also have those in church who are set in place who know what they're talking about, who can better explain the questions that they have that I may not be able or the areas I missed, they'll be able to pick those areas up." A white Catholic father from Indiana said, "I expect church to give them the basics, the foundations of our religion. Of course that's to be practiced at home, we're their first teachers and all that. But I do expect them to give a foundation for the kids to understand and see it in practice among the teachers and staff." Similarly emphasizing the home over church as the place where the most important religious formation happens, a conservative Protestant mother from Washington, DC, explained: "In church they're getting introduced to subjects, and you should go on and reiterate what they're learning. If your household isn't set to be a learning spot, then they're not gonna know anything about God. Some kids know nothing about the Bible, and I'm thinking that's weird, what happens in that household? You have to set up those learn-ing spots [at home]. Maybe it's a book they read at nighttime before bed or a certain reading schedule you have for them to explore those things." Mormon parents expressed the same view. A Mormon mother from New York City explained that, "In Mormondom, the church is supposed to be supplemental, and if it's not, it's less effective. So mostly what they get is from home, but that is certainly supported by the habits of church, no doubt about that. And in the social aspect church is so important that you have friends." And this Mormon father from Indiana told us, "I feel like it's my job to raise them religiously, so anytime their teachers at church can support what we're doing at home it's really nice. Kids might think maybe mom and dad aren't so smart, then they'll hear the same things at church that we're telling them, and I'll be so thankful. So yeah the church's responsibility is to back up what we're teaching at home."

A few parents we interviewed did place a somewhat greater respon-sibility on their religious congregations, but in the end it was the job of parents, not the congregations, to train their children properly.[3] Consider, for instance, the words of this mainline Protestant father from Los Ange-les, an immigrant from Cameroon: "The responsibility of the parents, first, is to remind the children of their obligation, get them ready for church, to encourage them to go to church and go with them. And you have to check with them, 'What did you learn in church?' You have to take them to church, it is not the church is going to get them from home, you have to make sure you take them to church every Sunday and let them attend church. The church's responsibility is for them to instill in them that value, tell them what God almighty is, why church is very important for their lives. I'm sure the church can better explain that more than I do, I can only explain my responsibility." And this Jewish mother from New York City spoke appreciatively about the supplemental educational role of her synagogue: "There are certain things that like I didn't grow up doing but now I'm doing that with the kids, surrounding holidays which she recog-nizes as certain things you do, light the candles, whatever. And then also through the synagogue we hear about other like holidays that I didn't even know about, like Simchat Torah and others that like never came into play. So they know about it now, they are learning certain things through the synagogue."

3. To be clear, it is not that parents saw their congregations as failing or weak; they simply wished to hold realistic expectations of their congregations and keep responsibilities and priorities in proper order.

At the same time, another Jewish mother from the same city expressed lower expectations from her synagogue: "My daughter went to our synagogue's Hebrew school for sixth and seventh grades, and then to a Hebrew high school for eighth and ninth grades that met once a week in the city. But she swears she is not going back, so we have to find something else. The truth is, the main reason is because in order to keep going to her camp, she has to be enrolled in a formal Jewish education program for three to four hours a week, otherwise I might just let it go for a little while." And this Hispanic Catholic mother from New York City spoke about Church, or some people in church, almost as influences from which they needed to protect their children, precisely to guard what is of real value in church: "No, I do not expect the Church to give anything to my children. What I do not want is [people in Church to] take away from my children [interest] in the Church [by teaching thing] like, 'The Church . . . [says such and such], and God . . . [says so and so].' I don't do that. If they stop going to church, it's because they want to, after they reach the age of majority. But now, I feel good that they are going, without me have to force them." A Hispanic Catholic father from Indiana expressed similarly low expectations of church: "What do I expect from the Church? Not to be alienating, not to push my kids away. Be welcoming, let them know they are part of us—that's important to make them want to stay, not wanna leave." The overall view of most parents, then, is summarized by this white Catholic mother from Indiana: "Whatever the parish offered we would try, but mostly we relied on the support from our families."

Most helpful is when congregations provide a general sense of an inviting, comfortable community and some positive experiences for children. Kid-appealing programs and some teaching of the moral "basics" (e.g., the Ten Commandments, the Parable of the Good Samaritan) are also great. Congregations that do things to make time spent there fun for children help the getting of kids to participate less of a headache, and so are particularly attractive and appreciated.

"I like that our church has children's programs," explained a white Catholic mother from Indiana. "Not all parishes have them but I think that is huge. There was a lull between the younger and older kids, wasn't a lot of youth anything, but now it's evolved much more and there's a lot more things for them to do, to still have fun." A black Protestant mother from Houston explained what she wants out of church for her children: "Just activities to let 'em know you can have fun at church, just like at Chuck E. Cheese or school, so they know you can have fun at church too.

Doesn't have to be a children's church where they're separated from family, just some activities like drill team or choir." A Hispanic Catholic father from New Mexico explained what he wants from church: "Basic things like catechism, the creed, we trust and delegate that part to the catechists. But we also need to understand what they are doing. It's one thing to recite the creed, know it by memory, but another thing to know why we do it, and we their parents have educated them more to understand what is not so visible." This mainline Protestant mother from Washington, DC, gives a flavor of what she is after from church for her children: "Every time we get to the Lord's Prayer in the liturgy, I look at both boys to make sure they memorized and say and process it. Involvement through the acolytes, they have got to get there early, put on the garments, be part of the service. I did that when I was a kid. You felt more attached when you're involved with what's happening. I feel less confident on the intellectual piece, teaching lessons, I've relied on Sunday school to do that. And then as the kids have gotten older, we haven't been as involved as I think we should have, but the youth group has provided a venue for them to talk about faith to other adults or older kids in an environment that's safe. Sometimes those conversations are richer than what we may have at home as they get older." Another mainline Protestant mother from Los Angeles told us, "She feels so at home at church, ever since she was a baby she was passed around from pew to pew, went from this person to that person during the worship service, so she feels so safe and at home. I hope she's strong enough in her mind and soul to stand up and say this is who I am and this is what I believe in, and stick with it." A Muslim mother from Chicago reiterated the centrality of a sense of community for children in their congregation: "We go to the prayers during Ramadan because my kids love that, it's our holiday time. It makes them feel the community, that there's other Muslims like them. It's important for the kids to see everybody else in the mosque doing the same thing as we do. That helps us teach them everything else. So, yeah, that's the only time when we go to the mosque, during Ramadan."

A white Catholic father from Indiana expressed his modest hopes about church this way: "I expect CCD to teach them the basics of the religion, essentially the historical teachings, but I'm more concerned that they teach them the Golden Rule and that kind of thing, rather than particular scripture. If they get that message across, that's what I expect and not necessarily more." A conservative Protestant father from Los Angeles agreed: "They do like church, they do. My oldest goes to youth group, 'cause it's fun. For him he only sees the fun. He hears what's being taught but he's definitely going wholeheartedly for the fun. We know that. So just keep giving it to him [laughs] because it's there, he's just going to need a little more nurturing I guess." A conservative Protestant mother from Florida explained: "Church is secondary role, because I'm the primary, they can be secondary. But it teaches them about community and what it feels like to be part of the body of Christ and where if you're sad or something we could pray for you or at least walk over and hug ya. Then as they get older, if you need something like help or support, like your mom died, we could provide that kind of support or pray together if there's a problem. There's a lot of kids my children's ages that go to church and come to Christian school, so they have a big peer group. There were twenty-three kids in vacation Bible school, so there's a good network of believers they can rely on and help and talk to." Similarly, a Mormon mother from Indiana described her church this way: "Our church is focused on a lot of programs. Young women programs where you can meet and do arts and crafts, learn how to cook, teach us how to be a good wife and mother. I didn't grow up with a stable mom, and I've transitioned to knowing how to be a good wife through the church, the mom I'm supposed to be. So church is what has made me the person I am. In our church there's so many activities where it's easy to learn what to do and how to raise your kids." One Hindu mother from central New Jersey expressed that she primarily appreciates the social support her temple provides for what she and her husband teach at home: "Learning in a group or community, it's a better way of learning, so kids don't feel like, 'Oh my mom and dad are just telling me stuff,' in one ear and out the other, but like, 'Oh, all these people are listening.'"

Sometimes parents' expectations for what their congregations ought to be providing come out in their observations of what is lacking, as with the report of this Jewish mother from New York City: "Synagogues should be focusing on attracting and I mean not just catering to but making it a priority to keep young families by providing programming and making it comfortable for them, and making services that are interesting and welcoming. They don't do that, so people come in and then people leave." Other times, expectations are revealed in what parents praise, as with this Jewish father from the same city's observations: "The synagogue has phenomenal kids' programs. They didn't twenty years ago but now they have phenomenal programs, we love that."

Buddhist parents share the same views expressed above. "A huge part of the reason why it's important for me to have my kids go to the temple is to develop strong friendships there," reported a Buddhist mother from Chicago. Another mother from the same city told us, "My family comes to this temple, but when this temple didn't have [children's] teaching programs, I took my kids to the other temple three blocks away. Still, my family is here and the people here are friendlier." One Buddhist father reported temple as a place simply to observe others: "Sometimes my wife takes them to the temple, just for watching, not to enter the program." Important in all of this, as expressed by one Buddhist father also from Chicago, is that temple be fun: "They just like to go. They, don't say, 'Oh, it's boring' or something like that, and they know how to respect it because I taught them."

But specifically "religious" aspects of congregations—like theology, liturgy, and doctrinal teachings—are not especially important when it comes to parenting.

As with some of the beliefs already expressed, parents usually do not come straight out and say this. But it is implicit in other things they do say, including many of those observed just above and these last few quotes. Children having religious friends in congregations is often important to parents, sometimes seemingly more so than what they learn religiously. One mainline Protestant father from New York City, for instance, said, "When they go to youth group or Sunday school, that's their friends there, they consider them church friends, who outside of church he wouldn't see." Similarly, this conservative Protestant mother from Florida told us, "She loves being at church because of the friends she has there, it gives her a safe, secure home. She is so comfortable there and makes good, safe connections. The other piece is, she doesn't have a father and there are men there that really, she doesn't connect good with men, but there are a couple there that she'll hug and connect with, that gives some type of male connection." One white Catholic father from Indiana struck the same chord but focusing more on himself than the needs of his children: "I'm not a dogmatic person, not motivated by doctrine, Catholic doctrine or any other kind of doctrine. I see religion as interesting and beautiful and I like going to church with the kids, but it's not anything that I need to have a spiritual life. That to me is very intimate and prayerful and expressed in work and parenting, gardening, other things in my life, so I don't really depend on the teachings of a church to inform my spiritual life." And a Hindu mother from New York City related that, "It's more important to me for her to learn the values instead of the ritualistic aspect of religion. She participated once a year in a children's puja, was part of it until age eighteen. And we would take her to the temple, she would participate, but at the same time we gave her the more moral values at home. If you ask me can she recite all the mantras? I don't think so, she used to be, but at the same time does she have the basic values? I guess so." Much of American Judaism seems particularly suited to downplay the "religious" parts of congregational life, as expressed by this Jewish mother from New York City: "My Jewish connections are much more practice and community-based than theological. The theology is there, but I don't examine it too closely."

While rarely discussing the matter directly, parents' talk in interviews suggests various reasons why the "religious" aspects of their congregations seem less important to them than other features. For some, such as this Hispanic Catholic father from New Mexico, the more strictly religious parts of church are not so comprehensible: "There are always teachings [in church] that, as they say, sometimes go over your head, but not for other people. But no, I think it's been all right." Note, however, his satisfaction with church, despite not understanding some of its teachings. Similarly, this Muslim mother from Chicago confided to us, "The Quran, we still don't know a lot of it [chuckles]. We keep learning with them but there's lots of things we don't know. We should know but we don't." Other parents, such as this white Catholic mother from Indiana, think that the traditional religious aspects of their congregations are too narrow or particular to be too concerned about: "The Church's guidance is just more exact, mine is broader. I can't give you any answer, I don't know, I don't have all the answers, I don't know everything that the Church or all these other people know." Similarly, this Mormon mother also from Indiana said, "I'm not a fanatical whatchamacallit, 'cause some people are fanatical about Joseph Smith but I'm not like that, I am more progressive. I focus more on what is the church now."

Yet other parents, including this black Catholic mother from Indiana, believe that morality is more basic and important than "religion," so religion need not be made central if morality is intact: "For us, moral values are very important. Religion is just a vehicle to carry that through. As individuals we already subscribe to a type of moral code that really isn't different, one [religion] does not overwrite the other [morality]." Then again, the idea held by many American religious parents that all religions share the same essential beliefs relieves them of having to be much concerned with religious "details" and instead simply believe in something or other: "Sometimes I'll say, 'Whoever is up there, whatever the plan is, whether it's God, Buddha, or whatever.' Because in a way it's a lot of the same beliefs, though when you go down to the details and that's when it becomes complicated. But there's really no big difference as long as you believe in something." Whatever the various reasons, however, the outcome is similar across all religious types: what matters most about and from religious congregations are features other than their particularly religious activities and character.

How Parents Should Pass on Religion to Children

The final dominant cultural model that we examine concerns the best strategies and methods that most religious parents think they should use to transmit religion to their children.

> *How to Pass on Religion to Children*: Parents have only one good and hopefully effective way to raise children to understand and carry on their family's religion (or perhaps return to it someday after a period of disaffection). That is for parents simply to practice their own personal religious faith, naturally, for its own sake and as role models for their children. If all goes well, children will over time learn, absorb, and embrace their own version of that faith, almost unconsciously. Children are observant and malleable, especially when young; the key for parents is to provide them religious practices to observe and try out, such as prayer, worship, and volunteering. Raising religious children should thus primarily be a practice-centered process, not chiefly a didactic teaching program. If along the way children ask questions about religion out of curiosity, parents should answer as well as they are able. On occasion parents might also proactively share religious ideas and observations. But parents must never "preach" or be verbally overbearing in any way. Hypocrisy is the worst, so parents must be consistent and "walk the talk" (even if there is not much talk). Parents also need not expect dramatic religious experiences from their children; passing on the faith to the next generation can and should be a gradual, natural, intuitive process. Parents will need to insist that their young children attend religious services and other religious community activities, as appropriate, but when children become teenagers, parents must adjust their requirements to allow them as self-directed individuals to make "informed" religious decisions for themselves.

Parents have only one good and hopefully effective way to raise children to understand and carry on their family's religion (or perhaps return to it someday after a period of disaffection). That is for parents simply to practice their own personal religious faith, naturally, for its own sake and as role models for their children.

This general strategy works well for parents because, among other reasons, it does not require them to understand and explain orthodox content to their children, which most cannot. It avoids preaching or imposing religion on their children. Instead, it is seen as appropriately leading, not coercive, a semivoluntary socialization, not direct indoctrination or social control. While all parents across all traditions agree on this belief, some view modeling more as an intentional, strategic process, while for others it is "natural," unconscious, and automatic—in that, because children are always watching, they do not have actively to think about transmitting or teaching religion.

"First be an effective role model, to the extent we are able," explained a white Catholic mother from Indiana. "Do the right things and cheerfully, not be hypocritical about it, not say one thing and do another. That's first and foremost." "The biggest thing is trying to walk the talk, that's what we try to do, 'cause we never said we had all the answers," said a white Catholic father from Indiana. A Hispanic Catholic father from New Mexico said, "We have to be an example for them. It would be difficult to say, 'Be Catholics, go to Mass,' when I won't go. The most important thing I've done is to be consistent going to Mass, lead by example, so they can see it, or they will not believe me." This white Catholic mother from New York City agreed: "It's really practice, through your actions. We go to church, but I think it's really how we live our lives that sets the tone and makes you a role model for your kids, that's what sinks in, what trickles down. You can make the big speeches, a big deal out of Christmas or Easter, but everything in between is really what matters, those are the consistent lessons, the ones you show on a regular basis." Remembering her own childhood, this Hispanic Catholic mother from Indiana told us: "I go back to parents. You need to pray with kids, show them to pray at night. They may not like the rosary but you need to show how to do the rosary. I remember sitting with my grandma and my mom doing the rosary in the evening with my dad as well, and it's like a little flashback and somehow bringing up your own family, if I do that like my parents did maybe she'll do it." This white Catholic father from Indiana explained, "I go to church on Sunday because I want to be there but also because I want my kids to be there, to appreciate and learn right from wrong, what the good Lord has for you. I don't think I act differently or appreciate things just to set an example, it's also who I am, but [setting an example] is a big part of it as a parent." A white Catholic mother from New York City said, "First and foremost, we need to model it. If we want them to have the faith and understand the power and the community, we need to play our part, be part of the community. Which is why we're Eucharistic ministers, why they altar serve. It's about giving back and nourishing that community. They've balked a couple times, like [scoffing], 'why do I have to do this, this is such a pain,' and we say, well you have to give back, it's such a gift. It's beautiful to see young kids there participating and giving something back, not all kids, very few who will put in the time to train and commit to go. So the first is modeling and showing them it's not just about lip service, but also we make the time and it plays an important part in our lives." This black Catholic from Indiana said, "Being a good role model in the way you act or respond to things in life, a leader that kids really look up to." And this Hispanic Catholic father from Indiana said, "Family's gotta do it, and it's gotta be important to us, 'cause if we're just going through the motions, just go to Mass on Sundays and that's it, if we don't participate more, they're gonna see that. But if they see us set an example participating in retreats, small groups, helping with festivals, being part of the community, that's what they're gonna learn."

The agreement across religious traditions continue. "Kids pay attention to what you do," observed a Jewish mother from New York City. "You can talk till you're blue in the face but they look at how you live. You have to be consistent and live your values." A Mormon mother from Indiana said, "We're not perfect, but I think overall I'm a good person and I try to do good and try to lead a good example for my kids to follow, especially having four girls and me being their role model." "You have to teach the requisite knowledge," insisted a Muslim mother from New York City, "but more important is to model whatever you teach, that the transmission of knowledge is accompanied by behavioral modeling." This Hindu mother from New York City explained: "If you want your child to have a particular faith, the most important thing is you actually have to do what you want them to do. You have to practice the religion. There is a difference between being born a Hindu and practicing Hindu, right? I try to be a practicing Hindu. Do I succeed all the time? I don't know, but I try. If I want to be a Hindu but don't practice it, then how is she becoming a Hindu? Or a Christian, or whatever, a Jew. You have to practice it to model that for her." A Buddhist father from Chicago gave this specific illustration:

Respect, kindness. My wife gave them an example the other day. I was sweeping the floor and she called me to do something. I put the broom down and I walked to her to see what she needed. She said to them, "See, that's what I'm talking about, your father didn't say [in angry voice], 'hold on a moment' or 'what do you want, woman?' He just stopped what he needed to do and came out of respect and desire to help me." So hopefully I've set a good standard for the girls, a good role model.

A Muslim mother from New York City gave this example: "September 11 was a pivotal moment for Muslim women who covered, because you had to decide if you were gonna stay with it or not. A lot of women took off their scarves, but I chose to keep it on. I decided to cover after my son was born because of my awareness of myself as a Muslim role model, what I want to impart to my son about what it means to be Muslim now. I hoped by demonstrating my commitment he'll at least feel a connection to faith and choose whether or not he's gonna believe it and be Muslim and transmit it to his kids. At least he'll have an example in me of what it means to stay connected, that's been really important to me in his upbringing, just trying to be a good role model of what it means to be Muslim, from practicing rituals to being a not-dogmatic person in the work I do." Many Jewish parents, including this mother from Indiana, talked about volunteering as a way to model their values: "Modeling that behavior, just the same as everything else. Our kids, we're not just preaching to them, we're living it. So just modeling behavior. Control yourself and you can control your kid, model good behavior to your kid and they won't act out. Our kids are living proof of that. I try to instill in my kids the importance of volunteering and giving back to people who are less fortunate and financially donating to causes and things, and we let them know that we donate to these various causes that we believe in, and we really encourage them to volunteer." "By example, and talking," a Mormon mother from Indiana reiterated. "The parent has to set it, if you don't want somebody to do something, then you don't it. Just the daily routine of how you talk to them about what you believe in your faith."

Protestant parents talk the same way. "The most important thing is prayers, praying with them, them hearing me pray, just modeling how to pray," related a conservative Protestant father from Florida. "Then church, seeing us take leadership roles and serving and being a help to others. I never want them to see us act differently at church than we do any other time, so I keep going back to just be genuine and real." A black Protestant mother from Houston put it negatively:

> You can't lead and be a role model if you're not walking the walk. I see it around me all day every day, I tell these young single mothers that you all making a mistake bringing men in and out of your children's lives. These little girls gonna do the same thing they see their mothers do, that's what you teaching them. You're their front line, they're looking at you. Certain things you should not let them see and expose them. We make mistakes, but some things we don't have to do. When I came up,

my mother told me, "There's just things you don't do and bring home," and young parents have to learn that. Some say, "These are my children, I raise them the way I want." Yes, somebody has to tell you, because what you're doing is not good.

A mainline Protestant mother from New York City (who personally identifies as an atheist but is still involved in church) said, "My girl has some emotional maturing to do, that's why I haven't been able to give her some basic [verbal] lessons about being kind. Instead I try to demonstrate it to her. I will help someone on the street, I go out of my way to help people where others won't so she sees it. I just hope I can role model it." And this conservative Protestant mother from Florida projected, "By age thirty or thirty-five, I am praying for a confident, strong, Christian woman who walks in her faith. I'm not going to expect it, that's not my role. All I can do is give her the home that will teach her and try to mold her as best as I can, but then what she does afterward, I have no control over."

If all goes well, children will over time learn, absorb, and embrace their own version of that faith, almost unconsciously.

"She's a sponge," observed a mainline Protestant mother from New York City, "so we discuss sermons and talk about Good Friday and Easter and that whole process, what actually happened and what it meant. I'm not really a scripture person so [we discuss] mostly what we read in church during the service." "You set an example and then they just kind of do it," a Muslim father from Indiana reported. "I want the children to have absorbed so much from me that they realize, 'Hey, I can't live without God.'" A Jewish mother from Indiana said, "I can't even explain it, but Judaism really guides our life. Now my kids are all picking Jewish partners, so it's important to them. I would say it has really seeped into the soul of their lives, even if it's not religion, just the whole package of being Jewish and living their lives in those communities." A conservative Protestant father from Los Angeles recalled, "He has surprised us a few times, like we told him something and then later we see [from something he says or does that] he really listened, ya know?" Another conservative Protestant father from New York City observed, "I guess expectations would be that they will kinda follow in their parents' [footsteps], like going to college and finding a job and all those kinda things. I guess I would just expect that would kinda be their path."

This Hispanic Catholic father from New Mexico explained, "I am inculcating things in them, and they are learning. My intention is precisely for them to learn it, so I won't have to tell them later. We are giving them this so they have bases, and from these bases they can make their own decisions."

Children will learn and naturally absorb religion in various ways. Crucial, of course, are family religious practices at home, as described, for example, by this Mormon mother from Indiana: "We have family scripture every day, family prayer morning and night, and with each meal. We have family home evening once a week, a little song and prayer and lesson and then a treat. And when I help a family that needs a food order they'll go with me and help deliver. And their father helps out a lot with people that need things fixed and he'll bring the boys with him. We try to bring them whenever possible when we have opportunities to serve. We would love for them to be servers. That's how Jesus lived his life and nothing would make me happier than for my boys to emulate him." And a Hindu mother from New York City described her approach: "I started it very young for my daughter. We have an altar at home. I would give her bath and would chant the mantras with her, so by the time she was speaking, she could recite them. And I would take her to the temple and she would say 'Mommy, we have to go and say "hi" to Ganesha,' a residing deity. So you introduce it gently and from a very early age." Again, parental modeling is crucial to success, as one Muslim father from Indiana noted: "Having a mother at home from day one, it's a very important environment, the mother being at home constantly, all the time with them. Mother practice five times a day, when before the child walks, they see their mother. She passes God to them, you can never take away that from them." A Muslim mother from Indiana gave this testimony, for instance: "All of a sudden she told me, 'When I finish high school, I'm going to cover my head.' When you do actions the right way, you make it easy on people, you don't have to tell them what to do, they learn from your action, you set the example. She saw me, our relatives in Syria, saw a lot of girls her age cover, so that probably made her cover too."

But exposure to religious congregations is important too. "If I believe and go to temple," explained a Buddhist father from Chicago, "not even talking about such deep believing, just go to temple and take them with me, I know for sure it affects them. It's not even a choice, but now they just identify as, 'I'm Buddhist,' I don't have to teach them, they just heard us say it. That's one of the values, the family values and bond, and there's no reason to change that." And a black Protestant father from Houston remarked, "It's important the church address all the audience there, from the children to widows to the elderly, that everybody is incorporated.

Lately, I'm seeing the children, whatever they're hearing they're like sponges."

A Jewish father from Indiana's explaining how and why his children have learned music serves as a perfect analogy for how most parents believe their children should ideally learn religion:

> I definitely guide them. It hasn't really been a question whether or not they're going to do music, for example, it was just assumed that they all would. But it's not as though I had to force them. It's just an expectation that everyone in our family plays, and we love and are proud of it, and they want to be like their older brothers. So it's not like, "You are going to do music or else," but more like around four or five years old we asked, "What instrument do you think you're gonna play?" and, "What music are you excited about?" So they definitely gravitated toward their own musical interests, but also with some guidance.

How this works with religion is described by a white Catholic mother from Indiana as a "drip, drip, drip" effect:

> Look around the house and see the Catholic stuff of on the walls, it's hard to go into a room without seeing something. I think that has some subliminal effect over time. There's a statue of Mary, not in church, just something you have. That kind of little thing helps. Another thing is go to Mass every Sunday, period. It doesn't matter if you're on vacation or traveling or on a Boy Scout trip, we'll figure out a way to go to Mass. So it locks it in, the expectation, there's no exceptions. We don't start exploiting exceptions and turning them into the rules. The rosary in the car every time, period. And it gets easier, they don't argue about it. After the first 10,000 times they don't argue anymore. They're just accepting, like you go to a restaurant and you say grace, period. It doesn't matter where it is. It's consistency, not a lot of fanfare but just regular steady drip, drip, drip. And the Catholic schools are a huge help because they are systematizing faith as a regular part of our routine. I think that probably is what will prevail in the end, at least I'm hopeful.

Children are observant and malleable, especially when young; the key for parents is to provide them religious practices to observe and try out, such as prayer, worship, and volunteering.

"Now I have three souls under the same roof with me," observed a black Protestant mother from Houston. "They're innocent, they're basically clay to be molded, so it's really serious now, 'cause they're watching me, as a woman and as their mom. It's just me raising them, so I have a lot of responsibility." "You're molding these people," agreed a white Catholic mother from New York City, "and the way for it to really sink in is you live it and keep it part of your ongoing conversation." A Hispanic Catholic father from Indiana recalled, "When they were school age, we'd sit and pass around a little devotional booklet and ask, 'who wants to read?' Kids are like sponges, they're wanted to learn and volunteer and will read that." One black Catholic mother from Indiana argued, "It's better to expose rather than trying to influence, because sometimes influencing people backfires, especially with kids. It's better to expose them to things because that way they have questions they'll ask, then it's easier to explain something to a person [as an answer] than tell them this is how you're supposed to do it."

Parents believe that imitation is a key way their children will learn to practice their religion, sometimes to be followed by some verbal instruction about the meaning of the practice later. "I don't think I need to teach them to chant because my mom did not teach me anything," a Hindu mother from Chicago told us. "I just saw her doing it and I started doing it, that's how it came. So if I do, my kids, when they see me doing, they will start doing, and I will explain if she asks that there are great ancestors that have led a good life, so it's like guidance for us." A Muslim mother from Chicago explained similarly: "If I want to our children to grow up Muslim then we have to show them we are practicing Muslims, we are praying five times a day. We don't force them, but when they see us doing, they have to do it [laughs]. And they fast, since they were six or seven years old they've had practice and watched us doing it, we don't eat anything at home and then they have to do it, so we practice in the beginning and now they're in the habit." A Buddhist father from Chicago said, "I started to bring them to temple really young, because it's easier to convince a three-year-old to do something they don't understand than a seven-year-old, especially when it's long and boring. So if they start at three and it's something they do every week for years, by the time they're seven they're more comfortable to ask about it." Again, this Muslim mother from New York City related, "As a Muslim, I want to impart to my son what it means to be Muslim in this time, hopefully by demonstrating my commitment to faith he'll feel a connection to faith, he'll have an example of what it means to stay connected through me, and that's been really important to me as far as his upbringing."

Parents, like this mainline Protestant father from Indiana, sometimes remember having learned their faith and practice in exactly this way from their own parents: "We have tried to be that example to our kids, sometimes just a silent example. It doesn't mean that we have to talk to the kids, but just in our actions, that they would see us having devotions in the morning, on our own. I especially remember my dad as I was getting ready for school, always see him at the kitchen table with his Bible and his little booklet and I think that's where I get that from." This conservative Protestant mother from Washington, DC, likewise recalled, "I remember my mom always praying, it's something you see and over time start to understand that this is a tool I actually should use, through hard times, good times, you start to develop praying itself. I definitely saw her praying, that was something that stuck. Like the Bible says, raise your child in the way to go and they won't depart from it." A white Catholic mother from Indiana reported: "My parents were great role models, weekly Mass, Catholic schools, rosaries, all those things. But also more than that, at one point they sponsored a Cambodian refugee who lived with us and so we saw the service component first hand, joyfully."

Parents think it especially important to expose children to prayer. "The one explicit religious observance that we now undertake is saying grace before meals and the Lord's Prayer before she goes out to school in the morning," recounted a mainline Protestant father from New York City, "and if you forget, she will stand there and bow her head and it's, "Oh yeah." [chuckles] So yeah, she had definitely internalized that." A white Catholic father from Indiana told us, "Praying before meals is important, and we would take turns. It was so adorable to hear what they would say in the prayers and them knowing others were listening. So coming together as a family and praying at dinnertime was really important because that solidifies the family and makes them more receptive to what you have to say." Volunteering and service are other important activities in this process, many religious parents think. "They're learning about poverty and inequality through community service through school and everything I do too," explained a Jewish mother from New York City, "and they see that I volunteer to help other people, even though I'm not being paid." One Mormon father from Indiana said, "I believe they can attain a great deal of happiness within the church, the faith. That's my encouragement to them, to remain faithful to progress within the church where we can find service opportunities, leadership opportunities, and social connections that are very enriching." "To have the kids see me willing to dedicate the time to the church sends the message that it's important," claimed a mainline Protestant mother from Washington, DC. "If we're gonna be a part of that community, trying to be a leader to shape it for all of our benefit is important. Everyone in our family volunteers, actually."

Some parents, like this Buddhist father from Chicago, deploy even more crafty approaches to exposing their kids to religion: "We go to the temple to bring the kids, take them to the temple, it's good enough. And if you be there, you will learn something, will be a good person. I'm not expecting much. I want to get them the way my dad taught me, he took me there, I helped him do things, and then he taught. He said I don't have to go, but just come with dad and do some work for the temple. Then instead of waiting why don't you go to class, learn music, Thai dance, all those things. So I get them to go naturally, not forcing so much, though we do enforce them sometimes." In any case, parents need to start this process when children are very young, as this Muslim father from Indiana explained: "You gotta start faith from the beginning, teaching your children from day one. You can't just all of a sudden when they're teenagers bring something new into the picture. They have to grow up with it from the beginning and they have to hear about God. You don't go way into the whole fill of religion, but discuss enough for that child at that age, mental ability, maturity and it grows. Before you eat, you say in the name of God please bless this food, and they know the words but one day they'll ask, what am I saying? Then you talk about if it weren't for God we wouldn't have food, he's what makes it possible." With this general kind of approach, many parents, like this Buddhist mother from Chicago, feel confident about keeping their children within their religious tradition: "I don't think they will leave Buddhism, because they've been exposed, they've been going to temple since they're young, so I don't think that's gonna happen, but if it does, I guess I can't force them. I was raised this way so I never thought of that."

Raising religious children should thus primarily be a practice-centered process, not chiefly a didactic teaching program.

Parents modeling religious practices is primary, we have seen, and explaining belief systems is secondary. Parents can and should explain and teach some, but they also look to religious institutions—church, Sunday school, Hebrew school, youth group, temple classes, summer camps, and so on—to contribute the more "official" religious formation of children through the didactic teaching of religious knowledge. "The first thing you can do with your child is lead by example," said a mainline Protestant mother from Washington, DC, continuing: "If you're involved at church, you'll hope that sticks. You have kids and go to church more often, and then you begin to behave in a way that reflects the religion in front of the kids, expose them to what you would hope would graft into them in their faith and so it ups the game a bit. So go to church weekly, talk to them about their faith, hook them up with good role models, mentors for the confirmation process, good godparents who stay in touch with them." "Being a Christian just makes life better, you know," reported a conservative Protestant mother from Florida. "I can show them the way and lead 'em, that's all I can do." A Catholic mother from Indiana said, "I tried to lead by example. But with my divorce it is kinda hard, but I think they know I'm still a good person, things happen. I want to believe they think I'm a good example in our faith, so, yeah, parents I think they need to lead by example." A conservative Protestant father from Los Angeles explained, "Our goal is to be influential in the world around us. We model that by our friendships as a married couple and hopefully our kids will do the same. We don't steer our kids a ton into who they should be friends with or not, we do let them know that it's wise to choose good friends and that there's wisdom in being friends with kids who are not all goofy and stupid."

Some negative cases and exceptions are worth noting. One mainline Protestant father from Washington, DC, for example, explained that he and his wife are actually relying on the power of modeling and example to raise their children to be *not too* religious: "Our kids as adults will probably be like we are now, they will go so far and then start to question and maybe just give up on it or maybe dig in deeper. The example we're setting by not being fully committed to church and not being a super religious family, we're sort of setting that as the goal." Other parents, especially white Catholics, feel guilty about not modeling an example for their children that they know they should, as with the following three distinct white Catholic fathers all from Indiana:

What's hard for me about being Catholic is it doesn't fit my lifestyle all the time. I still feel Catholic guilt when I miss Mass, so then I try to do the prayer-and-reflect thing, confess and blah blah, and all that stuff. But it's a hard decision to make to miss Mass and then have to explain to my son why it's important to go, so I'm not setting a good example.

None of my kids got actively involved in the youth group because we're too busy in other areas. I don't get involved in the men's group either, so I don't lead by example.

My wife is the backbone of this family, she takes the kids to confession every Christmas, but I'm not always a good example [and the obvious question is:], "Why isn't dad going?" Because I don't have anything [sin] to confess? [laughs] Dad's not always the best example, often I'm busy, or I don't make time for it.

Finally, one mainline Protestant father from Los Angeles—who seemed especially concerned, nearly obsessed, with his children's public behavior—stood out as a clear exception to the "downplay didactic teaching" rule: "Children are children and sometimes they do dumb things out of ignorance. But we remind them that you go to church and we expect a different type of behavior from you. I have high expectations of them when it comes to their behavior, loving themselves, respecting people, to empathize with other people as they would want it, to do what's right, know the right thing. They absorb it, but I want that more, so I keep talking, telling them, telling them, telling them what I would like. I am very, very confident that the more I keep talking, telling them, telling them, it will stick, and then [I will enjoy] watching them as they move on, their examples. We'll see how it goes, but I will tell you they are good kids. I get reports that they are good kids, and my daughter who is twelve was elected the best student of the month for behavior." But this insistence on didactic teaching is a nearly singular exception to the dominant belief, which continues as follows. "I can't even think of all we did," said a Jewish mother from Indiana, "I guess we've passed on everything, we've demonstrated by our actions everything that we wanted to." A New York Jewish mother of a toddler girl told us, [on raising her Jewish] "I only know how to be a Jewish mother, don't know how to be any other kind of mother, and she already knows so much about Judaism. It's just what we do because it's us, it's very ritual based, so she has her own kiddush cup, her goblet, when we do havdalah, which is the ceremony to end the Sabbath, she holds the spice jar to the light, she knows to do this, it's very ritual, there's a lot of ritual." A Muslim father from Chicago explained: "I have experience teaching, but with your own children you cannot teach them. You practice and they see you. They're like monkeys. They will do what you do. The day you start preaching them, they might go against you. That's their nature. So as a parent, you just practice it. I am blessed that I have knowledge [about Islam]. But practicing does not really need knowledge, it's the basic things." Equating the "influence" of children with "forcing" them against their will, as many parents we interviewed do, this Buddhist mother from Chicago argued, "I think parents should just expose the kid to religion, not influence. I believe if you force them to follow you in your belief and devotion, and all these things, it's like brainwashing your kid." Enumerating the various family religious practices in which they engage, a Mormon father from Indiana stated, "Most important things are the daily prayer and scripture study and the weekly family home evenings and weekly church attendance," and a Mormon mother from the same area said similarly, "I read the scriptures both alone and with my children. I go to church, three hours sometimes more every week, and teaching Sunday school, and we do Family Home Evening." A Hindu father from New York City explained at some length:

> We do the festivals, fasting, she prays every day in our prayer room, goes to the temple, and from very young we did the ceremonies, washing the gods, getting new clothes for the seasons. That's how it is stamped in the brain as they grow, not only offerings but also washing and cleaning, different foods, a small piece of jewelry, everything going on in the household. That immediately puts the question in their mind, "Why is this happening?," [which you then explain]. The gods are also a part of your family, you eat, god eats, right? It's not just a piece of metal just sitting there, it's part of your family. You feed them, you bathe them, you see them every day, and in summer we have a small fan that turns on if the temperature goes up, 'cause the god is part of your family. It's all family based, my mother-in-law was a very practicing religious Hindu, she knew all the verses to explain their meaning. We are from Brahmin family so we have all this in our family traditions.

This Hispanic Catholic mother from New Mexico shares that approach:

> Small words, I speak to her in small words. I don't talk to her a lot, so she won't tell me later that I talk too much and she gets bored. I don't want for her to get to that point, so two, three small words, nothing more. I limit myself to small things only, like, "Trust in God," "God will take care of you," "You are not alone," "God is with you." I don't inculcate much. She is still young to speak much with. But as the years pass and she prepares in catechism, she is also going to learn. So I shouldn't talk much, not to confuse or anger her. I think the moment or occasion will be given when we would have to talk.

If along the way children ask questions about religion out of curiosity, parents should answer as well as they are able.

We have seen this belief expressed in sundry quotes above, which we support with a few more here. Parents mostly wait for their children to ask them questions, but on occasion the more intentional parent, like this white Catholic father from Indiana, will be more proactive: "Trying to point out [to my kids] 'God incidences' is huge, because otherwise they might not notice. So I might say, did you see what just happened there? I think that was an act of sheer prayer." When asked by children, parents often confess, like this white Catholic mother from Chicago, that they do not have answers to their questions: "Most of our conversations about faith are after CCD classes, she'll have more questions. And then whatever my response was, I guess she wasn't happy and she just gave me 'that look,' so I said well go and ask your teacher. I can't remember the specifics but I do remember we had a conversation [laughs]."

More important than parents having answers, however, is showing their children how to find them. The answers may be believed to be found in the Bible, as this Hispanic Catholic father from New York City explained: "We sometimes talk about Christians and moral topics and I give them my opinion. Or we say, 'let's see what the Bible says,' we talk like that. There are always doubts, like I say sometimes, 'Hey, my God, where [in the Bible] is it?,' but that they break the faith, no, no breaks, because that is the strength in my life, have faith, strength to keep going ahead." Or the answers may be online. "I'm always pretty available to them if they have a question," said a (non-theistic) Buddhist mother from Chicago, "and if I don't know the answer, we go find it together, that's my favorite way of solving problems. 'I don't know,' I'm honest with them, 'I don't know. Let's go look together,' and we get on the internet together." Or the answers may be found in the Bible and on the internet: "When they ask tough questions," a black Protestant mother from Houston reported, "I go to the word [Bible] and see if I can find it, or go on Google and find the answer. Go to sources."

For other parents, the answers can be given by clergy, as noted by this Hispanic Catholic mother from Chicago: "I speak about God, about how great God was with them, that he blessed them. They once asked why different candles were lit in church at different seasons and I did not know what to answer, so quickly I say let's go ask father, the father knew how to explain." Or a parent may simply say, like this Hindu father from Chicago: "Depending on what the question is, if it's something very specific I will tell them I will do my own study and then get back to them." If a question is unanswerable, some parents may use it to teach children that someday they will meet God face to face, as exemplified by the story of this Mormon father from Indiana: "The other day our son asked at dinner, 'if God is Jesus's father, who is God's father?' Great question! I don't have the answer and that's what we talked about at dinner, we said that's part of faith some questions are just going to be unanswered until we can ask God directly, and that was all he needed." Alternatively, parents can explain that some questions have no good answers but people still need to believe in faith anyway, as this black Catholic father explained: "When they would ask difficult questions, I would be truthful and tell 'em pretty much we don't know why, that God said he doesn't put anything more in life than you can bear, so it's kinda hard to answer. You try to be a parent but you don't have all the answers yourself, so a lot of times you just try to think of an appropriate answer and reply truthfully at that given time." Crucial in every case, as we just read, however, is that parents be honest about their lack of knowledge. "We talk about morality," a conservative Protestant father from Florida reported, "and we told them be open and honest and we'll be open and honest with you. If you ask me the question, I'll give you the best answer I can."[4]

Not all parents are bereft of answers to their children's religious questions, however. Some, like this Muslim mother from Chicago, seem able to provide adequate answers: "They asked questions many times, 'Did you ever see God?' 'What did God look like?' And we just tell them our beliefs." With younger children the task can be easier, as this Hindu mother from central New Jersey explains: "He asked, if we pray to God, 'Where is God?' We tell him that he lives in us, in all living things, and he took that at face value and didn't really ask any further questions. The conversations are pretty quick, for the most part, as a kid at that age they get distracted easily and then it's on to the next question." Other parents, like these two Muslim fathers, from Indiana and New York City, respectively, simply try to answer as well as they can: "They have come and asked questions about God, faith, religion, and we have tried to explain the best possible," and, "They ask questions, like, 'What happens when

---

4. A significant theme in the sociology of childhood in recent years is the bidirectional nature of parent-child influence, that children can influence parents as much as the reverse (Leon Kuczynski and C. Melanie Parkin, "Agency and Bidirectionality," in *Handbook of Socialization*, ed. Joan Grusec and Paul Hastings [New York: Guilford Press, 2007], 259–83). We did not hear much evidence for this in our interviews, but that could be because of the design and focus of our study. Even so, a few cases of children shaping parents did emerge from our interviews. One mainline Protestant father from Indiana, for example, told us: "We talk about religion in the family, but I don't advise. They're adults. We advised them when they were young. Why do we make these choices, what does God want for us? We would drive together a lot, but not me instructing her. We would just talk and debate things and often I would end up changing my mind. I think that's important that a parent should not feel they have all of the answers, because life is hard and we don't have all of the answers. It took me a while to learn that." And a black Protestant mother from Houston recounted: "My kids [when they want to go out] say, 'But mommy, God is gonna protect us, Jesus is gonna protect us.' And I say, 'Yeah, you're sure right.' I say 'Go ahead all.' How you gonna teach them to believe and you sittin there not believing it yourself, you not trusting yo self enough to let your kids go? So I let 'em go, and they come back just fine."

you die? Where do you go?,' stuff like that. We try to answer to the best of our ability. Sometimes we'll be driving in the car, coming from an Islamic school, they cover some of these topics, one of them will ask a question and we'll answer it."

Finally, many of the Jewish parents we interviewed either don't believe or are not sure they believe in things like God, heaven, and other topics that often preoccupy children's questioning minds. For them, Judaism is not about the supernatural, which can often puzzle kids. As a result, their explanations to children about religious matters, if and when they take place, tend to sound different from those of believers in most other traditions. For example, the Jewish parents we interviewed were typically less concerned with providing correct answers to their children's questions (which comports with what we said above about their relative lack of interest in knowing "the truth") than with encouraging their children simply to ponder, to explore, and to search for their own best understandings—to see "what speaks to them," as one mother says in a quote a few pages further on. Their answers also struck us as expressing more confidence in their children's own capacities to think and learn for themselves about life's Big Questions. Consider, for instance, the two quotes, the first from a Jewish mother from Indiana:

> A little while ago, he was looking out the window at the universe and wondering where does it all come from, and he muses out loud, "Wow Mom, isn't it amazing when you think about it?" Occasionally my kids will ask questions about God. I've never been comfortable being didactic with them, never comfortable saying, "Well, you know, of course we believe in a God," that kind of thing. I've never wanted to do that, but I've always kind of mused with them, and led them to just wonder. Because to me wonderment is what God means, really. So at times when questions come up about God, I kind of deflect a little bit and just say, "Well you know, look around you. Don't you think maybe that's what God means?" I've never wanted to just say yes or no to questions. Or every once in a while I'll say, "Wow, you know, I actually never thought about that, but it's a great question. Let's talk to Rabbi about it next time."

This second quote is from a Jewish father from New York City:

> When discussions about God come up, I get very torn because I don't really believe in God, but I think they do. I feel like there's some uniqueness about [pause], especially when you're young and don't really

understand the world, you have to believe there's something in control of everything. I guess they also get it from Hebrew School. But I would like for them to reach these decisions on their own. So you don't want to lead your children in any direction, just give them an orientation and then they'll figure it out eventually.

This seemingly distinctive American Jewish approach to parental religious transmission may help to explain the apparent paradox that many Jewish parents, in our observation, are seriously committed to passing on Judaism to their children but not very interested in talking with them about the Jewish religion. It may also shed light on the seeming division of labor between the home/family and the synagogue, in which the home takes the lead in passing on Jewish identity and the family holds primary responsibility for instruction in religious matters. All of this helps to make sense of the report by this Jewish mother from Indiana, who otherwise made clear in her interview the importance of Judaism in and for her family: "I rarely talk about religious things, because my daughter has such a good relationship with our Rabbi, she's getting religion and spirituality every week in that class, she can ask or say anything in class she wants, so, no I really don't talk about it."

On occasion parents might also proactively share religious ideas and observations. But parents must never "preach" or be verbally overbearing in any way. Hypocrisy is the worst, so parents must be consistent and "walk the talk" (even if there is not much talk).

Parents are very straightforward about this. "Parents need to be active, to show by example; no, you don't have to volunteer at everything, but volunteer with some things," recommended a mainline Protestant mother from Indiana. "Play a part, play a role, listen, all that stuff. [Kids will call you out if] you're a hypocrite, well don't be a hypocrite, show by example." "I think every day little lessons on kindness and love," said a conservative Protestant mother from Florida. "You may not necessarily preach at them, because that would get old quickly, but teaching the whole 'Do unto others' thing." "They see us walking the walk and talking the talk, so hopefully it'll trickle on down to them where they'll walk the walk," explained a black Protestant father from Houston. And this black Protestant mother from Houston told us: "You wanna pray for 'em, but you don't want to badger 'em, like [in a confrontational tone], 'You get out of my house.' You don't want to do that because pushing 'em makes matters worse. You just have to continue to talk to 'em, pray for 'em, let 'em know, and hopefully they get to swing it on back in before time is too late." A white Catholic father from Indiana said, "With my boy, I didn't force him to go to church, but I strongly encouraged it as a 'you should do' something." One Hispanic Catholic father from New Mexico expressed his anti-preachy view this way: "I don't like how people tell you, 'You have to become closer to God,' or you go to their house to visit them and they only want to talk to you about religion. That doesn't work with me. No, no, no. My relationship with God is really, really, really intimate, even if I don't go to church [much]. I feel that God loves me greatly. So, I go to church less than a lot of people and I think that you don't have to. To God, it's God, and we must respect him, but we can't force that of others." Similarly, a Mormon mother from Indiana said: "Be a good role model. It's kind of hard to be a hypocrite and say you shouldn't do something and then you're doing it. Practice what you preach. Teach them but actually follow what you say. That's hard, as a parent, actually [chuckles], like with the cussing thing, I cuss and am not happy with that, and my kids have brought it up, so you know what, you're right, and let me stop doing this."

In keeping with the discussion of Jewish parents' approach to answering children's questions, this Jewish mother from Indiana described the approach in her family: "Things naturally come up in the course of conversations, most nights we have family dinners around the table and stuff comes up, 'cause we're talking, we are communicating all the time. I feel my leadership as a parent is more about talking about stuff and sharing how I feel about it, my value system, my decisions, why I made them, what I think about them, then ask what do you guys think about it? We'll talk, have conversations, and that way kids actually tend to end up believing the same thing as parents because it's done as a conversation, a shared kind of coming together of values, a subtle kind of teaching as opposed to, 'this is a no-no.' I don't think that's effective." A Muslim father from Indiana explained, "Kids will look up to you, and that's what we did, when my mom was raising us up, she was very religious, but I mean she didn't force a religion on us, if we want to go pray, we pray. She gave us freedom to do whatever we want to do really. A mother is always an influence when it come to the family." "I just wanna bring them and expose them," explained a Buddhist mother from Chicago. "This religion has this, this, this, or if you wanna know more you can research from the library or whatever, and then they can make a decision." And a Hindu mother from New York City said, "I do the ritualistic aspect every single day, because you don't raise your child by preaching, you raise your child by doing it.

So she won't come back and say, 'Mommy, you drink and you're telling me you can't drink.' Well no I don't, so I have the right to tell you not to, I practice it."

Parents also need not expect dramatic religious experiences from their children; passing on the faith to the next generation can and should be a gradual, natural, intuitive process.

Some parents had their own religious conversion or other "religious" experiences earlier in life. But none we interviewed seem to expect anything like that from their children—including Protestant parents from revivalist traditions historically emphasizing individuals at some discreet time "making a decision for Christ," raising a hand or walking down the aisle of an evangelistic or revival meeting, or even youth at some "age of accountability" simply "becoming a Christian" and being baptized. No parent we interviewed focused on the idea of religious conversions or the need to have a "religious experience." They instead expressed confidence in their own ability, sometimes with the help of God, and often with some support from their religious congregations, to pass on religious faith and practice to their kids in an ongoing life process. This attitude and belief about what is *not* necessary was not often an explicit point of discussion by parents, so us suggesting its being part of this cultural model is partly an argument from silence. But some parents did say some things that implied the belief or perhaps made it explicit. Almost no parents spoke about "religious experiences" either positively or negatively. Religion for nearly all of them is mostly about being a good person, not a dramatic enlightenment or personal encounter with God, Jesus, or any other superhuman force. At most, a few parents might have said something like what this Mormon mother from Indiana mentioned: "I think it is wonderful to have intense spiritual experiences, but they're not something that can be manufactured or manipulated."

The dominant view sounded something like what this mainline Protestant mother from New York City told us: "Just let them participate with what we're doing, and naturally they learn and pass on." And this conservative Protestant father from Florida: "A lot of our family life revolves around church, so as I continue to make that a part of our lifestyle, things naturally fall in place. That's sort of my idea." Or this Muslim father from Chicago: "I've never been the type of person that tends to do 180-degree turns. I would like to think of it more as an organic, gradual process. Obviously events can happen in people's life that cause them to change that way, but I like to think of it more as an organic process." And this

Jewish mother from Indiana: "I don't have any really definite dogmatic beliefs. There's certain ethical principles that are very much a part of who I am, and I don't even know if I ever taught my kids that, but they're the same way." Similarly, this Hindu father from Chicago reported, "I don't have to even remotely pretend to instruct them into good behavior, they just have it. It's a lucky thing for me and my wife, but that's how it's turned out. Maybe they just observed at home that this is how this family is and picked up." And a white Catholic mother from Indiana observed, "We as a family are just going to go to church, we always did this together, if I am going, you're going, if we're getting up, you're gonna get up. So it wasn't so much a requirement, just something we just did as a family." In these ordinary, natural, organic ways, parents believe that kids will "pick up" their religion, as this black Protestant father from Houston said: "I hope he picks up praying, thanking God for whatever he does, and learning from his mistakes, trying to follow in my footsteps and stay grounded."

Parents will need to insist that their young children attend religious services and other religious community activities, as appropriate, but when children become teenagers, parents must adjust their requirements to allow them as self-directed individuals to make "informed" religious decisions for themselves.

The idea is self-explanatory, although it applies most clearly to Christian religious traditions where attendance and participation in congregational activities is theologically normative. So, a white Catholic mother from Indiana said, "Obviously at a young age children don't know, but as they get older, they need to make an informed decision and stand behind it, whether it's Catholic or atheist or Jew or whatever. Just make sure it's an informed decision, doing it for the right reason, it's truly what you believe, and not just because others are doing it." A Hispanic Catholic father from Indiana agreed: "I would not force them, maybe the little ones, our duty is to take them when young children, but when older, I could not force them, because they will no longer receive it with faith. If they go voluntarily, they will receive the faith, but without interest to learn in church, do not force them." "Certain things they're forced to do because they're children," explained a Jewish mother from New York City, "but then when they're adults they have the knowledge to say, this speaks to me or this doesn't speak to me, and whatever they choose, at least they'll know, they will be making an informed choice." A white Catholic father from Indiana repeated this theme: "Early in life, children are not capable of making certain decisions, so you have to guide them in a way. As they reach adulthood, you shouldn't try to force your religion on them, they should be able to explore other opportunities. They should still seek a religion, but the ones who get it forced on them end up flying out, rebelling." One black Protestant father from Houston extended this principle to children deciding which church they prefer to attend: "We let him go to two churches then decide. That's the right way to do it, don't force it on your child, instead let them make the decisions. We are at church a lot so that was his choice. We didn't force him to get baptized, to be active, we did force him to participate in things, but only because we wanted him to have those experiences."

Different parents have different ideas when children should be free to decide on religion for themselves. Some Catholics, like this white Catholic father from Indiana, focus on an unspecified age after "the foundation" is laid and required sacraments are completed, the last of which would be confirmation: "As practicing Catholics, our kids are Catholic, so we sent them to the Catholic faith, baptism, first reconciliation, first communion. Obviously later in life they can make a choice, but giving them that foundation of religion is what counts, no matter what the religion, 'cause then they have a base to go off of. It's a parent's right to give them some sort of foundation when it comes to religion so as they get older they can make an informed decision." Others, such as this mainline Protestant father from Washington, DC, think the middle to late teenage years is the best time of transition: "My influence is positive, I think, a role model, it's all on how devout you are. I believe that they should be exposed to religion and practice it, and then when they become adults, whether that's fifteen, sixteen, seventeen, whatever it is, then it's on them to choose." Yet others, including this black Catholic father from Indiana, call it "late high school": "Oblige kids to go to church only for so long, 'cause kids don't know what's good for 'em. You got to lead 'em in the right direction just to see how they respond. So, obligation until a certain age, late high school, but as they get older, once kids get to being a junior or senior, you can't make them." Still other parents, like this mainline Protestant mother from Indiana, name age eighteen as the specific age of self-determination: "After age eighteen, they're adults, they have a right to make their own choices. My daughter stepped away from church altogether. It didn't mean she wasn't a person of faith, and she's been going back and looking at different churches for several years now." A black Catholic mother from Indiana said children can make their own religious choices when they've become financially independent: "We have Sunday school so children are exposed to the doctrines of the faith at an early age. But just because it works for me does not necessarily mean I'm going to shove it down anybody's throat. My job is to raise her with what I know. It worked for me, so I'm going to expose her to it, take her to church and everything. If she turns eighteen and decides she doesn't want it, I'm not going to be happy but I'm not going to stop her either. She's an adult, she can make her own decisions. [But as long as she's dependent] no, she's coming to church [laughs]. My house, my rules. You're coming with me, you can decide to do whatever you want when you start paying your own bills. That's how my mom did it, that's how I'm gonna do it." One Mormon family, typical of many Mormons, has a rule that children attend church as long as they live at home: "We don't want to be their friend until they're older, we want to be their parent first. Going to church is not an option for them here. When they've said I don't want to go to church, we say this is what we do as a family and we're going to church." A white Catholic father said the same as the deciding factor: "It's very important while they're under our care and our responsibility that we share the same views. We have to have a cohesiveness as a family unit to operate and live and love, so there's an understanding of why we're doing what we do. But once they're out of the house, hit college, graduate, move on to what they want to do with life, if they decide their values change, that's really up to them. But before they're eighteen and out of the house, it's very important that they share those values with us while we have responsibility for them." Whenever the transition point is, parents ought not to try to oblige their older children religiously, since that will backfire at worst and at best be a waste of time, as this Hindu father explained: "You put all the values in there and what you taught them they are practicing when under your wings, and then if they decide not to practice it I will not force them, because if they're not going to do it, I'm wasting my time, because I already invested enough time to educate, teach, and practice."

A Disagreement: Exposure to Other Religions?

Some American religious parents disagreed about one point that would fit under the "How to Pass on Religion" cultural model. This proposition is not a dominant view, but held by only a minority of parents. For some parents it is quite contentious. The belief is this: *In order to help children to be truly informed about their personal religious decisions, parents should purposefully expose children to the practices and beliefs of other religions, so they have a better sense of the range of choices and become more informed and tolerant.* The more liberal among mainline Protestants especially espouse this belief. One father in that tradition from Washington, DC, for example, told us: "No, I can't expect them to be religious, because we aren't, that wouldn't be me, especially if I am not actively trying to indoctrinate them myself, I can't expect that. I want them to choose, if they want to be Buddhist, Jewish, whatever, be agnostic. I want to sort of expose them and let them make a choice." A mainline Protestant mother from Indiana explained, "The beauty of being an individual is if my children grow up and decide that they don't want to practice religion or not believe in Jesus, that's their choice. It would be no different than if they decided they were homosexual, I would still love them regardless and be pretty open to whatever they want to believe as they grow up." And a mother in the same tradition from New York City said, "I think parents should expose kids to other religious traditions, like if they wanna go to a Passover seder or a Hanukkah party or something." Another New Yorker mother affiliated with a mainline Protestant church who does not believe in God described her struggle to teach her twelve-year-old daughter, who loves church and pressures her mother to believe and attend like she does, that she as an adult should have the right *not* to do so. To her, an important principle and lesson is at stake: "She wants to know why I don't go to church, why I don't believe in God. I say I totally get you have this belief and I support it and it's a good thing, but I just don't have that belief, I believe other things instead, and sometimes that frustrates her. She would like for me to go to church regularly, to be Christian. That's about her being a kid and not understanding that difference can still be positive, if you are different from someone else, that is okay. She does feel a little like I am judging her by not wanting to do what she wants to. But I'm still not going, because the lesson I want her to learn is that it's okay to do the thing you want to do, but, you know, to love someone is to set them free and let them be who they are, rather than forcing them into a particular mold." Most Jewish parents want their children to remain Jewish, but the notion of "informed choice" is also deeply compelling to many of them, including this Jewish mother from New York City, who wants her kids' possible choice not to be Jewish to be well informed so they do not end up rejecting something about which they are ignorant: "Informed choice. One studies, one learns all about Judaism, the history, the rules, and then one has the personal choice to do or not do as it fits one's lifestyle. Most people are not informed about anything and choose to not do things. But for my kids, I really want them to know what they're not doing, that they really know what's involved, and whatever they choose to do, at least they'll know, they will be making a choice." Also balancing a worry not to be closed-minded about other religions with a definite interest in successful religious reproduction, this Jewish mother from New York explained, "I don't think I could say don't explore something [in another religion], but I would hope that the fundamentals [of Judaism will stick]. You know I plan on sending her to the Jewish camp that lots of our kids attend, I think that camp is a thing that hooks kids in." Resistance of exploring alternatives is not quite acceptable, but hopefully the whole problem of defection will be avoided and the fundamentals solidified through a positive social experience of Jewish summer camp.

Most Mormons also very much want their children to remain Mormon. But some on the liberal end of the church also believe in proactively fostered education and informed choice. This Mormon father from Indiana, for example, drew on the internal resources of his own tradition—"because we are a persecuted church"—to justify actively exposing his children without prejudice to other religions: "If you're going to allow your children to make choices, you need to educate them on what those choices are, which means you have to teach them about evangelical, Muslim, Buddhist, any religion. You give them the basis, the foundation of Christianity but allow them or teach them to be open-minded and not to persecute any other religion. Just because there are Muslim extremists doesn't mean that Islam is a bad religion. Just because Latter Day Saints have reorganized congregations out there that do crazy stupid stuff doesn't mean all LDS are like that. Or just a few Catholic priests are pedophiles. I really try hard to teach my children not to persecute, because we are a persecuted church. You can give a very firm Mormon upbringing but also teach open-mindedness at the same time as a big value." Most Catholics likewise hope their children remain Catholic, but some liberal white Catholics, such as this mother from Chicago, subscribe to the "expose and choose" belief: "I'd rather expose them to religions and see what they like, because if you force your kid to do whatever, they're gonna rebel and not be happy and you're not gonna be happy. Just let them do what they think they like, let them get to know a bunch of different religions and then choose."

Because some religious traditions, such as Hinduism and Buddhism, tend not to be exclusive but may allow adherents to also follow other faiths, these issues are less pressing. Still, for many parents in these traditions, the underlying principles are the same. "They need to choose for themselves," reiterated a Hindu mother from central New Jersey. "I don't think forcing anything works, on religion or anything. You just give them the options and show them, they need to be exposed to know it, you definitely have to show them. But to believe or not it's up to them, I don't think we can force that." And one Buddhist father from Chicago reported, "She's been to the Baha'i temple with me, to the Hindu temple, not been to a Muslim temple yet but that's one of my goals. She goes with me and sees all the different faiths, and we discuss it. If our girls ask us something, we tell them."

Furthermore, some Muslim parents we interviewed who believe that all religions are ultimately the same when it comes to what really matters about religion—namely, being a good person—also spoke in ways reflecting this general idea. A Muslim father from Indiana, for example, said, "Every parent will bring kids up regarding the values of being a good person, whether it's Muslims or Christians, it doesn't matter as a parent, it's just the same thing. There's different ways of doing stuff, but every parent probably wants kids to be good and nice to people. I think we do pretty much the same thing, the only difference is religion, and everybody has their choice of religion." Finally, parents who believe that being "spiritual" is more important than being religious were also vocal about helping children to choose whatever religion or nonreligion they want, since for them being spiritual is what really matters. One white Catholic mother from Indiana, for instance confessed, "I really don't care if my kids share my Catholic faith, I don't care. They can become atheists like their father, that's fine. But I would hope they be spiritual people, because life is hard."

To be sure, however, this proposition was only advocated by the more liberal and open parents we interviewed. As we have seen, most parents would concede that, in the end, when one's children are adults, no parent can force them to believe or practice anything. But few parents endorse *proactively* exposing their children to significantly different religions in order to guarantee that their eventual choices would be thoroughly informed. That would seem like overkill and counterproductive to keeping children in the family's faith, which is what most parents desire. Sometimes, combinations of the interest in family and cultural solidarity, plus some unfamiliarity about other religions, can motivate parents to avoid proactively exposing children to other religions. Consider, for instance, the words of this lapsed white Catholic father from Chicago, who is married to a Thai Buddhist woman and who together are raising their children as Buddhists: "I would be disappointed if they didn't wanna do Buddhism anymore, 'cause I would feel then like Thai culture, they're half Thai, would just kinda stop right there. And then when they have children, are they gonna do anything Thai? I would want them to stay around my beliefs, as weird as that sounds, because I guess it's what you understand, as yourself, would make you feel better. Like I don't know anything about, you know, Jewi-, Jewi-, the religion of the Jewish, or if I'm saying that right I . . . Judaism, sorry. Or Muslim, or anything like that. So I guess it's that fear of me not knowing about it. I would be disappointed and would want them to stay around like what I raised them with." Beyond that approach, a few parents from more conservative religious traditions went out of their way to critique as unrealistic the logic and practice of "exposure," "informed consent," and "free choice" with religion. One conservative Protestant mother from Los Angeles, for example, took a "let's get real" approach to the matter: "You have a way you believe and live in your household. Every home has rules, no matter how many times you may say you don't, every home has rules. So somehow you are teaching them something. It's silly to let kids decide for themselves because first they are kids who don't understand anything, really. We have so much power over our kids in good and bad ways, and we're so foolish to not use it or think we don't have influence on them. I even see it with my kids now, there are times when the girls get mad at me, but when it comes down to it you realize, well, you're still their mom or dad and they want to please you." More liberal religious parents would suggest that proactively educating children about different religions should be done precisely to change the fact that "kids don't understand anything." They may also concede that her view might apply to younger children, but not teenagers. However, a white Catholic father from Chicago offered what could be a response, arguing that precious few parents are actually qualified to educate their children about other religions, that it is impossible really to understand "the other" without first being rooted in one's own tradition, and that such superficial interreligious instruction is actually often motivated not by ecumenically generous spirits or what is best for children but rather the personal desire on the part of parents for positive moral affirmation and social validation for being such good liberals:

> I don't think people honestly know enough [about religions] to expose kids with any intentional planning. "Exposing to many different religions" sounds good, but you're really not exposing them to anything, you're essentially reading them the Wikipedia page, which isn't anywhere close to the same thing as really exposing someone, actually having that be an option for them. You need to start with what you know. That can form the basis of relationships that can take a lot of different forms. There's a lot of similarities between religions, so in some ways by exposing them to the one tradition, you are exposing all the traditions. It doesn't really do anybody any favors to pretend. Like *I* can't expose

anybody to Buddhism, 'cause I don't know what the heck I'm talking about. My "exposing" them to it would be just for show, just so I can tell my friends, "Aren't I great?"

So this specific "how to" belief about the best ways to pass on religion to children is, unlike the other propositions already explored, held by only a minority of more liberal parents.

CHAPTER FIVE

Theorizing Cultural Models

OUR EMPIRICAL FINDINGS in the previous chapters challenge some theories of culture that have dominated cultural sociology and parts of anthropology for decades. As we noted in the introduction, we went into our interviews with religious American parents from many backgrounds expecting to encounter diversity, but instead we heard something approaching hegemonic consensus. We anticipated parental conversations about life, religion, and children to display internal inconsistences, but instead we discovered an underlying coherence and reasonable intelligibility. We sampled our interview respondents intentionally to examine differences between religious traditions, race and ethnicity, social class, gender, household type, and rural-urban background, but we encountered instead beliefs, goals, and purposes that are widely shared across those differences. Rather than rummaging their "tool kits" of culturally acceptable explanations for "talk" that would rationalize their actions, our interviewed parents expressed beliefs and purposes that were clearly internalized and dear to their hearts. After finishing our interviews, we coded and analyzed our data as the standard "variables sociology" mentality would commend, but in the end we found not varying outcomes associated with differing categories, but a general approach shared across those categories, as if it had been methodically indoctrinated. Having worked through this research project from beginning to end, we could not avoid the unorthodox conclusions we report here.

If our empirical findings are valid and the particular question of parents passing on religion to children does not represent an anomaly to the normal workings of culture, then at least some of the assumptions of what we next describe as the post-Parsonian paradigm of culture are wrong at least some of the time, and perhaps much of the time. That paradigm rightly sought to correct flaws in the old Parsonian approach. But in the process, it overcorrected, swinging to opposite extremes, when it should have shifted more carefully to a complex, balanced middle ground. A growing number of voices have recently raised doubts about different aspects of the post-Parsonian approach to culture, to which we add ours. We also want to advance an alternative theoretical understanding that returns us to a more realistic, complex ground that can improve our understanding and analyses of culture.

Described in most general terms, the old Parsonian view (named after the influential Harvard sociologist, Talcott Parsons, 1902–1979) assumed that culture is a unified system that is internally coherent, logically consistent, normative, well integrated, consensual among populations, resistant to change, clearly bounded by nation-states ("societies"), and personally internalized through institutional processes of socialization. Culture causes actions by instilling in new members of society an understanding of and personal commitment to "values," the realization of which becomes the motivation and directive for correct behavior at the microlevel and the source of social order at the macrolevel (see the far left column in table 2).

Post-Parsonian approaches to culture emerging in the 1970s rejected these assumptions and turned them upside down—so arguably they might better be called *anti*-Parsonian approaches (the center column in table 2). Culture was theorized by post-Parsonians as disjointed, its coherence thin at most. The cultural beliefs and values that people professed were said to be inconsistent or incompatible with one another. The elements of culture, far from being well integrated in a normative system, are often fragmented, at best loosely coupled. Rather than being consensually shared by members of populations, culture is believed in post-Parsonian approaches to be contested, unevenly engaged and embraced, and (in some accounts) manipulated both by ordinary cultural users and powerful actors. Culture is also changeable in its relevance and uses, readily adapted to different contexts as situations demand. Culture has a fluid, ambiguous nature that works its way in and out of multiple levels of life, including the local and subcultural in different expressions. If culture is in any way socialized and internalized, that happens selectively and inconsistently. In fact, the very existence of a centered subjectivity of the self may be thought to be doubtful. Better to conceive of culture as external to persons, objective to their thoughts and feelings. Culture's work is not to normatively govern people's actions but to help people "make meaning," to claim significance for different aspects of life, and to attach intelligibility to people's behaviors, often in post hoc, rationalizing ways.

Table 2. Governing Assumptions about Culture of Three Different Theoretical Approaches

The Parsonian View	Post-Parsonian Approaches	Cultural Models Theory
Unified systems	Assemblages of pieces	Networks of schemas
Internally coherent	Thin coherence, disjointed	Variable but potentially highly coherent
Logically consistent	Often internally self-contradictory	Reasonable when properly reconstructed
Normative	Instrumental, justifying	Constitutive, orienting, and telic
Highly integrated	Disjointed, loosely coupled	Intelligibly linked schemas
Resistant to change	Situationally highly adaptive	Normally durable, susceptible to change
Consensual	Contested, manipulable, emphasizing difference	Potentially highly consensual, but also often local and subcultural
Power relations ignored	Power relations central (in some theories), ignored in others	Powerful interests variably able to shape, dominate widespread cognitive beliefs
Clearly bounded by nation-state borders	Fluid, ambiguous, local	Boundaries variable, an empirical question
Subjectively internalized through socialization	External, selectively internalized if at all	Subjectively internalized, primarily in practical consciousness
Specifies "ultimate values"	Makes provisional meaning	Guides practices through constitutive and normative belief orientations
Causally motivates means-ends actions	Nonmotivational, post-hoc sense-making, rationalizing	Motivates action, but in complex, multicausational, many-leveled processes

These post-Parsonian assumptions about culture have dominated theory in cultural sociology and anthropology for decades. Names and ideas sometimes associated with post-Parsonian views include James Clifford, Ann Swidler, cultural "tool kits," "strategies of action," and some approaches under the influence of pragmatism, situationism, and postmodernism. But the post-Parsonian approach to culture is not best thought of as specific theories or theorists, but a paradigmatic outlook that can pervade entire fields. Meanwhile, however, advances in other disciplines and fields have laid the groundwork for a basic rethinking of its approach. Since the 1980s, the cognitive sciences have given us much better knowledge about how human minds work. Moral psychologists have complicated our understanding of how evaluative judgments and decisions operate. A school of theoretically grounded and empirically driven cognitive anthropologists has developed and flourished. Social theorists more broadly offered helpful insights into how social structure and active agency are dynamically related.[1] A younger generation of sociologists has reconsidered the once passé concepts of values, morality, and norms, resurrecting an appreciation for their actual importance for understanding and explaining social life.[2] Other sociologists have advanced new methodological arguments about how to access motivating culture through indirect means.[3] And yet other young sociologists have published impressive accounts of how culture works that do not follow the dominant line.[4] With these and other developments, discontent with the post-Parsonian approach has been growing. We too are discontent and wish this book to contribute to the broader reconsideration of post-Parsonian theory of culture now underway.

1. For example, William Sewell Jr., "A Theory of Structure: Duality, Agency, and Transformation," *American Journal of Sociology* 98, no. 1 (1992): 1–29; Margaret Archer, *Realist Social Theory: The Morphogenetic Approach* (Cambridge: Cambridge University Press, 1995); Anthony Giddens, *The Constitution of Society* (Berkeley: University of California Press, 1984).

2. For example, Steven Hitlin and Stephen Vaisey, eds., *Handbook of the Sociology of Morality* (New York: Springer, 2010); Steven Hitlin and Stephen Vaisey, "The New Sociology of Morality," *Annual Review of Sociology* 39 (2013): 51–68; Kraig Beyerlein and Stephen Vaisey, "Individualism Revisited: Moral Worldviews and Civic Engagement," *Poetics* 41, no. 4 (2013): 384–406; Elizabeth Christine Victor, Andrew Miles, and Stephen Vaisey, "The Role of Moral Worldviews in Predicting Adolescent Sexual Behavior from Adolescence to Emerging Adulthood," *Journal of Adolescent Research* 30, no. 6 (2015): 779–99; Andrew Miles and Stephen Vaisey, "Morality and Politics: Comparing Alternate Theories," *Social Science Research* 53 (2015): 252–69; Steven Hitlin and Stephen Vaisey, "The New Sociology of Morality," *Annual Review of Sociology* 39 (2013): 51–68.

3. For instance, Allison Pugh, "What Good Are Interviews for Thinking about Culture? Demystifying Interpretive Analysis," *American Journal of Cultural Sociology* 1 (2013): 42–68; Stephen Vaisey, "Is Interviewing Compatible with the Dual-Process Model of Culture?" *American Journal of Cultural Sociology* 2 (2014): 150–58; Stephen Vaisey, "The 'Attitudinal Fallacy' Is a Fallacy: Why We Need Many Methods to Study Culture," *Sociological Methods and Research* 43, no. 2 (2014): 227–31; Stephen Vaisey, "Socrates, Skinner, and Aristotle: Three Ways of Thinking about Culture in Action," *Sociological Forum* 23, no. 3 (2008): 603–13.

4. For example, Justin Farrell, *The Battle for Yellowstone: Morality and the Sacred Roots of Environmental Conflict* (Princeton, NJ: Princeton University Press, 2015); Robert Brenneman, *Homies and Hermanos: God and Gangs in Central America* (New York: Oxford University Press, 2011).

We believe the most promising way forward has been developed by the cognitive anthropology school, which we examine next. The far right column of table 2 summarizes the key points of that theory. We understand the internal dimension of culture as most basically cognitively constituted in neurological systems, organized in networks of structurally durable beliefs and schemas, often widely shared by varieties of types of populations (involving dominant but also supplemental and alternative themes), and motivationally directive of action and practices. Our empirical case in this book has not attempted to substantiate every aspect of this cultural models theory—more and different types of research will be necessary to do that. We have focused instead on driving home a few limited but crucial points, key building blocks in a larger argument—namely, that culture can be *coherent, consensual, reasonable, internalized,* and *teleological* in its orientation to *guiding* life practices.[5] This is not an argument for a return to Parsonianism, since our approach is different from that in important ways. Instead, we wish to move forward into a post-post-Parsonian era that corrects the numerous over-reactions and mistakes of the dominant approach of recent decades.

Reconstructing Cultural Models

Our empirical purpose in this book has been to identify and analytically represent the cultural models that inform how American religious parents approach the transmission of religious faith and practice to their children. But what is a "cultural model?" Here we follow the ideas of a school of cognitive anthropologists—especially Naomi Quinn, Claudia Strauss, Dorothy Holland, and Roy D'Andrade—whose thinking we find helpful.[6] The

5. The word *orientation* is a crucial qualifier here. We do not mean that culture has simple, direct, and full causal power to produce consistent human actions, but rather that culture is by nature oriented toward the guiding of life practices, even if it is only one force at one level among many that shape those practices.

6. See Naomi Quinn, ed., *Finding Culture in Talk* (New York: Palgrave Macmillan, 2005); Naomi Quinn, "An Anthropologist's View of American Marriage: Limitations of the Tool Kit Theory of Culture," in *Advances in Culture Theory from Psychological Anthropology*, ed. Naomi Quinn (New York: Palgrave Macmillan, 2018), 139–84; Claudia Strauss and Naomi Quinn, *A Cognitive Theory of Cultural Meaning* (Cambridge: Cambridge University Press, 1997); Roy D'Andrade and Claudia Strauss, *Human Motives and Cultural Models* (Cambridge: Cambridge University Press, 1992); Giovanni Bennardo and Victor de Munck, *Cultural Models: Genesis, Methods, and Experiences* (New York: Oxford University Press, 2014); Dorothy Holland and Naomi Quinn, *Cultural Models in Language and Thought* (Cambridge: Cambridge University Press, 1987); also see Richard Shweder and Robert Levine, *Culture Theory* (Cambridge: Cambridge University Press, 1984); Roy D'Andrade,

idea of cultural models "begins with the assumption that people in a given group share, to greater or lesser extent, understandings of the world that have been learned and internalized in the course of their shared experience, and that individuals rely heavily on these shared understandings to comprehend and organize experience, including their own thoughts, feelings, motivations, and actions, and the actions of other people."[7] The key feature of "culture" in this approach operates in human *cognitions*, in how people *believe* and *think*, both tacitly and explicitly. People's cognitions are organized in "schemas" that are normally neither systematically organized nor entirely random or disorderly, but are rather variably coherent and structured.

An important task in the study of culture is to identify the more or less organized mental schemas and structures that compose people's cognitions and that organize and help direct their life practices, what we are calling their cultural models. How can that be done? Researchers do not have direct access to people's minds, so how can we identify cognitive suppositions and beliefs—especially when they are tacit, not explicit? One answer is through the careful analysis of people's discourse. Get people to talk a lot and from different perspectives about a subject of interest, study closely and systematically what they say and how they say it, and from that analysis can emerge a systematic understanding of the cognitive assumptions and beliefs that people hold in their minds, even when they are not fully aware of or articulate about it. The job of the researcher is to help "bring to the surface" through lots of talk people's actual cognitive suppositions and beliefs about which they may not often be consciously reflective.[8]

Social scientists have usually understood culture to have both internal and external dimensions. The internal side involves people's subjective assumptions, beliefs, attitudes, values, and dispositions. The external is reflected in objective material artifacts, the built environment, embodied practices, and publicly available symbols and signs. Both can be

---

The Development of Cognitive Anthropology (Cambridge: Cambridge University Press, 1995); Brad Shore, *Culture in Mind: Cognition, Culture, and the Problem of Meaning* (New York: Oxford University Press, 1998).

7. Quinn, *Finding Culture in Talk*, 2–3.

8. This process roughly parallels with cultural cognitions what psychoanalytic therapists try to accomplish with their clients when it comes to their unconscious emotions, desires, and thoughts: to bring them through extended talk to the surface of consciousness for recognition, inspection, and evaluation—the difference being that scholars of cultural models are not trying immediately to help people therapeutically.

interpreted to understand their cultural meanings, though doing so entails methodological assumptions and challenges. Absolute certainty is never feasible, though reliable understanding is quite possible. Providing such interpretive understandings is the job of the cultural analyst, and is what we hope to offer here. Our focus is not the external side of culture (about which more further on)—although we did collect data on the religious artifacts in parents' homes, neighborhoods, and often places of worship to provide some context for our interview analyses. Our primary focus instead is culture's internal dimension, on religious American parents' cognitive assumptions and beliefs. That, we think, following the cognitive anthropologists who inform us, is best done through the careful study of discourse, which is why we focus on the analysis of in-depth interviews with parents.

Some sociologists have argued that "if we want to learn about culture, the last thing we should do is to conduct in-depth interviews."[9] We completely disagree. It is true that people cannot simply sit down and tell you about all of their assumptions and beliefs. Most are too obvious and too opaque to explicate them systematically. People do know and believe a lot more than they can directly and immediately tell, however.[10] And with the right research methods we believe that much of people's cognitive cultural suppositions and beliefs can be identified and understood. Discourse is "the best available window into cultural understandings and the way that these are negotiated by individuals. Culture in this sense of understanding encompasses the largely tacit, taken for granted, and hence invisible assumptions that people share with others in their group and carry around inside them, and draw upon in forming expectations, reasoning, telling stories, and performing a plethora of other ordinary everyday cognitive tasks."[11] What of particular value that social scientists like us bring to this process are systematic research methods and the trained ears and eyes for noticing patterns in discourse that those

9. John Levi Martin, "Life's a Beach but You're an Ant, and Other Unwelcome News for the Sociology of Culture," *Poetics* 38, no. 2 (2010): 240.

10. Michael Polanyi, *Personal Knowledge: Towards a Post-Critical Philosophy* (Chicago: University of Chicago Press, 1974).

11. Quinn, *Finding Culture in Talk*, 3. Our approach also assumes, however, that most of what people say in in-depth interviews is sufficiently trustworthy to be used as raw social science data. Not every social scientist believes that. Some skeptics claim that talk is little but talk, disconnected from the real causes of behavior in life. But see arguments that stand the test of time in Steve Bruce and Roy Wallis, "Rescuing Motives," *British Journal of Sociology* 34 (1983): 61–71; and Roy Wallis and Steve Bruce, "Accounting for Action," *Sociology* 17, no. 1 (1983): 97–110.

speaking may only partially understand consciously. "Cultural analysis, then, refers to the effort to tease out, from discourse, the cultural meanings that underlie it."[12]

What then is the idea of a *cultural model*? First, we must remember that the *actual cognitions* that operate in people's minds versus our *scholarly representations of them* are different things. The cognitions are the first-order reality; our interpretive descriptions and analyses of them are second-order representations of that reality. Reality is always more complex, subtle, and difficult than the representations that social scientists present in their findings. Good scientific representations identify the key conceptual and causal features of reality and describe their internal relations and structures in ways that enlighten and inform observers. Good science makes reality conceptually clearer for human understanding than does un-interpreted reality itself. If that were not the case, then science would be unnecessary. Still, scientific descriptions and analyses are never the first-order reality itself, only second-order representations.[13]

By our account—following the theory in cognitive anthropology on which we draw—the concept of "cultural models" refers to the first-order reality of the mostly tacit, cognitive assumptions and beliefs that people in groups more or less intersubjectively share and use to make sense of their experiences and to understand how to act in the world. In this view, cultural models belong to the internal side of culture. Cultural models are what people have learned and internalized, subjectively, in cognitive memory systems. They are largely taken for granted by those who hold them—in Naomi Quinn's words, they are "referentially transparent," that is, mostly invisible to their "owners" in ordinary circumstances.[14]

Yet cultural models are not entirely private as a result of their being internal or subjective in cognition, but are also publicly available for recognition, analysis, and understanding through their expression in speech and other representations. If that were not true, then cultural models could not be intersubjectively shared in the first place, and people in ordinary life could not navigate their interactions and the world with their help. Of course, cultural models cannot be directly accessed, as if under a microscope. But that does not make them empirically inaccessible. They can be systematically studied, in the same way we study most everything

12. Quinn, *Finding Culture in Talk*, 4.

13. Although, to necessarily complicate things, the second-order scientific knowledge then becomes its own reality, though of a different nature than the referents that they are *about*.

14. Quinn, *Finding Culture in Talk*, 3.

else that matters in the social sciences, namely, indirectly, through indicators, inference, retroduction, and abduction. What the study of cultural models is attempting to identify and understand then are the "mental representations shared by members of a culture," the "understandings of the world that have been learned and internalized" that "people in a given group share, to greater or lesser extent," which make ongoing experience comprehensible and maneuverable.

What then about our second-order, scholarly representations of people's cultural models? The language here can become confusing because these are also models, but of a different type; they are abstract conceptual models resulting from scholarly analyses represented with words and diagrams, not actual cultural models operating in the neural systems of people in the real world.[15] To keep things clear, then, we propose to call what we present in this book *analytic models*. They are our scholarly descriptions of the real cultural models with which the parents we interviewed make sense of the world and their lives. As models of models, analytic models are scaled-down and simplified representations of real objects or processes that facilitate the visualization and comprehension of their qualities and dynamics. An analytic model is thus a simplified, organized representation of the real cognitive assumptions and beliefs that comprise some internal aspect of people's culture. Analytic models organize and systematically structure those assumptions and beliefs more than they usually actually exist and operate in people's minds.[16]

But good analytic models are always "true" to the realities they represent, neither enhancing nor distorting them but rather bringing clarity, insight, and comprehension. So analytic models present in *condensed propositional form* the kind of statements that people *would* make about their cultural cognitions *if they were fully self-aware, honest, and articulate* about the assumptions and beliefs that compose their cultural models.

15. Actually, to make matters more complicated, we must acknowledge that analytic models are also "real" in their own way, even if their reality is of a different type than those of cultural models, and, if and when analytic models become part of a social group's shared cultural knowledge at a popular level, as can happen with the ideas in some scholarly works, then they can also influence actual cultural models in the "real world." So, to be precise, we must say that both types of models are real but in different ways, and that at least potentially their relation could be one of reciprocal influence.

16. Cultural models also usually entail both models *of* (representing the way things really are) and models *for* (representing the way people ought to live, how things ought to be), to reference the well-known distinction of Clifford Geertz. Quinn, *Finding Culture in Talk*, 61.

The task of the scholar in forming analytic models is the "reconstruction, from what people said explicitly, of the implicit assumptions they must have had in mind to say it."[17] Behind and beneath what people are able to explain in interviews lay complex networks of real assumptions and beliefs that directly and indirectly inform what they do say. Scholars like us analyze people's actual discourse in order to identify and represent those internal, subjective cognitive suppositions and beliefs, which tend to lay in the background, unrecognized, or often so taken for granted that they seem obvious and are not typically expressed.

Identifying cultural models and forming descriptive analytic models requires exercising the dual capacities of skilled *perception* and *reconstruction*. We use our ears and eyes to *perceive* as correctly as possible the often-tacit cultural assumptions and beliefs that lay behind and beneath discourse. This means not only taking at face value what people say on the "surface" but also listening to and interpreting their discourse at a variety of levels and in different ways.[18] We must also faithfully *reconstruct* those observed networks of cognitive assumptions and beliefs in simplified propositional forms that represent their content and internal relations (and possible variants across different social groups). If we do it well, the analytic models will "ring true." In that, insightful, conceptual, interpretive understanding and representation are crucial. Simply following methodological procedures and formulas is never enough.

Another question: do the parents we interviewed idealize their own thinking and practices of parenting in their talk? Probably, on at least some points. But that is not a problem for our purposes. It does not distort our results. Our primary interest is not an accurate accounting of what parents actually do, but rather the cognitive cultural models with which they operate, which we think (though do not demonstrate in this book) imperfectly motivate and guide what they do, among other factors. We want to learn about the *culture* of parenting for religious transmission, not parents' actual particular behaviors of transmission. The exact causal connection between culture and actions is a related but distinct

---

17. Quinn, *Finding Culture in Talk*, 45. The "what must be the case if . . ." feature of this form of analysis reflects what critical realists, like ourselves, call "retroductive" analysis, that is, the use of "transcendental" reasoning to identify directly nonobservable conditions that must be true if the facts of a given case are what they are; see Berth Danermark et al., *Explaining Society: Critical Realism in the Social Sciences* (New York: Routledge, 2002), 73–114.

18. Allison Pugh, "What Good Are Interviews for Thinking about Culture? Demystifying Interpretive Analysis," *American Journal of Cultural Sociology* 1 (2013): 42–68.

analytical concern than our immediate interest here. So, if parents idealized in their interviews, that itself is actually part of the culture we seek to discern and reconstruct, which creates no serious problem for our purposes.

In our view, then, central to cultural sociology is *the interpretive, rational reconstruction in condensed, organized, propositional forms (analytic models) of the networks of people's actual, subjective, cognitive assumptions and beliefs (cultural models), through the careful, systematic analysis of extended discourse.* The goal is to identify and represent in analytic models the content and structure of real cognitive cultures in order to understand and explain (as a next analytical step) how culture shapes people's actions, practices, and experiences, and produces external cultural objects, symbolic systems, built environments, and so on.

Methodological Implications

So what kind of data are needed to do this kind of cultural analysis well? How much discourse do we need to reconstruct analytic models of people's real assumptions and beliefs that compose their cultural models? The answer is: it depends on how much complexity, coherence, and diversity exists in people's networks of cultural cognitions. The simpler and more coherent and similar are people's cultural assumptions and beliefs, the smaller the sample one needs. If everyone in a social group literally held exactly the same cognitions, then we would only need to interview one member to get it right (although more than one to confirm that we got it right). But people in social groups never think exactly alike. So we need to interview enough people to make sure we identify people's real cultural cognitions well enough to model them correctly and to confirm with confidence that we are not missing some important but as-yet undetected cultural belief content, complexity, tension, qualification, or exception. The sample needs to be large enough to capture the breadth, depth, and complexity of people's real cognitions and to be reasonably confident that we have not missed something important. So how large is enough? Unfortunately, there is no one right answer. It depends on how much agreement and complexity exist in the cultural cognitions among the social groups being studied.

The cognitive anthropologists we follow here tend to believe, based on their decades of research experience, that most social groups embody fairly high levels of agreement about core cultural assumptions and beliefs. Roy D'Andrade, for instance, writes that "cultural models tend to be strongly shared. . . . My personal estimate is that a sample of 20–30 is sufficient to obtain a reasonable estimate of the degree of agreement for the items of a cultural model."[19] This, he observes, cuts against the natural tendency of sociologists to assume that large samples are needed to confidently represent a group's views. But that assumption, he argues, is biased by sociology's typical interest not in identifying what is shared, but rather in differences, variables, contrasts, and comparisons across categorical groups: "It is not surprising that a small sample shows high agreement about certain things *if those things are highly agreed about in the whole population.* . . . Much of the attitude/belief research in sociology is oriented toward those attitudes and beliefs that vary across social divisions such as gender, class, ethnicity, and region. Typically, such research does not focus on beliefs and attitudes that are part of the high concordance code because shared beliefs yield no interesting information about social differences."[20]

We went into our interviews as typical sociologists primed to look for expected comparisons and differences between the various demographic and religious subgroups that we sampled. We were surprised, however, to find relatively few differences. The empirical evidence we confronted forced us to realize that the main story to be told was one about similarities and shared views—the account we told in the previous chapters—and not comparative differences. That required a definite shift in our expectations and analyses. But it was also reassuring that the empirical data rather than our preconceived ideas had the power in the end to determine our findings and story.

If our task is building analytic models that represent "high concordance codes" in people's cultural models, smaller samples may be all that is needed. Whether or not groups of people's tacit and explicit cognitive assumptions and beliefs involve high agreement is in the end an empirical question that can only be answered in the very process of research. If one has sampled interview respondents well, once one begins to hear the same discourse repeated, one can reasonably judge that additional data will not contribute much to the reconstruction of good cultural models. That is called "interview saturation." Such methodological limits usually cannot be determined at the outset of a study, but only during the process of interviewing. In the end of our research,

---

19. Roy D'Andrade, "Some Methods for Studying Cultural Cognitive Structures," in Quinn, *Finding Culture in Talk*, 99.

20. Ibid.

we came away confident that our sample of 235 interviews provides us with enough evidence to present solid findings and draw reliable conclusions.[21]

Unpacking the Theory of Cultural Models

Our empirical observation is that culture can be *coherent, consensual, reasonable, internalized,* and *teleological* in its orientation to guiding life practices. We believe cognitive anthropology's theory of cultural models helps explain that well. Since cognitive anthropologists have already developed their approach elsewhere, we do not need to recount the entirety of the theory here. Full understanding and appreciation requires reading their work. For our purposes and to contribute our perspectives, we offer the following.

Internal Culture. We recognize a distinction between internal and external culture, and we feel no need to insist that culture is "really" either one or the other. Internal culture, as we already noted, is made up of cognitions, beliefs, values, assumptions, schemas, meanings, dispositions, and the like. It is formed in persons through bodily experience and governed and stored in the body, especially the brain, particularly in memory. This is the realm of human subjectivity, embodied experience, and personal understanding and agency. External culture is composed of public symbols, material artifacts, the built environment, bodily inscriptions and presentations, art, print publications, electronic and digital media, and so on. It consists of material and institutional expressions and outcomes of internal culture (and possesses the capacity to shape internal culture in turn). External culture involves the realm of humanly created, objective, and publicly observable objects, such as tools, buildings, languages, and practices.[22] Various theorists have argued over the decades about whether culture "really" is internal or external. Anthropologist Ward Goodenough, for instance, insisted that culture was internal and subjective, located "in the minds and hearts of men," while Clifford Geertz contended that

21. In fact, we began our study with a rough sense of how many total interviews we wished to complete, which informed our stratified quota sample design, and, if anything, in retrospect, our final dataset was perhaps oversaturated with more interviews than would have been necessary to make our case—although we are happy to have erred on the side of completing too many than too few interviews.

22. For a parallel distinction made between "personal" and "public" culture, see Omar Lizardo, "Improving Cultural Analysis: Considering Personal Culture in Its Declarative and Nondeclarative Modes," *American Sociological Review* 82, no. 1 (2017): 88–115.

culture is external and public.[23] That is a fruitless disagreement. Culture has both internal and external dimensions that we need to recognize and distinguish.

Other theorists have argued more recently against the empirical accessibility, explanatory importance, or even basic reality of human internal experience, people's capacity to internalize things like beliefs and values, and the realm of subjectivity in general.[24] Such arguments are interesting and must be seriously considered, but in the end they are not persuasive. When we eliminate cognitive subjectivity, we are left with behaviorism—a lesson learned in the 1950s. We will not spend our effort here disputing antimentalist arguments but simply proceed on the assumption that subjective experience is real and that people can and do internalize things like beliefs, identities, and values.[25] Clearly, any cognitive approach to culture, including ours, must take human "internality" seriously, since cognitions are by definition entities that exist and operate in people's subjective mental lives. That said, our focus in this book is exclusively on the internal aspect of culture. When we say "culture" here, we mean its internal, subjective, especially cognitive dimension. How that interacts with external features of culture raises crucial and fascinating questions that are beyond our capacity to address in this book.

Cognitive Beliefs. The theory of cultural models is built on the fact that human beings are embodied animals possessing brains with amazing

23. Goodenough: "A society's culture consists of whatever it is one has to know or believe in order to operate in a manner acceptable to its members. . . . Culture is not a material phenomenon; it does not consist of things, people, behavior, or emotions. It is rather an organization of these things. It is the forms of things that people have in mind, their models for perceiving, relating, and otherwise interpreting them." (Ward Goodenough, *Cultural Anthropology and Linguistics* [Indianapolis: Bobbs-Merrill, 1957], 167); Geertz: Culture "consists of socially established structures of meaning. . . . Culture, this acted document . . . is public. . . . Though ideational it does not exist in someone's head. . . . Culture is public because meaning is. . . . My own position . . . has been to try to resist subjectivism . . . to try to keep the analysis of symbolic forms as closely tied as I could to concrete social events and occasions, the public world of common life" (Clifford Geertz, "Thick Description: Toward an Interpretive Theory of Culture," in *The Interpretation of Cultures* [New York: Basic Books, 1973], 3–30). In our view, Geertz confused "public" with "shared," as culture is first and primarily intersubjectively shared, and only then and as a result can it be publicly enacted, meaningful, and interpretable.

24. See Robert Sharf, "Experience," in *Critical Terms in Religious Studies*, ed. Mark Taylor (Chicago: University of Chicago Press, 1998), 94–116.

25. See, however, Christian Smith, *What Is a Person? Rethinking Humanity, Social Life, and Moral Good from the Person Up* (Chicago: University of Chicago Press, 2010); Christian Smith, *To Flourish or Destruct: A Personalist Theory of Human Goods, Motivations, Failure, and Evil* (Chicago: University of Chicago Press, 2015).

capacities of thought, memory, and causal understanding. Humans do not simply "make meaning" or rationalize actions post hoc but continually perceive and interpret their environments, form beliefs that they take to be justified, and develop belief-shaped intentions to engage in activities in order to realize certain ends.[26] Humans then more or less consciously and effectively pursue those ends through various actions and practices.[27] That does not describe all human activity but it does much of the most important of human activities. Such observations we can frame in either pragmatist or personalist terms, but for present purposes it makes little difference.[28] What does make a critical difference is recognizing the essential human need to form cognitive beliefs about reality in general, particular environments, causes and effects, and goods worth realizing. Internal culture largely consists of conglomerations of such beliefs.[29]

By "beliefs" we do not primarily mean propositional ideas that people actively consider, adopt, reflect on, and readily express when questioned—the equivalent of an official Protestant confession of faith.[30] That is only one possible kind of belief, and a relatively rare type. Beliefs come in a much broader range of forms. Here "beliefs" refers to premises or propositions that people consciously or tacitly regard to be true. Stated precisely, beliefs are mental attitudes of a certain kind directed toward premises or propositions, specifically, those which are taken to be true.[31] Human beliefs encompass a wide range of attitudes and supposi-

26. Antonio Damasio, *Self Comes to Mind: Constructing the Conscious Brain* (New York: Vintage Books, 2010); Damasio, *Descartes' Error*; Mark Johnson, *The Body in the Mind* (Chicago: University of Chicago Press, 1987); George Lakoff and Mark Johnson, *Philosophy in the Flesh* (New York: Basic Books, 1999); Francisco Varela, Eleanor Rosch, and Evan Thompson, *The Embodied Mind* (Cambridge: MIT Press, 1991).

27. Our definition of "action" is Weberian, that is, subjectively meaningful human behavior or activity; "practices" are repeated actions, similar activities that recur over time for meaningful reasons.

28. Smith, *What Is a Person?*; Smith, *To Flourish or Destruct*.

29. "Cognitions" in our approach is not intended to signify merely the "cerebral" and intellectual. Further on we signal the tight connection between cognitions, feelings, and desires, especially as cultural models relate to motivations. Claudia Strauss has attempted to recognize these connections by suggesting that cognitions are "thought-feelings" (D'Andrade and Strauss, *Human Motives and Cultural Models*, 3, 15). We do not seek to spell out the precise relations between cognitions, affect, and volition, but see Smith, *To Flourish or Destruct*; and Pugh, "What Good Are Interviews?," on "the visceral" and "meta-feelings."

30. Smith, *To Flourish or Destruct*.

31. The belief per se is the mental attitude of taking a premise or proposition to be true, not the content of the premise or proposition itself. Philosophers take different views of the finer points of the exact status of beliefs. Our position aligns with that of Lynne Rudder

tions about what people regard to be true, only some of which are the result of or represented by active reflections or expressed propositions. Beliefs may be mindful or thoughtless, vehemently defended or taken for granted as obvious, reflected on or accepted without consideration, and objectively veritable or false. Thus, on reflection we can rightly say things like, "I believe that George Washington was the first US president even when I am not thinking about it, indeed, even when I am asleep."[32]

Understood this way, we see that people's beliefs are crucial in forming their identities, orientations to the world, and ways they live their lives—and are therefore crucial in the constitution of internal culture. But, again, few such beliefs are of the actively considered, propounded, explicitly propositional sort.[33] Most are highly mundane and operate in the background as attitudes or suppositions that people regard to be true. *In principle*, all of people's beliefs *should* be able to be "surfaced" and expressed in propositional form—which is precisely what the analysis of cultural models does. But in reality, only a small fraction of ordinary people's beliefs are expressed that way on an everyday basis.[34] Our position, then, is that a host of people's beliefs are real, truly believed, and (we believe) influential on their patterns of action—but that does not mean people can or do ordinarily bring them to conscious awareness for direct inspection and expression.[35]

Clusters, Constellations, Schemas. Cognitive science tells us that people's beliefs and other mental objects are organized in something like packets, often called "schemas." Schemas are preconceived mental patterns that organize categories of information and their relationships, which aid people's perceptions, ordering, and comprehension of new information and experiences.[36] Internal culture is built out of schemas.

Baker, *Saving Belief: A Critique of Physicalism* (Princeton, NJ: Princeton University Press, 1987).

32. Quoting John Searle, *Making the Social World: The Structure of Human Civilization* (New York: Oxford University Press, 2010), 26.

33. Fritz Strack, Roland Deutsch, and Regina Krieglmeyer, "The Two Horses of Behavior: Reflection and Impulse," in *Oxford Handbook of Human Action*, ed. Ezequiel Morsella, John Bargh, and Peter Gollwitzered (New York: Oxford University Press, 2008), 104–17.

34. Melvin Spiro, *Culture and Human Nature* (New Brunswick, NJ: Transaction, 2003), 162.

35. Stephen Vaisey, "Socrates, Skinner, and Aristotle: Three Ways of Thinking about Culture in Action," *Sociological Forum* 23, no. 3 (2008): 603–13; Stephen Vaisey and Margaret Frye, "The Old One-Two: Preserving Analytical Dualism in Psychological Sociology," in *Oxford Handbook of Cognitive Sociology*, ed. W. Brekhus and G. Ignatow (New York: Oxford University Press, 2019), 101–14.

36. Paul DiMaggio, "Culture and Cognition," *Annual Review of Sociology* 23 (1997):

It is thus best understood as organizations of components, structuring of parts, arrangements of schemas. Humans do not work directly up from individual beliefs, such as "I am the parent of two children," to systemically integrated holistic worldviews (which very few ever get to anyway). This is where post-Parsonian theorists are correct. That kind of building up instead involves multiple levels of vertical integration of packets of beliefs and a lot of possible variance in the tightness of their integration and consistency. In fact, at a level "below" (in the sense of less complex) the simple belief just noted exist multiple, more basic beliefs on which it rests, including, "I exist," "the I that I am has a certain nature," "I have children," "human relationships vary by type," "I am made what is called a 'parent' by virtue of certain biological or legal facts," and so on.

Once formed and accepted, these beliefs can produce the more complex belief first stated, which can then connect to other closely related beliefs, such as "parents have certain identifiable responsibilities for their children." Such related beliefs tend to link together cognitively in more or less reasonable ways, forming intelligible clusters of beliefs. They are not randomly or chaotically connected. Internal culture is thus made from countless clusters of beliefs that human brains form, connect, store in memory, act on, and recall when necessary or primed. Cultural models of specific topics can consist of what can be reconstructed in about a paragraph's worth of propositions, like those we presented in the preceding chapters. The analysis of cultural models conducted in order to answer

263–87; Beate Hampe and Joseph Grady, *From Perception to Meaning: Image Schemas in Cognitive Linguistics* (Boston: De Gruyter, 2005); Mark Johnson, *The Body in the Mind* (Chicago: University of Chicago Press, 1987). Others describe schemas as "recurring, dynamic pattern[s] of our perceptual interactions and motor programs," which compose "gestalt structures, consisting of parts standing in relationships and organized into unified wholes, by means of which our experience manifests discernible order" (Johnson, *Body in the Mind*, xiv–xix); "a recurring, dynamic pattern of our perceptual interactions and motor programs that gives coherence and structure to our experience" (Johnson, *Body in the Mind*, xiv); "the recurring patterns of our sensory-motor experience by means of which we can make sense of that experience and reason about it, and that can also be recruited to structure abstract concepts and to carry out inferences about abstract domains of thought" (Mark Johnson, "The Philosophical Significance of Image Schemas," in *From Perception to Meaning: Image Schemas in Cognitive Linguistics*, ed. Beate Hampe [Berlin: Mouton de Gruyter, 2005], 15–33); "structures that organize our mental representations at a level more general and abstract than that at which we form particular mental images" (Johnson, *Body in the Mind*, 23–24); "schemata exist at a level of generality and abstraction that allows them to serve repeatedly as identifying patterns in an indefinitely large number of experiences, perceptions, and image formations for objects or events that are similarly structured in the relevant ways" (Johnson, *Body in the Mind*, 28); "mental representations of fundamental units of sensory experience" (Hampe and Grady, *From Perception to Meaning*, 44).

larger research questions, such as "how do parents approach the transmission of religion to children?," usually requires linking together a collection of cultural models that collectively help to answer the questions. Our explanation answering our research question thus required us to identify and present a constellation of cultural models, as we said in chapter 1.

Networks of Beliefs. Cultural models are networks of clustered cognitive beliefs that people hold about some matters of relevance to them (although, admittedly, presenting clustered beliefs in the form of paragraphs of propositions tends to obscure this networked aspect of the models). Fully explicated constellations of cultural models that answer research questions are networks of networks of such cognitive beliefs (see figure 2). The idea of networks here is important. Culture is not a single, tight "system" of norms, values, or beliefs, on the one hand. Nor is culture an assemblage of disparate discursive tools in a bag to be pulled out as needed to make sense of what one is already doing, on the other hand.[37]

---

37. Here we obviously refer to the "Swidlerian" "tool kit" or "strategies of action" theory, after the cultural sociologist Ann Swidler, whose seminal publications defined this approach (Ann Swidler, *Talk of Love: How Culture Matters* [Chicago: University of Chicago Press, 2003]; Swidler, "Culture in Action," *American Sociological Review* 51 [1986]: 273–86). The Swidlerian account exerted a major influence in cultural sociology for decades in ways we think have distorted its view not only of culture but also human motivations, reasons, beliefs, and accounts of action. One of us has criticized aspects of the Swidlerian view of culture elsewhere (Christian Smith, *To Flourish or Destruct*, 298–303; Christian Smith, *Moral, Believing Animals: Human Personhood and Culture* [New York: Oxford University Press, 2003], 133–36; also see Quinn, "Anthropologist's View of American Marriage"). This book carries such criticisms further. Here we demonstrate empirically what the Swidlerian view denies: the existence of deeply internalized, widely shared, complex cultural models that comprise the near consensus of large groups of otherwise very different types of people (and which we have good reasons to believe help to motivate and guide their actions and practices). The cultural models we explicated here are not external instruments of rationalizing "talk" that people pull out from cultural "tool kits" in order to defend post hoc questioned behaviors that may not actually be motivated by the ideas in the talk. They are instead internal, collectively shared in people's long-term cognitive memory and motivational systems. As internalized facts of social order, they precede the actions and experiences of the individual people who believe in and (we think) at least somewhat seek to live by them. Such cultural models are methodologically not obviously accessible on the "surface" of interview discourse—which seems to be the rejected assumption of some critics of the ability of interview data to tell us about culture. But they can be accessed and reconstructed through the careful study of extended interview discussions. The genealogy of Swidler's approach is similar to that of the larger field's. The old Parsonian account viewed culture as a clearly bounded normative system of ultimate ends and values that were socialized into dependent children to grow up and behave in ways that sustained the function of normative social relations and institutional social systems. Culture was thought to be the common operating system of entire social groups (nations for sociologists, tribes for anthropologists), the direct motivations for individual actions, and methodologically

Culture consists of networks of beliefs residing in the memory systems of embodied human brains that orient people to reality and help motivate and guide their life practices. The image of networks is intended to suggest that people's belief clusters are connected by more or less reasonable links between the nodes of cognitive schemas. Unlike tightly integrated and well-bounded "systems," these networks can be organized tightly or loosely, clearly delimited or frayed on many sides, reasonably justified in some ways but perhaps not others. Unlike the contents of cultural "tool kits," the belief clusters in the network are actually linked together in some intelligible and often reasonable way, and they do not merely "make sense" of ongoing practices but actually help to determine, motivate, and guide those practices.

Grasping the idea of culture as networks of beliefs and belief clusters also helps to explain the relative stability and durability of most cultural models. Distinct clusters of beliefs comprising cultural models are not only linked together internally in part by some intelligible relation of sets of ideas (for example, the reasonable implications of beliefs about the limited importance of religious congregations for the central responsibilities of parents, and vice versa). In addition, most of the specific clusters of ideas in any larger cultural model (as defined by the relevance of a particular issue or question) also likely connect as nodes to other networked cultural models. In other words, cultural models of specific issues do not stand alone in distinct compartments disconnected from cultural models of different issues. Rather, central belief clusters in one cultural model

---

accessible in the values and norms that people professed and acted on and that social institutions embodied. The Swidlerian approach capitalized on growing discontents in anthropology and sociology in the 1970s and '80s about that view, arguing that cultures are not clearly bounded, coherent, internally integrated, behavior-directing systems. Most human action, it claimed, is not motivated to realize or affirm prespecified ends, values, and norms. People, in fact, are not very reflective about their actions, but normally simply carry on repeating familiar repertoires of behavior they are competent to perform and that pragmatically seem to work. Only when people's strategies of action fail, when they are asked by others to account for the behaviors, or when they encounter "troubled times" do people start reflecting on and trying to give explanations for their doings. Most of what they say, however, is viewed in the Swidlerian approach as post hoc rationalizations trying to make actions appear sensible and legitimate to themselves and others, not as reliable accounts of their actual beliefs and purposes. Culture thus consists of assortments of familiar routines, tactics, categories, explanations, skills, habits, and other odds and ends that enable and make sense of certain kinds of practice-competences, constrain what is conceivable and doable, and try to provide acceptable reasons for behaviors that may actually be driven by other forces. A fuller account of post-Parsonian paradigms would have to delve further into the theories of Pierre Bourdieu and Michel Foucault, a task we cannot take on here but which we note deserves further exploration.

also function as clusters in other cultural models. For example, the Purpose of Life cluster of beliefs composing one cultural model described in chapter 1, which operates as essential background cognitions for understanding the question of religious transmission to children, also certainly operates as a relevant component in other cultural models, most likely including models about education, marriage, recreation, and vocation and occupation. That means that a variety of cultural models of different parts of life are tied together by the central node of the one Purpose of Life cluster of beliefs.

As a consequence, changes in one belief cluster will have ramifications for the whole constellation of cultural models that it is part of. If people's cognitive beliefs were fragile or highly pliable, this would make many cultural models vulnerable to transformation simultaneously, in something like a domino effect or ripple effect that rocks all conceptual vessels. Significant cognitive beliefs tend not to be fragile or pliable, however. They are established early in life and tend to resist change. Therefore, the multiple interconnections of various constellations of cultural models by belief clusters of high centrality stabilize people's cultural models, since to profoundly change one model would also require changing other models. And the wholesale transformation of people's broad cultural outlooks on many domains of life is difficult and rare. In effect, any person's total internal cultural assets consist of networks of networks of networks of vertically, horizontally, and diagonally linked clusters of cognitive beliefs. No one cultural model is isolated and so vulnerable to dramatic transformation or collapse. The more "connected" and therefore more central a particular cultural model is, the more durable it is likely to be. Likewise, the more connected are certain constellations of cultural models about various topics, the more they as a whole are likely to be stable. Cultural models can and do change. But their default state is stability and durability, in part because of the network structure of their organization, which is ultimately driven by the functioning tendencies of the human brain.

Background Cognitions. The theory of cultural models that we employ comports with the familiar distinction in various sociological theories between "practical consciousness" and "discursive consciousness," as Anthony Giddens coined it.[38] The same is true with the "dual process" model of human cognition and judgment, which sociologists have

---

38. Anthony Giddens, *The Constitution of Society* (Berkeley: University of California Press, 1986).

imported from the cognitive sciences.[39] The relevant idea behind both is that ordinarily, only a small part of human activity at any given moment is governed by cognitions that are consciously attentive to the activity. The majority of human doings instead operate by cognitions that are automatic, habitual, unconscious, or unfocused; they run on some kind of mental autopilot.

The idea of cultural models fits these understandings perfectly. The beliefs composing cultural models are real, just as real as human practical consciousness and the "hot" and "fast" judgments in dual-process theory. But they act mostly not on "front stage" but in the background of attention, beneath the threshold of people's awareness. Effectively internalized cognitive beliefs that compose people's cultural models are mostly so obvious that they are invisible to their adherents. Also contributing to such cognitions remaining largely out of sight is the fact that few people have the time, energy, and mental skills to bring up for inspection and evaluation all of their internalized assumptions and beliefs about life and how it is best lived. Fortunately, humans' embrained bodies do not require that to function. Nevertheless, most automatic, habitual, unconscious human activity is still significantly governed by real, internalized, intelligible, and relatively coherent, stable, and potentially shared belief cognitions. Such cognitions simply need not belong to "discursive consciousness" and the realm of "slow" or "cold" (that is, consciously considered) judgments.

All of this (the agreement between the cultural models approach, the distinction between practical and discursive consciousness, and the dual-process theory of cognition and judgment) explains why people sometimes struggle in interviews to express the basic beliefs that they genuinely internalize and embrace. It also helps illuminate why attempts to express those beliefs can involve inconsistencies. And it explains why culture researchers cannot simply report people's exact words, like stenographers, but must instead analyze their discourse to identify what lays behind and beneath it—to try to retroductively reconstruct the cultural models that people must believe if they are in fact sincerely saying what they say in interviews.[40] The cultural models are really there and operative in people's cognitive systems and practical lives. But they do not sit on the tips of people's tongues, nearly ready to be enumerated and explained when requested.

39. For example, Stephen Vaisey, "Motivation and Justification: A Dual-Process Model of Culture in Action," *American Journal of Sociology* 114 (2009): 1675–715; Michal Pagis, "From Abstract Concepts to Experiential Knowledge: Embodying Enlightenment in a Meditation Center," *Qualitative Sociology* 33 (2010): 469–89.

40. Pugh, "What Good Are Interviews?"

These facts are now well known and accepted in the cognitive sciences and attentive parts of social science.

Furthermore, these observations interpret very differently evidence from interviews that post-Parsonians have often said demonstrate the incoherence, externality, and post hoc instrumental use of culture. These insights about the reality and power of practical consciousness in human activity and the dual-process character of human cognitions and judgments explain why and how the evidence of post-Parsonian accounts can be descriptively valid but their interpretations of it misguided.[41] The cultural models view of the evidence considered as a whole is more consistent with current knowledge about human cognitions, more in harmony with human phenomenological experience of subjectivity and lived practices, and so more persuasive as an account of culture.

Memory and Internalization. The theory of cultural models highlights the importance of memory in culture. Most people think of memory as an effort to remember something. But cognitive psychology and neuroscience tell us there are many types of human memory processes that operate in distinct parts of the brain.[42] All memory involves the encoding, storing, and retrieval of information or competencies. But memory can be *sensory* (e.g., retaining for a few seconds the auditory impression of fingernails just scratched on a chalkboard), *short-term* (e.g., repeating to oneself a telephone number to call), or *long-term* (e.g., remembering events in one's childhood). Sensory memory can be *iconic* (based on visual perceptions), *echoic* (auditory), *haptic* (touch stimuli), *olfactory* (smell), or *taste* memory (palate flavors). Memory is also divided into the two major types of *explicit* (also called *declarative*)—the conscious, purposeful recollection of information, ideas, or prior events (e.g., remembering a new acquaintance's name)—and *implicit* (also called *nondeclarative*), which is the unconscious storing and recall of knowledge (e.g., automatically knowing the lyrics while singing a familiar song). A main type of implicit memory is *procedural* memory, which concerns knowing how to perform

41. Quinn, "An Anthropologist's View of American Marriage."

42. The relevant literature is immense, but see Michael Eysenck, *Fundamentals of Cognition* (New York: Psychology Press, 2012); Michael Ullman, "Contributions of Memory Circuits to Language: The Declarative/Procedural Model," *Cognition* 92 (2004): 231–70; Alan Baddeley, *Working Memory, Thought, and Action* (Oxford: Oxford University Press, 2007); Larry Squire, "Memory and Brain Systems: 1969–2009," *Journal of Neuroscience* 29, no. 41 (2009): 12711–16; Karin Foerde and Russell Poldrack, "Procedural Learning in Humans," in *The Encyclopedia of Neuroscience*, vol. 7, ed. Larry Squire (Oxford: Academic Press, 2009), 1083–91.

actions without conscious attention (e.g., riding a bicycle). Explicit memory comes in two main kinds, *semantic* memory, which concerns general knowledge about the world in the form of ideas, facts, concepts, and meanings (e.g., who Moses was); and *episodic* memory, which is the recall of autobiographical events involving places, times, people involved, reasons for the events, and emotions related to them (e.g., what happened at one's sixteenth birthday party). Semantic memory is thus associated with "knowing that," while episodic memory is "remembering" specific occurrences with a particular sense of self-involvement (dubbed "autonoetic consciousness"). A subtype of episodic memory is *flashbulb* memory, concerning highly emotional or extraordinary events (e.g., exactly where one was and what one was doing the morning of September 11, 2001). *Topographic* memory can combine explicit, semantic, and episodic memories to provide a specific kind of recall about known places, orientations to space, and itineraries. Memory is also divided into two types by temporal bearing, with *retrospective* memories involving past matters (e.g., recalling yesterday's argument) and *prospective* memories concerning future intentions (e.g., remembering one's dentist appointment tomorrow).

These distinctions are not simply conceptual. Different types of memory operate through distinct regions of the brain. For example, short-term memory depends on neural communications linking the dorsolateral prefrontal cortex and the parietal lobe. Long-term memory works through the medial temporal lobe. Emotional memories are processed by the amygdala, while the hippocampus is involved in spatial and declarative memories. And procedural memory operates in the dorsolateral striatum. Indeed, some parts of the brain appear to be dedicated entirely to very specific types of memory—for instance, the fusiform gyrus of the brain is devoted exclusively to recognizing people's faces. But such neurological divisions of labor are not always so clean-cut, since some parts of the brain act as information reception, integration, and transfer sites linking numerous other parts of the brain. All of these biological memory functions also continually interact with other biological and environmental factors, including genetics, neurochemistry, diet, bodily exercise, stress, sleep, and the availability of cultural categories involved in remembering.

Findings from the cognitive sciences and neuroscience about human memory systems now provide us with a far clearer understanding of how "internalization through socialization" actually works, compared to the days when that phrase was commonly used as a black box in sociology and anthropology. During the Parsonian era, scientific knowledge about memory systems was primitive, so "internalization" stood in as a concept for learning and recall processes that were real but not well understood. Post-Parsonian theories of culture emerged in the 1980s when sophisticated cognitive and brain sciences were still in their infancies and their findings had not yet penetrated the social sciences. (Consider, for example, that in sociology, Paul DiMaggio's groundbreaking chapter on "Culture and Cognition" was not published until 1997.) As a result, it was easy for post-Parsonian theorists of culture to question and discount the whole idea of the internalization of beliefs, values, and norms. "Who knows what goes on in the murky world of human subjectivity?," they asked. But such skepticism is now outdated. Massive research in multiple fields of science has dramatically improved our understandings of the reality of and cognitive and neural-substrate mechanisms involved in the memory processes that produce "internalization through socialization." When we say "internalization" today, we have a pretty clear idea of what that means and how it works.[43]

Cultural models are grounded in long-term memory functions, which, with recurrent use, sustain their durability over time. But cultural models are not adequately described only as types of long-term memories, since they often involve all but two of the memory input, storage, and recall systems just named (sensory and short-term memory being the exceptions, unless information from them is transferred into long-term memory systems). Consider the memory systems that must be active in the formation, consolidation, and deployment of parents' cultural models of religious transmission to children that we presented as analytic models in chapters 1–4:

- explicit/declarative (e.g., recalling during hard times that one can turn to a loving God for comfort, remembering that children who have left the faith may not be able to enjoy an official church wedding)
- implicit/nondeclarative (e.g., being flooded with feelings of spiritual peace on the whiff of burning incense, involuntarily feeling anger and resentment on seeing religion being forced by a parent on a child, having suffered the same as a youth)
- procedural memories (e.g., knowing how and when to recite a common prayer, genuflect, make an offering, take Eucharist, and kneel, stand, sit, raise hands, and so on)

43. Also see Lizardo, "Improving Cultural Analysis," on "enculturation."

- semantic (believing that everyone needs a stable home base from which to navigate life's journey, knowing that the youth leader of one's congregation is not entirely reliable)
- episodic (e.g., reminiscing about the warm happiness of lighting candles as a youth on religious holidays, reliving the shock of Uncle Fred's drunk driving death after he left the faith and his life went downhill)
- flashbulb (e.g., recalling the joy of one's child's baptism, remembering the grief of one's parents after an older sister declared in the living room one hot summer's night that she was an atheist)
- topographic (e.g., knowing which part of one's house faces east, remembering which pews or seats have the best visual advantage for keeping kids interested in what is happening in religious services)
- retrospective (e.g., recalling that one's father faithfully read scripture and prayed every day, remembering the hypocrisy of some religious adults while growing up)
- prospective (e.g., remembering that one must register one's children for religious summer camp before the end of the week, remembering and feeling guilty that Little League will mean missing church for the next two months)
- iconic (recognizing a statue or icon), echoic (soaring to beloved music), haptic (knowing the feeling of ritual embraces of fellowship), olfactory (breathing in the particular, familiar smell of one's house of worship), or taste (knowing the special flavor of sanctified bread, wine, juice, or other offered foods).

Theorists who brush aside "culture as inside the minds of actors . . . for the simple reason that our minds are not good at holding lots of connected things in them" could not be more wrong.[44] The exact opposite is true. Human brains are fantastic information processors that encode, store, retrieve, connect, express, and set into action incredibly complex "things." How such ill-informed pronouncements are taken seriously in culture scholarship is beyond us. Of course, human memory and cognitive systems can be corrupted by various well-known factors that introduce biases and blockages. But that in no way means that human brains and mental lives are so limited that they cannot serve as the central processing

---

44. John Levi Martin, "Life's a Beach but You're an Ant, and Other Unwelcome News for the Sociology of Culture," *Poetics* 38, no. 2 (2010): 240.

units of internal culture. They can and do. And our powerful if imperfect human capacities for memory play a key role in making that happen.

Intersubjectivity. Some social scientists went through a phase of doubting intersubjectivity, the notion that people can share subjective beliefs, understandings, and meanings. Some still seem caught in that phase. "How can the sharing of subjectivities between different 'interiors' actually happen?," they asked. Even more problematically, how can we *know* it happens? Studying the insubstantial "insides" of individual people's mental, volitional, and affective lives is already difficult if not impossible. How can we also believe in and empirically study people *sharing* what goes on in their insides with each other? By what kind of telepathy or ESP is that possible? Plus, the very ability to prove intersubjectivity seems to depend on the prior acceptance of intersubjectivity. Isn't that circular? Besides, philosophers wrestle with what they call "the problem of 'other minds,'" namely, the difficulty of one mind knowing whether other minds really exist.[45] As obvious as it seems, when we push hard on that question, can we really verify the existence of other minds? How do we know that reality does not boil down to a single mind (ours) that incorrectly projects or perceives that other minds like ours coexist? What if they are merely creative artifices of our own mind? How can we possibly get outside our subjectivity to validate the objective actuality of other people's minds? And if serious philosophers wrestle with this problem, why should the social sciences assume intersubjectivity as an unproblematic fact?

These doubts left some scholars determined to avoid what they view as the morass of intersubjectivity.[46] In sociology, for example, Robert Wuthnow once argued that "the methodological limitation posed by the subjective approach arises principally from the difficulties associated with making verifiable claims about subjective phenomena." Research interviews, he said, cannot be assumed to provide "evidence of an internal psychological state," so we should "admit our lack of knowledge about hidden states" and "try to move away from focusing . . . on the radically subjective

---

45. For example, Anita Avramides, *Other Minds (Problems of Philosophy)* (New York: Routledge, 2001).

46. The larger species of this kind of skepticism is known as antimentalism. In sociology, Émile Durkheim was an antimentalism; George H. Mead was a moderate antimentalism. Claude Lévi-Strauss, much of practice theory, Michel Foucault and the poststructuralists, B. F. Skinner and behaviorism, Robert Wuthnow of the 1980s, Pierre Bourdieu, and various streams of postmodernism share this skepticism about the existence, accessibility, or methodological relevance of mental states.

beliefs, attitudes, and meanings of the individual."[47] Clifford Geertz notably suggested that "subjectivism" obscures interpretations of culture with "appeals to dark sciences" and the "search of all-too-deep-lying turtles."[48]

Our theory of cultural models, however, rests squarely on a belief in the reality of intersubjectivity. So how can we answer skeptics? The key is to recognize and reject the impossible philosophical presuppositions that give rise to this skepticism: positivism and empiricism. They cannot work and do not deserve our assent. We need instead to adopt some philosophy of social science that takes the approach of "transcendental realism" and employs the reasoning operations of analytical "retroduction" and "abduction." ("Transcendental" here does not refer to the Transcendentalism of Ralph Waldo Emerson or the religious positing of a transcendentally divine realm, but rather the realist equivalent of the reasoning procedure involved in Immanuel Kant's "transcendental idealism," namely, considering what must a priori be the case if reality is a certain way—in Kant's view, that our minds have an a priori, not experience-based understanding of quantity, space, time causation, and so on.) We believe the best philosophy to do this is critical realism. With a good philosophy in hand, we have warrant for believing that, contra empiricism, some things that are not directly empirically observable are nonetheless real, causally powerful, and so important for explanations. We also no longer aspire, contra positivism, to a (social) science that is allegedly able and obliged to "prove" through empirics that it possesses "positive" and indubitable knowledge. Instead, we are freed to operate the way the best science actually works— the ideas of positivism and empiricism notwithstanding—which is systematically to use all relevant empirical evidence and our best reasoning abilities to learn about entities, structures, and causal relations that we mostly *cannot* observe.

Doing so requires analytical retroduction, that is, working backward from what we have the best reason to believe is true to identify the conditions and occurrences that must be or most probably are the case for it actually to be true. This sounds complicated, but it is actually straightforward, and people use retroduction all the time. A simple example: You and your friend suddenly feel nauseous—what must be or most probably is the case if that is true? Oh, some of the food at the sketchy buffet restaurant where you ate two hours ago must have been spoiled. Now you know that

47. Robert Wuthnow, *Meaning and Moral Order* (Berkeley: University of California Press, 1987), 334, 336, 340, 63, 338, 65.

48. Geertz, *Interpretation of Cultures*, 33.

you suffer food poisoning and why. To increase your confidence in this retroductive conclusion, you might investigate how others who ate the same
dish are feeling. But that is not necessary. You have warrant to believe the
explanation. Do such retroductive conclusions enjoy the same degree of
rational certainty of conclusions from, say, deduction? No. You *could* be
sick because a wicked neighbor hit you with imperceptible poison darts as
you walked from your car to the door—that is not impossible. But it also
does not fit well your best picture of all the facts that you rightly believe
you know about reality, so you stick with the food poisoning explanation.

The ideal model of retroductive reasoning is the crime scene investigation. Detectives arrive on the scene of a murder, search for and collect all
seemingly relevant observable evidence, and then work backward from
that evidence to figure out the truth about what they did *not* observe: who
committed the murder, how, and why. Rarely are the results utterly "positive," as positivism would demand. But with enough good evidence and
retroductive analysis, the results can usually tell through "inference to the
best explanation" what reasonable people have warrant to judge to be true.

"Abduction," then, is the process of reaching a holistic explanatory
understanding of all of the evidence that works backward from the conclusions of retroduction. Abduction begins with a coherent interpretive
theoretical framework, a narrative that purports to explain the observed
evidence (e.g., Marxism, functionalism, Goffmanian dramaturgy, neoliberal economics, psychoanalytic psychology, behaviorism). It asks inquirers
to interpret the available evidence through the perspective of that framework or narrative. It attempts to explain how all of the empirical pieces fit
into a coherent scenario that makes the most sense. Abduction's goal is to
persuade oneself or others to adopt the interpretive explanatory framework or narrative. When abduction is successful, people say, "Ah-ha, I see,
yes, that is what happened [or is happening]." When it fails, people say,
"I don't buy it."[49] Like retroduction, the logical operation of abduction
is straightforward, and people do it all the time in various ways. But the
knowledge that results from abduction is even less certain than knowledge
from retroduction, because often more than one interpretive framework
can account for the observed evidence. Which to believe? Does the sun
revolve around the earth (geocentrism) or does the earth revolve around

---

49. Note that our critical realist understanding of abduction (see Danermark et al.,
Explaining Society, 41–70) differs from that of Iddo Tavory and Stefan Timmermans,
Abductive Analysis: Theorizing Qualitative Research (Chicago: University of Chicago
Press, 2014).

the sun (heliocentrism)? For some time, of course, that was a hot debate in astronomy that the available empirical evidence could not resolve. Are masses of poor people in the Global South who work for less than subsistence wages in nasty factories experiencing a necessary phase in a process of economic development that will eventually produce national prosperity (neoliberalism) or are they the latest victims of globalized capital seeking the highest profit margins by exploiting vulnerable wage laborers and stealing the surplus value of their work (neo-Marxism)? Sometimes the available evidence underdetermines the conclusions. Nevertheless, abduction is an unavoidable, commonly practiced, and often useful method of reasoning we can employ to better understand and explain reality.

But cannot science do better than offering uncertain, competing interpretive frameworks and narratives? Sometimes. But not necessarily or always. To believe otherwise is again to indulge the delusions of positivism and empiricism. Science is a human practice for producing warranted beliefs about what is real and how it works. And as a *human* practice, it is ultimately subject to all of the limitations of human knowing.[50] Nevertheless, science successfully gives us an immense amount of knowledge that we have great reasons to believe. We should be happy for what we can learn about reality and not demand what we cannot. And this realization returns us to the question of cultural intersubjectivity.

If we hold our social science to the impossible epistemological standards of positivist empiricism, then intersubjectivity goes down the toilet. And so, for that matter, does any hope of producing any plausible social science explanations, if we apply our standards consistently. But with critical realism (or some other philosophy embracing transcendental realism) and the help of retroductive and abductive analyses, we can affirm as warranted the belief that people intersubjectively share beliefs, understandings, and meanings. Start with everything you (have good reason to believe you) know about reality and life experience, and then consider the conditions that must pertain for what you know to be true (retroduction). Among them will be the reality and adequate functioning of intersubjective understanding. Things could not be what they are or work as they do without that. And that realization entitles you to believe in intersubjectivity with confidence.[51]

50. Michael Polanyi, *The Tacit Dimension* (1974; Chicago: University of Chicago Press, 2009).

51. For comparison, see Erika Summers-Effler, Justin Van Ness, and Christopher Hausmann, "Peeking in the Black Box: Studying, Theorizing, and Representing the

The burden now rests with skeptics to come along with better reasons than yours that overturn many of your warranted beliefs about reality and experience, which will not happen. Next, take the theory of intersubjectively shared cultural models that we have described and interpret the world as you know it through its explanatory framework (abduction). Does it make sense? Do the pieces fit well? Does it avert the invalidation of fatally significant counterevidence? Does it seem inferentially to provide the best explanation of your understanding of reality? We think so and expect that others will, too. Having thus deservedly come to believe in people intersubjectively understanding and sharing cultural models, explaining *how* it works turns out to be not that hard: people share similar life experiences and then talk together and influence each other's cognitions about those experiences, which, in the context of the operation of other tendencies and mechanisms,[52] has the effect over time of aligning their beliefs.

Metaphors We Think and Live By. Our approach and analysis emphasize the centrality of metaphors in parents' cultural models. In chapter 1, we showed parents' common use of the "life is a journey" and "religion is a foundation" metaphors, among many others. These metaphors defined the contours of parents' understandings and led to inferences about how to act. Cultural models, it turns out, can hardly function without heavy reliance on hosts of metaphors. Metaphorical analysis has gained attention in the social sciences since the publication of George Lakoff and Mark Johnson's groundbreaking work *Metaphors We Live By*, which claimed, "Our ordinary conceptual system, in terms of which we both think and act, is fundamentally metaphorical in nature."[53] Through meticulous analysis of texts across a variety of conceptual domains, Lakoff and Johnson detailed how humans constantly use metaphors to express abstract and difficult ideas as concrete concepts.

People's use of conceptual metaphors is typically not a conscious process, nor are the metaphors always directly expressed in speech. Instead, they function as implicit maps that guide reasoning. Lakoff and Johnson argue that people constantly employ metaphors by drawing on humanity's

---

Micro-Foundations of Day-to-Day Interactions," *Journal of Contemporary Ethnography* 44 (2015): 450–79.

52. Such as the effects of the desires to be accepted, to belong in solidarity to social groups, to maintain ontological security, to know and affirm what is believed to be morally right, and to enjoy the approval of reference groups.

53. George Lakoff and Mark Johnson, *Metaphors We Live By* (Chicago: University of Chicago Press, 1980), 3.

sensorimotor apparatus, in which, through a process of "phenomenological embodiment," primal bodily experiences like moving, balancing, supporting, pushing, and pulling become concrete images for understanding other abstract causes and forces we encounter.[54] Bodily experience also provides orientations to space, such as front-back, high-low, near-far, and up-down, to generate metaphors for reasoning. Even the most mundane experiences, like pouring water into a glass and seeing it rise vertically, enable metaphorical associations like "more is up," "good is up," and thus "more is good."[55] From ordinary interaction with the material and social world every day, people develop primary metaphors, such as "actions are motions" and "purposes are destinations." These primary metaphors can then be pieced together to form more complex conceptual metaphors such as "life is a journey."[56]

Operating typically below the level of conscious thinking, these conceptual metaphorical understandings have implications for how people perceive, reason about, and act in the world. If one understands life as a journey, for example, one will readily recognize the importance of planning a route, staying on course, expecting obstacles, preparing the necessary belongings to bring, and remaining aware of one's location along the way. Knowledge about physical travel thus generates normative guidelines for life.[57] In the previous chapters, we showed that American religious parents frequently described their lives in terms of different *tracks* they have taken, *turning points* they have made, circumstances they had to *go through*, and the future they anticipate as they *look ahead*. Of course, people in different cultures and subcultures will highlight certain metaphors and ignore others as they construct the cultural models by which they make sense of and live life. Part of the job of the cultural analyst is to map and explain those variations and their consequences for people's life practices.

While usually unnoticed, metaphors are ubiquitous in ordinary speech. To sociologists, they should be "like flags waving, or Xs that mark the spot" because people use them to attempt to express their understandings of something.[58] The metaphors people employ are so deeply embedded in their ways of understanding that they rarely realize how or why they

54. Lakoff and Johnson, *Philosophy in the Flesh*, 17, 46.

55. George Lakoff, *Women, Fire, and Dangerous Things: What Categories Reveal about the Mind* (Chicago: University of Chicago Press, 1987).

56. Lakoff and Johnson, *Philosophy in the Flesh*, 63.

57. Lakoff and Johnson, *Philosophy in the Flesh*, 62.

58. Quinn, *Finding Culture in Talk*, 49.

employ them, nor the assumptions or causal reasoning that these meta-phors entail.[59] Although some dual-process theories doubt that interview data can reveal unconsciously motivating processes through respondents' conscious and deliberative speech, the analysis of metaphors seems at least partly able to sidestep this problem, for metaphors draw on previously formed associations and sometimes prelinguistic understandings grounded in people's experiences. Thus, Naomi Quinn suggests that "at this level of cognitive processing, speakers do not, indeed cannot disguise or twist, much less suppress, what they say and how they think about it. This task, of talking at the speed of speech, demands that we have assumptions at hand to contextualize our talk, making sense of statements and filling in unstated meanings as we go."[60] Metaphors "are used by speakers to clarify the points they are trying to get across to listeners. For this purpose, speakers choose metaphors that are cultural exemplars of the point being made."[61] In short, research on cognitive cultural models must attend closely to the metaphors people use as they talk about their lives, not only their propositional claims, just as we have tried to do in the chapters above.

Cultural versus Analytic Models. We proposed above the distinction between people's actual *cultural models* (the real networked clusters of beliefs that operate in people's brains) and the *analytic models* that we scholars formulate as the results of our empirical research on people's cultural models. The former is the subject of cultural analysis and the latter describes its results. Both are real, but in different ways. Cultural models exist in the embodied cognitions of every normally functioning human person. Analytic models exist as scholarly knowledge, conceptual descriptive models of people's actual cultural models. They are simplified scholarly versions of people's simplified cognitive versions of a very complex reality. In critical realist parlance, cultural models are the "intransitive" and analytic models the "transitive" objects of study. We do not claim there is a simple, one-to-one correspondence between the cultural models "out there" in people's brains and lives and the scholarly analytic models presented in these pages. Analytic models do not mirror cultural models. The transitive never perfectly reflects the intransitive. Nonetheless, a genuine representational validity of correspondence should exist between the two if the research and analyses are done well, and the more closely

59. Quinn, "An Anthropologist's View of American Marriage," 51.
60. Quinn, "An Anthropologist's View of American Marriage, 52.
61. Quinn, *Finding Culture in Talk*, 49.

analytic models represent cultural models, the better the research has been conducted.[62]

Motivating Models. One of the central tasks of social science is to investigate people's cultures in order to understand how they causally constitute, generate, and guide people's understandings of reality, social institutions, and lived practices and experiences. (Other related tasks include explaining where those cultures came from, how and why they have changed over time, and what cultural dynamics tell us more generally about humanity.) The systematic analysis of cultural models enables us to accomplish that task in a way that best accounts for the realities of embodied human cognitive processes and the complex character of human motivations, actions, and practices. Cultural models are real, not merely useful analytical constructions of scholars, because people's beliefs are real and organized in particular structures. And they are *models* because as belief clusters, they interpretively simplify reality in cognitive forms and offer both cognitive understandings *of* reality and motivators and guides *for* purposive living (referencing Geertz's distinction between "models of" and "models for"). In the latter sense, "models for," cultural models are not merely the product of human "meaning making," as some theorists conceptualize culture; they also help to motivate and direct human activity.[63]

The majority of human activities are motivated. Human motivations are not straightforward but complex, multiple, and sometimes not easy to understand. Crucial for comprehending motivations is identifying the clusters and constellations of cognitive beliefs that define people's view of reality, what they consider to be good and right, and how they understand how they ought to live and why. In short, we need to comprehend people's cultural models to understand their motivations. Cultural models are not the only source of people's motives, but they are critical in generating many of those that most interest us.

---

62. "Just because knowledge and its referents are usually different, it does not follow that there can be no relationship between them. If we are to allow a notion of correspondence, it must involve conformability and intelligibility rather than replication." Andrew Sayer, *Realism and Social Science* (London: Sage, 2000), 42. Also see Gerald Visions, *Veritas: The Correspondence Theory and Its Critics* (Cambridge, MA: MIT Press, 2004); John Searle, "Truth and Correspondence," in *The Construction of Social Reality* (New York: Free Press, 1995), 199–226; Andrew Newman, *The Correspondence Theory of Truth: An Essay on the Metaphysics of Predication* (Cambridge: Cambridge University Press, 2002); and Paul Boghossian, *Fear of Knowledge: Against Relativism and Constructivism* (New York: Oxford University Press, 2006).

63. See D'Andrade and Strauss, *Human Motives and Cultural Models.*

One of us (Smith) has written extensively elsewhere about the reality and nature of motivations for action, an argument we need not repeat here.[64] Suffice it for present purposes to define motivations as "the causal energy and direction provided by the organized patterning of people's beliefs, desires, and emotions that move people to choose, initiate, and often persist in particular actions or general strategies in specific contexts."[65] Motivations provide energy and direction for action. They come from the complex, ongoing interaction of desires, beliefs, and emotions. Stated precisely, motivated actions are thus behaviors performed when (1) there is some goal G that person P affectively desires or intends to bring about, (2) P believes that by performing action A he or she will likely help achieve G, and (3) this (i) emotionally laden desire or intention for G, (ii) the belief in the causal effects of A regarding G, and (iii) the desire to employ the means of A together *cause* P to do A.

The primary energy for motivations comes from desires. But of the three component parts of motivations (beliefs, desires, emotions), cognitive belief is the most basic. That is because some beliefs are necessary preconditions for desires and emotions, while the reverse is not true. We can in principle hold cognitive beliefs (for example, that George Washington was our first president) without experiencing desires or emotions related to them. Yet we cannot feel desires or emotions without first holding some beliefs that ground, define, and orient them (I desire to . . . *what*? I feel . . . *what* and *why*?[66]). Cognitive beliefs are thus the fundamental basis on which more complex motivations are built.

Beliefs that contribute to motivations must possess some degree of *stability* if they are to sustain actions and practices. Constantly changing beliefs motivate little but erratic behavior. Beliefs that give rise to motivations also need to be *salient* enough to generate significant desires and affects. One's cognitions about George Washington as first president may not do that, but beliefs about the policies of the next president may (that is, they may generate the desire to vote). Cultural models are composed of beliefs. Most of them are fairly stable, according to our theory. And as part of people's cultural models, they are normally salient to everyday life (unimportant beliefs do not end up in cultural models). Minor and trivial

64. Smith, *To Flourish or Destruct*.

65. Smith, *To Flourish or Destruct*, 67.

66. Note that people can have purely physiological (noncognitive) bodily sensations that are an essential part of emotional events, but to experience them as emotions and not merely sensations requires holding some background beliefs about situations and causes that help to interpret them as particular types of affects.

beliefs either function as sub-cognitions (e.g., "children exist") supporting the more salient beliefs of cultural models ("I am a parent of children") or remain irrelevant to motivations. We see then that cultural models involve precisely the kind of things that can generate motivations for action.

Cultural models involve interactive beliefs about both the way things are (descriptive, analytical) and the way things ought to be (normative, axiological, moral). In cultural models, is-beliefs and ought-beliefs are not categorically disconnected (per David Hume's misunderstood objection to what later was dubbed the "naturalistic fallacy"). Rather, they interact in mutually defining ways, in a more Aristotelian fashion. For example, part of a cultural model might be represented as follows: "Family solidarity increases happiness [causally descriptive], which is good [axiologically descriptive], therefore we should behave in ways that increase family solidarity [normatively prescriptive]."

People must engage in some or other actions and practices. Completely inert existence is not an option (even if some people seem to act as if they think it is). Important actions and practices do not generate, energize, and direct themselves; they must be motivated in some way. Motivations consist of combinations of beliefs, desires, and emotions—of which beliefs are the most fundamental—that together generate energy and direction for intentional activity. That can happen in different ways, sometimes as lifelong projects and other times as spontaneous acts. But most human motivations—especially those that shape life *practices*, that is, meaningful, ongoing behaviors—derive from and are oriented by the beliefs that define people's cultural models. At the heart of people's motivational systems stands their cultural models. To act purposively requires knowledge of what exists, how reality is organized, how causation works, and what is good to realize and experience in life. Cognitive cultural models provide exactly that kind of knowledge. Indeed, the primary "task" of cultural models is to select, assemble, and sustain the very kinds of beliefs that provide such knowledge. Somewhat like basic natural science and social science texts, they provide elementary knowledge about what is (believed to be) real (e.g., "I am a parent"). Like road maps and geography books, they describe the terrain of reality (e.g., "Life is a difficult journey"). Like advice manuals, they explain relevant causal relations ("Children rebel when forced into religion"). And like moral philosophies and shared social values, they tell us what is good to pursue and enjoy (e.g., "Children need to choose independently for themselves").

When people wake up in the morning and need to know what to do next and why, they normally turn to their ongoing routinized practices to provide the answer. We typically do next what we did at the same time and in the same situation as before. But the key question remains about what motivates those practices in the first place. Some of them may be random and inexplicable. But most human practices are indeed motivated, even if those performing them at any given time are not reflecting on the motivations (practical consciousness again). The theory we advocate here says that people carry out actions and develop and sustain their practices primarily because they are motivated by the defining, orienting, informing, and guiding capacities of their cultural models. To repeat, those motivations need not operate at the forefront of conscious awareness. They do only rarely. They are normally submerged, in the background, unconscious, operating on autopilot. Yet that does not make cultural models less causally potent but actually more so, since they direct action without requiring people's conscious attention and evaluation.

Now let us bring this discussion back to the substantive topic of our book. A religious man or woman finds him- or herself the parent of a child. What to do? Among the myriad possibilities, these parents must decide whether and how they will raise the child with regard to their religion. Many will choose for intelligible reasons to try to pass on their religion to their children. So they deploy certain strategies and tactics to transmit their religious practices, identity, and beliefs. Why will they do that? And how will they go about it? The answers to those questions will be determined by many factors, perhaps including pragmatic ones, such as the convenience of access to religious activities and the expectations of extended family. If so, then cultural models about the value of convenience and efficiency and of pleasing one's family will pertain as well. But among the potentially many factors, very influential will be parents' most important beliefs, desires, and feelings about life, success, religion, family, and children, especially as they were shaped by their evaluation of the way they were raised by their parents. And those beliefs are what make up parents' cultural models. That is what we showed in the previous chapters.

But how does that actually work? In effect, parents raising children more or less (and often less) consciously negotiate their way forward by coordinating their actions and practices with the beliefs of their cultural models of life and the world. That does not normally happen through conscious deliberations and declarations of the form, "I believe B_1, B_2, and B_3, therefore I will perform P." Most people are not like that. Rather, parents most often proceed with what makes sense to them intuitively (given their background cognitive beliefs) and adjust when situations seem "off" from what seems right and amenable to improvement. For instance, few parents march into the office of clergy, lay out their expectations for good religious congregations, and ask for programs and cultural environments to meet them. But when a parent concludes after some experience that a congregation seems inattentive to children, cold, overly zealous, or too demanding, parents will respond accordingly. What determines their responses is not mysterious. They derive primarily from the cognitive beliefs that make up their cultural model that we called the Proper Role of Religious Congregations. Cultural models thus guide the religious transmission practices of parents.

But cultural models do more than guide. They also motivate the religious practices in the first place, in the sense of providing the energy to initiate and often sustain them. How so? Recall our definition of purposively motivated action provided above. The constellations of beliefs that form parents' cultural models provide them the necessary (1) goals to achieve (successful religious transmission), (2) beliefs about actions that will likely achieve those goals (modeling by example, avoidance of force, strategically timed discussions), and (3) emotionally laden desires to realize the goals (because religion is good for children and families). Together these provide the energy generating and sustaining parents' actions, which often become practices, oriented toward transmitting religion to children. Crucial to parents' motivation to pass on their religion to their children, we have shown, are their beliefs that religion is good for children, will help them navigate life's journey, provides an essential foundation for life, helps them be good people, offers resources for support and comfort during hard times, contributes when shared to family solidarity, and so on. Nearly all religiously involved American parents genuinely believe these things, and those internalized cognitions provide them all the motivation they need to attempt to pass on their religion to their children. Cognitive beliefs not only orient parents to reality but also help to create affectively charged desires to realize certain outcomes, which then produce their motivated actions and practices.

To help make our case more plausible, let us run a mental experiment. Imagine the world exactly as it is, except that some evil villain (let's say an economist) presses a button that deletes every living person's cultural models, as we have described them. Everyone's networks of functional beliefs (about reality, one's place in it, and goods to enjoy) disappear. What would happen in the next hours and days? How would life in that world function? Well, it could not function. Chaos would ensue. Lacking the stable clusters of core beliefs that define, orient, inform, and guide action, nobody would know what is real, what is what, how things work, or what they should do. They would not be able to form intelligible and sustainable desires or understand the emotional significance of many of their physiological sensations. They would, for example, feel what we call hunger or the need to defecate, but they would not know how to respond to those sensations properly. Functional human life requires that people hold cultural models. If they did not, those would certainly be "unsettled times," to say the least.

Imagine next that some well-meaning soul (let's say a sociologist) manages to distribute to every living person a tool kit containing sundry cultural items (recognized vocabularies, discourses, explanations, and so on) that they hope people will pull out and use to bring some order, meaning, and direction back to their lives. Would that project succeed? We think not. Mere collections of tools are useless without some larger framework of understanding specifying what they are designed to tear down, fix, and build. Cultural tools cannot bring order without some larger, prior order in place within which their usefulness can be understood and capitalized on. Tool kits only become valuable when found in competent hands in auto repair shops, carpenters' trucks, and model ship builders' desks; they are useless in the hands of someone who lacks basic, stable cognitive beliefs about what needs doing and why. The usefulness of cultural tools, in other words, is only realized when people possess cultural models by which they orient their lives.

Power and Interested Interventions. Questions of power in human relations are central in sociology and parts of anthropology, so a theory of culture that ignores issues of power, domination, and ideology will be deficient. Accounts that claim culture is all about power and domination, however, such as most Marxist and some postcolonial theories, will also be inadequate. We said earlier in this chapter that the Parsonian view of culture all but ignored power, and that some post-Parsonian theories of culture made power relations central to their accounts. How, then, does our theory of cultural models treat power? The answer is straightforward and can be stated concisely.

Internal culture is essentially networks of cognitive knowledge, consisting of orienting and action-directing beliefs, which are linked to related desires and emotions. These beliefs are organized in clusters as cultural models about different parts of reality. Cultural models exist as cognitive entities in the embodied brains of people, but they are also intersubjectively shared among groups of people. Cultural models, we claim, have the ability not only to explain actions and practices in retrospect, but also prospectively to motivate and guide them. That is the key point of relevance for the issue of power relations. Because cultural models have the capacity to arouse, direct, and sustain meaningful behavior, anyone who wants to influence (not simply coerce) the actions and practices of other people will want to shape the content of those people's cultural models, and so too their associated desires and emotions, or to activate certain but not other already-held cultural models to focus and frame matters in a way that serves their interests.

Cultural models as we describe them are cognitive and subjective. They constitute the internal side of culture. However, cultural models are obviously also shaped in myriad ways by the institutions, public narratives, and objects of external culture (a matter we do not discuss in this book). People do not create their cultural models from scratch inside their heads, but form them over lifetimes, not only as embodied creatures in time and space, but also as social animals being continually enculturated in schools, families, the media, religious associations, workplaces, consumer markets, entertainment experiences, and so on. Every institution, setting, product, and narrative of external culture is potentially susceptible to being shaped by powerful actors in ways that enhance their influence over the formation, plausibility, and resonance of other people's cultural models. The powerful can thus exploit culture to serve their own interests. Unequal power relations and conflicts of interests are thus reflected and inscribed in the content and structure of both external and internal culture. The accomplishment is most effective, however, when the influence of the powerful is not even detectible by those who believe in and act on cultural models—just as the "best" computer malware accomplishes its malicious activities without computer users ever learning their devices had been infected.

Our approach to cultural models has no particular investment in specific applications of the concepts of ideology, hegemony, false consciousness, and so on. Their usefulness can be sorted out on their own terms, although we think that each idea points to something real and consequential related to culture. More important for us is the basic theoretical recognition of the connections between (1) the motivating potential of internal cultural models, (2) the susceptibility of internal cultural models to being shaped by external cultural forces that are influenced by powerful actors, and (3) the consequences those cultural interventions can have in serving the political, wealth, and status interests of the powerful. Again, if culture were not motivationally potent, it would be of little interest or use to those who wish to shape the thinking and practices of others. But cultural models *are* causally powerful, and so they do attract the interest and interventions of institutionally powerful people and groups.

These processes can operate at a microsocial level, as with "family myths," for example, that serve some family members' interests more than others.[67] They also occur at the meso-social level, when, for instance, objectively exploited residents of Appalachian coal mining communities are persuaded to believe that the coal-extraction industry serves their best interests.[68] And these processes occur at the macrosocial and global levels, as, for example, when whole populations are convinced that spending money on and consuming material products and exciting experiences (that increase the riches of a few) will make them happy (or, to shift frameworks, that sacrificing oneself entirely for the Communist Party is one's highest possible purpose in life).[69] These processes occur, but, we think, not necessarily inevitably, all the time, and everywhere. Cultural models are highly susceptible to being formed in ways that serve the interests of the powerful. But culture itself is not merely a medium of social domination (any more than computer systems exist for the exploitations of malware). Most basically, culture exists to define what is real, locate and orient people within that reality, and tell them what is good to pursue.[70] The exploitation of culture by the powerful is a secondary malignancy.

Centering Persons. The theory of cultural models offers (what in our view is) the advantage of being a *person*-centered, not society-centered or other kind of approach. As theoretical personalists, we believe that human

67. Arlie Hochschild, *The Second Shift* (New York: Penguin Books, 2012); also see Sherryl Kleinman, *Opposing Ambitions* (Chicago: University of Chicago Press, 1996).

68. John Gaventa, *Power and Powerlessness: Quiescence and Rebellion in an Appalachian Valley* (Champaign: University of Illinois Press, 1982).

69. Roger Rosenblatt, ed., *Consuming Desires: Consumption, Culture, and the Pursuit of Happiness* (Mercer Island, WA: Island Books, 1999); Douglas Hyde, *Dedication and Leadership: Learning from the Communists* (Notre Dame, IN: University of Notre Dame Press, 1971). How does all this relate to this book's substantive inquiry into religious transmission? In brief, it seems to us that the apparent transformation of American religion—from historically being (a) authoritative communities that define transcendent interests and standards with some autonomy from immanent mass-consumer capitalism and liberal individualism, to having primarily become instead (b) sources of personal therapeutic resources for coping with life's difficulties and achieving success and happiness—clearly serves the interests of those who benefit from our current political economy and its attendant cultural institutions, such as the mass media. Spelling out those relations would require the writing of an entirely different book (but see Christian Smith with Melinda Lundquist Denton, *Soul Searching: The Religious and Spiritual Lives of American Teenagers* [New York: Oxford University Press, 2005], 172–92).

70. The causal agency here resides in the people, who form and believe cultural models, while the causal power to define, orient, and direct resides in the cultural models.

persons—not social forces, society, practices, or variables—are in reality, and so ought to be treated in theory as, the prime movers and value centers of human social life. By contrast, the later-career theory of Talcott Parsons centered the functional requisites of social systems.[71] Post-Parsonian theories took a variety of angles on this matter, sometimes centering persons, but other times centering practices or power relations, or even purposively decentering and dissolving persons.

The theory of cultural models, however, takes as its primary unit of analysis persons and the cultural models they hold. According to Claudia Strauss, being a "person-centered" account means, among other things, "tak[ing] into account three complexities of the socialization process: (1) public social messages may change, be inconsistent, or hard to read; (2) internalizing these messages does not mean copying them in any straightforward way; and (3) motivation is not automatically acquired when cultural descriptions of reality are learned."[72] That is to say, persons are treated as complex, discerning, active participants in and agents of the process of their own cultural formation, not as "cultural dopes," automatic reproducers of "habitus," or mere sites where power relations intersect. Rather, "to understand why someone acts the way they do it is not enough to know the discourses, objects, and events to which they have been exposed; we need to know the psychic structures [of that person] that assimilate those things and render them a basis for meaningful action."[73] We would add that the theory of cultural models fits well a larger personalist conception of human beings and society, about which one of us (Smith) has written much elsewhere.[74] One need not be a personalist to believe in and analyze cultural models, but if one is a personalist, then the theory of cultural models becomes attractive for this additional reason.

Objections Anticipated and Answered

The cultural models theory we advocate encounters predictable objections, which we answer preemptively as follows.

---

71. Parsons's first major book, *The Structure of Social Action* (1937; New York: Free Press, 1967) took a largely person-centered approach, but his career subsequently moved in a social systems–centered structural-functionalist direction.

72. Claudia Strauss, "Models and Motivations," in D'Andrade and Strauss, *Human Motives and Cultural Models*, 9–10.

73. Strauss, "Models and Motivations," 7.

74. Smith, *What Is a Person?*; Smith, *To Flourish or Destruct*.

Objection #1: Cultural models do not actually exist in and for real people, but are the post hoc fabrications of scholars who impose thematic order on the actually disorganized discourse of research subjects. The question here is whether our scholarly analytic models that (purportedly) describe people's actual cultural models are in fact (a) representational reconstructions of something real in people's cognitions (as we claim) or (b) merely the original constructions of researchers like us who foist the appearance of organization and intelligibility onto jumbled and confused discourse data.

Our first response is to place the burden of proof where it belongs, on the objection and not our theory, and to question why we should think the objection valid. Its skepticism enjoys no obvious epistemological advantage over the view that cultural models do exist. Furthermore, the kind of theoretical social situationism that generates this kind of objection is fraught with debilitating flaws, as one of us (Smith) has shown elsewhere.[75] At the same time, the theory of cultural models has significant support in that it is consistent with and backed up by important findings in cognitive science.

The existence of something like cultural models is also phenomenologically demonstrable in the ordinary lives of normally functioning people. Would any of us deny that we ourselves have myriad beliefs about the world that tend to assemble together in reasonably clustered ideas, that those clusters relate in complex and intelligible ways to other belief clusters, and that our clusters of beliefs have some influence on our intentions and actions? If so, what account of him- or herself could such a belief-denying person offer as an alternative? That they are simply buffeted about by external social forces or unconscious psychological drives? That their seemingly intelligible actions are actually random and uncaused? That they lack cognition and, like animals, only respond to the conditioning of rewarding and punishing stimuli? In fact, skeptics who deny the reality, intelligibility, and potential causal power of organized human beliefs have in doing so negated their capacity to offer the objection already given, since a necessary condition for the ability to offer that objection is the possession and operation of intelligible, causally efficacious beliefs. The objection is thus self-defeating. If it were actually true, then no person would be able to make it.

Meanwhile, we have offered in the preceding chapters a great deal of empirical evidence for the existence of shared, coherent, teleologically

75. Smith, *To Flourish or Destruct*, 91–118.

oriented cultural models based on a dataset gathered using sound methods of data collection and analysis. We spared no pains in analyzing our data systematically and in detail. And in the presentation of our argument, we have erred on the side of evidentiary overkill to make clear our point about shared cultural models. We stand accountable to critics. But it is not enough for skeptics to dismiss the reality of cultural models without presenting more compelling evidence and cogent reasoning than ours. Until skeptics can deliver that, we will have no reason to find this first objection persuasive.

One last, related empirical point before moving on. At the end of each of our interviews, we closed by asking our parent respondents whether they had any further thoughts they wished to express. Our invitation was open-ended and made clear that no further comments were obligatory. Many parents did offer parting reflections, however. One of the most common was the grateful observation that participating in the interview had helped them articulate some of the things they believe and care about but usually do not have occasion to think about and talk through. One Hispanic Catholic father from Chicago, for example, ended his interview by saying: "I can tell you this has been very, very helpful to me. I'll be honest, this is the first time that I've sat with someone who's questioned me and given the opportunity of expressing my views, my beliefs, without having the fear of someone judging back. It's been a great experience for me, it puts my thoughts in more perspective, more concrete. I might never see you again, so it makes it easier [to think and talk openly]. It also teaches, 'cause it makes you reflect and understand. I really enjoyed it." These are the words, if we take them seriously, of a person who does not exemplify a post-Parsonian user of culture. They are the words of someone in possession of internal "views and beliefs" and "thoughts"—that is, who operates in life with cultural models running in the background that are rarely systematically examined and discussed, and who thus appreciates the chance to reflect on, clarify, and express the beliefs that constitute his cultural models. These words, if we trust his testimony, which he said was "honest," also tell us that this man's thoughts and beliefs *preexist* the research interview. The interview primarily functioned as a context for him to better illuminate for himself and express those beliefs with greater perspective, solidity, self-understanding. We also hear someone who is grateful for that opportunity, who enjoyed the process, since better understanding the beliefs that define our understandings of reality and guide our actions is an intrinsically rewarding experience. Aristotle was right: "Humans by nature desire to know."

Other parents expressed similar reactions in their final comments. A white Catholic father from Chicago said, "It's always good to talk these things out loud, and you learn things about yourself." A white Catholic mother from Indiana remarked, "It was interesting, I was glad 'cause I don't get to articulate all these ideas all the time, so hopefully that makes some sense." A Jewish mother from New York City said, "Thank you for giving me a way to talk about things that matter the most to me in the world, the people that matter the most to me." Likewise, a Hispanic Catholic father from New York City stated, almost as if he had completed a therapy session, "Thank you very much for letting me participate, because [what I discussed] it's something I have remembered, it has come out what for so long I had kept inside." And a Muslim father from Chicago told us, "Actually, it's kind of interesting, [our interview] made me think about a lot of things. These are the types of question that me and my wife would always talk about. Definitely a lot of interesting parenting questions." Even in this case, in which the father had (unusually) talked about the transmission of religion frequently with his wife, he still found thinking about the issues in the interview to be stimulating. Again, something about clarifying and articulating their existing beliefs about important matters was stimulating to many parents. "You got deep and you made me think! You really made me think," observed a black Protestant father from Houston, appreciatively.

Nothing in what parents told us in closing suggested that they were floating answers they did not really believe or forcing a coherence or harmony of ideas that did not exist. People's beliefs already "matter" to them and just need expression; they are true in people's minds already, but voicing them fosters deeper learning about themselves. And when parents did not believe a statement or know how to answer a question, they readily said, "I don't really know," "I'd need to think more about that," and "That's a tough one." When they did share their thoughts in interviews, they seemed for all the world to us to be genuine and honest—as expressed, for instance, by the final words of this Hispanic Catholic father from New Mexico: "I believe that what I've been asked [by you], I have answered as I have lived it, and from what I know. Thank you."

Of course, the skeptical objector may respond, these parents are just saying the kinds of polite things that people are trained and expected to say in such situations. Who knows what they *really* think and mean? A headstrong skeptic can never be satisfied. Still, the researchers who conducted our interviews are not especially gullible conversationalists, and our shared conclusion after conducting the interviews was that we encountered little but candor and sincerity from the parents. Those we interviewed believed the subject of conversation to be important, they wanted to help us, and they usually found our conversations stimulating and enjoyable. None seemed to feel the need to impress us. If anything, again, they found it to be a relief and a pleasure to be able to reflect and speak freely without worrying they would pay a price for saying the "wrong" thing. We told them that we wanted to hear the honest, unvarnished truth, whatever that was, and we think that is basically what we got.

"But wait!," the skeptic may yet insist, "all of you, including you researchers, are just playing an encompassing interactive discourse game that has nothing to do with people's alleged beliefs, desires, and feelings." If that is true, then the entire enterprise of social science research melts down, liquidating along with it the objections of the skeptic. For if all of us are only playing a self-deceived and other-deceiving language game, then that includes the skeptic too, so his or her sustained objections become self-defeating in yet another way. The waters of radical skepticism, when allowed to flow freely, never stop at the doorstep of the skeptic but engulf and destroy the skeptic's house too. We all need to be intelligently skeptical with focus, not comprehensively skeptical as a default.

Let us suppose instead that the final reflections of these parents can be trusted until proven untrustworthy. Might the background presence of cultural models show up in their comments, even faintly, if their remarks are carefully interpreted? We think so, even in some nonobvious cases. Consider the somewhat cryptic words of this conservative Protestant mother from Indiana, who observed at the end of her interview, "This was real interesting for me to put [into] words, 'cause I usually don't put words to these things, and those aren't things that I think about and try and put into words." We might interpret this statement skeptically and claim that it shows that people do not reflect much on what they believe and so have few coherent, intelligible beliefs. But it does not follow from people's lack of reflection and talk about beliefs that they do not have beliefs that are coherent and intelligible. We all hold many important beliefs that we rarely think and talk about. But note that this woman repeatedly stands her "words" and "thinking" in relation to the vague referents "this," "these things," and "things." What does she mean? "This" appears to refer to the interview itself ("This [interview] was real interesting . . ."). But "these things" and "things" seem to refer to something else. Maybe she meant the interview questions. But people do not talk about "putting words to" and "putting into words" interview questions. Maybe she instead meant her answers to the interview questions. That would make sense. But if so, the question remains about what her answers to the questions really represent. Do they reference underlying, preexistent, internalized if unclarified beliefs that function as cultural models? Or are they "disorganized discourse," as the objection above suggests, perhaps serving to justify practices that are not shaped by beliefs? If the former, then we would expect her to say "this was interesting," just as she did. Thinking and talking about the beliefs that define our cultural models is interesting. But if the latter, we would not expect her to experience the interview as interesting. Presumably she would in that case be relieved to have survived the interview without coming off as totally incoherent. We think the best interpretation of "these things" and "things" are the substantive topics of conversations about which she has beliefs that are so deeply internalized that she rarely has to think about and articulate them, yet that are "interesting" to reflect on and articulate when she is asked to do so.

Objection #2: The cultural models that we present cannot really be shared *by parents if the way they voice them and the specific examples they give to illustrate their points differ.* The question is whether people really share coherent, substantive beliefs that they express in various ways, or whether instead we analysts are abstracting from dissimilar discourse to a higher level of generality in order to make it appear that parents share the same cultural models when in fact they do not. At issue is not so much whether people possess something like cultural models (Objection #1) but *just how shared* among different people they actually are. Our reply is this.

First, if shared cultural models exist as we argue they do, it would be unrealistic to expect everyone who holds them to express them identically. The idea of cultural models is not that people read verbatim from the same scripts or offer cookie-cutter examples and narratives. It is rather that some people share the same underlying beliefs about certain domains of life (of course, different groups of people often hold different cultural models). The fact that they are *models* means that they operate at a certain level of generality. To express them in the same specific terms would make them not cultural models but technical instructions or paint-by-numbers pictures. We are not transforming or inventing through abstraction what people only allegedly believe. We are seeking to represent in concise form what people actually do believe.

One test exists for whether we are authentically representing people's underlying clusters of beliefs and not creating the illusion of belief agreement through abstraction. That would be if interview respondents reviewed the analytic models resulting from analyses of their different conversations and declared, "Yes, that is essentially what I think, that resonates, so thank you for putting it into those words." That is, assuming people are basically honest and not swayed by social desirability to agree with our conclusions, an assumption that is our default until it is shown to be invalid. Such a test faces logistical methodological challenges, but we think conducting this kind of validity check should be one of the next steps for research in cultural models. We are confident based on our experience in this and other projects that our analytic models of religious transmission would pass that test.

The fact that different types of people narrate and illustrate their cultural models in different ways strengthens rather than weakens our reasons for believing that they are shared across the different groups. Of course many American Jewish parents will describe the texture and particulars of a good life or the valuable resources offered by their religious traditions differently than, say, evangelical Protestant or Buddhist parents. So what? Consensus in basic beliefs and differences in particular descriptions are not contradictory. They operate at different levels and for distinct purposes. The same cultural models can be expressed through diverse vocabularies, styles of discourse, and illustrations. What else would we expect? Yet different types and styles of discourse can point back to similar underlying perceptions, beliefs, values, and goals that make up shared cultural models. By analogy, when we hear varying dialects, favored lexicons, and manners of speech expressed by different kinds of Americans in different regions of the country, we do not conclude that they are not all speaking English or that the English language does not exist. We conclude that the same shared language can be spoken in quite different ways. The same logic applies to cultural models: the particularities of their expression do not negate their underlying shared character.

Moreover, to keep perspective, let us not exaggerate the differences between the ways our parents expressed their cultural models. Skeptics may purposefully look for the most dissimilar terminology, examples, and stories offered by parents, and then conclude that they do not share similar beliefs. But that would be the real imposition of scholarly biases on the data. Reading closely the myriad quotes in chapters 1–4, most striking is the high degree of similarity of discourse across otherwise very different kinds of parents. The images, themes, metaphors, explanations, and feelings expressed are not wildly divergent. If anything, they are often boringly repetitive—which is why we felt the need to implore readers in the introduction to read them all carefully. We cannot guarantee that all studies of cultural models in other areas of life will reveal the same similarity.

But our empirical case, at least, was not fraught with such dissimilarities of talk that we had to move to higher levels of abstraction. So one of the premises of this objection is not valid in our case.

Let us remember, too, that our analysis revealed among some different types of parents not only many shared cultural models but also certain specific issues about which parents disagreed. Amid the overwhelming similarity of beliefs, we found significant divergence on the questions of the importance of salvation and the afterlife, the value of proactively exposing children to other religious traditions, and the extent and style of parents' definitive authority over their children. If we had found 100 percent agreement among parents in our research, we too would worry that we were creating and not discovering consensus. But we did not. The fact that some disagreements among parents did register in our analyses should increase confidence about the consensus among parents that we found in most areas. Sometimes parents disagreed, and we reported that; most of the time, they agreed, and we showed that. We did our best to represent accurately the degrees of agreement and disagreement that we heard. We did not have to fabricate basic agreement among parents; it clearly existed in and behind what they said and often even how they said it.

Objection #3: Inconsistencies in expressed beliefs in interviews show that culture is not subjectively internalized, as the cognitive cultural models approach says, but rather exists external to people as disconnected pieces of publicly available discourse deployed to make sense of questioned behaviors or practices after the fact. We offer three brief replies to this objection. First, as we just said, our empirical findings about parents' expressed beliefs reveal few inconsistencies and contradictions, and little incoherence, so at least in our case we have little explaining to do. Second, even if our findings did involve rational inconsistencies in the explanations of our interview respondents, they would not substantiate this objection. The question of the consistency of expressed beliefs in interview conversations and the matter of whether culture is subjectively internalized are two separate issues. People can be consistent or inconsistent in their talk, whether or not culture is deeply internalized.[76] There is no logical connection

76. As Quinn observes ("An Anthropologist's View of American Marriage," 48–49): "Anthropologist Claudia Strauss, who studies the inconsistencies in her interviewee's talk, has shown that, over longer stretches of interview, this talk is in fact chock full of contradictions. However, Swidler's and Strauss's interpretations of these inconsistencies are different. While Swidler takes them as evidence that the variant views expressed are not

between the two issues. In fact, many if not most people internalize and genuinely embrace beliefs that are inconsistent. Observed inconsistencies themselves prove nothing about internalization.

Third, in many cases, some incoherence in interview talk results, we think, from the very deep internalization of the beliefs expressed, rather than the opposite. Subjective internalization works at multiple levels, from close to the surface to deeply buried. The more deeply a set of beliefs has been internalized, the harder we should expect it to be for people to bring them to the surface and express them, and the greater the chance that people will struggle, hesitate, and fail to explain well integrated, coherent belief systems. But that does not show they are not internalized. Very deeply internalized beliefs are simply obvious and therefore usually invisible to people. (Here we reference again the helpful distinction between "practical consciousness" and "discursive consciousness."[77]) Until a sociologist shows up asking questions, people rarely need to consider their deeply internalized beliefs. And when the sociologist does show up, laying all those beliefs on the table in neat order can be difficult. That does not show that beliefs are not subjectively internalized; it may instead reflect the fact that they are *very deeply* internalized.[78]

Objection #4: Whether or not actions and practices are motivated and however that may work, we know that the old Weberian model of means-ends motivated action is wrong; thus, your theory's discussion of beliefs, desires, and actions believed to achieve goals is obsolete and erroneous. Our response to this objection is two-pronged. First, we deny the assertion that Max Weber's theory and ours are fairly characterized as merely being about choosing means to specified ends. That is a caricature of both accounts, which are more complex and realistic than this objection recognizes. Second, we reject the premise that means-ends models of motivated action are categorically wrong. Most human actions are motivated one way or another, and motivations are always about the energy and direction to

---

'internalized' but simply variant 'public codes,' Strauss assumes that these contradictory views are indeed inside people's heads, but finds that her interviewees are typically unaware of holding them simultaneously. How we manage these inconsistent views is the subject of much of her work."

77. Giddens, *Constitution of Society*.

78. By analogy, someone who claims to own an artificial Christmas tree and ornaments might, when asked to display them, only be able to produce some of them after much difficulty and angst. That does not prove that he or she does not own them; it may just reveal that the tree and ornaments are packed away in various boxes in the deepest recesses of the attic.

realize certain desired outcomes. This is both phenomenologically obvious to any self-reflexive person and the universal common sense of humanity. Attempts to deny it (which are themselves motivated actions wishing to achieve a particular goal) are indefensible and self-defeating. This objection also falls apart, then, with only brief consideration.

Objection #5: Human subjectivity may be real, but it cannot be studied empirically because it is not directly observable. Really? Then what exactly does the one voicing this objection mean by it? And how could we know? Does it involve thoughts, ideas, concerns? Is it offered sincerely, with the intention to improve social science? Because if this objection is correct, then we can know nothing reliable about the thoughts, ideas, concerns, sincerity, and intentions behind and informing it, since they supposedly cannot be observed. All that we have, in such a case, is a string of words that fit the syntax of a language. But what they are intended to accomplish and how seriously we ought to regard them we cannot discern, since the reliable knowledge of the subjectivity that would be required to do that has been ruled out.

No, engaging in meaningful arguments, taking one's critics seriously, being persuaded (or not), and working together in knowledge communities of social science necessarily presuppose the possibility and reliability of intersubjective understanding. We cannot have it both ways. Either we can achieve adequate understanding or we cannot. In reality, we can and do manage it, at least enough to make life work. The fact that you are now reading and hopefully understanding this book shows, for example, that intersubjective understanding is possible.

Objection #5 derives from the hopelessly flawed philosophies of positivism and empiricism, which we already encountered. It is naive about the philosophy of social science and unreflective about our normal social science practices. People who buy this objection need to think harder about what good social science does. To be empirical does not mean being directly observable. It means being based on some relevant kind of observation or experience, as opposed to being purely theoretical or logical. Depending on the subject of study, there can be many relevant kinds of observations. In (social) science, what we directly observe are usually indicators and consequences of things that we cannot directly observe, yet about which we care much more than about the observable. Take the operation of causation, for instance. It is not directly observable, as (the empiricist) David Hume convincingly showed in the eighteenth century. Yet identifying the causes of outcomes lies at the heart of science. Causes are real and can be empirically identified, but normally (when true, controlled experiments are impossible, which is most of the time[79]) this must be done indirectly through retroduction and inference to the best explanation, joined with theoretical abduction.

Knowledge about human subjectivity is at least as accessible and potentially warranted as that about physical causation, insofar as each of us, for starters, possesses, continually experiences, and can closely examine our own personal subjectivities. We know from at least one observation, of ourselves, that subjectivity exists and has a certain character. We also have very good reasons to believe that others also possess subjective experience. Furthermore, people possess an amazing capacity called language with which we communicate with others about subjective experience, sometimes with difficulty, of course, but nonetheless feasibly and often reliably enough. Indeed, all of us routinely engage in (generally successful) attempts at intersubjective understanding based on empirically accessible evidence, usually in the form of speech exchanged between ourselves and others. There is nothing strange or impossible about that. So why, after spending their whole lives doing exactly that, do some scholars feel the need to claim that human subjectivities are inaccessible to systematic study, and so understanding of it is beyond us? The idea that such an objection could torpedo the theory of cultural models—or any other social science analysis that references human subjectivities, which is nearly every approach going except the pure behaviorism that was shown long ago to be impossible—is just strange.

Too many social scientists remain haunted by the ghosts of positivism and empiricism. Those spirits provoke confusion and anxiety among even the smartest of scholars, despite their philosophical bodies having been killed off long ago. To be free of the troubling visitations of those ghouls and so enlightened about the real nature of the world we live in and study, we need to silence our falsely protective incantations of "direct observability" and renounce every lingering vestige of positivism and empiricism. Such an exorcism can be accomplished by recognizing, believing, and acknowledging four obvious yet sometimes apparently scandalous antipositivist and antiempiricist facts, namely:

1. Many immaterial and directly unobservable entities exist in reality that possess causal powers. These include our thoughts,

---

79. Even when the best experiments are conducted, causation is not observed but merely isolated.

desires, intentions, reasons, self-consciousness, and the nonphysiological aspect of our emotions (human subjectivities), as well as microwaves, magnetic and gravitational forces, and the causal potentialities of physical objects.

2. We rarely enjoy direct observations of the subjects of research that most interest us, despite their real existence. This is true of social structures, causal processes, and institutional transformations (democratization, for instance), as well as quarks and leptons, the extinction of the dinosaurs, and (as yet) cosmic dark matter. It is also true of human subjectivities.

3. We normally produce (social) scientific knowledge about reality not by staring at and measuring our objects of study (direct observation) or even running experiments on them. We do so rather through more complex processes of conceptualization, inference, retroduction, and abduction, which apply reasoned and personally insightful reflection to the empirical evidence that we can access in order to understand and theorize entities and processes that we cannot observe.

4. Even the very best (social) science only ever provides us empirically grounded, warranted beliefs about the nature and operation of reality. It never grants indubitably certain knowledge (more on this further on).[80] And those beliefs are warranted only within the context of a variety of other interrelated presuppositions, many of which are empirically unverifiable or based on yet other assumptions that are empirically unverifiable, that constitute the enterprise of scientific inquiry justifying the findings as beliefs meriting acceptance.

By grasping and professing these four truths, we can dispel the ghosts of positivism and empiricism that still haunt some halls of social science, and without apology or misplaced confidence we can make human subjectivities the objects of our social science research—as indeed we must if human activities are to be properly understood.

Objection #6: Research interviews are artificial and leading in their pre-determined questions, so they cannot be relied upon to reveal what is really going on in people's natural subjectivities. Actually, we reply, what social

---

80. For an elaboration and defense of this fourth point, see Smith, *Moral, Believing Animals.*

scientists call interviews are not artificial in comparison with people's experience in ordinary life. Normal social life regularly involves something like "interviews" taking place between people.[81] In everyday life we call them "conversations," but like interviews, they involve the ongoing exchange of thoughts prompted by questions, observations, and expressed interests, which evoke interactive responses. Most people are familiar and comfortable with "conducting interviews," especially with friends and confidants to whom they are prepared to open up their true thoughts and feelings, but also with people who are unfamiliar and hold different power or status positions. Of course poor research interviewers can conduct bad interviews. But bad researchers can ruin any method of data collection. And skilled research interviewers can conduct very productive and revealing interviews. In-depth personal interviews suffer no comparative disadvantage of artificiality or "external invalidity." In fact, interviews feel more natural to most people than the other common research method in the social sciences: forced-choice questions on lengthy survey questionnaires. That, if anywhere, is where we should really be concerned about artificiality and validity.

Returning to the specific objection, the worry about semistructured interview questionnaires being leading is also groundless. Again, poor research interviewers can lead and bias the replies of their respondents. But in an interview that is designed and conducted well, that need not happen. Questions are structured to lead from very broad to more focused queries, and conversations are free to range far from the script. Interviews working from the theory advocated here in particular seek not to force expected answers, but instead to facilitate lengthy and open-ended conversations that can indirectly reveal the assumptions and beliefs that make up respondents' cultural models. Given that our access to other people's subjectivities is indirect, it seems to us that well-conducted research interviews, far from being questionable, are the best method available for identifying and reconstructing people's real cultural models.

Furthermore, if our standard is to establish with certainty "what is really going on" in people's subjectivities, all research involving any aspect of human subjectivity is doomed. Such an impossible standard reflects an outdated and failed epistemological "foundationalism" that demands indubitable knowledge. That standard and its resulting expectations are totally naive. Of course, social science interviews can never prove what is "really" true about subjective beliefs, assumptions, motivations, and

---

81. Charlotte Linde, *Life Stories: The Creation of Coherence* (Oxford: Oxford University Press, 1993); Quinn, "The So-Called Interview," in *Finding Culture in Talk*, 41–43.

intentions. But neither can survey researchers prove that reported answers to survey questions are valid. Nor can symbolic interactionists verify that some observed behavior recorded in their field notes was "really" a gesture of hostility or romantic advance or whatever else they tell us. The content and authenticity of other people's subjectivities (and often even some of our own to ourselves) are not a realm where certainty and proof obtain. But that does not make them inaccessible, mysterious, or incomprehensible.

This idea applies in a different way in the natural sciences. Even there, what can be "verified" usually depends not on direct observation or experiment but on indicators and inferences to the explanation that seems best. What, for example, is "really" the temperature of a mass of material? We can't know directly. But we can use an instrument as an indicator of the temperature, a thermometer. We do not ever observe the temperature; instead, we see a digital reading on a gadget (or, previously, a red line in a glass tube). That seems to work for our purposes, so we trust and rely on it. Or, for another example, how did our universe "really" come into existence? We cannot prove the Big Bang or any other theory through observation. But again, we can fit together the empirical pieces that we are able to assemble (usually through indirect indicators) and infer through retroduction that the Big Bang is the best available explanation (even though some of our observations, such as the apparent accelerating expansion of the universe, do not square with that accepted theory).

The same is true of interviews seeking to access people's beliefs. We have no direct access for observation. But we do have empirical indicators of the unobservable that are sufficiently trustworthy for the carrying on of human social life generally—that is, shared language deployed in answers, reports, explanations, testimonies, and so on. If this were not true, if linguistic utterances could not under the right conditions be trusted, then all of human social life would break down. And what generally works for the discerning communicator in schools, marriages, businesses, friendships, and book writing also generally works for the discerning researcher conducting in-depth interviews. Obsessive skeptics demanding certainty about what is "really" going on with people's beliefs need to drop their impossible and inconsistent epistemic requirements and focus instead on how we can improve the validity and reliability of interview-based research findings that are indeed possible to produce.

The correct standard in (social) science is not indubitable certainty, which is impossible, but *warranted belief*. In fact, the latter is something that all people continually seek to discern in most domains of life. What do we have good reasons to believe is true? That is a universal question that in practical consciousness occupies a great deal of human attention. People's talk can tell us a lot that we have good reasons to believe is true (and under other conditions, probably false) about their subjectivities. Rather than dismissing the good and mostly reliable because it is not perfect and certain, we should work toward improving our skills as interviewers and analysts so we can more accurately understand and represent the contents of people's subjectivities.

Research Questions

Suppose readers find our theory of cultural models persuasive. Beyond its helping to interpret our specific empirical findings on American religious parents' approaches to transmitting religion to their children, what more general research agendas and questions might this theory suggest? Many, we believe, but here are some questions we consider interesting and important:

- *Formation of Models*: How are people's core cultural models initially formed and possibly subsequently transformed? How do toddlers and children negotiate the myriad pieces of cognitive input and interpretive narratives they encounter to select and cluster beliefs into the cultural models they embrace?
- *Sharedness and Difference*: What cultural models in specific empirical cases are shared across groups that are categorically different, and why? And when and why do different social groups diverge on their embraced cultural models when they do? What explains patterns of similarity and solidarity versus difference and disagreement?
- *Professed and Unconscious*: What if any patterns are discernable in and across specific empirical cases in those elements of cultural models that tend to operate tacitly and unconsciously versus those that are consciously affirmed and expressible? And when and why do specific cognitive beliefs move between those fields of (lack of) awareness?
- *Articulation of Models*: What types of models, people, or environmental conditions are associated with interview respondents' being more articulate about their tacit or backgrounded beliefs? When might respondents intentionally misrepresent their beliefs and why? What methodologies can researchers use to increase the

self-reflexivity of interview respondents and render their cultural models more transparent to their conscious reflections?

- *Metaphors and Image Schemas*: How do metaphors, which are pervasive in discourse, work to represent the beliefs composing people's cultural models?

- *Universality and Relativity*: Are there formal structural aspects or substantive contents of cultural models that hold across all human cultures (as the result, say, of our common embodiment in space and time), or are the organizations and substance of cultural models always particular to specific groups of people in varying times and places?

- *Radical Change*: When and why do people dramatically transform their cultural models? What explains different kinds of radical changes in cognitive beliefs? To what extent does profound change in one cultural model entail changes in others (or not) and why?

- *Desires and Emotions*: How and when do cognitive beliefs generate (or not) volitional desires and emotions? How might desires and emotions reinforce or weaken certain cognitive beliefs?

- *Motivation for Action*: What kind of cultural models tend to motivate and direct people's action and practices, and why and how so? Under what conditions are otherwise-motivating cultural models neutralized or counteracted?

- *Interested Interventions*: How are power, wealth, and status converted into effective interventions in external culture in ways that alter the contents of people's cultural models so that they better serve the interests of those who intervene? What kinds of causal relations link the interests of the powerful, their interventions in external culture, the (re)shaping of popular cognitive beliefs, and the means by which that benefits the powerful? How do ideology, distraction, and hegemony work? To what extent are these processes intentional and strategic versus "natural" and "automatic?" Under what conditions do people embrace or reject new or revised cognitive beliefs that seem objectively to contradict their own interests?

- *Validating Analytic Models*: How can we better use interview respondents' post-interview feedback to assess the representational validity of our analytic models? In what ways can we systematically test our analytic models by checking their resonance with the people whose cultural models they purport to represent?

Other important research questions no doubt exist, but these are some that particularly interest us, and we think answering them will advance the study of culture.

Conclusion

This book is not only about the substantive empirical question of the transmission of religion from parents to children but also the theoretical question of the nature and workings of culture. We have reconstructed from in-depth interviews with parents the cultural models that inform how they approach religious transmission, and that reconstruction reveals much about culture generally. The massive weight of the interview data presented in our findings demonstrates that the cultural models we have reconstructed are real, intelligible, complex, internally coherent, and almost universally shared among religious American parents across significant demographic differences. Furthermore, although this is not a study that tracks cultural models over time, the near-consensus and dominance of the cultural models we have reconstructed and the many spheres of life in which they are rooted (the purpose of life, family solidarity, and so on) suggest that they are durable, not fluid or readily changeable. Moreover, while our data cannot demonstrate this point directly, it is difficult to imagine that the cultural models described in the preceding chapters have little bearing on the practices of parents in raising their children. Nobody would suggest that parents enact them precisely in their behavior like obedient consumers following product instructions out of the box, but we believe and argue (although we cannot here demonstrate) that they play an important causal role in forming and motivating the everyday practices of parents. Our findings suggest the need to rethink post-Parsonian approaches to culture that have dominated theory for decades. We believe a cognitive theory of cultural models offers the most realistic, appropriate, and promising way to rethink and move constructively beyond those approaches. We hope this book provides a valuable step in that direction.

Conclusion

WE HAVE LEARNED much in this book about parenting, religion, and culture. In these final pages we review, highlight, and elaborate on some of the key points we wish to underscore.

Children as Projects. Implicit in all that we discovered above is that American religious parents approach children as "projects." They vary in how self-aware they are about adopting this outlook, but in most cases parents understand their role as tackling a long-term enterprise of planned work designed to achieve an intended (but broad and flexible) aim. As such, good parenting requires at least some tacit understanding of successful outcomes, risks, and strategies. For most, the tasks involve continually facing, navigating, and readjusting expectations, demands, and pressures. Children are thus a project "on a journey" on which parents need to perform well or jeopardize one of life's most important undertakings.

This observed outlook of children-as-projects may seem obvious to some readers—because they share the same cultural models of parenting. But let us remind ourselves that this view contrasts sharply with other historically widespread approaches to parenting that see children growing up as a natural or automatic development,[1] or as not entailing the dra-

1. This observation raises questions related to Annette Lareau's *Unequal Childhoods: Class, Race, and Family Life* (Berkeley: University of California Press, 2003), which observes two distinct parenting styles that vary categorically by social class: "concerted cultivation" (middle class) and "accomplishment of natural growth" (working class). On the question of religious parenting, we found no clear social class difference. Both working-class and middle- and upper-middle-class religious parents share the same cultural models and described engaging in similar strategies and practices. Unlike Lareau, we did not observe actual parental behaviors, and the shared cultural models we identified may work out in practice to reflect some of the differences Lareau observed. Still, the cultural models of religious parenting we discovered actually seem to combine in interesting ways

matically different progressive stages that many take for granted today, or as primarily the shared responsibility of the tribe, village, or kinship network.[2] The last two approaches have been the more common approaches of parents and other adults to the growth and "socialization" of children as new members of society.[3] By comparison, for many American parents today, nearly all of the responsibility for raising children religiously rests on their shoulders alone. Their children are their own projects to organize, implement, and hopefully bring to successful realization. Such an understanding of parenting begs for further research and explanation about the historically changing nature of society and family that would bring such an approach into being.

On a personal note, related to children as projects, we came away from our interviews quite impressed by the sincerity and underlying thoughtfulness of many different kinds of parents about raising their children and the importance of religion in their lives. Most struck us as truly caring and trying the best they knew how to be good and effective parents, even while often dealing with real pressures, burdens, and challenges. The point should not be overstated. Again, most parents do not reflect and strategize about religious transmission to children on a daily basis. And their strategy relies mostly on example setting and socialization through osmosis. Yet, as we have argued through this book, when asked to explain their approach, most parents' talk revealed underlying belief commitments that seemed to inform how they were tackling religious transmission. In contrast to common stereotypes about parents, for example, just

---

both of the two strategies that Lareau observed. Our parents' emphasis on purposefully arranging religious activities, exposures, and engagements to strategically achieve desired ends embodies at least some of the strategy of "concerted cultivation." Yet their trust in the efficacy of simply practicing their own religious routines and devotions without a lot of fanfare and instruction, of leading by everyday example, and expecting children to absorb most of religion by "osmosis" reflects something of Lareau's "accomplishment of natural growth" model. These observations are not a critique of Lareau's work but an encouragement for continued research into parenting cultures with an eye to possible greater complexities than perhaps previously realized. See Bridget Ritz, "Social Class and Cultural Conceptions of Religious Parenting." Paper presented at the American Sociological Association Annual Meeting, Philadelphia, August 2018.

2. We do not explore the historical comparisons that we suggest here. However, in another, related book, one of us (Smith) offers a historical interpretation of the transformation of American religion, families, and human selves that maps nicely onto our arguments here (see Christian Smith and Amy Adamczyk, *Handing Down the Faith*).

3. David Lancy, *The Anthropology of Childhood* (Cambridge: Cambridge University Press, 2015); Philippe Ariès, *Centuries of Childhood* (New York: Vintage, 1965); William Corsaro, *The Sociology of Childhood* (Thousand Oaks, CA: Sage, 2017), 65–90; Peter Stearns, *Childhood in World History* (New York: Routledge, 2016).

dropping kids off for Sunday school and then going out to enjoy coffee and the newspaper on their own, most of the parents we interviewed seemed personally engaged in their children's religious socialization.[4] This partly reflects the fact that our study's interview sample was not representative of all self-identified American religious parents of all levels of religious commitment, but of those having actual affiliations with some religious congregation, which provided a select sample of those more institutionally connected parents.

Religion as This-Worldly Resource. However serious and thoughtful many American religious parents may be about the religious enculturation of their children, we should not assume that they share the same ideal concerns and investments as the leaders of their religious traditions. We were continually struck during our interviews by what seemed to be a gap between what religious identity, practices, and beliefs meant to parents and what (we have good reason to believe) it means to the "professional" religious leaders of parents' religious institutions. The particular doctrines, standards, and priorities of their own religious traditions seem to be not terribly important to most American religious parents. Instead, for most, religion is primarily a good resource for getting along well in this life, for coping, succeeding, and maintaining good relationships. Things like correct doctrine, worship, spirituality, and denominational distinctives are not the issue. Practical this-worldly help is primarily what matters. For the majority of even quite religiously involved American parents, religion is a matter that is often essentially instrumental and therapeutic. It is useful for helping to get done important functional tasks, particularly for surmounting the many problems and obstacles that arise in life's journey. Few parents seem preoccupied with believing an orthodox truth, sustaining their religious tradition, or the question of who will go to heaven and hell. They more basically value religion's promise of support, comfort,

---

4. This contrasted with the indirect view of American parents that one of us (Smith) gathered through in-depth interviews with teenagers in an earlier project, the National Study of Youth and Religion (NSYR), in which many parents sounded more than a little disengaged from religious transmission to children. This difference we think is explained by two factors. First, the NSYR involved a representative sample of all US teenagers, not only ones whose parents were religiously affiliated, and so included many youth with parents who were only marginally religiously involved. By design, then, more religiously disengaged parents were involved in that study. Second, the picture of parents gained through NSYR was mediated through the perceptions and accounts of their teenage children, who surely did not understand everything about their parents' approach to religious transmission, and which no doubt introduced some subjective biases into their representations of their parents.

guidance, grounding, and family bonding, which they appreciate, even prize, for helping to make life's journey go well.

These more mundane concerns and appeals of religion in America are not new. The French social observer, Alexis de Tocqueville, for example, noted in the 1830s about religion in the United States that "I . . . do not believe that the sole motive of religious men is interest; but I think that interest is the principal means religions themselves make use of to guide men, and I do not doubt that it is only from this side that they take hold of the crowd and become popular. . . . American preachers constantly come back to earth and only with great trouble can they take their eyes off it. To touch their listeners better, they make them see daily how religious beliefs favor freedom and public order, and it is often difficult to know when listening to them if the principal object of religion is to procure eternal felicity in the other world or well-being in this one."[5] Our research shows that today we can simply substitute "being a good person" for "freedom and public order" and the same observation holds. Concerns with national welfare have been largely replaced by an interest in personal and family happiness and well-being. But the popular appeal of religion in the United States remains primarily immanent and practical, not doctrinal or otherworldly.

Here we connect the outlook of American religious parents with what one of us (Smith) has argued is the true, tacit, functional, de facto religion of the vast majority of American teenagers: Moralistic, Therapeutic Deism (MTD).[6] MTD can be summarized in five points: 1. A god exists who created and ordered the world and watches over human life on earth. 2. God wants people to be good, nice, and fair to each other. 3. The central goal of life is to be happy and to feel good about oneself. 4. God does not need to be particularly involved in one's life except when God is needed to resolve a problem. 5. Good people go to heaven when they die. MTD is the religion to which most US youth actually adhere, whatever are the official teachings of the particular religious traditions to which they belong. Findings from the National Study of Youth and Religion (NSYR), from which the idea was generated, suggested that most American youth adhere to MTD because they learn it from their parents, who are also its adherents. Our research in this project generally confirms that notion, but complicates it somewhat.

---

5. Alexis de Tocqueville, *Democracy in America*, ed. and trans. Harvey Mansfield and Delba Winthrop (Chicago: University of Chicago Press, 2000), 505–6.

6. Smith with Denton, *Soul Searching*, 118–71.

Both parents and their children, we suggest, share the same this-worldly, practical, moralistic, therapeutic understanding of religion. But American youth express simpler versions of it in MTD, while American parents, who have more life experience, usually hold somewhat more complex views of religion's purpose and values. (Again, this is surely partly due to the fact that the NSYR sample of youth was nationally representative, while our sample of parents was only of those affiliated with a religious congregation—had we sampled a broader array of American parents, we probably would have heard straighter versions of MTD from them.) Parents also emphasize certain points over others, especially MTD's emphasis on being good, nice, and fair, and on the purpose of life to be happy. Most religious parents simply take God's existence for granted (with the notable exception of some Jewish and Buddhist parents), and the question of who goes to heaven is just not especially relevant to most parents. In short, our research on religious parenting confirms the general parental source of MTD among American teenagers, but also reveals some complicating distinctions that manifest across generational differences. That suggests the need for further research on continuities and transformations in parent-child religious socialization, and the possible roles of age, cohort, and period effects in the process.

Ancillary Congregations and Traditions. Our observations about American religious parents' approaches to their religious congregations and traditions seems important for those very religious communities. First, consider parents' expectations of religious congregations. One stereotype in American religious communities concerns parents who expect their religious congregations, leaders, and programs to do all the work to train their children in religion. We have also heard at religious education and youth ministry conferences many youth pastors complain that "their" kids' parents often simply just hand over their children to them, saying, "We don't know what we are doing, you do it." We went into this research with those stereotypes and complaints in mind. But we were surprised to find something quite different.

The parents we interviewed unvaryingly believed it was their responsibility to pass on religion to their children and expressed confidence that their methods of religious transmission stood the best chance of success among all of the conceivable alternatives. Some parents did voice dissatisfaction with specific programs or leaders in their religious congregations. And some were less invested in congregational participation than others (because we intentionally sampled parents on that difference). But more obvious was the consistent view that parents believed it to be *their* job—not their church's, temple's, synagogue's, or mosque's—to raise their children religiously.

This may seem like good news for religious leaders and pastors. Perhaps most parents are taking more responsibility for raising their children religiously than the stereotypes and complaints suggest. But that positive message is also a double-edge sword for religious clergy, leaders, and youth workers, since it is associated with parents discounting the importance of religious congregations for family religious life. All of the parents we interviewed saw the activities of churches, temples, synagogues, and mosques as secondary in significance to their own efforts. Religious congregations, they said, exist to reinforce what parents do and say, and to provide hopefully appealing social environments that will not turn off their children to religion. Beyond that, parents hold fairly low expectations of their religious congregations. They do not want too much, nor do they demand much. They seem realistic about the limits of what religious congregations can provide them and aware of the problems that congregations can cause. So they limit what they expect and save themselves the trouble of disappointment and frustration. Furthermore, what most parents most value in religious congregations are friendly and appealing social and activity environments that will help keep their kids interested, not so much having to do with the specific contents of religion itself. And if they find their congregations sufficiently undermining what they want to do and say, they can leave to find a better match.

In short, the price to religious congregations of having parents who take nearly full responsibility to pass on religion to their children is those same parents holding somewhat low expectations of their congregations and, therefore, often making limited investments in the same. This is not true of every parent we met. Some were very involved in their religious congregations yet still managed realistically to limit their expectations of them. But the normal condition was essentially the deal one might expect: people not looking for big returns need not make major investments. The more serious investments, if made at all, are into family households.

Furthermore, since beliefs about the value of raising children in a religion in particular are located within and typically justified by the larger parenting job of preparing children for life's journey in many other ways, for most parents the demands of specifically religious socialization can readily be trumped by other demands, especially of sports, when those others compete and are seen as more pressing or valuable. Again, clergy, children and youth ministers, and congregational and denominational leaders occupy a relatively secondary and sometimes peripheral role in the eyes of most affiliated parents. Parents approach raising children religiously not as a shared community endeavor taking place under the authority of leaders of religious traditions but as family projects in which congregations play merely supporting roles as may be helpful.

In some sense, this approach to congregations extends to entire religious traditions. While only implicit in parents' talk, this fact became clear to us: few parents view themselves as the representatives, advocates, or "sponsors" to their children of the religious traditions to which they belong. Religion, they believe, is an important resource to help their children live good lives, in terms of both morality and well-being, and so worth implanting and cultivating in their children. But very few parents expressed an understanding of themselves as engaged in a larger collective task of transmitting their particular religious tradition from generation to generation for the sake of the life of the tradition itself. Most parents positively identified with their religious traditions and believed something between viewing their tradition as a good starting point for their kids and affirming it to be the highest truth. But another role or posture that parents might have also adopted, and that those who care about the future of particular religious traditions should wish them to adopt, was clearly missing. That was parents also acting as something like promoters or champions of their particular traditions, not simply because they are familiar and offered good resources for their children, but more compellingly because they believe in the importance of the long-term continuance of their traditions as a value itself. Stated differently, most American religious parents who are affiliated with a religious congregation do intentionally work to pass on religion to their children, but do so primarily for the sake of their children, not their religious tradition. They were not necessarily apathetic about their religious traditions. But they did not see themselves as sponsoring, representing, or advocating for it to their children.

This approach was especially apparent among mainline Protestant parents, which is not surprising, given that tradition's general ecumenical and sometimes liberal posture (although it is worth remembering that within the memory of persons still living there was a day when the differences between, say, Presbyterians, Methodists, and Baptists were thought truly significant and worth making an issue over). Perhaps somewhat more surprising, very few Catholic parents we interviewed seemed to view themselves as sponsors, promoters, or advocates of Catholicism or the Church. They generally want to see their children remain Catholic because they believe (per the cultural models already described) that would be good for them and their families. But little they said suggested that they view themselves as particularly responsible for the survival and continuance of the Catholic Church's doctrine, discourse, and (what remains of its) distinctive way of life as a tradition. That seemed either to be a taken-for-granted nonproblem or else not something of particular concern. Catholic parents, in other words, viewed themselves as stakeholders in religion for themselves and their children but not in the long-term future of the Catholic Church. Their parental interests and purposes were expressed in ways very different from that of the institutional Church. By comparison, the approach described above was less often expressed by Jewish, Mormon, and Muslim parents, who tended more to advocate to their children for the distinctive value of their minority religious traditions and the importance of their continued vitality. Hindu parents were similar in this respect, but often because of their greater investment in maintaining their Indian cultural identity across generations than in promoting Hinduism as a religion per se.

Still another angle on parents' discounting the particularities of their religious traditions relative to their own concerns is their prioritizing their "values" over religious denominational and tradition distinctives. The parents we interviewed spoke repeatedly of the central importance of "values" in life. Parents almost never spelled out the specific content of their values. But the idea suggested general concerns, standards, and principles that parents deemed vital to hold. Parents thought it absolutely crucial to pass on their values to their children, who they sincerely hoped would embrace and share them. Very rarely did parents speak as insistently about passing on the particular cultures, discourses, and rituals of their religious traditions. Religion actually seemed to comprise a subset of their larger body of values.[7] Indeed, it was common for parents to say that they would not mind too much if their children switched to a somewhat different religion or married someone of a dissimilar religion, as long as they all still shared the same "values."

The idea of "values" has as much to do with economic theory (monetary worth) and science (an assigned or calculated numerical quantity) as it does qualitative judgments of moral or functional desirability. The word "values" also strongly suggests individual preference orderings, not objective standards or truths. "Values" is not the language of traditional religious

---

7. Perhaps the old Parsonian theory of culture is actually the dominant "folk theory" of culture among ordinary Americans, leading to this emphasis on general values, which may too have something to do with the fact that America is a historically Protestant-dominant society.

discourses, which would use other terms like virtues, ethics, commands, truths, discipleship, practices, traditions, formation, and obedience. Yet the language of "values" seems to have displaced those more particular and sometimes exacting religious terms, even among many of the most religiously involved adults and many religious thought leaders. The idea of holding and espousing "values" functions to indicate some definite personal moral and identity allegiances—as opposed to drifting with no standards or commitments. But values talk is usually general, unspecified, and sometimes vague (consider, for instance, the nebulous politicized term, "family values," which itself says nothing substantive in particular). We could comment more about the significance of the cultural pervasiveness of the term "values," but our point here is more specific. That is simply that for most American religious parents, the priority of "values" consistently trumps commitment to the distinctive features of their own religious traditions and denominations. And that tells us something important about the relatively ancillary place of those traditions for religious parents.

Uniformity across Diversity. Given the vast pluralism and diversity of religions in the United States, we might expect conversations with religiously and demographically different kinds of parents unpacking their views of why and how to pass on religion to children to produce a cacophony of ideas, assumptions, opinions, feelings, goals, and strategies. But we found no such thing. Instead, the vast majority of religious parents from different religions, races, ethnicities, social classes, and family structures reflected and expressed highly similar cultural models concerning the transmission of religion to their children. And the underlying metaphors that helped define those models parents also shared with remarkable correspondence. That similarity across those differences was remarkable. It did not fit our expectations, our research design, or the standard assumptions about culture in much of cultural sociology and anthropology. We have already discussed and theorized the highly shared nature of these cultural models of religious parenting in the preceding chapters and will not iterate that here. Instead, we conclude with some observations about what that seems to tell us about American religion more generally.

One implication is that, for all of the seeming variety and diversity of American religion,[8] in at least some ways the religious field in the United States involves more than a little commonality if not uniformity. Dominant assumptions and beliefs about religious life and practice can and

---

8. Diane Eck, *A New Religious America: How a "Christian Country" Has Become the World's Most Religiously Diverse Nation* (San Francisco: HarperSanFrancisco, 2002).

sometimes do transcend the particularities of religious traditions and unite the majority of diverse adherents in shared outlooks. In a previous project, again, one of us argued something similar about the near ubiquity of Moralistic Therapeutic Deism among American youth.[9] Decades before, Robert Bellah observed something parallel about the permeating presence and power of American Civil Religion.[10] American religion is characterized by religious diversity, that is a fact. But it appears that the shared *American* aspect of "American religion" can sometimes play a more determining role than its more varied *religion* aspect. We would do well to attend more closely to such real but perhaps subtle forms of agreement and similarity across seemingly diverse and even fragmented religious groups in the American religious field.

For those who are invested in the life of diverse religious traditions themselves, the implications of the similarities that we have observed are significant. Religious institutions invest vast resources into developing leaders, programs, and curricula for religious education and youth ministry considered appropriate to their particular beliefs, histories, and cultures. Most clergy from many denominations spend countless hours preparing and delivering sermons, homilies, and teachings designed to form their congregations' members in ways that reflect the singularities of their specific traditions. And many religious leaders intentionally work to keep alive the distinctive vocabularies and styles of discourse inherited in their traditions. Yet when it comes to the crucial question of why and how parents should pass on religious practice and faith to their children, nearly all parents from all American religious backgrounds think, talk, and plan alike. The underlying cultural models and metaphors of religious transmission held by, say, Baptist parents have fundamentally more in common with those of their Catholic, Mormon, Muslim, and Hindu peers than anything distinctively Baptist in its content or texture. The same is true of nearly every other combination of religious parents in relation to other parents.

In other words, any distinctive teachings of American religious traditions about passing on faith and practice to children is overshadowed and overwhelmed by the governing power of the dominant cultural models and

9. Smith with Denton, *Soul Searching*.

10. Robert Bellah, "Civil Religion in America," *Journal of the American Academy of Arts and Sciences* 96, no. 1 (1967): 1–21. Also see Philip Gorski, *American Covenant: A History of Civil Religion from the Puritans to the Present* (Princeton, NJ: Princeton University Press, 2017); Nancy Ammerman, "Golden Rule Christianity," in *Lived Religion in America*, ed. David Hall (Princeton, NJ: Princeton University Press, 1997), 196–216.

metaphors shared by most religious parents across all traditions. That is to say, when it comes to the basic outlook of parents approaching religious transmission to children, we find few distinctives across different religious types. Of course, this observed near-uniformity comes across with reference to somewhat abstract and unspecified "values," which are always refracted through specific religious, ethnic, familial, and local experiences. Thus, for example, Jewish parents observe the Shabbat seder, unlike evangelical parents who read the Bible and pray, unlike Hindu and Buddhist parents who offer sacrifices of food at altars. Yet the more fundamental assumptions, concerns, and purposes that motivate those particular practices those parents actually largely share in common. Thus, the religious views of most American religious parents on at least some basic issues appear to be shaped more by general (and arguably sometimes even not-religious[11]) influences and beliefs than by the particularities of their own religious traditions. Sociologically, that belies the suppositions and hopes of many religious leaders (in our experience and observations) that their specific traditions and denominations cultivate and sustain distinctive worldviews and discourses in religious life. American parents from various religious traditions instead operate, at least on some issues, with a much more general and widespread outlook and plan. That raises questions about the reality and viability of genuinely particular religious communities in the United States today, at least on some levels and in certain ways.

A different aspect of the shared cultural models we discovered is that the underlying views of parents made a great deal of coherent sense. And we think the coherence of the cultural models help make their near uniformity possible. The dominant paradigm of culture theory primed us to expect plenty of incoherence, inarticulacy, and post hoc rationalizations in cultural discourse. We did encounter some of that, but beneath it we found even greater coherence and sensibility. Most of the parents we interviewed turned out to be serious, caring, thoughtful people trying their best to raise their kids in often difficult situations and in a culture they experience as seriously problematic. And, while they could rarely express it as systematically as we have in this book's exposition, the underlying reasoning of the beliefs that comprise parents' cultural models and metaphors proved to make logical, coherent sense. Whether or not we or any

11. An inquiry into the historical, institutional, and cultural influences on the formation of parents' shared cultural models of religious transmission could demonstrate, for example, the impacts of forces as disparate as the early twentieth-century rise of mass-consumer capitalism and compulsory mass public education, mid-twentieth century suburbanization and network television, and late twentieth-century neoliberal economic globalization.

reader agrees with the content of their cultural models, they at least work as internally sensible networks of ideas. That not only counters some standard views that parents today are rather clueless, apathetic, and ignorant about religion for their children, it also challenges some standard assumptions in contemporary theories of culture. That suggests the need for more empirically driven, historically contextualized research on the character and sources of cultural models, however they vary or not in their coherence and shared nature.

Dilemmas of Force and Choice. The hardest struggle American religious parents encounter in passing on religion to their children is navigating the tricky balance between force and choice. Parents want their children to embrace and continue their family's religion, and they feel authorized to compel their children to participate in and learn about their religious practices and beliefs. But parents also view religion as a personal, even private, individual, voluntary choice. They not only respect their children's right to choose their own religion but actually desire for them freely to embrace and affirm it, since in American culture such a voluntary personal choice is believed to make religion more meaningful and authentic. This assumption is of course not a religious universal, since religion in other times and places has operated and still operates as an ascribed identity and compulsory institution. Think of early puritan New England or of Saudi Arabia today.[12] But religion as voluntary individual choice is definitely the norm in contemporary America.

So the task of parents is to somehow use their authority to create conditions in which their children will voluntarily choose the religion they want them to choose. However open-minded religious parents may be, very few consider the choice of religion to be equivalent to an ice cream flavor or vacation destination. Nearly all parents have some investment in their children continuing their own religion, oftentimes a big investment. And therein lies the dilemma. How to arrange the lives of children and families in just such a way that parents can get the outcomes they want without it seeming to anyone to be manipulated or forced?

The most ominous worry for most parents is the hazard of provoking one's children to rebellion by forcing religion on them too strongly. The specter of teenage children becoming rebellious is a peril that determines the parameters and thresholds of parents' religious expectations

---

12. For an excellent discussion of related but often ignored issues, see Slavica Jakelić, *Collectivistic Religions: Religion, Choice, and Identity in Late Modernity* (New York: Routledge, 2016).

and demands of children. The default rule of thumb is prudence erring on the side of flexibility and choice rather than strictness and force. Potential deficits in religious enculturation resulting from parents being too easy on children are massively offset by the damage and setbacks that rebellion would cause, parents surmise. To be sure, American religious parents are not obsequiously bending over backward to accommodate their children's possible resistance to religion. Most parents push religion with children as much as they think they reasonably can, given however important it is to them as parents. But the structure of this larger situation means that in the end parents tend to undersell religion to their children—in a way they do not undersell when it comes to homework, sports, and music lessons— and that older children as ever-potential rebels end up holding the greatest negotiating power when it comes to doing religion.

A second rule of thumb for parents is to get as much as possible of "the basics" for "a foundation" in religion established while children are still young, before adolescence. That way, by the time children are old enough to think critically and perhaps resist their parents' religious transmission efforts, it is too late for children to expunge those early influences from their hearts. Hopefully then familiarity and momentum will carry children through to young adulthood with some continuity in their religion. This strategy is roughly analogous to driving friends deep into forested mountains while they sleep in the back seat, and then when they awake asking them whether they would like to go for a hike in the woods or instead to an art museum in the faraway city. The friends do get to choose, but the context governing their choice is predetermined before they realize any choice could be made.

Evident in our interviews was the fact that some parents felt an intuition that the force/choice binary does not adequately capture the full complexities and meaning of their situation, yet they had difficulty framing their dilemma in any different terms. That only tended to add to their worry about the matter. Am I really approaching this correctly, some parents wondered? Is providing the conditions in which my kids will choose what I want really forcing religion on them or is it still letting them choose for themselves? How and why is that different from parents strongly influencing their children in any other ways, which is clearly unavoidable? Some parents struggle with these questions, seeing their religious nurturing as not *exactly* force, but also not *exactly* choice, although being unable to describe things in another way. And that can produce even more anxiety, consternation, and guilt. All of this casts in stark relief the irresolvable conundrum that the very existence of dependent children creates in a liberal individualistic culture that prizes autonomy and free choice. And it highlights the cognitive power of the force/choice binary in American cultural models of religious parenting.

All of this varies somewhat by religious tradition. Mainline Protestants, Catholics, and Buddhists tend the least to "impose" religion on their children, although for different reasons and in diverse ways. Some Catholic parents rely on Church sacraments as semi-non-negotiable benchmarks of expectations of children, whereby children can do whatever they want afterward as long as they just complete their Confirmation. Most Catholic children end up complying with that deal, whether they like it or not. Conservative Protestant parents tend simultaneously to be highly invested in their children remaining "in the faith" *and* to view faith as needing to be an authentic, individual, personal choice, resulting in the force/choice dilemma impinging on these parents with particular force. Many Jewish, Mormon, and Muslim parents seem relatively comfortable communicating very high expectations and hopes that their children will carry on the religion (or at least, in the case of Jews, Jewish culture) of their parents, but do not especially rely on force to make that happen. Their religious minority status and cultural distinctiveness go a long way to substitute for compulsion. Of all the religious types we studied, as we noted, black Protestant parents feel the most comfortable demanding that their children engage in their religion for as long as they live at home, worry a great deal about children becoming rebellious and "going astray," and yet remain the most confident that children who are properly raised will eventually return to faith and church after a time of wandering. We of course found exceptions to these generalizations. Recall, for example, the Jewish mother in chapter 3 who worried that exposing her toddler to Jewish practices was depriving him of the right to full freedom of religious choice. But beneath these differences and exceptions, all parents wrestled hard with the same underlying dilemma of how to balance compulsion and free choice when it comes to shaping their children's religious commitments and practice.

To Conclude

Many scholars in the social sciences and the humanities study various aspects of religion. Some social scientists study parents and parenting. And a growing number of sociologists and anthropologists are researching the religious lives of teenagers and emerging adults. Despite it being a question of huge importance for religion and family life, however, extremely few scholars have studied how and why religious parents raise their children to pass on to them their religious practices and beliefs. We have engaged this question of intergenerational religious transmission taking a cultural approach, in the hope of further opening up this area for additional study and beginning to provide helpful answers and greater understanding. In the process we think we have learned some important things about the nature and workings of culture generally. But much more research on both religious parenting and cultural models is needed beyond what we have accomplished here, which we will be gratified if this book helps to prompt and inspire.

Research Methodology

Interview Data Collection Methods

The findings of this study are based significantly on in-depth, personal interviews and observations with 235 coupled and single parents living in the United States that we conducted in over 150 households. These parents were purposively selected from religious congregations to represent different religious traditions, regions around the country, racial and ethnic backgrounds, social classes, family structures, and other factors, based on their theoretical importance. Religious traditions represented included white evangelicals, white mainline Protestants, black Protestants, white Catholics, Hispanic Catholics, Mormons, Conservative Jews, Muslims, Buddhists, and Hindus. A sample of nonreligious parents was also interviewed for comparative purposes. The study included an oversample of Catholic households, including twenty-five parents who spoke Spanish at home. Each household study involved in-depth interviews with parent couples, single parents, or parent-figures living in residence. Children in the household were not interviewed.

The religious parents sampled to participate in this study were purposively selected from membership lists of religious congregations. The researchers collaborated with clergy and pastoral and administrative staff to select appropriate parents to study. Because this study is focused on the parental transmission of religious faith to children, the study design chose to focus on parents who had some membership connection to a religious congregation. This tilts the sample in the direction of parents who are more religious than the national average, but for the purposes of this study that is an advantage, not a weakness. The sampling of parents from congregations worked to obtain both high-involvement and low-involvement parents.

We wanted to be able to compare families who were more involved in their congregations with those who were marginally involved. The sampling of religious parents from congregations also strove to obtain variance when possible on families' social class and family structure. Some of our sample's nonreligious and "spiritual but not religious" parents—which we intended for more informal comparisons—also emerged from our selection of low-involvement parents formally tied to religious congregations. But most of our nonreligious parents were sampled using convenience methods relying on the weak social ties of interviewers. These parents had to have not been raised religious and not married to a religious spouse, in order to fit our nonreligious American parent type.

The sampling of households took place through a stratified sampling process. First, major regional areas of the United States were selected from which to collect data. Combinations of religious traditions most appropriate for those areas were then identified (e.g., black Protestants in the South, Conservative Jews in New York and Chicago). Specific locations in regions were then selected based on access to the researchers. Specific religious congregations in those locations from which to sample households were then identified, in part randomly and in part based on convenience, depending on possible insider contacts or "local knowledge" that researchers may have had. Once specific religious congregations were selected, project researchers contacted the relevant clergy or other leaders, explained the nature of the research project, and secured their cooperation to study a set of parents in the congregation. Using congregational membership lists and the sampling-type criteria described further on, project researchers worked with congregational leaders or administrators to identify potential subjects to participate in the study. The parents of these households were then contacted directly, explained the nature of the study, and asked to participate. The few sampled households that declined participation were replaced by a second-ballot household highly similar to them and the process of contact, explaining, and gaining cooperation began again. Regions, religious tradition types, and household demographic types were sampled and data collected from them until all of the sample types of cells were filled.

This study intentionally sought to be able to make numerous analytical comparisons among kinds of households and parents studied. We did not wish to be a study of basically white, middle-class, suburban Christians. Based on sociological criteria, the study sample was drawn from a purposive, stratified method in order to make empirically grounded analytical comparisons on the following key dimensions:

- *Religious Tradition*: white and Hispanic Catholic, white evangelical and mainline Protestant, black Protestant, Conservative Jew, Mormon/LDS, Muslim, Hindu, Buddhist, and nonreligious households
- *Social Class*: Middle/Upper-Middle vs. Working Class/Lower
- *Race and Ethnicity*: Hispanic, white, black, and other race/ethnicities
- *Family Structure and Type*: Two biological parents, remarried/mixed household types, single-parent households; heterosexual versus same-sex parents
- *Religious Commitment*: Higher and lower religious commitments in parents/families in the same congregations
- *Region of the United States*: the American Midwest, Northeast, and South, Southwestern, and Western regions
- *Urban-Suburban-Rural*: Type of population of residential contexts

The central, qualitative part of this study was not interested in and did not seek to construct a truly nationally representative, probability sample. Rather, our purpose was to understand, in greater depth than surveys can, things like the cultural assumptions, relative priorities, meanings, routine practices, aspirations and fears, relational dynamics, histories, rituals, material and visual household objects, and social and institutional contexts that shape different kinds of parenting to transmit religious faith to children. We found little extant research prior to this study that accessed and described the life narratives, emotional associations, cultural meanings, and causal mechanisms involved in the intergenerational transmission of religious faith comparing across different kinds of households. Our research design was thus dictated by the specific purposes of this project. We also proceeded on the belief that not every last sample cell representing every theoretical combination of features needed to be filled by empirical cases for our study. It was not necessary, for example, to find and interview Hispanic families who belong to black Protestant churches or lower-class Conservative Jews. The most socially important sample cells designed to achieve the most relevant analytical comparison are more limited in number.

Table 3 indicates the specific distribution of numbers of types of parents that our research project sampled and studied. There we see, for example, that the study samples and researches 29 conservative Protestant (evangelical) households, some of which were middle class and some working class/poor, and then each of those types representing different kinds of

Table 3. Final Stratified Quota Sample Distributions of Parent Interviewees

Religion	Social Class	Family Type	Religious Commitment High	Religious Commitment Low
White Catholic (N = 38)	Middle/ Upper Mid	2 Bio	14	10
		Blended		2
		Single Parent		
	Working/ Low Income	2 Bio	3	4
		Single Parent	2	3
Black Catholic (N = 4)	Middle/ Upper Mid	2 Bio	1	
		Single Parent		2
	Working/ Low Income	2 Bio	1	
Hispanic Catholic (N = 32)	Middle/ Upper Mid	2 Bio	4	1
		Single Parent	1	
	Working/ Low Income	2 Bio	13	1
		Blended	1	
		Single Parent	7	4
Conservative Protestant (N = 29)	Middle/ Upper Mid	2 Bio	11	1
		Blended	4	
		Single Parent	2	1
	Working/ Low Income	2 Bio	4	
		Blended	2	2
		Single Parent	1	1
Mainline Protestant (N = 23)	Middle/ Upper Mid	2 Bio	4	8
		Same Sex	1	1
	Working/ Low Income	2 Bio	3	1
		Blended	2	
		Single Parent	2	1
Black Protestant (N = 24)	Middle/ Upper Mid	2 Bio	5	1
		Blended	9	
		Single Parent		1
	Working/ Low Income	Blended	2	2
		Single Parent	4	
Conservative Jewish (N = 15)	Middle/ Upper Mid	2 Bio	7	3
		Same Sex	2	
		Single Parent	3	
Mormon (N = 10)	Middle/ Upper Mid	2 Bio	5	
		Blended	2	1
	Working/ Low Income	2 Bio		1
		Blended		1
Muslim (N = 13)	Middle/ Upper Mid	2 Bio	9	1
		Single Parent	2	
		Blended	1	

Table 3. (*continued*)

Religion	Social Class	Family Type	Religious Commitment High	Religious Commitment Low
Hindu (N = 14)	Middle/ Upper Mid	2 Bio	1	10
		Single Parent	1	
	Working/ Low Income	2 Bio	2	
Buddhist (N = 13)	Middle/ Upper Mid	2 Bio	6	3
	Working/ Low Income	Blended	2	
		2 Bio	2	
Nonreligious (N = 20)	Middle/ Upper Mid	2 Bio		9
		Blended		3
	Working/ Low Income	Blended		4
		Single Parent		4
Total (N = 235)			**148**	**87**

family structures and levels of religious commitment. Majority type religious traditions in the United States receive roughly proportionately most of the sample cases. Minority religious traditions are, at the same time, oversampled to provide enough data on them to be able to make meaningful comparisons. Mormons received the least attention here, because we already know a great deal from previous research about their expectations and practices, which, relative to most other groups, tend to be highly prescribed and standardized. Our sample also included twenty nonreligious parents and four same-sex-parent households.

Interviews with parents for this study were conducted by a team of twelve experienced and trained interviewers, most of whom were faculty, graduate students, and research associates in the Center for the Study of Religion and Society at the University of Notre Dame. Most of the personal interviews conducted for this study were completed in the homes of the parents being interviewed. If a parent preferred otherwise, interviews were also conducted in restaurants, coffee shops, work offices, and the buildings of their religious congregations. Steps were always taken in all contexts to insure the privacy of the interview conversations, so parents were able to speak freely and confidentially. Initially, we were concerned that parents would defensively feel as if they were being investigated or judged by researchers. But that concern passed quickly, as most parents proved to be open and frank in their interviews. After the initial greetings and required paperwork for informed consent were completed, the interviews were conducted and digitally recorded. Incentives were paid to interview respondents on completion of the interviews. The interviews with parents averaged a mean of 2.0 hours in length, with a range from 41 minutes to 4.2 hours, depending on the family structure, size of the household sampled, and the verbosity of the parent interviewed.

The interview questionnaire for this project (provided below) asked comparatively broad questions, especially at the beginning, relative to those asked in many other interview-based studies that closely follow predetermined scripts, intending to invite long, self-directed answers from parents. The strategy was to set a context of inquiry that focused on our interests but allowed plenty of leeway for parents to narrate their own stories, make their own crucial points, and provide their own examples. All of the interviewed parents were asked to address the same set of shared questions and speak to the same kinds of issues as all others, but room was allowed both interviewers and those interviewed to approach their discussions in ways that seemed to best suit the specifically sampled parents and households. This approach followed the method of many cognitive cultural sociologists and cognitive-psychological anthropologists, which commends not being too directive in interviews, but rather allowing for much open-ended talk to take place and conducting many levels and types of analysis of the transcripts, not merely "hearing" what is said "on the surface."[1] That improves the chances that the research discovers whatever reality is operative in households, rather than being too agenda-setting or leading in fixed questions and thus risking finding results that the study itself presupposed and to which it led. Only near the end of interviews conducted, in cases when interview respondents had not addressed important questions of concern, did we more directly probe for answers.

Our approach to interviews thus facilitated a complex, multileveled analysis of interviewee's talk, enabling us to pull apart different aspects of assumptions, claims, feelings, and judgments of those we studied. Allison Pugh ("What Good Are Interviews") puts it this way: "Interpretive, in-depth interviewing enables access to four kinds of information—'the honorable,' 'the schematic,' 'the visceral' and 'metafeelings'. . . . Although people surely evince different cultural schemas to explain away particular problems, they have a sense for what counts as honorable behavior in their

---

1. For example, Naomi Quinn, ed., *Finding Culture in Talk* (New York: Palgrave Macmillan, 2005); Allison Pugh, "What Good Are Interviews for Thinking about Culture?: Demystifying Interpretive Analysis," *American Journal of Cultural Sociology* 1 (2013): 42–48.

cultural world, which may or may not mesh with their innermost predilections. Their meta-feelings are a demonstration of the degree to which they are cultural migrants, a measure of the distances they have traveled from their early social contexts shaping the meanings of their early experiences, to the strictures of the cultural milieu in which they find themselves today." Intentionally conducting this kind of analysis helps us better to understand not only what is "on the surface" of the content of what parents say but also other levels of complexity, meaning, ambivalence, emotions, and evaluations that often come out when people are asked to talk at length about topics rather than asked pointed questions that evoke short answers.

After the interviews were completed, all of the interviewers met together for a two-day meeting to debrief on our experiences, share our notes and initial reflections on the interviews, and to begin to identify dominant themes and subsample differences in the interview conversations we had. The project principal investigator (Smith) took notes on the debriefing meeting discussions, which help inform the initial phase of the data analysis process. A team of three dozen undergraduate and graduate students and contract employees worked to transcribe the nearly five hundred audio hours of interview recordings, and as an extra measure of quality control, each transcript was thoroughly checked for accuracy. The twenty-five interviews conducted in Spanish were transcribed by a project researcher who is fluent in Spanish, and those Spanish transcripts were translated into English by ten Spanish-speaking undergraduate and graduate students.

We coded interviews over a ten-month period, involving a team of two dozen highly trained and closely supervised University of Notre Dame graduate and undergraduate student research assistants using the qualitative data analysis software, MAXQDA. An initial coding-methods workshop was with members of the coding team, to train them on the goals of the project, the purpose of and process for data coding, proper storage of interview data, inter-rater reliability, and the use of the MAXQDA software interface. After an initial foray into coding, inter-rater reliability was tested and coding protocols and rules were adjusted for consistency. The coding team then performed two stages of coding: (1) a first-order coding of passages in the transcribed interviews and (2) a second-order coding of the coded passages (see Heather Price and Christian Smith, "Procedures for Reliable Cultural Model Analysis Using Semi-Structured Interviews," Notre Dame Center for the Study of Religion and Society, working paper, 2019). First-order coding involved the direct selection of phrases and passages in the interview transcripts that provide qualitative evidence of the presence or absence of a particular idea, action, attitude, perception, intent, or other quality or disposition in the respondent, relating directly or indirectly to their transmission of faith to their children. Two dozen main themes were coded, including:

• Parents' role of religion in their own lives	• Approaches to passing on religious faith, belief & practices to children	• Motivations for passing on religious faith & practice (or not)
• Parents' assumptions and understandings about religion	• Practices and behaviors of children	• Parents' influence in thinking about passing on religion and faith—own experiences in church, influence
• Parents' connection between religion/ religious practice & belief and happiness/future happiness	• Gender division in teaching children about faith and beliefs	• Choice of congregation
• Parents' importance of particular beliefs & practices vs. general values or morals	• Career-household parent division in teaching children about faith and beliefs	• Role of congregations: fellow congregants, ministers, the general influence of the congregation and programs
• Importance/priority given to passing on religious faith to children	• Disagreements between parents about what/ how/ when/why to teach children about faith and beliefs	• Youth group, youth programs, youth ministers
• Parenting style	• Parenting influence	• Primary/secondary parent role division
• Discipline of child	• Challenges to parenting	• Trauma to parent: during any part of parent's life
• Particularly emotional passages	• Childhood demographics	• Demographics

Coders followed a systematic process to code each interview, first developing and continuing to refine the decision rules that determined the scope of their assigned theme. These decision rules guided the coding process and defined what data to include and what data to exclude from the parameters of the themes being coded. Each coder followed a coding method whereby the interview was skimmed for organization, passages related to main themes and subthemes were highlighted, keyword searches were used to increase reliability and reduce coder fatigue error, brief summaries for each interview were written, and codes were reviewed by a supervisor before being submitted and integrated into the larger dataset. After seven months of coding, the first-order coding process was completed.

To test for reliability, eliminate the chance of single-coder biases occurring, and reach near consensus of method, coders were paired and assigned for each theme. These pairs separately coded identical interviews, from which inter-rater reliability (IRR) statistics were calculated. Each themed pair also had assigned an external senior coder with whom an additional round of IRR testing was performed. Coders met with the coding supervisor to have explained their topic, to review the associated decision rules, and to discuss the scope of their assigned theme. After completing a limited amount of coding, the pairs of coders met in IRR sessions to discuss their working assumptions and revise their decision rules to achieve shared understandings of the themes. IRR sessions repeated during coding until consensus of a minimum of 80 percent of coded passages was achieved (as suggested by Matthew Miles and Michael Huberman, *Qualitative Data Analysis: An Expanded Sourcebook* [Thousand Oaks, CA: Sage, 1994]), meaning that highlighted and marked passages by two different coders overlapped 80 percent of the time. Once this minimum threshold was met, consensus was judged to have been reached and the pairs of coders proceeded to code the interviews.

Second-order coding works to code the first-order selected passages and the summary documents to further identify types within themes and underlying commonalities and differences across themes within interviews. In this phase of data preparation, coders did not use the primary transcript documents, but rather coded on the coded themes. Within themes, coders looked for clustering of ideas and presence or absence of common elements within the theme. These interpretations were then used to organize subsequent data analysis. For example, coders reviewed all of the passages about motivations of parents to transmit their faith and outlined the common ideas expressed by parents, such as the importance of keeping a heritage alive, reproducing fond memories from parents' childhood, or commitment to develop strong values within a secular society. The coders' interview summaries were also collated and analyzed for emergent themes across first-order themes. These cross-theme patterns were categorized and coded across all of the interviews. The authors of this book then took those coded interviews and studied them intently to discern what they might reveal about the operative cultural models giving rise to parents' talk about passing on religion to their children.

Our parent interviews followed the following common interview guide of questions, while allowing interviewers and interviewed parents the flexibility to explore promising questions and discussions not specified here:

"Intergenerational Transmission of Religious Faith" Interview Questionnaire

Introduction: "Thank you again for agreeing to do these interviews. Remember that all of your answers are totally confidential, so you can speak freely here. Also, you may skip any question you prefer not to answer."

CURRENT LIFE BIG PICTURE

Overview: So my goal here is to learn about you, your family, and your experience as a parent—especially as it relates to passing on (or not) of your religious or spiritual faith and practice to CHILD.

> Q: First, can you start off just telling me about the big picture of your life now? What's your situation when it comes to family, work, living, schools, friends, or whatever I need to get a context for you and your family?
>
> Q: What sorts of things do you hope to *accomplish* in the next 10 years of your life?
>
> Q: Do you feel like your life is generally on the *right track*? Tell me about why and how.

BACKGROUND

> Q: Stepping back, can you tell me about your *family situation growing up*, about your parents and other family members. How were you raised? And how has that shaped you into the person you became?
>
> • Social class, education, region/state, neighborhood, values, religion?
>
> • Happy times? Traumas? Difficulties? Highlights? - Childhood friends, school, play, interest, aspirations?
>
> • What kind of approach did your parents take in parenting you as a child and youth?
>
> • What about your teenage years?—Work or college experience?— Crucial moments/experiences? Turning points?

VIEW OF LIFE

Q: So back to today, can you tell me more about you *yourself as a person*? What are you like, your personality, values, interests, etc.?

Q: Can you tell me some about *yourself religiously*? Are you a religious person?

- What *kind* of religion? Tradition? Denomination? [Does particular denomination matter to you?]
- What *believe* religiously? Probe.
- Particular beliefs about or relationship toward *God* (or spiritual forces? Or?)? How do you view God? What do you think God might be like, if anything?
- Regular religious *practices*?
- *Importance* of religious faith and practice?—[IF] *Why* is religion *important* (or not important) to you in life?
- *How learned* religion or spiritual life?—Did *change* religiously over time or not? Why? How?
- Have *doubts* or *confusions* about religious or spiritual matters?
- [If involved at a place of worship] What are the *benefits* of organized religion in your life? Any *drawbacks* or problems or liabilities of your being religious?

  [*IF R THINKS SOMETHING WRONG WITH WORLD/LIFE*]

Q: What do you think is the *cause* or *source* of *what is wrong* with the world, humans, life? [trying to get at any notion of "sin"]

Q: How is religious faith or spiritual life expressed especially in *ordinary, everyday* life? Beyond possible formal, official CHURCH expressions of religion, are there any other ways faith or spiritual practices *show up in your "everyday" living*? (e.g., religious meanings of "secular" things, personal spiritual practices, private prayers) [looking for "everyday religion" here]

Q: What about PARTNER? Is religious, which, how, why? How *similar/different* is PARTNER?

Q: How would *family be different* if you *removed religion* or spiritual life from it? How? Why?

FAMILY FORMATION & BECOMING A PARENT
[IF SINGLE, PARTNER="THE FATHER/
MOTHER OF YOUR CHILDREN"]

Q: How did you and PARTNER *meet or get together*? What is your story there?

Q: What has your *experience* with PARTNER been like over the years? Probe.

Q: [*If not repetitive*] Can you tell me the specific story of *having* CHILD?

Q: Did becoming a parent *change you* in any particular ways? Change your *relationship* with PARTNER?

Q: Has becoming a parent changed your *views about religion*, God, religion, or spirituality in any way?

Q: Tell me about your CHILDREN [1, 2, 3]. What is he/she/they *like*?

Q: What is your *relationship* with him/her/them like? Has that changed over time? Close or distant?

Q: How is CHILD *doing in life*? Getting along with others? School? Attitude? Maturity?

Q: [IF SCHOOL AGE] What sort of *school* does CHILD attend? How did you decide where to send CHILD to school?
[*IF ALTERNATIVE/PRIVATE*] How did you decide you wanted that kind of school for CHILD?
[*IF PUBLIC*] Do you ever wish you could send CHILD to alternative or private schooling? Why?

Q: [IF PRESCHOOL] What are your thoughts or plans about schooling for CHILD when he/she is older?

FAMILY DESCRIPTION [IF NOT REPETITIVE]

Q: So how would you *describe your family* in general terms?
- What words or ideas best tell someone what your family is like, what you are all about?

Q: What do members of your family do with *free time*? Hobbies? Recreation?
- Time family/CHILD spends watching TV, using computer, or other visual technology?

Q: What sorts of organized or informal *activities* outside the home is CHILD engaged in?
- Sports? Music? Drama? Games? Playgroups? Scouts? Religious?

Q: How actively *involved* are *you* in these activities (e.g., going to games, seeing performances)?

Q: Does anyone in your family engage in any *volunteer* work? Is CHILD involved? Why or why not?

Q: [*IF NOT REPETITIVE*] Tell me more specifically about *religion* and your *family*—not just you, but your *whole family*. Very religious? What does that mean? How is religion or faith or CHURCH in your family?

Q: Who is more of the *"leader" or "point person" in religious matters* in the family?

Q: *Why* are you *part of* a CHURCH? How important is that? What does it do or mean for your family?

Q: What specifically do you *look for* in a CHURCH/place of worship? What are the most important things to you in deciding where to attend?—*music?—location?—style of service?—size?—children/ youth programs?*

Q: What specifically, if anything, do you *look to CHURCH to provide w/re to CHILD* in religious influence, teaching, support, or whatever?

- What has been your *experience* (re CHILD) with things like religious education classes, Sunday school, youth groups, religious travel, missions trips, etc.?

- Do you feel *cooperation* and shared purpose at CHURCH in the spiritual formation of CHILD? Or are there any *tensions* or people working at *cross-purposes*? Or?

ASPIRATIONS & CHALLENGES

Q: What are your *hopes and goals and dreams* for CHILD? What do you want to see him/her become or experience or achieve or enjoy in their life, w/re school, money, romance, sports, marriage, religion, etc.?

Q: What are the biggest *challenges or difficulties* for parents today? What makes parenting hard?

Q: Has CHILD been *easy or difficult to guide* in a positive direction? How so?

- Any particular *concerns about the wellbeing or development* of CHILD?

Q: What is your experience trying to manage or *negotiate the different demands* of various parts of CHILD's life—how do *you prioritize or coordinate* (or not) between different demands and activities?

Q: What do you think is *your influence as a parent* in CHILD's life *compared to other influences*, such as their friends and peer groups, the media, school influences, other adults, other institutions?

Q: Are any *groups or organizations or programs or institutions particularly supportive* of or helpful to you as a parent—like extended family, friends, neighbors, school or community groups, religious, recreation or sports leagues, support groups, play groups?

Q: Some parents we interview see *problems in the national and global economy* and they *worry* about whether or not their children will be [as] *financially secure/stable*; other parents do *not* seem to see a cause for concern here. Do you ever worry about your child about financial security? Why or why not? [IF SO] What do you do to alleviate that?

PARENTING STYLE

Q: What kind of *general style or approach* do you take to parenting?—Strict or lenient?
- *Boundaries or limits or rules* set? - freedoms and self-directions you allow?
- Punishments or disciplines? (did ever spank?)
- How much can *trust* CHILD with independence, or need for oversight?
- Feel responsible to *protect*, versus allowing CHILD to *take risks*?
- Relate as *friend* of or *authority* over CHILD?—*explain* things, or just say how it's gonna be?

Q: Is CHILD *required* to go to [RELIGIOUS ACTIVITIES] or is that up to them?

Q: How *well* do you think your overall parenting style *works*? Has it *changed*? Why, how?

Q: Do you and PARTNER ever *disagree* about parenting styles/ approaches? How do you handle that?

IMPORTANCE OF (RELIGIOUS) REPRODUCTION

Q: Generally, how important is it to you that CHILD ends up *sharing* most of your personal general beliefs, values, and lifestyle?

Q: How would you feel if CHILD grew up to look, believe, live *very differently* from you in lifestyle?—re: family, social class, sex, religion, politics, work, possessions, financial security, cars, vacations, entertainment, etc.

Q: How *important* is it to you that CHILD grow up believing and practicing the *same religious* faith as you? [NR="beliefs about religion"]

Q: Why [IF] do you want CHILD to grow up to be a religious or spiritual person?

Q: What, if any, are the *essential* spiritual beliefs or practices that you hope CHILD will adopt?

Q: How *religiously different* from you could CHILD grow up to be before it would bother you?

Q: Do you think CHILD should *marry* someone of the *same religion* as you are, assuming they get married, or not necessarily? [NR="someone not religious"] Why?

Q: How much would it bother you if your *grandchildren* grew up being *non-religious*? Of a totally *different* religion? Why? [NR="very religious"]

Q: Some youth *drop out of religion* as teenagers until their earlier 30s, when they have their own children. Would it be *okay* with you or it would *bother* you if CHILD did that?

CONVERSATIONS AND CONFIDENCE

Q: Do you and CHILD *have conversations* about significant things? How easy or hard is that?
  • Topics? Dealing with hard moral questions? Topics avoided? Why?

Q: Have you had any conversations with CHILD *about God, spiritual matters or religion*? How did that come up and go?

Q: Has CHILD ever asked you questions about God, religion, or spirituality that you've found *difficult to answer*? How? Why?

Q: Do you ever feel *you don't understand* your own religious tradition/faith well enough to convey it effectively to CHILD? If so, how do you deal with that? (*Probe*: Q: Some parents feel generally *confident and secure* in shaping their children's religious and spiritual lives; others feel *uncertain, hesitant, or insecure*. How do you personally feel? [IF UNCERTAIN] Areas that are particular challenging for you? Why?)

Q: Some parents we talk to seem to feel the need to "*outsource*" the religious training of children to "specialists," like CHURCH, youth ministers, religious camps. Have you ever felt that? [IF SO] Why?

Q: Has CHILD ever known someone who *died*, or ever been to a *funeral* that provided the occasion to talk with CHILD about *death*? Describe.

Q: Do you ever talk with CHILD about *your* or *their* religious *doubts*, confusions, disbelief, etc.?

Q: Has talking with CHILD *influenced you*, your own religious beliefs or knowledge or practices?

RELATION TO RELIGIOUS COMMUNITIES

Q: Does CHILD generally *like CHURCH* or not? Why or why not?
  • Do you ever have to negotiate or argue *about going to CHURCH*? What is your approach?

Q: What *role does CHURCH* play (or not) *in shaping* CHILD religiously or spiritually? Or otherwise?

Q: Who, if anyone, at CHURCH has been *helpful* to you as a parent or has *most influenced* CHILD?

Q: Have you had any *disagreements* or *conflicts* with anyone at CHURCH about the approach to the religious or spiritual formation of CHILD or other children at CHURCH?

Q: How helpful or not is your CHURCH in *equipping or supporting you as a parent* for the job of passing on your religious faith and practice to your children? Describe/explain.

Q: Is there *anything* your CHURCH *could do better* to equip or support you in this way? What? How?

RELIGIOUS TRANSMISSION

Q: What role do you think that *parents ought* to play in helping to *form* the religious faith and practices of their children? That is . . .
  • Do parents have the *right* or *obligation* to influence children to accept and practice their own faith?
  • Or should they *just expose* children to different religious options and leave choosing up to them?

Q: Are parents or CHURCH more *responsible* for passing on religious faith and practice to children? Why?

Q: What are the most important things, if any, that you as a parent *have intentionally done in the past or do now* to try to pass on religious faith and practices to CHILD?

> Probe: Reading scripture or other religious texts together? Praying together at meals?
> - Family devotions or prayers apart from meals? Play spiritual/ religious music/talk radio in home?
> - Watching religiously oriented TV shows or movies together?
> - Enrolling CHILD in catechism class/confirmation/other sacramental prep programs?

Q: Is CHILD interested in religious things, or not? What do [WOULD] you do if/when CHILD expresses *resistance* to religious activities inside or outside of the home?

Q: Is there anything you have decided definitely *not* to do as a parent in passing on your religious faith or practices to CHILD? Anything you *avoid*? What and why?

Q: Are there other people *outside* of your family *who have significantly influenced* CHILD's *religious formation*, of beliefs, identity, practices, etc.? Describe.

Q: What about CHILD's friends and *peers*? Are they a *positive or negative influence* on CHILD's *religious* faith or practices?

Q: Does your church have a *youth group*? [IF SO] Does CHILD participate in it? Do they like it? What kind of influence do you think it might have on them?

Q: Do you and PARTNER *agree* or ever *disagree* on what sorts of spiritual beliefs or practices you would like CHILD to adopt? [IF SO] How do you handle those disagreements?

Q: [IF *INTERFAITH* HH] Do you try to pass on both your own *and* PARTNER'S religious tradition? Or just one or the other? How does that work?

Q: Are there *other adults* beyond your immediate family who play a role in the formation of CHILD's religious faith (i.e. grandparents, family friends, school teachers, etc.)? What do they do?

Q: Do you have any *visual or material religious objects* in your home (e.g., pictures, statues, icons, candles, wall hangings, etc.)?

Q: Do you have religiously oriented *media* (playing) in your house (or car), like magazines, TV, CDs, radio, literature? What? What role does that play?

Q: If you had to make your best guess, what do you think CHILD will look like religiously or spiritually at age 30 or 35?

[IF CHILD IS OLDER] Q: Looking back, do you *wish you would have done anything differently* in raising CHILD, either generally or religiously?

Last Opportunity: Okay, so I have asked a lot of questions and we've discussed a lot in depth. Are there any other ideas we have not already discussed that you'd like to share before we stop? Anything that did not come up in our talking so far that is worth adding?

[**CODES**: CHILD = name of child if only one, "children" if 2+ children. CHURCH = "church" for Christians & LDS, "synagogue" or "temple" for Jews, "mosque" or "prayer center" for Muslims, "temple" for Hindus and Buddhists.]

A NOTE ON THE TYPE

{⊶⊷}

THIS BOOK has been composed in Miller, a Scotch Roman typeface designed by Matthew Carter and first released by Font Bureau in 1997. It resembles Monticello, the typeface developed for The Papers of Thomas Jefferson in the 1940s by C. H. Griffith and P. J. Conkwright and reinterpreted in digital form by Carter in 2003.

Pleasant Jefferson ("P. J.") Conkwright (1905–1986) was Typographer at Princeton University Press from 1939 to 1970. He was an acclaimed book designer and AIGA Medalist.

The ornament used throughout this book was designed by Pierre Simon Fournier (1712–1768) and was a favorite of Conkwright's, used in his design of the *Princeton University Library Chronicle*.